11345112

MULTINATIONALS AND TRANSFER PRICING

MULTINATIONALS AND TRANSFER PRICING

Edited by
Alan M. Rugman
and
Lorraine Eden

ST MARTIN'S PRESS
New York

© 1985 Alan M. Rugman and Lorraine Eden
All rights reserved. For information, write:
St. Martins Press, Inc., 175 Fifth Avenue, New York, NY 10010
Printed in Great Britain
First published in the United States of America in 1985

Library of Congress Cataloging in Publication Data
Main entry under title:

Multinationals and transfer pricing.

"Based on the proceedings of a conference on
Multinationals and Transfer Pricing held at Dalhousie
University, Halifax, Nova Scotia, Canada in October
1983. The conference was sponsored by the Centre for
International Business Studies and the Social Sciences
and Humanities Research Council of Canada"— Pref.
    Bibliography: p. 316
    Includes indexes.
    1. Transfer pricing — Congresses. 2. International
business enterprises — Congresses. 3. Transfer pricing —
Government Policy — Congresses. I. Rugman, Alan M.
II. Eden, Lorraine. III. Dalhousie University. Centre
for International Business Studies. IV. Social Sciences
and Humanities Research Council of Canada.
HD62.45.M835   1985   338.5'2   84-22336
ISBN 0-312-55257-2

CONTENTS

PREFACE

This volume is based on the proceedings of a conference on 'Multinationals and Transfer Pricing' held at Dalhousie University, Halifax, Nova Scotia, Canada in October 1983. The conference was sponsored by the Centre for International Business Studies and the Social Sciences and Humanities Research Council of Canada.

The conference was organized by Alan M. Rugman, director of the Dalhousie Centre for International Business Studies. He wishes to express his deep appreciation to Jennifer Barr, John McIlveen and Pat Zwicker for their help in assisting with local arrangements.

The original idea for this conference arose out of a suggestion from Jack Hirshleifer to Lawrence Copithorne, while help in its actual implementation was received from Donald Brean. However, the major source of inspiration for the conference, and the greatest amount of support, came from Lorraine Eden. Dr Eden serves as co-editor of the book, reflecting her insight and energy in refereeing and editing the papers to integrate them into a unified structure.

The first step in the organization of the conference was to extend invitations to a group of leading scholars who had made major contributions to the literature on transfer pricing. A public call for papers was also issued. Finally, over a dozen papers were accepted for the conference, and several discussants were invited to add balance to the programme. From the conference proceedings the editors of this volume have prepared an integrated book on transfer pricing. The result is offered as a contribution to the literature on multinational enterprises in general and to the theoretical, empirical and public policy aspects of transfer pricing in particular.

Alan M. Rugman
Dalhousie University

1 INTRODUCTION

Alan M. Rugman and Lorraine Eden

What is Transfer Pricing?

A 'transfer price' can be defined as the price used for internal sales of goods and services between the divisions of a business enterprise. When some of the divisions are located in different countries this type of firm is called a multinational enterprise (MNE). The intra-firm sales which take place between the branches of such an MNE create the need for internal prices to value the exchange of these divisions. Transfer prices are necessary to manage efficiently the internal markets of the MNE, and keep track of the performance of the divisions.

From the viewpoint of the MNE transfer prices are a means to an end; they are used to facilitate decisions about the organization of the firm's internal markets. Yet from the viewpoint of nation states transfer prices themselves are a potential problem, especially if governments believe that the transfer prices set by the MNE do not reflect open market values. For example, the ability of MNEs to set their own internal prices is often perceived by nation states as a mechanism to avoid payment of taxes. A division located in a high-tax area can reduce its profits (and taxes) if other divisions overcharge it for supplies and underpay it for purchases of its output. (Indeed, the MNE would not be operating in a profit-maximizing manner if it failed to take advantage of whatever market power it had to improve its global performance.)

For these, and related, reasons the interests of MNEs and nation states are often in conflict. These conflicts arise from a fundamental difference in the roles of business and government: business enterprises are responsible for the efficient management of their operations while governments have a wider mandate than efficiency. Political responsibilities of governments lead them to introduce taxes, tariffs and other regulations designed to increase the welfare of certain groups in the nation state. Multinationals must live within this environment of national controls and

1

respond as best they can. Many writers have argued that transfer prices are often used as a method of evading such government controls.

When governments impose various tax, commercial and regulatory policies on their citizens, the MNE by using transfer prices can (to a degree) reallocate resources and redistribute profits between countries. This not only weakens these regulations and thus national sovereignty, but is often perceived to have undesirable effects on variables such as national output and employment levels, consumer prices, factor incomes and the balance of payments. Whether the MNE actually has the power to do this is an unresolved matter, yet it is the perception that it has the power that matters. As a result governments view transfer pricing with suspicion and attempt to prevent such transfer price 'manipulation' (note the pejorative sound of this expression). In many nations, transfer prices are regulated to conform with an idealized 'arm's-length standard', i.e. the market price that would have been negotiated by unrelated parties bargaining at arm's length. The best known of these regulations is Section 482 of the United States Internal Revenue Code which offers three ways to measure an arm's-length price: the comparable uncontrolled price, resale value and cost-plus methods.

To these considerations must be added the problem of natural market imperfections. Whenever external markets are missing (e.g. as in intermediate products such as knowledge) or function poorly (e.g. where transactions and information costs are high) MNEs can create internal markets which are more efficient than these external ones. The problem of pricing knowledge generated by the MNE and the costs of information and transacting in regular markets can be reduced or eliminated by the use of internal markets.

To the extent that the MNE is an internalizer of exogenous imperfections, both natural and government induced, it is in a special position *vis-à-vis* national firms operating at arm's length in regular markets. This has implications for transfer pricing. If MNE internal markets exist because they are more efficient than regular markets, does this mean that transfer prices must also be more efficient than regular market prices? If the answer to this question is 'yes', clearly government regulation of transfer prices on *efficiency grounds* is unnecessary (although there may still be *distributional* reasons for such regulation). Even if the answer is 'no', on many occasions transfer prices cannot be compared to arm's-length market prices, since the latter simply may not exist.

In this book these paradoxes are examined in detail. Our knowledge of transfer pricing is enhanced by a series of analytical, empirical and policy papers which explore the depths of the transfer pricing controversy. We argue that the conflict between multinationals and national governments over transfer pricing can best be analyzed by separating the controversy into three questions: first, does transfer pricing by MNEs in a world of government regulations improve or worsen global welfare, i.e. are transfer prices efficient? Second, do arm's-length prices exist for purposes of comparison with transfer prices? And third, is regulation of transfer pricing necessary on efficiency and/or distributional grounds?

This book is organized around these three themes. In it, blame is not pointed at either multinationals or at national governments. The book aims for a better understanding of the economic reality of intra-firm trade and of ways to increase the benefits, both to MNEs and to governments, from this trade. By adopting a non-partisan stance, this book should help to defuse some of the 'we' against 'they' attitude towards transfer pricing. Hopefully, it will lead to more efficient and/or equitable methods of operating and regulating multinational enterprises.

Structure of the Book

This book arose out of papers invited for the conference on 'Multinationals and Transfer Pricing'. Yet it is much more than the proceedings of a conference. The editors went to great lengths to ensure that all the contributors prepared papers both at the frontiers of knowledge in the area and related to other papers in the book. It is organized to reveal a development of thought as the papers are read in sequence.

(i) Theory

First, several papers examine the theory of transfer pricing in MNEs from the viewpoint of economic theory, especially neoclassical microeconomic analysis. They start from elementary principles illustrated verbally and in geometric presentations, then move to mathematically more demanding partial and general equilibrium models using calculus and duality theory. The first two papers by Eden and Diewert lay the foundation for critical understanding of the several key postulates made in this book.

Eden reviews most of the existing theoretical literature on transfer pricing, and then synthesizes and extends it in one model of transfer pricing by horizontally and vertically integrated multinationals. She argues that transfer pricing in response to tariff barriers is welfare increasing, but that welfare is reduced when the MNE uses transfer prices in response to corporate profit tax differentials. The powerful paper by Diewert is a major development since duality theory allows him to advance significantly upon the work of previous theorists in the area. The paper identifies and relates five different types of transfer prices: efficient, profit-maximizing, decentralized, arm's-length and optimal regulated. His proofs of the conditions under which these various transfer prices are efficient or inefficient are major innovations as are his deadweight loss measures for these conditions.

The controversy over the efficiency of transfer pricing is clearly brought out by comparing the Eden and Diewert papers with that by Aliber. Aliber shows that attempts by governments to segment markets and assert national sovereignty create market imperfections that reduce global welfare. By using transfer prices to arbitrage these government-induced market imperfections, he argues that multinationals can improve efficiency and raise world welfare.

The theory of transfer pricing is next addressed in papers by Samuelson on multinationals and exhaustible natural resources, and by Itagaki on the equivalence of tariffs and quotas on intra-firm trade. The book then switches from economic theory to a more business school emphasis on transfer pricing from the viewpoints of accountants and those in financial management. Papers by Quirin and Brean deal with real world accounting and taxation aspects of transfer pricing and with the ways in which manoeuvring of liquid assets by the MNE are alternative techniques to transfer pricing. Lastly, Grubert comments on some unresolved issues in the theoretical work on transfer pricing.

(ii) Evidence

Second, there follows a series of empirically based papers which examine the evidence on transfer pricing by MNEs. The first paper by Rugman interprets the results of the Bertrand Report on transfer pricing in the Canadian petroleum industry. Benvignati reports on a major study of transfer pricing practices in US corporations. Then two papers examine transfer pricing in lower income nations: Natke, on Brazil, and Lecraw, on South-East Asia. Helleiner shifts the focus to the distributional implications of transfer pricing and its importance to lower income nations. It is difficult to generalize the findings of this disparate group of case studies, but some of their implications for arm's-length prices and the use of data on transfer prices are discussed later in this Introduction.

(iii) Policy and Regulation

Finally, public policy implications of transfer pricing are examined in papers by Plasschaert, Chudson and Shoup. Plasschaert relates the theoretical work on the efficiency of transfer pricing to the actual practices of multinationals in lower income nations. Chudson summarizes the conflicting positions of those in favour of either more or less regulation of transfer prices by developing countries together with an analysis of various direct and indirect methods of regulation. In an ambitious paper, Shoup calls for an international agency to be used for the voluntary arbitration of transfer pricing disputes. This is a clearly articulated call for action and it merits serious consideration by those concerned with the alleged abuse of transfer pricing policy by multinationals. Lastly, McGuinness comments on the distortionary effects transfer price regulations can have on multinationals.

Themes in the Book

While there exists a wealth of other ideas that only a careful reading of the papers will suggest to the reader, we believe that the three key themes emphasized in the book are on the leading edge of thought in this field.

(i) Are Transfer Prices Efficient?

First is the debate about the extent to which transfer prices are efficient. Some authors, such as Aliber and Rugman, argue that the MNE uses 'shadow' transfer prices to clear transactions among its divisions. The reason for transfer pricing is the existence of trade between separate divisions, and the MNE uses shadow transfer prices at marginal cost to clear these internal markets. Such transfer pricing is efficient, i.e. it raises global welfare. More specifically, transfer prices are efficient under two conditions. First, they are efficient when used to price intangibles such as knowledge which are intermediate products to the MNE (and for which regular markets do not exist). Second, transfer prices are also efficient when the MNE responds to government imposed market imperfections such as taxes and tariffs. In response to both types of market imperfections the MNE creates internal markets and uses shadow transfer prices to clear them. Since these transfer prices are chosen by the MNE, and set at marginal cost, they are efficient by definition.

While authors such as Eden and Diewert accept that the shadow transfer price is generally efficient, they argue that in a world with tariffs and corporate profit taxes the MNE would not set a marginal cost transfer price. A global profit-maximizing multinational chooses a transfer price that trades the gain from minimizing tax and tariff costs against the loss in misallocated resources (from not using the marginal cost price). This 'profit-maximizing' transfer price can be above or below the shadow price. Similarly, Diewert shows that the transfer price chosen by a decentralized MNE generally also differs from the shadow price. As a result, transfer pricing may or may not improve global welfare in a world of government imposed trade barriers. One of the main contributions of this book is the precise specification of conditions under which these apparently paradoxical results hold.

There are also contributors, including Quirin, Brean and Helleiner, who argue that tax laws allow and even encourage multinationals to 'keep two sets of books', i.e. to use shadow transfer prices to allocate resources within the MNE, and use 'accounting/money' transfer prices for tax purposes to determine the location of profits. For this group, efficiency is not of paramount interest; the equity implications of money transfer prices is the important issue, particularly with respect to the distribution of MNE income and profits between developed and lower income nations. For example, tax regulations such as accelerated depreciation encourage the use of two sets of books: the MNE uses the shadow transfer price to value true depreciation of its capital stock, and the accounting transfer price for tax purposes. Also, where the multinational runs a division at an overall loss for strategic reasons, a separate set of books based on money transfer prices can be used to evaluate management performance.

The business school literature on transfer pricing has extensively analyzed the use of money transfer prices for management evaluation. While these prices can be used to redistribute revenue and thereby profits between divisions of the MNE, they should not be confused with the transfer prices used to value intra-firm trade flows and clear the MNE's internal markets. However, an unanswered question is the extent to which money transfer prices can also affect allocative efficiency of both the MNE and the nation states involved. This is not an easy problem to resolve, and the answers seem to depend critically upon the precise manner in which the models of the MNE are specified.

In evaluating the efficiency of transfer pricing it does not seem particularly helpful to contrast these prices with arm's-length competitive prices which may or may not exist. When regular markets are absent, or constrained due to information and transaction costs, it is necessary to model the MNE in its own right as a special institutional response to market imperfections and to analyze transfer prices accordingly.

(ii) Do Arm's-length Prices Exist as a Basis for Comparison with Transfer Prices?

The second major theme of this book is also of a theoretical nature, but it arises as a particular problem in the case studies and empirical papers. Data on transfer prices are hard to come by. This provides a great obstacle to objective empirical work conducted by researchers and, to some extent, it constrains the analysis undertaken in this book. For example, the empirical results of both Natke and Lecraw are weakened by the lack of hard data. Benvignati has access to a large survey, but again much of the data available to her does not lend itself to rigorous econometric testing of the transfer pricing controversy.

Not only is there an empirical problem in finding (often unobservable) transfer pricing data, but there is also a theoretical problem in using arm's-length data which also may not be reliable. For example, Rugman finds that the Bertrand Report falls into this trap. While Rugman acknowledges that data on transfer prices used by multinational oil firms are available in the Canadian case for the 1958 to 1973 period studied, he discovers that there is no single arm's-length price, even for a tangible good such as crude oil, in this period. Instead, there is a wide range of estimates for such market prices which appear to exceed the differential between the observed transfer prices and the arm's-length price chosen in the Bertrand Report.

This leads to a fundamental conceptual problem in the treatment of transfer pricing by MNEs, one which is identified but not resolved here. Many tax authorities and economists, concerned about the abusive nature of transfer price manipulation by multinationals, especially in lower income nations, use the arm's-length standard to value intra-firm transfers. However, arm's-length tests implicitly assume that the divisions of the MNE operate as independent profit centres, and that market prices exist somewhere as a standard of comparison for inter-divisional transactions. Neither of these two assumptions is generally true.

Although multinationals are often organized into divisions along profit centre lines, the autonomy of the divisions is more apparent than real. MNEs are structured as integrated units to reduce the transaction costs which would otherwise prevent the organization of a market. In addition, MNEs sometimes operate an affiliate at a loss in order to retain market share in a region or for other strategic reasons. Within the integrated internal markets of MNEs there are frequently transfers of intangible knowledge and management know-how for which no market prices can be observed. This hinders the attempts of tax authorities to assign arm's-length prices for inter-affiliate transactions on the assumption that the divisions are separate entities. As a result, imposition of the arm's-length standard can cause serious distortions to the internal systems of MNEs.

If comparable arm's-length prices do not generally exist, there is no clear rationale on efficiency grounds for using the arm's-length standard to regulate transfer prices. As an alternative, Diewert shows that it is possible to calculate an 'optimal regulated' transfer price which is globally efficient. However, the informational requirements are so steep that he is, justifiably, pessimistic as to any government's ability to find such a regulatory standard. Even if the arm's-length principle is not unambiguously more efficient than unregulated transfer prices, it may be possible to justify the standard as the 'least inefficient' standard, or on distributional grounds. Economists, such as Shoup, argue that, putting the question of efficiency aside, the arm's-length principle is still necessary to ensure a fair international distribution of the MNE's world-wide income.

(iii) Is Regulation of Transfer Pricing Necessary?

The final key theme debated in this book is the perceived need for regulation of multinationals on efficiency and/or distributional grounds. It arises because there is more than one viewpoint about transfer pricing. One group feels that the use of transfer pricing by the MNE is efficient; another group believes that transfer pricing can be inefficient. The concern of both home and host governments with distributional aspects of transfer price manipulation inevitably conflicts with those who see the MNE as an efficient business organization. The MNE itself regards international tax rate differentials and exchange controls imposed by nation states as exogenous market imperfections to which transfer pricing is a legitimate internal response. On the other hand, nation states view the power to manipulate transfer prices as a method of evading legal obligations, thus eroding national sovereignty.

It is clear that most of the contributors to this volume would agree that, in the *presence* of natural market imperfections but in the *absence* of government induced market imperfections, transfer pricing is efficient, and therefore regulation, on efficiency grounds, is unnecessary. Similarly, most authors would agree that if all government tax, commercial and regulatory policies were harmonized internationally, regulation of transfer pricing on efficiency grounds would again be unnecessary. However, a consensus emerging from this volume is that the nation state is not dead. Governments retain sovereign powers of taxation, regulation and ultimate banishment of multinationals. This power leaves the state with the residual authority to change and control the environment within which MNEs operate. Therefore, international harmonization of national policies is not a practical solution to the transfer pricing problem. As a result, the view of several authors is that regulation of transfer prices is necessary on efficiency grounds.

One of the contributions of this book is the demonstration that unregulated transfer prices may be either more or less efficient than regulated ones. Even though it cannot be demonstrated that there is a clear efficiency rationale for such regulation, some contributors argue that regulation is still necessary on distributional grounds. In future years, these authors expect international intra-firm trade to be more closely managed by governments as they adopt mercantilist policies in an attempt to appropriate larger rents from MNEs. As a result they argue that the distributional effects of transfer pricing on the allocation of the MNE's world-wide income between shareholders, factor owners, home and host governments will become increasingly important, and more closely managed through transfer pricing regulations.

Since it appears that such controls are here to stay, it is crucial that there be more open discussions between the regulators, government and multinational business. In this regard, the call by Professor Shoup for voluntary international arbitration of transfer pricing disputes is probably a necessary intermediate step towards a deeper understanding of the causes and effects of transfer pricing. An awareness of the complexities and roles of the respective bureaucracies and organizations of multinationals and governments would eliminate much of the controversy over transfer pricing, based as it is on misconceptions of the constraints imposed on either side.

In conclusion, we hope that this book will provide challenges (and perhaps some answers) to the issue of transfer pricing by multinationals, and that greater understanding will result from the clearer analytical framework, more detailed empirical knowledge and sharper policy analysis which the papers in this book provide.

PART ONE
THE THEORY OF TRANSFER PRICING

2 THE MICROECONOMICS OF TRANSFER PRICING

Lorraine Eden

I. Introduction

In this paper the 'transfer price' is defined as the price that applies to intra-firm trade in tangible goods between affiliates of a multinational enterprise (MNE). Because the affiliates are related, the transfer price is an internal price to the MNE, serving to allocate profits between exporting and importing firms. In the absence of tariffs or corporate profit tax differentials constraining the MNE, Hirshleifer (1956) proved that the efficient or shadow transfer price should be marginal cost of the selling division. If a perfectly competitive outside market exists and there are no costs of transacting in this market, the MNE should set the shadow transfer price equal to market price. The shadow price is efficient in the sense that it induces a resource allocation between the divisions of the MNE that maximizes global MNE profits. Hirshleifer (1957) proved that this shadow transfer price is also the decentralized or arm's-length transfer price that would be chosen if the individual divisions of the MNE were run as profit centres and were required to maximize their separate profits.

However, when the MNE is constrained by tariffs and corporate profit tax differentials, the transfer price that maximizes global profits net of taxes and tariffs — the external or profit-maximizing price — in general differs from the Hirshleifer shadow/decentralized transfer price. This was first proved in seminal papers by Horst (1971) and Copithorne (1971). Motivated by these two articles, a growing literature has developed over the past twelve years which models MNE behaviour when transfer prices are constrained by tax and tariff authorities. These partial equilibrium microeconomic models assume the MNE chooses transfer prices and resource levels so as to maximize global profits net of taxes and tariffs. The articles model either horizontally integrated trade in secondary processed goods

13

(following Horst) or vertically integrated trade in primary processed goods (following Copithorne). The research to date has determined profit-maximizing transfer prices and resource allocation decisions for given corporate profit tax, tariff and exchange rates. The comparative static effects of changes in these rates, and optimal commercial policies for intra-firm trade, have also been investigated. The first task we undertake in this paper is to review and synthesize the transfer pricing literature based on Horst (1971) and Copithorne (1971).

The second purpose of our paper is to develop a model that encompasses and extends the Horst-Copithorne literature. The major extensions we develop are:

(1) horizontally and vertically integrated trade are simultaneously modelled;
(2) the implications of setting the profit-maximizing transfer price above, below or equal to the shadow transfer price for the comparative static effects of changes in corporate tax, tariff and exchange rates are determined;
(3) the welfare effects of tariffs on intra-firm trade are examined; and
(4) the efficiency of transfer price manipulation in response to tariffs and corporate profits tax differentials is addressed; i.e. we determine which transfer price, Hirshleifer shadow/ decentralized or Horst/Copithorne profit-maximizing, generates an allocation of resources closest to that generated by the MNE in the absence of tax and tariff constraints.

Lastly, section IV concludes the paper by briefly outlining possible directions for future transfer pricing research.

To facilitate comparison among the various transfer pricing models, we use one set of symbols and the same general assumptions throughout the paper. We assume firm 1 is the parent firm located in the home country, country 1, and firms 2 and 3 are subsidiaries located in host countries 2 and 3, respectively. Firm 3 produces a primary product for sale to the two secondary firms, 1 and 2, which process the primary good into a final product for sale in their local markets. The secondary firms are assumed to face downward-sloping demand curves and the MNE can price discriminate between these markets. Firms 1 and 2 can also engage in intra-firm trade where, for simplicity, we assume exports flow from firm 1 to firm 2. Exports from firm 3 to firms 1 and 2, therefore, involve vertically integrated trade while trade between firms 1 and 2 is horizontally integrated. We assume one unit of primary output is required per unit of final output. The following symbols and assumptions are used throughout (where i, j = 1, 2, 3 and i $\neq$ j):

Q_i = volume of output produced by firm i;

Y_i = volume of domestic sales by firm i;

X_{ij} = volume of exports from firm i to firm j;

P_{ij} = the profit-maximizing transfer price firm i charges firm j per unit of X_{ij};

λ = the shadow transfer price per unit of X_{ij};

C_i = total cost of producing Q_i where $C_i = C_i(Q_i)$, $\partial C_i/\partial Q_i = MC_i > 0$, $\partial^2 C_i/\partial Q_i^2 = MC_i' \gtreqless 0$;

R_i = total revenue from sales of Y_i where $R_i = R_i(Y_i)$, $\partial R_i/\partial Y_i = MR_i$, $R_i/Y_i = P_i$, $\partial^2 R_i/\partial Y_i^2 = MR_i' < 0$; and $\varepsilon_i = \partial Y_i/Y_i \cdot P_i/\partial P_i$;

r_{ij} = *ad valorem* tariff rate levied by country j on X_{ij};

t_i = proportional corporate profit tax levied by country i;

b_i = proportion of firm i's profits, net of corporate taxes, remitted as dividends to firm 1 where $0 \leq b_i \leq 1$ (i = 2,3);

e_i = country i's exchange rate measured in terms of country 1's currency (where $e_1 = 1$);

π_i = profits received by firm i after tariffs but before taxes;

T_i = proportion of π_i that is left for firm i after profit taxes are paid, i.e. the after tax return per dollar of π_i where $0 \leq T_i \leq 1$;[1]

Y = $(T_i - T_j)/T_j$, the profit tax differential between the exporter, firm i, and the importer, firm j;

L_i = $e_i T_i \pi_i$ = after tax or net profits of firm i; and

L = $\Sigma e_i T_i \pi_i$. = global net profits of the MNE.

The relationships between the three divisions of the MNE are illustrated in Figure 2.1. As a heuristic example we assume the Mexican affiliate, firm 3, produces and sells crude petroleum to the US and Canadian affiliates, firms 1 and 2, which process it into plastics for their domestic markets. The US affiliate exports its surplus plastics to the Canadian firm. The vertically integrated

Figure 2.1: A Heuristic Example of MNE Intra-firm Trade Flows

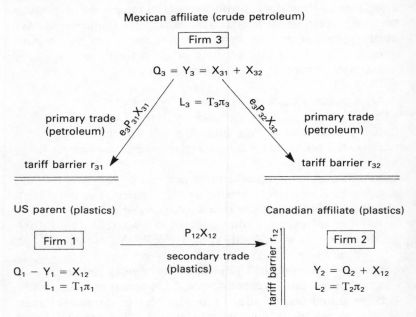

trade flows are $e_3P_{31}X_{31}$ and $e_3P_{32}X_{32}$, while the horizontally integrated trade flow is $P_{12}X_{12}$, all measured in US dollars. We assume $X_{31} = Q_1$, $X_{32} = Q_2$ and $Q_3 = X_{31} + X_{32} = Y_3$. Also $Q_1 - Y_1 = X_{12} = Y_2 - Q_2 > 0$.

II. Review of the Transfer Pricing Literature

A. The Horst Model

The first microeconomic model of horizontally integrated MNE intra-firm trade is developed in Horst (1971). He outlines the global net profit-maximizing strategy for an MNE with monopolistic power in two national markets where the MNE chooses its optimal transfer price and allocates resources, given corporate taxes and tariffs. The analysis breaks down into four cases depending on whether $MC_i' \lesseqgtr 0$ and the MNE can or cannot price discriminate between its markets. We review only the first case where $MC_i' > 0$ and price discrimination is possible.

We set up the initial 'free trade' (i.e. no corporate profit taxes and no tariffs so $t_i = t_j = r_{ij} = 0$) situation as follows. Firms 1 and 2 produce and sell an identical final good. Firm 1 also exports its surplus production to firm 2. The MNE's global profit function under free trade is:

$$L = [R_1 - C_1 + P_{12}(Q_1 - Y_1)] + [R_2 - C_2 - P_{12}(Y_2 - Q_2)] \\ + \lambda(Q_1 + Q_2 - Y_1 - Y_2) \tag{1}$$

where $R_i = R_i(Y_i), C_i = C_i(Q_i)$ and $Q_1 - Y_1 = X_{12} = Y_2 - Q_2$ as outlined in section I. The first (second) square bracket in (1) represents the profits of the exporter (importer) firm. The Lagrange constraint forces total MNE output to equal total MNE sales. Differentiating (1) with respect to Y_i and Q_i and setting the results equal to zero, we have the first order condition for a global profit maximum under free trade:

$$MR_1 = MC_1 = MR_2 = MC_2 = \lambda \tag{2}$$

Equation (2) proves that the Hirshleifer shadow price λ should equal marginal cost of the exporting division under free trade. Let us call this shadow price λ_{12} to identify it as the shadow price of X_{12}. Note that the profit-maximizing transfer price P_{12} does not appear in (2). Under free trade P_{12} divides profits between the divisions of the MNE (i.e. it affects the distribution of MNE income among countries), but does not affect total MNE profits (i.e. it does not influence the efficient levels of output, sales and trade flows). This is illustrated in Figure 2.2 which is based on Figure I in Horst (1973).

The MR_i, MC_i and P_i curves are shown for firm 1 in Figure 2.2(a), and for firm 2 in Figure 2.2(c). Figure 2.2(b) derives the marginal cost and revenue curves for intra-firm trade in X_{12}. The marginal cost of exporting curve MC_x is the horizontal distance between the MR_1 and MC_1 curves while the marginal revenue from importing curve MR_x is the horizontal distance between the MR_2 and MC_2 curves. Where MR_x crosses MC_x (point A with trade of $X_{12}°$) equation (2) is satisfied. The shadow transfer price λ_{12} is determined by this intersection and equals $MC_1°$, the marginal cost of exports at $Q_1°$. Reading across from A we can find $Q_1°$, $Y_1°$, $Q_2°$ and $Y_2°$ where $Q_1° - Y_1° = Y_2° - Q_2° = X_{12}°$.

Figure 2.2: The Effects of a Tariff on Horizontally Integrated Trade (The Horst Model)

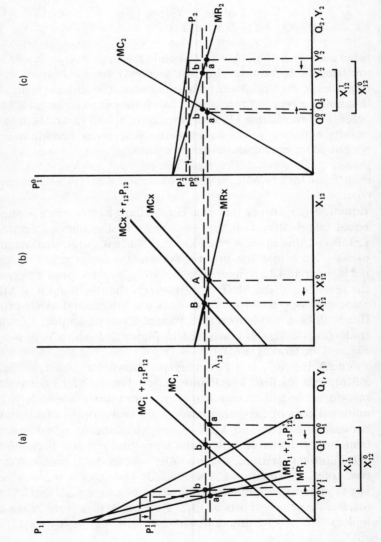

When the MNE is constrained by corporate profit taxes t_1 and t_2 and a tariff r_{12}, Horst (1971) shows that the MNE's global profit function is:

$$L = (1 - t_1)(R_1 - C_1 + P_{12}X_{12}) + (1 - t_2)(R_2 - C_2 - (1+r_{12})P_{12}X_{12}) \qquad (3)$$

He then shows that the profit-maximizing transfer price P_{12} depends upon the tax differential γ (which equals $(t_2 - t_1)/(1 - t_2)$ in Horst's model) compared to the tariff rate r_{12}. Horst was the first to realize that global net profits would be larger if the MNE set a maximum (minimum) value for P_{12} whenever γ was larger (smaller) than r_{12}. Because he expected tax and tariff authorities to impose MC_1 as an effective lower bound and P_1 as an upper bound to P_{12}, he assumed $MC_1 \leq P_{12} \leq P_1$. For $\gamma < r_{12}$, the MNE then chooses $P_{12} = MC_1$ which implies 'a high-tariff policy . . . has the unfortunate side effect of rendering tax policy impotent' (Horst, 1971, p. 1068). We can see this in his first order conditions for a global profit maximum under tax and tariff barriers:

$$MR_i - MC_i = 0 \quad (i=1,2) \qquad (4)$$

$$MC_2 - MC_1 - r_{12}P_{12} + \gamma(P_{12} - MC_1) = 0 \qquad (5)$$

Sales in each market are determined by $MR_i = MC_i$ while intra-firm trade depends on relative marginal costs adjusted for taxes and tariffs on X_{12}. Based on (5) Horst argues that, for $\gamma < r_{12}$, the last term in (5) becomes zero so small changes in the tax differential have no effect on X_{12} while tariffs remain trade-contracting. Horst's conclusion that tax policy is impotent unfortunately generalizes too much from (5). As we show in section III, changes in γ do have predictable effects on intra-firm trade even when $\gamma < r_{ij}$ if the MNE can set P_{ij} below the shadow transfer price λ. It is true that if $P_{ij} = \lambda$ (i.e. $P_{12} = MC_1$ here), both exporting and importing firms earn zero marginal profits on X_{ij} so that tax changes have no impact on the MNE. Tax policy is actually impotent because P_{ij} equals marginal export costs, not because the tax differential is less than the tariff.

We can illustrate the impacts of the secondary tariff r_{12} on the MNE using Figure 2.2. If $\gamma = 0$, equations (4, 5) can be rewritten as:

$$MR_1 + r_{12}P_{12} = MC_1 + r_{12}P_{12} = MR_2 = MC_2 \qquad (6)$$

The secondary tariff shifts the MR_1 and MC_1 (and therefore the MC_x) curves up by $r_{12}P_{12}$. The new equilibrium is at point B with lower level of trade X_{12}^1 and a higher level of foreign production Q_2^1. Note that the profit-maximizing transfer price P_{12} should now be set as low as possible to minimize tariff costs since $\gamma = 0$.

Horst's model is incorporated as the first tier in a two-tier model of the importing country's market in Adler and Stevens (1974). In the second tier third-country imports and domestic firms compete with foreign subsidiary sales Y_2 ($= Q_2 + X_{12}$). In the first tier Adler and Stevens show the export displacement effect $dX_{12}/d\bar{Q}_2$ is negative, i.e. foreign subsidiary production displaces MNE exports. They also show that $dY_1/d\bar{Q}_2 \gtrless 0$ for $MC_1' \gtrless 0$, i.e. home country sales increase as foreign subsidiary output expands. An inspection of Figure 2.2 confirms this: decreases in X_{12} correspond with increases in Y_1 and Q_2 (and decreases in Q_1 and Y_2). Adler and Stevens then empirically test these hypotheses in the full two-tier model for the chemical and electrical engineering industries and find the displacement effect is generally confirmed.

B. The Copithorne Model

The first partial equilibrium micro model of vertically integrated MNE trade is Copithorne (1971) which models firm 3 exporting raw materials to firms 1 and 2 for processing and local sale. The global profit function of the MNE under free trade ($r_{ij} = t_i = t_j = 0$) in this model is:

$$L = [R_1 - C_1 - P_{31}X_{31}] + [R_2 - C_2 - P_{32}X_{32}] + [P_{31}X_{31} + P_{32}X_{32} - C_3] + \lambda_1(Q_1 - X_{31}) + \lambda_2(Q_2 - X_{32}) \qquad (7)$$

where $Q_i = Y_i$ and the Lagrange expressions constrain $Q_1 = X_{31}$ and $Q_2 = X_{32}$. The first order condition is:

$$MR_1 - MC_1 = MR_2 - MC_2 = MC_3 = \lambda_1 = \lambda_2 \qquad (8)$$

where $MR_i - MC_i$ equals the net marginal revenue NR_i from producing and selling Y_i. The two shadow transfer prices for primary trade should, therefore, both equal MC_3, marginal export cost. Let us identify the shadow price of X_{31} as λ_{31} and of X_{32} as λ_{32}.

Figure 2.3: The Effects of a Tariff on Vertically Integrated Trade (The Copithorne Model)

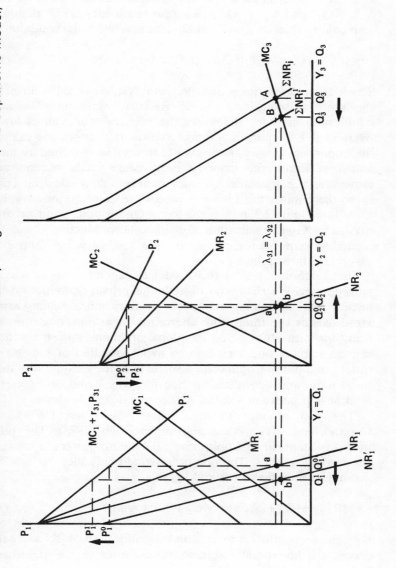

Figure 2.3 illustrates Copithorne's model. The NR_i curve is the vertical distance between the MR_i and MC_i curves. The NR_1 and NR_2 curves are then horizontally summed as the ΣNR_i curve in the right-hand graph. The intersection of ΣNR_i and MC_3 curves at point A determines $Y_3^o = Q_3^o$. Reading back from A we find $Y_1^o = Q_1^o$ and $Y_2^o = Q_2^o$. (See also Hirshleifer, 1957, p. 104.)[2]

If country 1 levies a tariff on X_{31}, the new first order condition is:

$$MR_1 - (MC_1 + r_{31}P_{31}) = MR_2 - MC_2 = MC_3 \qquad (9)$$

The MC_1 curve shifts up by $r_{31}P_{31}$, and NR_1 curve shifts down by the same amount, and the ΣNR_i curve shifts in. The new equilibrium at point B implies the primary tariff causes lower overall MNE output, in addition to a smaller output and sales in the importing country. Note that both the Horst secondary tariff and the Copithorne primary tariff cause trade to contract. However, primary trade X_{31} is an input into domestic production Q_1 so the primary tariff is antiprotective to domestic industry, i.e. Q_1 falls in Figure 2.3 in response to r_{31}. On the other hand, secondary trade X_{12} is a substitute for domestic production Q_2 so the secondary tariff is protective to domestic industry, i.e. Q_2 rises in Figure 2.2 in response to r_{12}.

In Copithorne (1976) this model is expanded to include an entrepôt division that buys or sells the primary product on the outside market, and any number of primary and secondary firms. He discusses the interesting aberration of a 'maverick' primary firm (one with $MC_i' < 0$ at the global optimum) and shows there can be at most one such firm to avoid violation of the second order conditions. Copithorne also reviews the existing literature on shadow and decentralized transfer prices, and discusses the relationship between shadow and external transfer prices.

The first attempt to amalgamate the Horst (1971) and Copithorne (1971) models appears in Eden (1978). The Eden model is identical to Copithorne's but allows for trade between the secondary firms. The first order condition under free trade is a simple extension of (2) and (8):

$$MR_1 = MC_1 + MC_3 = MC_2 + MC_3 = MR_2 \qquad (10)$$

We can use Figure 2.4 to explain this model. The MR_1 and MR_2 curves are horizontally summed and shown in the right-hand

Figure 2.4: The Effects of a Primary Tariff on a Horizontally and Vertically Integrated MNE (The Eden Model)

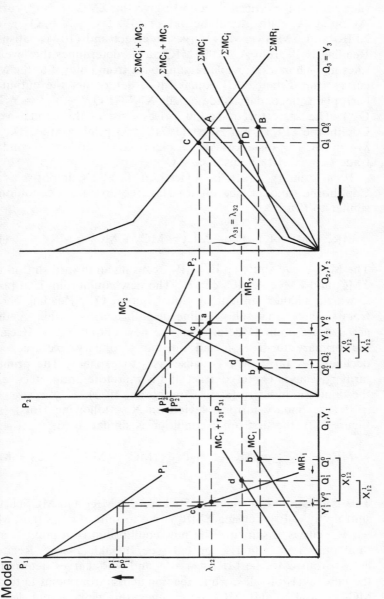

graph as the ΣMR_i curve. Similarly the horizontal sum of the MC_1 and MC_2 curves is the ΣMC_i curve, to which the MC_3 curve (not shown) is vertically added to give the $\Sigma MC_i + MC_3$ curve. At point A, with global output of Q_3^o ($= Q_1^o + Q_{2o}$), the ΣMR_i and $\Sigma MC_i + MC_3$ curves intersect and (10) is satisfied. Reading back from A to the MR_i curves determines the level of sales in each market, while reading back from point B to the MC_i curves (the distance AB equals MC_3) determines the output of each plant. Secondary trade equals X_{12}^o ($= Q_1^o - Y_1^o = Y_2^o - Q_2^o$). The same three shadow prices exist in this model as in Copithorne (1971) and Horst (1971): two primary trade ($\lambda_{31} = \lambda_{32} = MC_3 =$ distance AB in Figure 2.4) and one secondary trade ($\lambda_{12} = MR_1 =$ distance AQ_3^o).

If a primary tariff is levied on firm 1's imports as in Copithorne's model (see Figure 2.3), the first order condition is similar to (9):

$$MR_1 = MC_1 + r_{31}P_{31} + MC_3 = MC_2 + MC_3 = MR_2 \qquad (11)$$

The MC_1 curve shifts up by $r_{31}P_{31}$, causing an inward shift in the ΣMC_i and $\Sigma MC_i + MC_3$ curves. The new equilibrium is at point C with a smaller amount of global output Q_3^1. Reading across from C shows that sales decline in both markets, while reading across from point D determines the new output levels. Because the primary tariff is levied on the secondary exporter, X_{12} declines. (A tariff on X_{32} causes X_{12} to expand.) The primary tariff r_{31} causes Q_1 to contract and is therefore antiprotective to the domestic industry (as in Copithorne, 1971).

If a secondary tariff is levied on X_{12}, following Horst (see Figure 2.2), the first order condition is similar to (6):

$$MR_1 + r_{12}P_{12} = MC_1 + r_{12}P_{12} + MC_3 = MR_2 = MC_2 + MC_3 \qquad (12)$$

This is illustrated in Figure 2.5 where the MR_1 and MC_1 curves shift up by $r_{12}P_{12}$, causing ΣMR_i curve to shift out and the $\Sigma MC_i + MC_3$ curve to shift in. The new equilibrium is at point C and total output Q_3 can rise or fall (see Itagaki, 1980).[3] Reading across from C to the $MR_1 + r_{12}P_{12}$ and MR_2 curves determines the new levels of sales, while reading across from point D to the $MC_1 + r_{12}P_{12}$ and MC_2 determines the new output levels. Secondary trade X_{12} declines while subsidiary output Q_2 expands

Figure 2.5: The Effects of a Secondary Tariff on a Horizontally and Vertically Integrated MNE (The Eden Model)

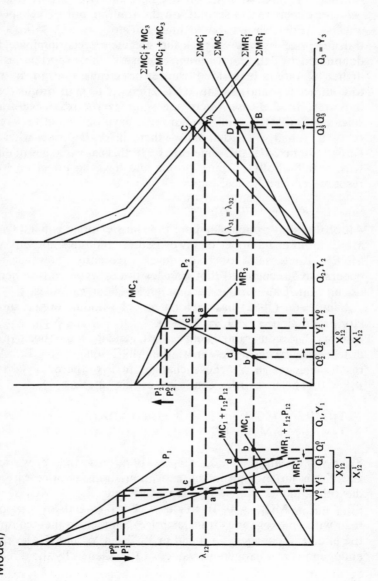

so the secondary tariff offers direct protection to the domestic industry (as in Horst, 1971).

Eden (1978) also investigates the effects of home and host country corporate profit taxes on the MNE. Corporate taxes have two sets of impacts: first, on the MR and MC curves (the '*ad valorem* effects'), and second, on the transfer price (the 'specific effects'). Eden shows that a high transfer price $P_{ij} > \lambda$ (a low transfer price $P_{ij} < \lambda$) implies the specific effects dominate (are dominated by) the *ad valorem* effects. If the exporter has the higher tax rate, a high (low) transfer price causes intra-firm trade to contract (expand) as the MNE attempts to shift profits to the importer. In the case where tariffs are zero, residence-branch rules apply ($b = 1$), and foreign firms have deficits of tax credits ($t_1 > t_i$, $i = 2, 3$), Eden shows that all MNE profits wherever earned are taxed at the same rate t_1. In this case changes in either t_1 or t_i fall wholly on pure profits and have no effect on MNE resource allocation decisions.

C. Endogenous Transfer Prices

All of the above papers assume the transfer price is fixed by the MNE at either its upper or lower bound, and does not vary with MNE output, sales or trade levels. Recently, however, two papers have recognized that transfer prices when constrained by tax and tariff authorities become endogenous variables.

Samuelson (1982) has a Horst model without foreign subsidiary production, i.e. $Q_1 = Y_1 + X_{12}$, $Q_2 = 0$ and $Y_2 = X_{12}$. He assumes P_{12} is constrained between MC_1 and P_1. If the (positive) tax differential exceeds the tariff, the MNE sets $P_{12} = P_1$. As a result, changes in Y_1 cause changes in P_{12} where $\partial P_{12}/\partial Y_1 = P_1' < 0$. The first order condition in this case is:

$$T_1(MR_1 - MC_1) + (T_1 - T_2(1 + r_{12}))X_{12}P_1' =$$
$$T_2MR_2 - T_1MC_1 + (T_1 - T_2(1 + r_{12}))P_1 = 0 \qquad (13)$$

Since $\gamma > r_{12}$ and $P_1' < 0$, $MR_1 - MC_1 > 0$ so that Y_1 is smaller and X_{12} is larger than in the exogenous transfer price case. On the other hand, if $\gamma < r_{12}$, the MNE sets $P_{12} = MC_1$ so that $\partial P_{12}/\partial Q_1 = MC_1' > 0$. In this case, both Y_1 and X_{12} are lower than with an exogenous transfer price. Samuelson then compares the effects of changes in r_{12} and in T_2/T_1 on Y_1 and X_{12} levels for endogenous and exogenous values of P_{12}. Generally the direction of change is the same. However, if $P_{12} = MC_1$, in the exogenous case a change in T_2/T_1 has no effect on the MNE (as in Horst, 1971), whereas it does in the endogenous case. (See also Eden, 1976, pp. 184-5.)

Eden (1983a) extends her earlier 1978 paper to cover transfer pricing policies imposed on the MNE by tariff authorities, such as the fair market value, cost-plus, resale value and GATT transfer value methods. Eden shows that most customs valuation methods generate endogenous transfer prices because $\partial P_{ij}/\partial X_{ij} = P_{ij}' \gtreqless 0$. For a given tariff rate, a $P_{ij}' > (<) 0$ method implies X_{ij} falls (rises) relative to an exogenous transfer price, $P_{ij}' = 0$, because the tariff wedge, $r_{ij} (P_{ij} + X_{ij}P_{ij}')$, is larger (smaller). She then uses the tariff wedge concept to analyze the impacts of changes in tariff rates on X_{ij}, domestic production Q_j and tariff revenues.

D. Uncertainty

The basic Horst and Copithorne models have recently been extended to incorporate uncertainty about exchange rates and foreign demand and cost conditions.

In the exchange rate uncertainty papers, exports are measured in the currency of the exporting country and the MNE is assumed to maximize the expected utility from global net profits. The first paper, Batra and Hadar (1979), uses the Horst model to prove that a rise in the exchange rate e_2 causes X_{12} to increase. The first order condition, assuming $r_{12} = 0$, is:

$$T_1(MR_1 - MC_1) = e_2T_2(MR_2 - MC_2) =$$
$$T_1(P_{12} - MC_1) - T_2(P_{12} - e_2MC_2) = 0 \qquad (14)$$

From (14) we see that devaluation of the home currency implies the cost of foreign subsidiary production rises relative to the cost of exports, causing the MNE to reduce Q_2 and expand X_{12}. Under floating exchange rates, the MNE enters the foreign exchange market and buys currency at a spot price of q_2. If $q_2 > (<) \bar{e}_2$, the MNE's expected exchange rate, Batra and Hadar prove that X_{12} rises (falls) relative to its level under a fixed exchange rate. They conclude that the absence of a forward market generates uncertainty, causing the MNE to reduce X_{12}.

Itagaki (1979, 1981, 1982) models the behaviour of a vertically integrated, two-firm MNE under fixed and flexible exchange rates. (In his 1982 paper horizontally integrated trade is also separately treated.) In Itagaki (1979) the comparative static effects of changes in T_1, T_3 and e_3 on the MNE are determined for a high transfer price $P_{31} > MC_3$. This is expanded in Itagaki (1981) to include uncertainty about e_3, and in Itagaki (1982) to examine the effects of repeal of deferral and the foreign tax credit. He argues (1979, p. 447) that with MNEs 'the income tax is no longer neutral in general, but has wide-spread effects' and that the size of the transfer price in relation to marginal export cost (i.e. whether P_{ij} is high or low) has a critical influence on these tax effects.

Das (1983) uses the Horst model to analyze the effects of demand or cost uncertainty in the foreign market on MNE resource allocation. He shows that cost uncertainty (i.e. C_2 includes a random term) causes Q_2 to decline while Q_1 and X_{12} increase. Demand uncertainty (i.e. R_2 includes a random term) causes Q_1, Q_2 and X_{12} to decline. He then analyzes the comparative static effects on the MNE of a change in T_2 under demand uncertainty (assuming $T_1 > T_2$ and $P_{12} > MR_1$) and of a change in r_{12} under cost uncertainty. The results are shown to depend upon the MNE's measures of absolute and partial relative risk aversion.

E. Optimal Commercial Policies

This last group of papers all model horizontally integrated MNEs although they are not directly based on Horst (1971). Katrak (1977) examines the optimal tariff or consumption tax a host country should levy on MNE intra-firm imports. If there is no foreign subsidiary production ($Q_2 = 0$), he argues an optimal commerical policy should equate the marginal utility from consumption of Y_2 ($= X_{12}$) to the marginal cost of imports. If the host country can tax profits earned on X_{12}, the optimal tariff rate is lower since a higher tariff reduces profits and therefore taxes. (See also Svedberg, 1979.)

Katrak (1980, 1981) examines optimal government policies towards exporting MNEs. His 1980 paper, which is based on Horst (1973), argues that the social optimum for the exporting country requires the MNE to allocate resources so that $P_1 = MC_1 = MR_2 = MC_2$. Since the MNE equates $MR_1 = MC_1 = MR_2 = MC_2$, its exports are too large. The optimal policy is to order the MNE to produce Q_1 where $P_1 = MC_1$ and also to levy an export tax (subsidy) on X_{12} equating $P_1 = MR_2 = MC_2$ when MC_1' is positive (negative).

Katrak (1981) determines the revenue-maximizing export tax for given profit tax rates. His basic result is similar to his 1977 optimal import tariff result, i.e. higher trade taxes imply lower profit tax revenues. However, Katrak (1981) extends this to incorporate transfer price effects. The optimal specific export tax on exports of X_{12} for country 1 (see Katrak, 1981, p. 464, equation (9)) is:

$$t_x^* = -T_1 X_{12}/(dX_{12}/dt_x) + ((1 - T_1)T_2/T_1)(MR_1 - P_{12}) \quad (15)$$

Since $dX_{12}/dt_x < 0$ the first term in (15) is positive implying $t_x^* > 0$. The second term disappears if $T_1 = 1$ (the home country profit tax rate is zero), $T_2 = 0$ (the foreign profit tax rate is 1), or $P_{12} = MR_1$ (the marginal profit on X_{12} is zero for both exporter and importer firms). However, if the MNE sets a high transfer price ($P_{12} > MR_1$) the exporter earns a marginal profit on export sales so that the profit tax loss from raising the export tax is larger. Since the second term in (15) is negative, the optimal export tax is therefore lower. On the other hand, if the MNE sets a low transfer price ($P_{12} < MR_1$), the second term is positive and the optimal export tax is higher. (Note that Katrak's interpretation of (15) is correctly stated in the text (1981, p. 461) but incorrectly reversed in the Appendix (p. 465).)

F. Summary

In section II we reviewed the transfer pricing literature based on Horst (1971) and Copithorne (1971). We discussed the two basic models of horizontally integrated and vertically integrated trade and identified the shadow and profit-maximizing transfer prices in each model. Using graphs, we explained the effects of primary and secondary tariffs on the MNE. We noted the importance of a high or low transfer price for the allocation of profits between exporter and importer and the comparative static effects of corporate profit taxes. Papers incorporating uncertainty and optimal commercial policies towards MNEs were also reviewed. In section III we build a model that incorporates the basic advances in the above literature and that has the major advantage of simultaneously modelling horizontally and vertically integrated trade.

III. A General Model of MNE Intra-firm Trade

A. The Static Model

We assume the MNE consists of three firms as outlined in section I with the following profit functions valued in country 1's currency (see Figure 2.1):

$$L_3 = e_3 T_3 [P_{31} X_{31} + P_{32} X_{32} - C_3] \qquad (16)$$

$$L_2 = e_2 T_2 [R_2 - C_2 - (e_3/e_2)(1 + r_{32})(P_{32} X_{32} - (1 + r_{12}) P_{12} X_{12}/e_2] \qquad (17)$$

$$L_1 = T_1 [R_1 - C_1 - e_3(1 + r_{31}) P_{31} X_{31} + P_{12} X_{12}] \qquad (18)$$

Substituting in the relationships assumed in section I, we have the global net profit function of the MNE:

$$L = T_1(R_1 - C_1) + e_2 T_2(R_2 - C_2) - e_3 T_3 C_3 + (T_3 - T_1(1 + r_{31}))e_3 P_{31} Q_1 + (T_3 - T_2(1 + r_{32}))e_3 P_{32} Q_2 + (T_1 - T_2(1 + r_{12}))P_{12} X_{12} \qquad (19)$$

The profit-maximizing transfer prices are determined by taking the partial derivative of (19) with respect to P_{ij} and using the envelope theorem:

$$\partial L / \partial P_{ij} = [T_i - T_j(1 + r_{ij})]e_i X_{ij} \gtreqless 0 \text{ as } T_i \gtreqless T_j(1 + r_{ij}) \qquad (20)$$

From (20) we see that P_{ij} should be set at its upper bound (lower bound) whenever T_i, the net return to the exporter, is higher (lower) than $T_j(1 + r_{ij})$, the net return to the importer, per dollar of profits on X_{ij}. (This is equivalent to Horst's $\gamma \gtreqless r_{ij}$.)[4] We consider two cases which are (loosely) referred to as the 'surplus of foreign tax credits' and 'deficit of foreign tax credits' cases. (See note 1 and Eden, 1983b, for detailed explanations of these two cases.)

In the surplus of tax credits case we assume both subsidiaries have effective tax rates in excess of the parent firm which implies $T_1 > T_2$ and $T_1 > T_3$. Therefore $T_3 < T_1(1 + r_{31})$ so the MNE sets P_{31} at its lower bound to shift profits on Q_1 to the importer, firm 1. However, we can assume any combination of $T_1 \gtreqless T_2(1 + r_{12})$ and $T_3 \gtreqless T_2(1 + r_{32})$ since r_{12} may be large enough to offset $T_1 > T_2$, and $T_3 \gtreqless T_2$. We assume $T_3 < T_2(1 + r_{32})$ and T_1

$> T_2(1 + r_{12})$ on the grounds that (1) tax authorities in country 3 would probably prevent large discrepancies between P_{31} and P_{32} and (2) these assumptions generate the largest number of unambiguous comparative static results. (The reader is invited to substitute the other assumptions and trace their implications in what follows.) Therefore in the surplus of tax credits case the MNE sets a high value for P_{12} (to shift profits to the exporter) and low values for P_{31} and P_{32} (to shift profits to the importers).

In the deficit of tax credits case we assume both subsidiaries have effective tax rates below the parent firm (note that we must have $b_i < 1$) which implies $T_1 < T_2$ and $T_1 < T_3$. Therefore $T_1 < T_2(1 + r_{12})$ so the MNE sets a low value on P_{12} to shift profits to firm 2. However, we can have $T_3 \gtreqless T_1(1 + r_{31})$ and $T_3 \gtreqless T_2(1 + r_{32})$. We assume that $T_3 > T_1(1 + r_{31})$ and $T_3 > T_2(1 + r_{32})$ on the grounds noted above and leave the other cases to the reader. Our transfer pricing bounds are, therefore, reversed — the MNE chooses a minimum value for P_{12} and maximum value for P_{31} and P_{32}. In the rest of this section we analyze the surplus of tax credits case, briefly commenting on the effects of the deficit of tax credits case at the end.

The first order conditions for a global net profit maximum are found by differentiating (19) with respect to Q_1, Q_2 and X_{12}:

$$\partial L/\partial Q_1 = [e_3T_3(P_{31} - MC_3)] + [T_1(MR_1 - MC_1 - (1 + r_{31})e_3P_{31})] = 0 \qquad (21)$$

$$\partial L/\partial Q_2 = [e_3T_3(P_{32} - MC_3)] + [e_2T_2(MR_2 - MC_2 - (e_3/e_2)(1 + r_{32})P_{32})] = 0 \qquad (22)$$

$$\partial L/\partial X_{12} = [T_1(P_{12} - MR_1)] + [T_2(e_2MR_2 - (1 + r_{12})P_{12})] = 0 \qquad (23)$$

The first square bracket in ((21), (22), (23)) shows the marginal profit of the exporter, firm i, while the second square bracket measures the marginal profit of the importer, firm j, in the 'market' for X_{ij}. Each first order condition can be interpreted as the condition for 'market equilibrium', i.e. summed global MNE marginal profits on X_{ij} must equal zero (see also Eden, 1983b).

If the MNE sets P_{ij} equal to the shadow transfer price λ (i.e. $P_{31} = P_{32} = \lambda_{31} = \lambda_{32} = MC_3$ and $P_{12} = \lambda_{12} = MR_1$), each firm earns a zero marginal profit on X_{ij}. However, the first order conditions only require that summed marginal profits are zero. From (20) we see that global MNE net profits are higher if P_{ij} is set above (below) λ when T_i is greater (less) than $T_j(1 + r_{ij})$. The relationship between P_{ij} and the marginal profit/loss of the exporting and importing firms is clear from ((21), (22), (23)). If P_{ij} lies above (below) λ, the exporter receives a marginal profit (loss) and the importer receives an equal in value marginal loss (profit) with zero summed marginal profits overall.[5] Assuming $T_3 < T_1(1 + r_{31})$, $T_3 < T_2(1 + r_{32})$ and $T_1 > T_2(1 + r_{12})$, firm 1 earns marginal profits in both the Q_1 and X_{12} markets, firm 3 earns marginal losses in both the Q_1 and Q_2 markets, and firm 2 earns a marginal profit in the Q_2 market and a marginal loss in the X_{12} market. Let us now turn to the comparative static effects of 'small' changes in T_i, r_{ij} and e_i on the MNE (i.e. we assume the sign of $T_i - T_j(1 + r_{ij})$ does not change).

B. The Comparative Statics

Totally differentiating ((21), (22), (23)) and setting the results in matrix form we have:

$$\begin{bmatrix} T(MR'_1 - MC'_1) - e_3 T_3 MC'_3 & -e_3 T_3 MC'_3 & -T_1 MR'_1 \\ -e_3 T_3 MC'_3 & e_2 T_2 (MR'_2 - MC'_2) - e_3 T_3 MC'_3 & e_2 T_2 MR'_2 \\ -T_1 MR'_1 & e_2 T_2 MR'_2 & T_1 MR'_1 + e_2 T_2 MR'_2 \end{bmatrix} \begin{bmatrix} dQ_1 \\ dQ_2 \\ dX_{12} \end{bmatrix} = \begin{bmatrix} A \\ B \\ C \end{bmatrix} \quad (24)$$

where

$$A = (MC_1 + (1 + r_{31})e_3 P_{31} - MR_1)dT_1 + e_3(MC_3 - P_{31})dT_3 + (e_3 T_1 P_{31})dr_{31} + (T_1(1 + r_{31})P_{31} + T_3(MC_3 - P_{31}))de_3$$

$$B = e_2(e_3(1 + r_{32})P_{32}/e_2 + MC_2 - MR_2)dT_2 + e_3(MC_3 - P_{32})dT_3 + (e_3 T_2 P_{32})dr_{32} + T_2(MC_2 - MR_2)de_2 + (T_2(1 + r_{32})P_{32} + T_3(MC_3 - P_{32}))de_3$$

$$C = (MR_1 - P_{12})dT_1 + ((1 + r_{12})P_{12} - e_2 MR_2)dT_2 + (T_2 P_{12})dr_{12} + (-T_2 MR_2)de_2$$

Denoting the element in the ith row and the jth column by a_{ij} and its cofactor by D_{ij} we assume $a_{ii} < 0$ $(i = 1, 2, 3)$, $a_{12} < 0$, $a_{13} > 0$, $a_{23} < 0$ so that $D_{ii} > 0$ $(i = 1, 2, 3)$, $D_{12} = D_{21} < 0$, $D_{13} = D_{31} > 0$, $D_{23} = D_{32} < 0$ and the determinant $D < 0$.[6] We use Cramer's Rule to determine the impacts of T_i, r_{ij} and e_i on Q_1, Q_2 and X_{12}. Noting the relationships $dY_1 = dQ_1 - dX_{12}$, $dY_2 = dQ_2 + dX_{12}$ and $dQ_3 = dQ_1 + dQ_2$, we can also determine the effects on Y_1, Y_2 and Q_3. The proofs are left for the reader. The results are summarized in the eight propositions and note 9 below.

Proposition 1. $dQ_1/dT_1 > 0$, $dQ_2/dT_1 < 0$, $dX_{12}/dT_1 > 0$, $dY_1/dT_1 \gtrless 0$, $dY_2/dT_1 > 0$ and $dQ_3/dT_1 \lessgtr 0$

Because firm 1 earns a marginal profit in both the Q_1 and X_{12} markets, a rise in T_1 increases these marginal profits (see (21) and (23)). Both markets are now in disequilibrium because summed marginal profits are positive. Since the global profit function is concave with respect to X_{ij} (i.e. $\partial^2 L/\partial X_{ij}^2 = a_{ii} < 0$) the rise in T_1 causes the MNE to expand both Q_1 and X_{12}. The impact of T_1 on the Q_1 market is illustrated in Figure 2.6(a) which shows total MNE net profits in the X_{ij} market. Market equilibrium is at point A where summed marginal profits are zero. In the traditional analysis of a profits tax a rise (fall) in the tax rate shifts the total profit curve L down (up) without altering the equilibrium level of output. However, in the MNE case, only part of the profits from X_{ij} are affected by a change in T_i so the shift in the global profits curve is not uniform. (A proportionate

Figure 2.6: The Effect of a Rise in T_i on Global MNE Profits from X_{ij}

(a)	(b)
Assuming Firm i Receives a Marginal Profit on X_{ij}	Assuming Firm i Receives a Marginal Loss on X_{ij}

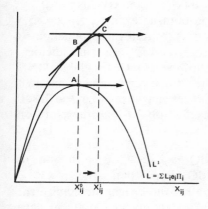
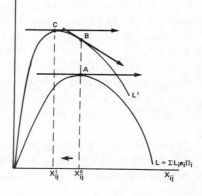

change in T_i and T_j, however, would uniformly shift the L curve, leaving X_{ii} unchanged.) Since firm 1 earns a marginal profit in the Q_1 market, a rise in T_1 creates positive summed marginal profits at $X_{ij}{}^o$ (point B), inducing the MNE to move to point C where summed marginal profits are again zero. Therefore dQ_1/dT_1. Figure 2.6(a) can also be used to explain $dX_{12}/dT_1 > 0$. The increases in Q_1 and X_{12} have secondary effects on the MNE: Q_2 falls, Y_2 rises, the effects on Y_1 and Q_3 are ambiguous.

Proposition 2. $dQ_1/dT_2 < 0$, $dQ_2/dT_2 > 0$, $dX_{12}/dT_2 < 0$, $dY_1/dT_2 > 0$, $dY_2/dT_2 \gtreqless 0$ and $dQ_3/dT_2 \gtreqless 0$

Firm 2 earns a marginal profit on Q_2 and marginal loss on X_{12}. A rise in T_2 generates summed marginal profits in the Q_2 market (see (22)) and summed marginal losses in the X_{12} market (see (23)). Since Q_2 and X_{12} are substitutes, these effects reinforce one another and Q_2 expands and X_{12} contracts. Figure 2.6(b) illustrates the effects of a rise in T_2 on the X_{12} market. (The effect on Q_2 is illustrated by Figure 2.6(a).) The market is initially in equilibrium at point A. Since firm 2 earns a marginal loss on X_{12}, the rise in T_2 causes the global profit curve to shift up and to the left. Summed marginal losses are now earned at point B, inducing the MNE to move to point C and a lower level of X_{12}. The rise in Q_2 and fall in X_{12} have second round impacts on the MNE: Q_1 falls, Y_1 rises, the effects on Y_2 and Q_3 are ambiguous.

Proposition 3. $dQ_3/dT_3 < 0$, and iff $P_{31} = P_{32}$, $dQ_1/dT_3 < 0$, $dQ_2/dT_3 < 0$, $dX_{12}/dT_3 \gtreqless 0$, $dY_1/dT_3 \gtreqless 0$ and $dY_2/dT_3 \gtreqless 0$

Firm 3 receives marginal losses on both its exports, $X_{31} (= Q_1)$ and $X_{32} (= Q_2)$, but Q_1 and Q_2 are substitutes in production so the impacts of a change in T_3 on Q_1 and Q_2 are contradictory. The impact on $Q_3 = Q_1 + Q_2$, however, is clear: global MNE output declines. If $P_{31} = P_{32}$, the firm receives equal marginal losses in both markets. Only in this case can we prove $dQ_1/dT_3 < 0$ and $dQ_2/dT_3 < 0$. However, the effect on X_{12} and therefore on Y_1 and Y_2 remain ambiguous.

Proposition 4. $dQ_1/dr_{31} < 0$, $dQ_2/dr_{31} > 0$, $dX_{12}/dr_{31} < 0$, $dY_1/dr_{31} < 0$, $dY_2/dr_{31} < 0$ and $dQ_3/dr_{31} < 0$

A glance at Figure 2.4 shows that all of these signs are confirmed. From (21) we see that a rise in r_{31} causes the MNE to earn summed marginal losses on X_{31} and to contract Q_1. This has second round impacts on the other markets. Note that domestic sales fall (and consumer prices rise) in both countries 1 and 2.

Proposition 5. $dQ_1/dr_{32} > 0$, $dQ_2/dr_{32} < 0$, $dX_{12}/dr_{32} > 0$, $dY_1/dr_{32} < 0$, $dY_2/dr_{32} < 0$, and $dQ_3/dr_{32} < 0$
The interpretation is the same as above; however, note that X_{12} now rises instead of falls.

Proposition 6. $dQ_1/dr_{12} < 0$, $dQ_2/dr_{12} > 0$, $dX_{12}/dr_{12} < 0$, $dY_1/dr_{12} > 0$, $dY_2/dr_{12} < 0$, and $dQ_3/dr_{12} \gtreqless 0$
These signs are all confirmed in Figure 2.5. The interpretation is again similar to Proposition 4.[7]

Proposition 7. $dQ_1/de_2 > 0$, $dQ_2/de_2 < 0$, $dX_{12}/de_2 > 0$, $dY_1/de_2 < 0$, $dY_2/de_2 > 0$, and $dQ_3/de_2 \gtreqless 0$
A rise in the value of country 2's currency has two effects on the MNE. First, firm 2's marginal profit from Q_2 increases by T_2 $(MR_2 - MC_2)de_2$. Second, its marginal loss on X_{12} falls by $T_2MR_2de_2$. (Since P_{12} is already valued in country 1's currency, the rise in e_2 has no effect on it.) The rise in e_2 therefore causes positive summed marginal profits in both the Q_2 and X_{12} markets. Because Q_2 and X_{12} are substitutes, the impacts are contradictory. However, an inspection of the two Cramer's Rule terms shows that the rise in marginal profit on Q_2 must be less than the fall in its marginal loss on X_{12}. As a result, the second effect dominates the first and the net impact is a rise in X_{12}.

It is interesting to compare this result with Batra and Hadar (1979). They also have $dX_{12}/de_2 > 0$ based on the positive impact of a rise in e_2 on the X_{12} market (our second effect). However, because they ignore primary trade, their first order condition requires $MR_2 = MC_2$ in the Q_2 market so the first effect we note above does not occur in their model (see (14)). Note also that in their model the rise in e_2 is referred to as a 'devaluation of the home currency'. In our three-country model, a devaluation of currency 1 implies e_2 and e_3 both rise proportionally so that e_2/e_3 remains constant. An examination of ((21), (22), (23)) shows that the effects of a devaluation of the home currency are probably ambiguous. The rise in e_3 causes summed marginal losses in the Q_1 market, inducing a fall in Q_1. Since e_3/e_2 is constant, there is no direct impact on the Q_2 market.

The rise in e_2, however, causes summed marginal profits in the X_{12} market, inducing a rise in X_{12}. Since Q_1 and X_{12} are complements and either effect could dominate, we predict, contrary to Batra and Hadar, that a devaluation of the home currency has ambiguous effects on the MNE.

Proposition 8. $dQ_3/de_3 < 0$

An inspection of (21) and (22) shows that a rise in e_3 causes summed marginal losses in both the Q_1 and Q_2 markets. Since Q_1 and Q_2 are substitutes, the net effect is ambiguous (even if we assume $P_{31} = P_{32}$). The only unambiguous result is $dQ_1/de_3 + dQ_2/de_3 = dQ_3/de_3 < 0$; a rise in country 3's currency causes the MNE to contract global output. This is easily explained: the MNE earns overall marginal losses in country 3. A rise in its currency increases these losses, and causes the MNE to reduce firm 3's total exports.

Our comparative static results for the surplus of tax credits case are summarized in Table 2.1. In the deficit of tax credits case the MNE sets $P_{31} > MC_3$, $P_{32} > MC_3$ and $P_{12} < MR_1$. As a result the comparative static effects of tax changes are reversed because

Table 2.1: The Comparative Static Effects of Changes in T_i, r_{ij} and e_i on the MNE (assuming $P_{31} < MC_3$, $P_{32} < MC_3$ and $P_{12} > MR_1$)[a]

Exogenous Variables	Effects on Endogenous Variables							
	Q_1	Q_2	X_{12}	Y_1	Y_2	Q_3	P_1	P_2
T_1	+	−	+	A [b]	+	A	A	−
T_2	−	+	−	+	A	A	−	A
T_3	−[c]	−[c]	A	A	A	−	A	A
r_{31}	−	+	−	−	−	−	+	+
r_{32}	+	−	+	−	−	−	+	+
r_{12}	−	+	−	+	−	A	−	+
e_2	+	−	+	−	+	A	+	−
e_3	A	A	A	A	A	−	A	A

Notes: a. If $P_{31} > MC_3$, $P_{32} > MC_3$ and $P_{12} < MR_1$, the tax signs are reversed, the tariff signs are unaffected, the signs on e_2 are unaffected, and the sign on e_3 is reversed.
b. A = ambiguous.
c. if $P_{31} = P_{32}$.

they depend on whether P_{ij} is high or low. The tariff effects are unchanged as long as P_{ij} is positive. The effects of a change in e_2 are also unchanged since the net impact on X_{12} is positive regardless of the values of P_{32} and P_{12}. However, $dQ_3/de_3 > 0$ if the MNE sets high values on firm 3's exports because a rise in e_3 increases the value of these marginal profits.

Lastly, let us look at the case where all three profit-maximizing transfer prices are set equal to their shadow prices. An examination of ((21), (22), (23)) shows that changes in T_i or T_j now have no effect on MNE resource allocation because zero marginal profits are earned by both the exporter and importer affiliates. As in Horst (1971) tax policy is impotent when the MNE sets 'equilibrium' transfer prices, i.e. when $P_{ij} = \lambda$. (See also Eden, 1976, p. 195.)[8] The tariff effects are unchanged as long as $P_{ij} > 0$. The effects of a change in e_2 are now the same as Batra and Hadar (1979); only the X_{12} market is affected and X_{12} expands. Lastly, a rise (fall) in e_3 causes summed marginal losses (profits) in the Q_1 and Q_2 markets so Q_3 contracts (expands).

C. Tariffs and Economic Welfare

In this section we address two issues: (1) the revenue-maximizing tariff for an importing country; and (2) the impact of tariffs on global welfare. The welfare effects of tariffs have been thoroughly analyzed in the general equilibrium model of international trade between unrelated firms. We examine whether a similar analysis applies to our partial equilibrium model of international trade between related firms.

If an importing country has some monopoly power in trade, it can increase its national welfare by imposing an optimal tariff. Let us assume that welfare in the importing country is positively related to total revenues received from corporate profit taxes and tariffs.[9] We can use Katrak's method for calculating the optimal export tax (1981, p. 464) to determine the importing country's optimal tariff for a given corporate tax rate.

Let us derive the optimal *ad valorem* tariff r_{12}^* for country 2 for a given tax rate $1 - T_2$ and given transfer price P_{12}. (The analysis and final formula are identical for changes in a primary tariff.) We assume firm 2 has a surplus of foreign tax credits so the effective tax rate on π_2 is the foreign tax rate. Total tax and tariff revenues paid by the MNE in country 2, measured in country 1's currency, are:

$$TTR_2 = e_2(1 - T_2)[R_2 - C_2 - (e_3/e_2)(1 + r_{32})P_{32}Q_2 - (1 + r_{12})P_{12}X_{12}/e_2] + r_{12}P_{12}X_{12} + e_3(1 + r_{32})P_{32}Q_2 \tag{25}$$

Differentiating this with respect to r_{12} we have the first order condition for a revenue maximum (since $\partial^2 TTR_2/\partial r_{12}^2 < 0$):

$$\partial TTR_2/\partial r_{12} = e_2(1 - T_2)(MR_2 - (1 + r_{12})P_{12}/e_2)dX_{12}/dr_{12} + T_2 P_{12}X_{12} + (r_{12}P_{12})dX_{12}/dr_{12} = 0 \tag{26}$$

Now substituting the first order condition (23) into (26) and solving for r_{12}^*, the optimal *ad valorem* tariff rate is:

$$r_{12}^* = - T_2 X_{12}/(dX_{12}/dr_{12}) + ((1 - T_2) T_1/T_2 (P_{12} - M_1)/P_{12} \tag{27}$$

First note the similarities between Katrak's optimal export tax in (15) and the optimal tariff in (27). Since $dX_{12}/dr_{12} < 0$ from Proposition 6, the first term is positive as in (15). The sign of the second term depends upon the sign of $P_{12} - MR_1$ (i.e. $P_{ij} - \lambda$) which is the reverse of (15). A high (low) transfer price implies the optimal tariff r_{12}^* is larger (smaller) than if country 2 simply ignored the impact of transfer pricing on its profit tax revenues. The second term in (27) is zero if either $1 - T_2 = 0$, $T_1 = 0$, or $P_{12} = MR_1$, generating zero marginal tax revenue. (Compare this with the second term in (15).) If $T_2 = 1$ so the profit tax rate is zero, $| (dX_{12}/X_{12})(r_{12}/dr_{12}) | = 1$ and r_{12}^* simply maximizes tariff revenues. If $P_{12} < MR_1$, the second term in (27) is negative so the optimal tariff is smaller. With a low transfer price the importer earns a positive marginal profit on X_{12}. Since marginal profit tax revenues are positive, the optimal volume of imports should, therefore, be larger and r_{12}^* smaller. On the other hand, if $P_{12} > MR_1$ the second term is positive and the optimal tariff rate is higher. The effect of the transfer price on the optimal tariff in (27) is, therefore, exactly the reverse of its effect on the optimal export tax in (15), i.e. a high (low) P_{ij} implies a higher (lower) tariff but a lower (higher) export tax.

Now let us examine the impact of tariffs on global welfare. In the traditional two-country/two-good model of international trade, tariffs lower world welfare because (1) global output falls and (2) the tariff drives a wedge between domestic and foreign consumer prices (see Caves and Jones, 1981, pp. 208-10). Can we draw a similar conclusion in our three-country/one-good model, i.e. that a tariff causes Q_3 to fall and the gap between P_1 and P_2 to widen? (Note that, in general, $P_1 \neq P_2$ even if $t_i = t_j = r_{ij} = 0$ since the MNE can price discriminate between markets.) Surprisingly, the answer is 'yes' for primary tariffs but 'no' for secondary tariffs.

The reasoning behind this conclusion lies in the domestic elasticity of demand in the two countries and in the way a tariff affects the MNE's first order conditions. For a global profit maximum under free trade the MNE sets $MR_1 = MC_1 + MC_3 = MR_2 = MC_2 + MC_3$ as in (10). Since $MR_i = P_i(1 - 1/\varepsilon_i)$ where ε_i is the domestic elasticity of demand, and $MR_1 = MR_2$, we have $P_1 \gtreqless P_2$ as $\varepsilon_1 \lesseqgtr \varepsilon_2$. We know that, in general, home firms view their domestic demand as less elastic than their demand in foreign markets (Caves and Jones, 1981, pp. 171-2). Therefore $\varepsilon_2 > \varepsilon_1$ and $P_1 > P_2$ under free trade.

Now if either country 1 or 2 levies a primary tariff, Propositions 4 and 5 prove that consumer prices in both countries rise. The primary tariff drives a wedge between the marginal cost curves of the two plants but does not affect the $MR_1 = MR_2$ equality (see (22)). As a result $\Delta MR_1 = \Delta MR_2$ and since $\varepsilon_2 > \varepsilon_1$ we have $\Delta P_1 > \Delta P_2$. Thus the consumer price gap $P_1 - P_2$ widens if either country levies a primary tariff. (See also Figure 2.4). At the same time, primary tariffs unambiguously cause global MNE output Q_3 to fall. We therefore conclude the primary tariffs do lower global welfare because Q_3 falls and $P_1 - P_2$ widens. (Note that this conclusion holds: (1) only in a partial equilibrium sense because this is a one-good model; (2) if the MNE's ability to price discriminate does not depend on the tariff; and (3) assuming the transfer price remains fixed.)

When a secondary tariff r_{12} is levied on intra-firm trade, Proposition 6 proves that consumer price in the importing (exporting) country rises (falls). Since $P_1 > P_2$ under free trade the secondary tariff causes the consumer price gap to shrink. (See also Figure 2.5.) At the same time, the effect of r_{12} on Q_3 is ambiguous. Therefore we cannot prove that a secondary tariff lowers global welfare (in the sense that Q_3 falls and $P_1 - P_2$ widens) although this is true for primary tariffs.

However, we do know that tariffs contract intra-firm trade *per se*, i.e. $dX_{ij}/dr_{ij} < 0$. In this sense a tariff must be global welfare-reducing because the tariff causes the MNE to contract X_{ij} below its free trade level. Since it is the size of the tariff wedge $r_{ij}P_{ij}$ that determines the amount of trade contraction (see (11) and (12)), the inefficiency induced by the tariff can be partly or wholly offset by a lower transfer price P_{ij}. The possibility that transfer price manipulation can reduce the welfare loss caused by tariffs and other trade barriers is explored in the next section. (See also Itagaki (this volume) where the choice between a tariff or quota can be affected by the MNE's ability to change P_{ij} in response to an *ad valorem* tariff.)

D. *Transfer Pricing and Economic Efficiency*

One important current debate in the transfer pricing literature concerns the efficiency of transfer pricing by MNEs in comparison to the so-called 'arm's-length' price. In the internalization literature (see Rugman, 1981, p. 83) transfer pricing is regarded as an 'efficient response by the MNE to exogenous market imperfections' such as corporate tax differentials and tariffs. MNEs are seen as overcoming these exogenous imperfections by creating an internal market with transfer prices. For Rugman, arm's-length prices do not exist; the MNE's chosen transfer prices are the correct efficient ones. Internalization theory sees transfer pricing as reducing the global inefficiency caused by government interventions designed to segment national markets. Since MNEs can use transfer prices to arbitrage trade barriers between countries, market segmentation is reduced and global welfare improves. (See also Aliber (this volume).)

On the other hand, Diewert (this volume) shows that the deadweight loss due to international tax differentials is larger when the MNE sets the transfer price above or below the optimal regulated price. Similarly, Bond (1980, p. 192) argues that transfer pricing distorts resource allocation as the MNE trades 'the gains from tax evasion against the efficiency losses resulting from resource misallocation' when transfer pricing in response to tax differentials. Most developed countries have regulations (e.g. Section 482 of the US Internal Revenue Code) to force transfer prices equal to arm's-length prices, both on efficiency grounds and to prevent either erosion or double taxation of the revenue base. (See Shoup, this volume, on the arm's-length price as a standard in international transfer pricing disputes.) The popular view clearly is also that transfer pricing worsens global resource allocation.

In this section we try to shed some light on this debate by

asking how corporate profit tax differentials and tariffs affect resource allocation when the transfer price is, first, the Hirshleifer shadow price and second, the profit-maximizing price that minimizes these exogenous imperfections. As a benchmark, we assume resources are allocated efficiently by the MNE under free trade. If all corporate taxes and tariffs are zero, the MNE allocates resources so as to satisfy (10). Let us call the free trade level of intra-firm exports X_o. The Hirshleifer shadow price is λ, the marginal cost of the selling division as determined by the intersection of the marginal revenue and marginal cost of export (i.e. excess demand and excess supply) curves (see Figure 2.2). The profit-maximizing transfer price (let us call it P) differs from the shadow price whenever there is a difference between the net returns to the exporter and importer of X. Now let us compare the effects on X under tax and tariff barriers when the MNE is constrained to use the Hirshleifer transfer price λ and when it is free to use P. We define the 'efficient' transfer price as that price which produces an allocation of MNE resources closest to that under free trade, i.e. closest to X_o.

First, if MNE trade is constrained by a tariff only and λ is chosen, the tariff wedge is $r\lambda$ and X_o contracts to X_λ. On the other hand, if the MNE can choose its transfer price, it sets $P < \lambda$ to minimize tariff costs. Because the new tariff wedge rP is less than $r\lambda$, trade contracts to X_P where $X_\lambda < X_P < X_o$. The distortion in resource allocation due to the tariff is less when the MNE can manipulate P compared to the Hirshleifer price. Transfer pricing is therefore an efficient response to tariffs, as argued by Rugman.

Second, if trade is constrained by tax differentials only and the MNE set $P = \lambda$, each firm earns a zero marginal profit on intra-firm trade. Changes in the tax differential γ thus have no effect on MNE resource allocation so $X_\lambda = X_o$. If the MNE can choose P, it sets $P \gtreqless \lambda$ when $\gamma \gtreqless 0$ to shift profits to the lower taxed firm. Because either profit-maximizing transfer price ($P \gtreqless \lambda$) causes positive summed marginal profits in the market for X, intra-firm trade expands. As a result, $X_\lambda = X_o < X_P$.[10] Shadow transfer pricing in response to corporate tax differentials is, therefore, inefficient in the sense that $X_\lambda = X_o \neq X_P$, as argued by Diewert.

Now let us analyze the efficiency of transfer price manipulation when the MNE is jointly constrained by taxes and tariffs. If

$P = \lambda$, γ has no effect on X whereas r causes X to contract. We conclude that $\gamma \gtrless r$ for $P = \lambda$ implies $X_\lambda < X_o$. On the other hand, if profit-maximizing transfer prices can be chosen, r causes X to fall so that $X_\lambda < X_P < X_o$, whereas the tax differential causes X to expand so that $X_\lambda = X_o < X_P$. If γ dominates r we therefore argue $X_\lambda < X_o < X_P$, whereas if r dominates γ we have $X_\lambda < X_P < X_o$, and if $\gamma = r$ we have $X_\lambda = X_P < X_o$. Therefore the profit-maximizing transfer price is unambiguously more efficient than the Hirshleifer price (in the sense that X_p is closer to X_o than X_λ) when the tariff rate dominates the tax differential, inducing the MNE to set $P < \lambda$. If the tax differential dominates the tariff, neither transfer price is umabiguously more efficient; whereas if $\gamma = r$, both prices imply the same (i.e. too low) level of intra-firm trade. Therefore we conclude that the profit-maximizing transfer price P can be either more or less efficient than the shadow price λ in a world of government-induced market imperfections. Note that although in certain circumstances Hirshleifer and arm's-length prices are the same (see Diewert, this volume), this does not answer the question as to whether profit-maximizing transfer prices are more or less efficient than the arm's-length price rules arbitrarily defined by government regulations such as Section 482. Clearly this is the crucial question and one that is not answered here. Diewert (this volume) does show that an optimal regulated transfer price can be determined which will generate an undistorted level of intra-firm trade, but he is, justifiably, pessimistic as to any government's ability to determine such a price. He does prove, however, that relaxing the regulatory constraints (i.e. moving away from the optimal regulated transfer price) worsens global efficiency. Lastly, we should stress that although the rationale for regulation of transfer pricing on efficiency grounds may not be clear, arm's-length rules may still be justifiable on distributional grounds, as argued by Shoup and Helleiner elsewhere in this volume.

IV. Conclusions: Where Do We Go from Here?

The purpose of this paper was to review and synthesize the existing partial equilibrium microeconomic models of international transfer pricing of tangible goods. In section II we showed how the theory has progressed from the early models by Horst and Copithorne to the recent work incorporating uncertainty, endogenous transfer prices and optimal commercial policies. In section III we drew on this literature to build a general model of transfer pricing that simultaneously modelled horizontally and vertically integrated trade and incorporated the major results to date. In both sections we developed the concept of a high/low transfer price and stressed its importance for the static and comparative static results of the various models.

Where do we go from here? Several directions are possible:

1. An obvious omission is the failure to model factor markets; i.e. to go behind the MNE's cost curves to determine the impacts of transfer pricing, taxes and tariffs on factor demands and factor incomes. Related to this is the assumption that corporate profit taxes fall only on pure profits and not on equity capital. Incidence effects of the corporate income tax have not been modelled in the transfer pricing literature.

2. The welfare and income distributional effects of transfer pricing on home and host countries need further development, e.g. producer and consumer surplus effects, the index of monopoly power, calculation of optimal commercial and tax policies. (See Bardhan (1982) for some work in this area.)

3. The work on exchange rate and foreign demand/supply uncertainty needs to be extended to a general theory of the MNE under uncertainty.

4. Some of the assumptions of the basic model should be relaxed to determine the implications of oligopolistic domestic markets, imperfectly competitive products and rivalrous behaviour by affiliates for our static and comparative static results. The implications of the recent literature on cross-hauling and intra-industry trade for the MNE model also need examination.

5. The impacts of other exogenous market imperfections on the MNE should be modelled, e.g. exchange controls, price controls, voluntary export quotas. Also the theory of the MNE should be extended to make environmental variables such as government regulations endogenous.

6. The theory of financial manoeuvring of MNE liquid assets (as in Brean, this volume) and the theory of transfer pricing of tangibles need to be jointly developed into a general theory of fiscal transfer pricing. (For some work in this area see Horst (1977 and Rutenberg (1970).)

7. Outside the basic partial equilibrium static framework are other frameworks in which MNEs can be analyzed: general equilibrium models, dynamic investment models (see Samuelson, this volume), models using duality theory (see Diewert, this volume.) The incorporation of transfer pricing into these models lies at the forefront of MNE research.

8. A microeconomic theory of transfer pricing of intangibles, such as technology, in a world of taxes and tariffs has not yet appeared in the Horst-Copithorne literature. (See Horst, 1973, for some preliminary work on this assuming free trade.) Such common cost allocations have public good attributes that should provide interesting and policy relevant comparisons with the standard theory of transfer pricing of tangible private goods.

9. Lastly, we argue that future extensions in the theory of transfer pricing should be developed in the context of an MNE model incorporating both vertically and horizontally integrated trade. An amalgamation of the Horst and Copithorne models not only yields fruitful results, but also more closely approximates the reality of the multidivisional multinational enterprise.

In conclusion we stress that transfer pricing is a phenomenon unique to intra-firm trade. As a result, models of the MNE are incomplete without an explanation of transfer pricing — and the theory of transfer pricing must be an integral part of the theory of the multinational enterprise.

Notes

* Earlier versions of this paper were presented at the universities of Alberta, Regina and Saskatoon, and at Brock University. I would like to thank the participants and also L.W. Copithorne, W.E. Diewert, Larry Samuelson and Carl S. Shoup for helpful comments.

1. In the simplest case $T_i = 1 - t_i$ as in Horst (1971). However, this is complicated by extra home country taxes payable on dividends remitted to the parent if the home tax rate exceeds the foreign rate. If $t_1 < t_i$ (firm i has a surplus of foreign tax credits) then $T_i = 1 - t_i$. However, if $t_1 > t_i$ (firm i has a deficit of tax credits) dividends $b_i\pi_i$ are taxed at rate t_1 while retained earnings $(1 - b_i)\pi_i$ are taxed at t_i. The effective foreign tax is, therefore $t_i + b_i(t_1 - t_i)$ and $T_i = 1 - t_i - b_i(t_1 - t_i)$. (Note $T_i = 1 - t_1 = T_1$ if $b_1 = 1$ (no deferral and deficit of tax credits).) For more complicated definitions of T_i incorporating withholding taxes see Eden (1983b).

2. Note that Diewert (this volume) also proves more generally that in the absence of taxes and tariffs, the shadow transfer price λ^*, the arm's-length price $\bar{w}$, and the decentralized price w^* coincide, providing the profit functions of the divisions are differentiable and concave functions of the volume of intra-firm trade X. His equation (4) is also equivalent to our (8).

3. Total MNE output declines under a primary tariff (either r_{31} or r_{32}) because the tariff causes the ΣMC_i curve to shift inwards, contracting Q_3. The secondary tariff r_{12} also causes ΣMC_i to shift inwards; however, it simultaneously causes the ΣMR_i curve to shift outwards, and either shift may dominate. The difference between the two tariffs is simple: a primary tariff drives a wedge between the MC_1 and MC_2 curves; a secondary tariff drives a wedge between the MC_1 and the MC_2 curves and also between the MR_1 and MR_2 curves (compare (11) and (12) and Figures 2.4 and 2.5).

4. Diewert (this volume) provides a similar but more general proof in Theorem 4: the profit-maximizing transfer price w_o should be set at its upper (lower) bound as the difference between the net returns to the exporter and importer firms, $\sum_k T_k (1 + \tau^k)X^k$, is positive (negative). He also shows in (53) that the MNE can be decentralized and reach the same global net profit maximum and same level of trade X^k, if the appropriate decentralized transfer price w^k is used. (Contrast this with Bond (1980) where the decentralized levels of net MNE profits and intra-firm trade lie below the profit-maximizing levels when tax rates differ.)

5. We assume that corporate profit tax and customs authorities set the effective upper and lower bounds on P_{ij}. The tax officials in the exporting country tend to accept a high transfer price since that raises taxable profits of the exporter. Customs officials in the importing country also tend to accept a high transfer price to raise tariff revenues. Tax authorities in the importing country, however, prefer a lower transfer price to shift profits to the importer. Minimum profit targets for each affiliate, minority shareholders and strong labour unions can also affect the upper and lower bounds to P_{ij}. Several authors (e.g. Horst, 1971; Itagaki, 1979, 1981; Samuelson, 1982) assume marginal export cost as an effective lower bound so $P_{ij} \geq \lambda$. This implies that in equilibrium the exporter never earns a marginal loss, nor the importer a marginal profit, on intra-firm trade. We prefer the alternate assumption that the MNE can set $P_{ij} \gtrless \lambda$ so that either the importer or the exporter shows the marginal loss depending on $T_i \gtrless T_j(1 + r_{ij})$. Our assumption probably best suits MNEs that do not employ the profit centre concept (see Bond, 1980) and that engage in large numbers of intra-firm transactions (see Copithorne, 1976). See also Diewert (this volume) on the upper bound w_2 and lower bound w_1 to the profit-maximizing transfer price w_o.

6. Assuming $a_{12} = a_{21} < 0$ implies $MC_3' > 0$; that is, we ignore the possibility that the primary firm is a Copithorne maverick firm.

7. Note that the secondary tariff r_{12} causes Q_2 to expand while the primary tariff r_{32} causes Q_2 to contract. Eden (1983a) explores the circumstances under which net protection from the domestic tariff structure is positive.

8. Diewert (this volume) reaches similar comparative static tax results in (18).

9. Note that this analysis assumes changes in r_{ij} do not cause the MNE to

change P_{ij}. Also note that the optimal tariff policy should take consumer surplus into account. Since higher primary and secondary tariffs reduce final sales, causing consumer surplus to decline (see Propositions 4, 5 and 6), the optimal import tariff should be lower than that calculated here.

10. Differentiating the first order condition for X_{ij} with respect to P_{ij}, setting it equal to zero and solving (see Varian, 1978, p. 268), we find $dX_{ij}/dP_{ij} = -e_i(T_i - T_j(1 + r_{ij}))/\partial^2 L/\partial X_{ij}^2$. Since $\partial^2 L/\partial X_{ij}^2 = a_{ii} < 0$ from (24), we have $dX_{ij}/dP_{ij} \gtreqless 0$ as $T_i \gtreqless T_j(1 + r_{ij})$. Assuming $T_i > T_j(1 + r_{ij})$ implies the MNE chooses a high P_{ij}, so that increasing P_{ij} causes X_{ij} to expand. On the other hand, if $T_i < T_j(1 + r_{ij})$ the MNE chooses a low transfer price to shift profits to the importer, so that lowering P_{ij} also causes X_{ij} to expand. If $T_i = T_j(1 + r_{ij})$, $dX_{ij}/dP_{ij} = 0$. Diewert (this volume) also has similar proofs in (18).

3 TRANSFER PRICING AND ECONOMIC EFFICIENCY

W. Erwin Diewert

I. Introduction

Consider a firm which produces an (intermediate) output in one plant or division and uses it as an input in another plant or division. If there is a well defined external market for the good where units can be bought and sold at a common price w, then there is no transfer price problem: the firm should value the intermediate good at the price w in both plants. However, in many cases, such well defined 'arm's-length' transfer prices will not exist. In this case, how should the firm choose its transfer price for the good?

Hirshleifer (1956) and Arrow (1964, pp. 404-5) suggested the following conceptual framework for choosing a transfer price: it should be that price such that if both plant managers treat it as a fixed (parametric) price and maximize their individual plant profits subject to their own plant technological constraints, then the aggregate net supply of the intermediate good is zero. Thus the Hirshleifer *arm's-length transfer price* acts just like a market price. This concept for a transfer price is also known as a *decentralized profit-maximizing transfer* or a *marginal cost transfer price* and it will be discussed in detail in section IV below.

In the above framework for transfer pricing, the divisional managers maximized profits separately with the common arm's-length transfer price being the only link between the two maximization problems. Horst (1971, 1977) and Copithorne (1971) suggested an alternative conceptual framework for choosing a transfer price: it should be that price which allows the firm to maximize total profits (in a centralized manner) over the two plants. If there are no tax distortions, Copithorne (1971, p. 339) shows that the transfer prices are completely arbitrary. If the plants are located in different jurisdictions and there are unequal income tax rates in the two locations, Horst (1971, p. 1061) indicates that the firm will choose the *money* or *profit-maximizing transfer price* to be either the smallest (or largest) possible price that the tax authorities in the two jurisdictions will accept as reasonable. Booth and Jensen (1977) also discuss this concept for transfer prices. We shall discuss this type of transfer price in section III.

The first two concepts for a transfer price arose by considering alternative firm profit maximization models: the arm's-length transfer price arises from decentralized profit maximization while the money transfer price arises from centralized profit maximization. The third concept for a transfer price (due also to Hirshleifer (1956)), the *efficient transfer price*, arises when we consider the social maximization problem of maximizing the aggregate net output of the firm (valued at constant reference prices) excluding the intermediate good. This maximization problem is similar to the firm's overall profit maximization problem except that profit taxes and taxes on intermediate good transactions are ignored. This social profit maximization problem can be set up as a mathematical programming problem where one of the constraints appearing in it is that the output of the intermediate good produced by plant 2, say, has to equal or exceed the amount of intermediate input used by plant 1. Our *efficient transfer price* is defined to be the optimal Lagrange multiplier for the intermediate good constraint. The three types of transfer prices are not necessarily distinct. If there are no tax distortions, then an efficient transfer price is also a profit-maximizing transfer price. If, in addition, the divisional production possibility sets are convex (so that there are no divisions which have increasing returns to scale in production), then the efficient transfer price is also an arm's-length transfer price. We shall discuss efficient transfer prices in detail in section II. The idea of identifying a transfer price with an optimal Lagrange multiplier originates with Arrow (1964, p. 405, 1977, p. 138) and Copithorne (1976, p. 342).

The comparative statics properties of the profit-maximizing and the arms-length transfer prices are developed in sections III and IV respectively.[1]

Another issue which figures prominently in the transfer pricing literature is the issue of decentralization. The basic issue is: do there exist transfer prices such that if each division of a firm maximizes profits in an independent decentralized manner using its divisional transfer price to value the intermediate good, then overall firm profits are maximized? This issue will be discussed in section V below.

The efficiency aspects of transfer pricing are examined in section VI and VII. We ask the following question: how much aggregate net output (valued at constant reference prices) is wasted due to inefficient taxation schemes, including the tax authority's choice of admissible bounds for the transfer prices. We do not regard the transfer prices themselves as the source of the inefficiency; rather it is the unco-ordinated policies of the various layers of government in the different jurisdictions.

In section VII, we generalize our two-division model to a K-division model where each division either uses or produces a common intermediate good.

Sections V and VII may be omitted by the less technically oriented reader. Section V makes use of the theory of concave programming developed by Uzawa (1958) and Karlin (1959). The other sections make use of economic duality theory.[2]

II. Efficient Transfer Prices

Suppose that the set of feasible outputs and inputs for division i can be represented as a set S^i of $N_i + 1$ dimensional vectors (y_i, x_i) for $i = 1, 2$ where x^i is a scalar.[3] We index outputs by a positive sign and inputs with a negative sign.

Suppose division i faces the vector of positive prices $p^i \gg 0_{N_i}$ for goods $1, 2, \ldots, N_i$. Then for a given amount of the intermediate good x^i, it makes sense for the production manager of division i to maximize net revenue (excluding the last good). This leads us to define the division i *variable profit function* π^i by

$$\pi^i(p^i, x^i) \equiv \max_y \{ p^i \cdot y : (y, x^i) \, \varepsilon \, S^i \}, \, i = 1, 2. \tag{1}$$

We assume that the production possibilities sets S^i are sufficiently well behaved so that the maxima in (1) exist.[4] We also assume that $\pi^i(p^i, x^i)$ is a decreasing function of x^i where it is finite. This makes good economic sense: if $x^2 > 0$ so that division 2 is producing the intermediate good as an output, then as we increase x^2, the net cost of producing x^2 will increase, and the net revenue $\pi^2(p^2, x^2)$ will decrease. If $x^1 < 0$ so that division 1 is using the intermediate good as an input, then as we increase x^1, we decrease the absolute value of x^1 so that there is less intermediate input going into division 1 and hence $\pi^1(p^1, x^1)$ will decrease as x^1 increases.

Assuming that there is no external market for the intermediate good, the firm's overall profit maximization model in the case where there are no tax distortions may be written as follows:

$$\max_{y^1,x^1,y^2,x^2} \{p^1 \cdot y^1 + p^2 \cdot y^2 : x^1 + x^2 \geq 0, \\ (y^1,x^1) \, \varepsilon \, S^1, (y^2,x^2) \varepsilon \, S^2\} \tag{2}$$

$$= \max_{x^1,x^2} \{\pi^1(p^1, x^1) + \pi^2(p^2,x^2) : x^1 + x^2 \geq 0\} \tag{3}$$

where (3) follows from (2) upon maximizing with respect to y^1 and y^2 and using definitions (1).

We have written the intermediate good constraint $x^1 + x^2 \geq 0$ as an inequality instead of as an equality. This does no harm if the good can be disposed of freely; moreover, our assumption that $\pi^1(p^1, x^1)$ is decreasing in x^1 and $\pi^2(p^2, x^2)$ is decreasing in x^2 will ensure that the constraint will hold as an equality at an optimal solution to (3).

Assume a solution (y^{1*}, x^{1*}), (y^{2*}, x^{2*}) for (2) exists. Then x^{1*}, x^{2*} will also be a solution to (3). This solution maximizes the social product of the firm.

In order to define the efficient transfer price, we need to assume $\pi^1(p^1, x^{1*})$ and $\pi^2(p^2, x^{2*})$ are differentiable with respect to x^1 and x^2 respectively. With these differentiability assumptions plus the assumption that (x^{1*}, x^{2*}) solves (3), the Kuhn-Tucker (1951) theorem implies the existence of an optimal Lagrange multiplier $\lambda^* \geq 0$ for (3) such that the following first order conditions hold:[5]

$$\nabla_{x^1} \pi^1 (p^1, x^{1*}) + \lambda^* = 0$$
$$\nabla_{x^2} \pi^2 (p^2, x^{2*}) + \lambda^* = 0$$
$$x^{1*} + x^{2*} \qquad = 0. \tag{4}$$

The *efficient transfer price* is defined to be the optimal Lagrange multiplier $\lambda^* = - \nabla_{x^1} \pi^1(p^1, x^{1*}) = - \nabla_{x^2} \pi^2(p^2, x^{2*}) \equiv - \partial\pi^2(p^2, x^{2*})/\partial x^2$.

If $\pi^1(p^1, x^{1*})$ and $\pi^2(p^2, x^{2*})$ are twice continuously differentiable with respect to x^1 and x^2 respectively, then the following second order necessary conditions[6] must hold:

$$v_1^2 \, \nabla_{x^1x^1}^2 \, \pi^1(p^1, x^{1*}) + v_2^2 \, \nabla_{x^2x^2}^2 \, \pi^2(p^2, x^{2*}) \leq 0$$

for all v_1, v_2 such that

$$v_1 + v_2 = 0 \text{ and } v_1^2 + v_2^2 = 1.$$

It is readily seen that this condition is equivalent to:

$$\nabla_{x^1x^1}^2 \, \pi^1(p^1, x^{1*}) + \nabla_{x^2x^2}^2 \, \pi^2(p^2, x^{2*}) \leq 0. \text{[7]} \tag{5}$$

Note that (5) is consistent with one of the derivatives $\nabla_{x^1x^1}^2 \, \pi^1$ or $\nabla_{x^2x^2}^2 \, \pi^2$ being positive (this corresponds to Copithorne's (1976, p. 344) non-conformist division), but then the other derivative must be more negative so that the sum of the two derivatives is negative or zero. If for example $\nabla_{x^1x^1}^2 \, \pi^1(p^1, x^{1*}) > 0$, then $\pi^1(p^1, x^1)$ is a locally convex function[8] for x^1 close to x^{1*} and hence the division 1 production possibilities set S^1 is nonconvex.

Using Samuelson's (1947, p. 132) standard interpretation for a Lagrange multiplier, we may interpet the efficient transfer price λ^* as the marginal increase in the world-wide net output of the firm (valued at the reference prices p^1 and p^2) due to an exogenous gift to the firm of a marginal unit of the intermediate good. Copithorne (1976, p. 346) uses the term 'opportunity cost' transfer price in place of our term 'efficient'.

If there are no tax distortions, then competitive profit maximization on the part of the firm will lead to maximal world net output. For purposes of evaluating divisional profitability, the firm should use the efficient transfer price λ^* defined above in order to value the intermediate good in each division.

However, if the divisions are located in separate tax and legal jurisdictions (e.g. countries, states, provinces), then since the governments in each jurisdiction are not usually interested in maximizing world output, there will usually be tax distortions on the interdivisional intermediate good transactions. Thus in the following section, we indicate how these tax distortions affect the behaviour of the multi-divisional firm.

III. Tax Distortions and Profit-maximizing Transfer Prices

The overall profit maximization problems (2) or (3) neglect the fact that governments tend to tax profits. Since the two divisions may be located in different countries, the rate of taxation in location 1, $1-T_1$, say, may not equal the rate of taxation in location 2, $1-T_2$, say.[9] Thus, $0 < T_1 \leq 1$ and $0 < T_2 \leq 1$ are the proportions of before-tax net income that division 1 and 2 are allowed to keep.

Let us assume that the two divisions are in different governmental jurisdictions. The amount of taxes paid in each jurisdiction now depends on the transfer price that the firm assigns to the intermediate good for tax purposes. The firm will have an incentive to choose an 'official' (for tax purposes) transfer price that minimizes its tax payments or more generally that maximizes its overall profits. Of course, the tax authorities recognize this incentive so we assume that they place bounds on the range of transfer prices that they will accept. Let the lowest such admissible price be $w_1 \geq 0$ and the highest such price be $w_2 \geq w_1$.[10]

For the sake of definiteness, assume that the intermediate good is produced as an output by division 2 and utilized as an input by division 1. If the two divisions are located in different countries, then there is the possibility of trade taxes on transactions involving the intermediate good. Thus let t^1 be a specific tariff or tax and τ^1 be an *ad valorem* tariff or tax placed on each unit of the intermediate good imported into jurisdiction 1. (If $t^1 < 0$ and $\tau^1 < 0$, then jurisdiction 1 is subsidizing the importing of the intermediate good.) Let t^2 be a specific export subsidy and τ^2 be an *ad valorem* export subsidy placed on each unit of the intermediate good exported from jurisdiction 2. (If $t^2 < 0$ and $\tau^2 < 0$, then jurisdiction 2 is taxing the exporting of the intermediate good.)

Assuming that the firm is attempting to maximize after-tax profits, the counterpart to the profit maximization problem (2) is now

$$\pi(p^1,\ p^2,\ w_1,\ w_2,\ T_1,\ T_2,\ \tau^1,\ \tau^2,\ t^1,\ t^2)$$

$$\equiv \max_{y^1, x^1, y^2, x^2, \ w} \{ T \ [p^1 \cdot y^1 \ + \ w(1+\tau^1)x^1 \ + \ t^1 x^1] \ +$$
$$T_2[p^2 \cdot y^2 + w(1+\tau^2)x^2 + t^2 x^2] : x^1 + x^2 = $$
$$0, \ w_1 \leq w \leq w_2, \ (y^i, \ x^i) \ \varepsilon \ S^i, \ i = 1,2 \}$$

$$= \max_{x^1, x^2, w} \{ T_1[\pi^1(p^1, x^1) \ + \ w(1+\tau^1)x^1 \ + \ t^1 x^1] \ +$$
$$T_2[\pi^2(p^2, x^2) + w(1+\tau^2)x^2 + t^2 x^2] : x^1 + x^2 = 0,$$
$$w_1 \leq w \leq w_2 \} \tag{6}$$

using definitions 1

$$= \max_{x, w} \{ T_1[\pi^1(p^1, -x) \ - \ w(1+\tau^1)x \ - \ t^1 x] \ +$$
$$T^2[\pi^2(p^2, x) \ + \ w(1+\tau^2)x \ + \ t^2 x] : x \geq 0, \ w_1 \leq w$$
$$\leq w_2 \}. \tag{7}$$

Note that the intermediate good adding up constraint in (6) is now written as $x_1 + x_2 = 0$ in place of the earlier inequality constraint $x_1 + x_2 \geq 0$ in (3). This has been done in order to ensure that interdivisional cash payments sum to zero in the tax distorted case.

Equation (6) follows from the line above using (1), the definition of the plant net revenue functions π^1 and π^2. Equation (7) follows from (6) if we assume $x^1 + x^2 = 0$ and set $x^2 = x \geq 0$ and $x^1 = -x$.

We may set up a counterpart to (7) in the case where division 1 produces the intermediate good instead of using it as an input. Note that in this alternative case, the tariff and subsidy variables t^1, t^2, τ^1 and τ^2 must be redefined. The alternative profit maximization problem (8) may be written as (letting $x^1 = x = -x^2$):

$$\max_{x, w} \{ T_1[\pi^1(p^1, x) \ + \ w(1+\tau^1)x \ + \ t^1 x] \ + \ T_2[\pi^2(p_2^2, -x)$$
$$- w(1+\tau^2)x - t^2 x] : x \geq 0, \ w_1 \leq w \leq w_2 \}. \tag{8}$$

Analytically, we need to solve problems (7) and (8). The overall profit maximum will occur at one or the other of the two possibilities and only in knife edge cases will the maximum occur in both problems.

We assume for the sake of definiteness that the maximum attained in (7) is strictly larger than the maximum attained in (8) so that $x \equiv -x^1 = x^2 \geq 0$; i.e. division 2 exports the intermediate good to division 1. (7) may be rearranged to yield the following equivalent expression:

$$\pi(p^1, p^2, w_1, w_2, T_1, T_2, \tau^1, \tau^2, t^1, t^2)$$
$$= \max_{x,w} \{T_1[\pi^1(p^1,-x) + T_2\pi^2(p^2,x) + [T_2(1+\tau^2)$$
$$- T_1(1+\tau^1)]wx + [T_2t^2 - T_1t^1]x: x \geq 0,$$
$$w_1 \leq w \leq w_2\}. \tag{9}$$

The w solution to (9), w_0 say, is the firm's *profit-maximizing transfer price* or *money transfer price* to use Copithorne's (1976) terminology. Because w appears in the objective function of (9) in a linear manner and is subject to linear inequality constraints, it may not be too surprising to the reader to find that w_0 equals either w_1 or w_2.

Theorem 1.[11] If $T_2(1+\tau^2) > T_1(1+\tau^1)$, then the firm will maximize profits by setting its money transfer price $w_0 = w_2$, the maximum transfer price the tax authorities will allow. If $T_2(1+\tau^2) < T_1(1+\tau^1)$, then the firm will maximize profits by setting its money transfer price $w_0 = w_1$, the minimum transfer price the authorities will allow. If $T_2(1+\tau^2) = T_1(1+\tau^1)$, then the firm's profit maximum is unaffected by the firm's choice of transfer price.

Proof. Suppose $T_2(1+\tau^2) > T_1(1+\tau^1)$. Then for any $x \geq 0$ and
$$0 \leq w \leq w_2, [T_2(1+\tau^2) - T_1(1+\tau^1)] wx$$
$$\leq [T_2(1+\tau^2) - T_1(1+\tau^1)]w_2x$$
or
$$T_1\pi^1(p^1,-x) + T_2\pi^2(p^2,x) + [T_2(1+\tau^2) - T_1(1+\tau^1)]wx + [T_2t^2 - T_1t^1]x \leq T_1\pi^1(p^1,-x) + T_2\pi^2(p^2,x) + [T_2(1+\tau^2) - T_1(1+\tau^1)]w_2x + [T_2t^2 - T_1t^1]x \tag{10}$$
with a strict inequality in (10) if $x > 0$ and $0 < w < w_2$. Hence when maximizing the objective function in (9) with respect to x and w (this objective function is equal to the left-hand side of (10)), we may restrict attention to the case where $w = w_2$ using the inequality (10). Hence we need only set $w = w_2$ in (9) and then perform the maximization with respect to x.

The case where $T_2(1+\tau^2) < T_1(1+\tau^1)$ is established in an analogous manner. Finally, when $T_2(1+\tau^2) = T_1(1+\tau^1)$, the objective function in (9) no longer contains w and hence its choice by the firm is irrelevant to the solution of (9) (but not to the tax authorities in the two jurisdictions). (QED)

Thus if trade taxes are zero (i.e. $t^1=t^2=\tau^1=\tau^2=0$) and $T_2 > T_1$, the profit-maximizing firm will choose the highest admissible transfer price w_2 in order to maximize profits in jurisdiction 2, the low-tax jurisdiction. If trade taxes are zero and $T_2 < T_1$, then the firm will choose the lowest admissible transfer price w_1 in order to maximize profits in jurisdiction 1, the low-tax jurisidction. If $T_1 = T_2$ so that the jurisdictional income tax rates are equal and $\tau^1 > \tau^2 \geq 0$ so that government 1's *ad valorem* import tariff is higher than government 2's *ad valorem* export subsidy, then the firm will choose its money transfer price equal to w_1, the lowest transfer price.

When tax rates in the two jurisdictions differ, by comparing the tax distorted profit maximization problem (9) with the undistorted problem (2), it can be seen that it is unlikely that the (x^1, x^2) solutions to the two problems will coincide. Are there any conditions that will ensure that the solutions do coincide? Theorem 2 below indicates that there are such conditions. Before we state this theorem, it is convenient to recall that we assumed that x^{1*} and x^{2*} solved the socially efficient profit maximization problem (3) which had no tax distortions. Recall also that the optimal shadow price of the intermediate good in division i was $\lambda^* = \lambda_i(x^{i*}) \equiv - \partial\pi^i(p^i, x^{i*})/\partial x^i$ for $i = 1,2$. Define σ_i^* as the rate of change of the division i shadow price; i.e.

$$\sigma_i^* \equiv \partial\lambda_i(x^{i*})/\partial x^i = -\partial^2\pi^i(p^i, x^{i*})/\partial x^i \partial x^i; \quad i = 1,2. \tag{11}$$

If the divisional technology sets are convex, then the divisional profit function $\pi^i(p^i, x^i)$ will be concave in x^i and this in turn implies that $\sigma_i^* \geq 0$ for $i = 1,2$.[12]

Theorem 2. Suppose that x^{1*}, x^{2*}, is a solution to the no tax distortions profit maximization problem (2) and that the first order conditions (4) hold at this point. Hence, the efficient transfer price λ^* is well defined by (4). Suppose $T_1(1+\tau_1) \neq T_2(1+T_2)$ and define the *optimal regulated transfer price* w^* by

$$w^* \equiv [(T_2-T_1)\lambda^* - (T_2 t^2 - T_1 t^1)]/[T_2(1+\tau^2) - T_1(1 + \tau^1)]. \tag{12}$$

It the tax authorities set $w_1 = w_2 = w^*$, then the socially optimal solution x^{1*}, x^{2*} satisfies the first order necessary conditions for the tax distorted profit maximization problem (6), or alternatively, $x^* \equiv x^{2*} = -x^{1*}$ satisfies the first order conditions for the tax distorted private profit maximization problem (9). In addition: (i) if $T_1\sigma_1^* + T_2\sigma_2^* > 0$ where the σ_i^* are defined by (11), then x^* is a strict local maximizer for (9), and (ii) if the divisional technology sets S^i are convex, then x^* solves (9) or equivalently, x^{1*}, x^{2*} solves (6).

Proof. Let x^{1*}, x^{2*} solve (3) and suppose x^{1*}, x^{2*} and λ^* satisfy equations (4). Multiply the first equation in (4) by $-T_1$, multiply the second equation in (4) by T_2 and add the resulting equations. Letting $x^* \equiv x^{2*} = -x^{1*} > 0$, we obtain the following equation:

$$-T_1 \nabla_{x^1} \pi^1(p^1, -x^*) + T_2 \nabla_{x^2} \pi^2(p^2, x^*) + (T_2 - T_1)\lambda^* = 0 \quad (13)$$

If the tax authorities impose $w_1 = w_2 = w^*$, then the variable w in the tax distorted profit maximization problem (9) must be set equal to w^*. Now differentiate the objective function in (9) with respect to x and set the derivative equal to zero. We obtain the following equation:

$$-T_1 \nabla_{x^1} \pi^1(p^1, -x) + T_2 \nabla_{x^2} \pi^2(p^2, x) + [T_2(1+\tau^2) -$$
$$T_1(1+\tau^1)]w^* + T_2 t^2 - T_1 t^1 = 0. \quad (14)$$

Now replace x by x^* and w^* by the right-hand side of (12) and we find that (14) becomes (13).

To prove (i), differentiate (14) with respect to x and evaluate the resulting derivative at x^*. Using definitions (11), the resulting derivative is $-T_1\sigma_1^* - T_2\sigma_2^*$ which is less than zero if $T_1\sigma_1^* + T_2\sigma_2^* > 0$. Hence the second order sufficient conditions for x^* to be a strict local maximizer for (9) when $w = w^*$ are satisfied.

To prove (ii), note that the objective function in (9) is a concave function of x if the divisional technology sets are convex. Since w is fixed at w^*, x is the only remaining decision variable. It is well known that if x^* satisfies the first order necessary conditions to maximize a concave function then x^* globally maximizes the function (e.g. see Karlin, p. 405). (QED)

If there are no trade taxes (i.e. $t^1 = t^2 = \tau^1 = \tau^2 = 0$), but $T_1 \neq T_2$ so that income tax rates differ, then the optimal regulated transfer price w^* equals λ^*, the efficient transfer price. On the other hand, if $T_1 = T_2$, $t^2 = t^1$ but $\tau^1 \neq \tau^2$, then $w^* = 0$. In general, w^* could be negative. Note that if $T_1(1+\tau^1)=T_2(1+\tau^2)$, then transfer price regulation has no effect on the tax distorted profit maximization problem (9).

The 'practical' implications of Theorems 1 and 2 may be summarized as follows. If the technology sets S^1 and S^2 are convex, the tax authorities have two ways of ensuring that the firm's profit-maximizing quantity solution to the tax distorted maximization problem (6) and the undistorted problem (3) coincide: (i) choose $T_1 = T_2$ and $t^1 = t^2 = \tau^1 = \tau^2 = 0$ (harmonize tax policy in the two jurisdictions)[13] or (ii) force the firm to use the optimal regulated transfer price w^* defined by (12) (by setting the lowest admissible price w_1 equal to the highest admissible price w_2 equal to w^*). I do not believe that the second strategy is a viable one: the tax authorities simply do not have the information to be able to determine the efficient transfer price λ^*. Hence they will not be able to determine w^* either.

We turn now to the comparative statics of the tax distorted maximization problem (9) where division 2 is producing the intermediate good. From Theorem 1, the optimal money transfer price w_0 is equal to w_2 (if $T_2(1+\tau^2) > T_1(1+\tau^1)$) or w_1 (if $T_2(1+\tau^2) < T_1(1+\tau^1)$). We assume that $x^\circ > 0$ solves (9) and that the following first and second order conditions hold:

$$-T_1 \nabla_{x^1} \pi^1(p^1, -x^\circ) + T_2 \nabla_{x^2} \pi^2(p^2, x^\circ)$$
$$+[T_2(1+\tau^2) - T_1(1+\tau^1)]w_0 + [T_2 t^2 - T_1 t^1] = 0 \qquad (15)$$

$$T_1 \nabla^2_{x^1 x^1} \pi^1 (p^1, -x^\circ) + T_2 \nabla^2_{x^2 x^2} \pi^2(p^2, x^\circ) < 0. \qquad (16)$$

Assume $0 < w_1 < w_2$ and define $\sigma^\circ \equiv - \nabla^2_{x^i x^i} \pi^i (p^i, x^{i\circ})$, $i = 1,2$ where $x^{1\circ} \equiv -x^\circ$, $x^{2\circ} \equiv x^\circ$. Then (16) may be rewritten as

$$\alpha \equiv T_1 \sigma^\circ_1 + T_2 \sigma^\circ_2 > 0. \qquad (17)$$

Differentiate (15) with respect to x and the various exogenous variables. We obtain the following comparative statics results (where α is defined by (17)):

$$\alpha \partial x / \partial T_1 = -\nabla_{x^1} \pi^1(p^1, -x^\circ) - (1+\tau^1)w_0 - t^1$$
$$\alpha \partial x / \partial T_2 = -\nabla_{x^2} \pi^2(p^2, -x^\circ) + (1+\tau^2)w_0 + t^2$$

$$\alpha \partial x / \partial w_1 = \begin{cases} 0 & \text{if } T_2(1+\tau^2) > T_1(1+\tau^1) \\ T_2(1+\tau^2) - T_1(1+\tau^1) & \text{if } T_2(1+\tau^2) < T_1(1+\tau^1) \end{cases}$$

$$\alpha \partial x / \partial w_2 = \begin{cases} T_2(1+\tau^2) - T_1(1+\tau^1) & \text{if } T_2(1+\tau^2) > T_1(1+\tau^1) \\ 0 & \text{if } T_2(1+\tau^2) < T_1(1+\tau^1) \end{cases}$$

$$\alpha \partial x / \partial t^1 = -T_1 \quad ; \quad \alpha \partial x / \partial t^2 = T_2$$
$$\alpha \partial x / \partial \tau^1 = -T^1 w_0 \quad ; \quad \alpha \partial x / \partial \tau^2 = T_2 w_o. \tag{18}$$

Except for the first two derivatives, the signs of all of the other derivatives can be determined provided that we know the tax rates in the two jurisdictions. Thus if jurisdiction 1 increases either its specific or *ad valorem* tariffs on imports of the intermediate, trade in the intermediate good will decrease; i.e. division 2 will produce less intermediate good in the new higher tariff equilibrium. Using (15) and (18), it can be shown that

$$T_1 \partial x / \partial T_1 + T_2 \partial x / \partial T_2 = 0 \tag{19}$$

Hence the two derivatives $\partial x / \partial T_1$ and $\partial x / \partial T_2$ are either of opposite sign or both equal to zero.

It is also possible to develop the effects on x°, the optimal production of the intermediate good by plant 2, of changes in the prices of the other (net) outputs facing the two plants, p^1 and p^2. Differentiation of (15) with respect to x and p^i yields:

$$\nabla_{p^1} x^\circ = \alpha^{-1} T_1 \nabla^2_{p^1 x^1} \pi^1(p^1, x^{1\circ}) = -\alpha^{-1} T_1 \nabla_{x^1} y^1(p^1, x^{1\circ}),$$

$$\nabla_{p^2} x^\circ = \alpha^{-1} T_2 \nabla^2_{p^2 x^2} \pi^2(p^2, x^{2\circ}) = \alpha^{-1} T_2 \nabla_{x^2} y^2(p^2, x^{2\circ}).$$

The above equalities follow by applying Hotelling's Lemma; i.e. the profit-maximizing net output vector for plant i given the net amount of intermediate good $x^{i\circ}$ is

$$y^i(p^i, x^{i\circ}) = \nabla_{p^i} \pi^i(p^i, x^{i\circ}) \ ; \ i = 1,2.$$

Hence if we know the signs of the vectors of derivatives $\nabla_{x^i} y^i (p^i, x^{i\circ})$, we may determine the signs of the derivatives $\nabla_{p^i} x^\circ$. Typically, $\nabla_{x^i} y^i(p^i, x^\circ) \le 0_{N_i}$. Hence typically $\nabla_{p^1} x^\circ \ge 0_{N_1}$ and $\nabla_{p^2} x^\circ \le 0_{N_2}$. Hence usually increases in the prices facing division 1 will increase its demand for the intermediate good and increases in the prices facing division 2 will decrease its supply of the intermediate good.

We may use Theorem 2 and the comparative statics results summarized in (18) above in order to discuss the following transfer pricing controversy:[14] does transfer price regulation by governments improve or worsen resource allocation? We assume that the efficient world allocation of resources occurs when the firm solves the undistorted profit maximization problem (3). We assume that $x^{2*} = -x^{1*} = x^* > 0$ solves this problem and the efficient transfer price is λ^*. If $T_2(1+\tau^2) = T_1(1+\tau^1)$, then governmental regulation of transfer prices is irrelevant from the viewpoint of world efficiency; i.e. it does not matter what bound w_1 and w_2 governments impose on transfer prices since the term involving the transfer price w in the firm's global profit maximization problem (9) vanishes. Hence government regulation of transfer prices will be ineffective in this case. However, if $T_2(1+\tau^2) \neq T_1(1+\tau^1)$, then an omniscient world regulator who knew what the efficient transfer price λ^* was could force the firm to use the optimal regulated transfer price w^* defined by (12). The regulator would set $w_1 = w_2 = w^*$, and the profit-maximizing firm would be induced to allocate resources efficiently. Of course, there are at least two difficulties with this optimal regulated solution: (i) governments have no way of determining what λ^* is (even the firm may have difficulty) and (ii) even if governments knew what λ^* was, they would have no incentive to agree on a regulatory policy that induced world efficiency. Each government is usually concerned with its own jurisdictional welfare rather than world welfare.

Suppose initially, $w_1 = w^* = w_2$. What would be the effect of relaxing the regulatory constraints; i.e. suppose w_1 was decreased and w_2 was increased? As long as $T_2(1+\tau^2) \neq T_1(1+\tau^1)$, the effect of this deregulation would be to increase x above the efficient level x^*. Further increases in w_2 and decreases in w_1 would lead to further increases in x (this follows from the comparative statics results in (18)). Thus relaxing optimal regulation leads to inefficiency and the more we relax the regulation of transfer prices, the greater will be the amount of induced inefficiency.

We conclude this section by developing another comparative statics result that will prove to be useful in section V when we study efficiency more formally. It is of interest to determine the relationship of $x°$, the solution to the tax distorted private profit maximization problem (9), and $x^* = x^{2*} = -x^{1*}$, the solution to the undistorted profit maximization problem (3). It can be verified that the efficient solution x^* will also be a solution to (9) if $T_1 = T_2 = T^* > 0$ and $t^1 = t^2 = \tau^1 = \tau^2 = 0$, i.e. if the income tax rates are equal in the two jurisdictions but all trade taxes and subsidies are zero. Consider the following profit maximization problem which depends on a scalar parameter ξ where $0 \le \xi \le 1$ and w_0 is the optimal profit maximizing transfer price for problem (9):

$$\max_{x} \{[T^* + \xi(T_1 - T^*)]\pi^1(p^1, -x) + [T^* + \xi(T_2 - T^*)]\pi^2 (p^2, x) + \xi[T_2(1 + \tau^2)w_0 - T_1(1 + \tau^1)w_0 + T_2 t^2 - T_1 t^1]x : x \ge 0\}. \tag{20}$$

When $\xi = 0$, (20) is equivalent to T^* times the undistorted profit maximization problem (3); when $\xi = 1$, (20) becomes (9). Thus as ξ travels from 0 to 1, the problem (20) travels from the undistorted problem (3) to the distorted problem (9). The first order necessary condition for (20) is:

$$-[T^* + \xi(T_1 - T^*)]\nabla_{x^1} \pi^1(p^1, -x) + [T^* + \xi(T_2 - T^*)] \nabla_{x^2} \pi^2(p^2, x) + \xi[T_2(1 + \tau^2)w_0 - T_1(1 + \tau^1)w_0 + T_2 t^2 - T_1 t^1] = 0. \tag{21}$$

Let $x(\xi)$ solve (20) and (21) for each ξ between 0 and 1. Note that $x(0) = x^*$, the optimal solution to (3), and $x(1) = x°$, the solution to (9). Now differentiate (21) with respect to ξ and evaluate the resulting derivative at $\xi = 0$. The derivative $dx(0)/d\xi$ is a first order approximation to the change in x as we move from the undistorted equilibrium to the distorted one. Recalling that the efficient transfer price λ^* was defined by (4) and that the shadow price derivatives σ_i^* were defined by (11), we obtain the following formula for $x'(0) \equiv dx(0)/d\xi$:

$$T^* (\sigma_1^* + \sigma_2^*) x'(0) = (T_2 - T_1)(w_0 - \lambda^*) - T_1(\tau^1 w_0 + t^1) + T_2(\tau^2 w_0 + t^2) \tag{22}$$

We assume that (5) holds with a strict inequality, or equivalently, that $\sigma_1^* + \sigma_2^* > 0$.

If there are no trade taxes, so that $\tau^1=\tau^2=t^1=t^2=0$, and $w_1 <$ $\lambda^* < w_2$ (so that the efficient transfer price is within the interval of officially admissible transfer prices) and income tax rates are different so that $T_1 \neq T_2$, then using Theorem 1, it can be seen that $(T_2-T_1)(w_0-\lambda^*) > 0$ and the other two terms on the right-hand side of (22) are zero. Hence trade will be expanded above the efficient level x^* when we have different rates of business income taxation in the two jurisdictions (and no trade taxes).[15] Let us call the term $(T_2-T_1)(w_0-\lambda^*)$ *the business income tax effect*.

If $T_1 = T_2$ and $\tau^2=t^2=0$ (so that no trade taxes or subsidies are imposed by jurisdiction 2), then the right-hand side of (22) becomes $-T_1(\tau^1 w_0+t^1)$, *the jurisdiction 1 trade tax effect*. Thus if government 1 taxes imports of the intermediate good so that $\tau^1 w_0 + t^1 > 0$, then trade in the intermediate good will fall below the efficient level x^*.[16]

If $T_1 = T_2$ and $\tau^1 = t^1 = 0$ (so that no trade taxes or subsidies are imposed by jurisdiction 1), then the right-hand side of (22) becomes $T_2(\tau^2 w_0+t^2)$, the *jurisdiction 2 trade subsidy effect*. Thus if government 2 subsidizes (taxes) exports of the intermediate good so that $\tau^2 w_0+t^2 > 0$ (<0), then trade in the intermediate good will rise above (fall below) the efficient level.[17]

In the general case, the sign of $x'(0)$ is determined by the sign of the sum of the above three effects.

Thus far, we have defined three different transfer prices: (i) the efficient transfer price λ^* defined in (4); (ii) the profit maximizing transfer price w_0 defined in Theorem 1; and (iii) the optimal regulated transfer price w^* defined by (12). In the following section, we introduce a fourth type of transfer price.

IV. Arm's-length Transfer Prices

Instead of maximizing profits in a centralized manner, the firm could allow each division to maximize profits independently. The interdivisional transfer price $\bar{w}$ that would be used under these conditions is the parametric price that equates demand and supply for the intermediate good. This type of transfer price appears in Hirshleifer (1956) and is known as the arm's-length transfer price.

Assuming that division 2 produces the intermediate good and

making the same notational assumptions as in the previous section, the divisional profit maximization problems may be written as (23) and (24):

$$\max{}_X T_1\{\pi^1 (p^1,-x) - \bar{w}(1+\tau^1)x-t^1x\} \; ; \tag{23}$$

$$\max{}_X T_2\{\pi^2 (p^2,x) + \bar{w}(1+\tau^2)x+t^2x\} \; . \tag{24}$$

The arm's-length transfer price $\bar{w}$ which appears in (23) and (24) will be determined later. Assuming that $\bar{x} > 0$ solves both (23) and (24), the first order necessary conditions for (23) and (24) are:

$$T_1\{-\nabla_{X^1} \pi^1 (p^1,-\bar{x}) - \bar{w}(1+\tau^1)-t^1\} = 0 \tag{25}$$

$$T_2\{ \nabla_{X^2} \pi^2 (p^2,\bar{x}) + \bar{w}(1+\tau^2)+t^2\} = 0. \tag{26}$$

The second order necessary conditions are (25) and (26) plus (27) and (28) below:

$$\nabla^2_{X^1 X^1} \pi^1 (p^1,-\bar{x}) \leq 0 \text{ and} \tag{27}$$

$$\nabla^2_{X^2 X^2} \pi^2 (p^2,-\bar{x}) \leq 0. \tag{28}$$

The first order conditions (25) and (26) may be rearranged to yield separate expressions for $\bar{w}$ which we then equate to each other and solve the resulting equation for $\bar{x}$. Thus we obtain the following equations:

$$\bar{w} \equiv - (1+\tau^1)^{-1}[\nabla_{X^1} \pi^1 (p^1,-\bar{x}) + t^1] =$$
$$- (1+\tau^2)^{-1} [\nabla_{X^2} \pi^2 (p^2,\bar{x})+t^2]. \tag{29}$$

The second equation in (29) is solved for $\bar{x}$ and then the first equation serves to define $\bar{w}$, the *arm's-length transfer price*. However, we must check that $\bar{x}$ satisfies both (27) and (28) or more generally, that $\bar{x}$ solves *both* (23) and (24).

As usual, it is interesting to compare the resource allocation generated by arm's-length transfer pricing compared to efficient transfer pricing. Let ξ be a scalar between 0 and 1 and consider the following equation:

$$\nabla_{x^2} \pi^2 (p^2, x) - \nabla_{x^1} \pi^1 (p^1, -x) + \xi[\tau^1 \nabla_{x^2} \pi^2 (p^2, x) -$$
$$\tau^2 \nabla_{x^1} \pi^1 (p^1, -x) + t^2(1+\tau^1) - t^1(1+\tau^2)] = 0. \qquad (30)$$

When $\xi = 0$, (30) is equivalent to the first order conditions (4) for the efficient profit maximization problem and hence x^* will satisfy (30) when $\xi = 0$. When $\xi = 1$, x satisfies (30), since when $\xi = 1$, (30) is equivalent to the second equation in (29). Let $x(\xi)$ solve (30) for $0 \le \xi \le 1$. Differentiate (30) with respect to ξ and evaluate the resulting derivative at $\xi = 0$. The derivative $dx(0)/d\xi = x'(0)$ is a first order approximation to the change in x as we move from the undistorted equilibrium to an arm's-length transfer pricing equilibrium. Recalling that the efficient price λ^* was defined by (4) and that the shadow price derivatives σ_i^* were defined by (11) with $\sigma_1^* + \sigma_2^* > 0$, we find that

$$(\sigma_1^* + \sigma_2^*) x'(0) = (\tau^2 - \tau^1)\lambda^* + (1+\tau^1)t^2 - (1+\tau^2)t^1. \qquad (31)$$

Thus if jurisdiction 2 imposes no trade taxes, the right-hand side of (31) becomes $-\tau^1\lambda^* - t^1 < 0$ if government 1 taxes imports. Under these conditions, trade in the intermediate good will fall below the efficient level x^*. If jurisdiction 1 imposes no trade taxes, the right-hand side of (31) becomes $\tau^2\lambda^* + t^2 > 0$ (<0) if government 2 subsidizes (taxes) exports. Under these conditions, trade in the intermediate good will rise above (fall below) the efficient level x^*.

Note that in contrast to formula (22), formula (31) does not involve T_1 and T_2 which are the rates of return net of business taxes in the two jurisdictions. Does this mean that if there are no trade taxes but there are different rates of business taxation in the two jurisdictions, then arm's-length transfer pricing will lead to an efficient allocation of resources while profit-maximizing transfer pricing will not? In general, the answer to this question is no. If one of the divisions (division 1 say) has a technology set that exhibits increasing returns to scale so that $\sigma_1^* < 0$, then it can be verified that although x^* solves the efficient profit maximization problem (3), x^* will not solve the decentralized division 1 profit maximization problem when $\bar{w} = \lambda^*$ and $\tau^1 = t^1 = 0$. Under these conditions, $x \equiv x^*$ will satisfy the first order condition (25), but it will *not* satisfy the second order condition (27) for division 1 to maximize profits in a decentralized manner. Hence if there are: (i) no trade taxes (so that $t^1 = t^2 = \tau^1 = \tau^2 = 0$), or more generally, there are harmonized trade taxes (so that $t^1=t^2$ and $\tau^1=\tau^2$); (ii) different rates of business income taxation (so that $T_1 \neq T_2$); and (iii) increasing returns to scale in one division, then arm's-length transfer pricing will not lead to an efficient allocation of resources.[18] However, if (i) and (ii) above hold and the divisional technology sets are convex (which rules out increasing returns to scale in both divisions), the arm's-length transfer pricing *will* be efficient, whereas joint profit-maximizing transfer pricing (recall Theorem 1) will usually be inefficient under these conditions.[19]

An arm's-length transfer price $\bar{w}$ is an example of a *decentralized* transfer price; i.e. each division maximizes profits independently given $\bar{w}$. Recall the centralized profit maximization problem (9) and the corresponding profit-maximizing transfer price w_0 defined in Theorem 1. In the following section, we ask whether a firm's central office could determine divisional transfer prices w_1^* and w_2^* such that if division i used the price w_i^* to value the intermediate good and maximized profits in an independent manner, then the centralized profit-maximizing allocation of resources could be achieved.

V. Profit-maximizing Decentralized Transfer Prices

Consider the (centralized) tax distorted profit maximization problem (6). Decentralized transfer prices will not exist in this tax distorted situation if there are increasing returns to scale in either division. However, they do exist if the divisional technology sets S^1 and S^2 are convex or if $\pi^1(p^1,x^1)$ and $\pi^2(p^2,x^2)$ are concave functions of x^1 and x^2 respectively.[20]

Assuming that the $\pi^i(p^i, x^i)$ are concave functions of their x^i arguments, we may set w in (6) equal to w_0 ($=w_1$ or w_2), the profit-maximizing transfer price, and apply the Karlin (1959, p. 201)-Uzawa (1958, p. 34) Saddle Point Theorem to the resulting version of (6). Thus we find that the firm's total after tax profits π may be written as follows:

$$\pi(p^1,p^2,w_0,T_1,T_2,\tau^1,\tau^2,t^1,t^2)$$
$$\equiv \max\nolimits_{x^1,x^2} \{T_1[\pi^1(p^i,x^1) + w_0(1+\tau^1)x^1 + t^1x^1] +$$
$$T_2[\pi^2(p^2,x^2) + w_0(1+\tau^2)x^2 + t^2x^2]: x^1 + x^2 = 0\}$$
$$(32)$$

$$= \max{}_{x^1,x^2} \min{}_u \{T_1[\pi^1(p^1,x^1) + w_0(1+\tau^1)x^1 + t^1x^1]$$
$$+ T_2[\pi^2(p^2,x^2) + w_0(1+\tau^2)x^2 + t^2x^2] +$$
$$u(x^1+x^2)\}$$

$$= \max{}_{x^1,x^2} \{T_1(\pi^1(p^1,x^1) + w_0(1+\tau^1)x^1 + t^1x^1] +$$
$$T_2[\pi^2(p^2,x^2) + w_0(1+\tau^2)x^2 + t^2x^2] + u^*(x^1+x^2)\}$$
$$(33)$$

$$= T_1 \max{}_{x^1} \{\pi^1(p^1,x^1) + [w_0(1+\tau^1) + t^1 + T_1^{-1}u^*]x^1\}$$
$$+ T_2 \max{}_{x^2}\{\pi^2(p^2,x^2) + [w_0(1+\tau^2) + t^2 + T_2^{-1}u^*]x^2\}$$
$$(34)$$

where $u^* \ \varepsilon \ U$ where U is the closed convex set of u solutions for the saddle point maximum problem (33). We note that u^* could be positive or negative. In the differentiable case, U is simply the set of optimal Lagrange multipliers for the constrained maximization problem (32); in this case, U will usually be just a single multiplier.

Equation (34) tells us that decentralization is possible even in the tax distorted case. If the head office tells division 1 to use the transfer price $w_1^* \equiv w_0 (1+\tau^1) + t^1 + T^{-1} u^*$ and division 2 to use the transfer price $w_2^* \equiv w_0(1+\tau^2) + t^2 + T_2^{-1} u^*$ where $u^* \ \varepsilon \ U$, then each division can independently maximize profits and it will turn out that the resulting allocation of resources will maximize the firm's overall profits. Note that the resulting divisional decentralized transfer prices w_1^* and w_1^* will be generally unequal. Let W_i denote the set of division i *decentralized transfer prices*. Then we have

$$W_i \equiv \{w_i^*: w_i^* = w_0(1+\tau^i) + t^i + T_i^{-1}u^* \ ; \ u^* \ \varepsilon \ U\},$$
$$i = 1,2. \qquad (35)$$

We note that the Karlin-Uzawa Theorem does not require differentiability of the divisional variable profit functions π^i. Hence the sets U, W_1 and W_2 are well defined even in the nondifferentiable case.

The above results on the theoretical possibility of decentralization may seem to be a bit artificial to the reader. The entire procedure rests on the head office's ability to discover an optimal Lagrange multiplier u^* for the constrained maximization problem (32). If the head office can do this, there is no need to decentralize: the constrained maximization problem (32) will have been solved already, and the head office can simply tell division i to produce the optimal net output x^{i*} of the intermediate good. However, Arrow (1977, p. 139) and others have argued that the theoretical possibility of decentralizing decisions is useful in the context of planning algorithms. For further discussion of this topic, see Arrow and Hurwicz (1960), Malinvaud (1967) and Heal (1969, 1971).

VI. Efficiency Effects

Suppose y^{1o}, x^{1o}, y^{2o}, x^{2o}, w_0 solve the tax distorted profit maximization problem (6). Recall the efficient profit maximization problem (2). Let y^{1*}, x^{1*}, y^{2*}, x^{2*} solve (2). We wish to compare how much output is produced in the tax distorted equilibrium compared to an efficient equilibrium where $T_1 = T_2$ and trade taxes are zero.

We define the output loss L due to the inefficient tax system as the total (world) value-added produced by the two plants when $T_1 = T_2$ minus the corresponding value-added when there are tax distortions, where the net outputs of the plants are valued at the reference world price vectors p^1 and p^2:

$$L \equiv p^1 \cdot y^{1*} + p^2 \cdot y^{2*} - [p^1 \cdot y^{1o} - p^2 \cdot y^{2o}]. \qquad (36)$$

Theorem 3. $L \geq 0$.[21]

Proof. Note that $y^{1*}, x^{1*}, y^{2*}, x^{2*}$ solves (2). Moreover, the distorted equilibrium $y^{1o}, x^{1o}, y^{2o}, x^{2o}$ is feasible for the maximization problem in (2). Hence the inequality $L \geq 0$ follows. (QED)

The result in Theorem 3 is nice but it does not give us any idea of the magnitude of the loss. In order to accomplish this task, we assume smoothness or differentiability and form a second order approximation to the loss.

Our starting point is an efficient equilibrium where $T_1 = T_2 \equiv T^*$ and trade taxes are zero. Thus we assume that x^{1*}, x^{2*} solves (3). We also assume that π^1 and π^2 are twice continuously differentiable with respect to x^1 and x^2, that the first order conditions (4) hold, and the second order conditions (5) hold with a strict inequality. We also assume that plant 2 is producing the intermediate good (as usual), so that $x^{2*} = x^* > 0$ and $x^{1*} = -x^*$. Now recall the analysis at the end of section 3 where we mapped the undistorted equilibrium into the tax distorted profit maximization problem (6) or (9) by means of a scalar ξ that went from 0 to 1. Recall that $x(\xi)$ was defined as the solution to equation (21) and the derivative $x'(0)$ was defined by (22).

Define the value-added produced by the firm[22] as a function of the scalar parameter ξ as follows:

$$Y(\xi) \equiv \pi^1(p^1, -x(\xi)) + \pi^2(p^2, x(\xi)). \tag{37}$$

We calculate the first and second order derivatives of Y evaluated at $\xi = 0$:

$$Y'(0) = [-\nabla_{x^1} \pi^1(p^1, -x^*) + \nabla_{x^2} \pi^2(p^2, x^*)]x'(0)$$

$$= [\lambda^* - \lambda^*]x'(0) \quad \text{using (4)}$$

$$= 0 ; \tag{38}$$

$$Y''(0) = [\nabla^2_{x^1 x^1} \pi^1(p^1, -x^*) + \nabla^2_{x^2 x^2} \pi^2(p^2, x^*)][x'(0)]^2 + 0 \, x''(0)$$

$$= -[\sigma_1^* + \sigma_2^*][x'(0)]^2 \quad \text{using definitions (11)}$$

$$= -[(T_2 - T_1)(w_0 - \lambda^*) - T_1(\tau^1 w_0 + t^1) + T_2(\tau^2 w_0 + t^2)]^2 / T^{*2}[\sigma_1^* + \sigma_2^*] \quad \text{using (22).} \tag{39}$$

A second order approximation to the loss L is

$$L_A \equiv Y(0) - [Y(0) + Y'(0)(1-0) + (1/2)Y''(0)(1-0)^2] \tag{40}$$

Now substitute (38) and (39) into (40) and recall the definition of the profit-maximizing transfer price w_0 given in Theorem 1. We find that a second order approximation to the loss of output induced by profit-maximizing transfer pricing behaviour is:

$$L_A \equiv [(T_2 - T_1)(w_0 - \lambda^*) - T_1(\tau^1 w_0 + t^1) + T_2(\tau^2 w_0 + t^2)]^2 / 2T^{*2}[\sigma_1^* + \sigma_2^*] \geq 0 \tag{41}$$

where $w_0 = w_2$ (w_1) if $T_2(1+\tau^2) - T_1(1+\tau^1) > 0$ (<0) and T^*

may be defined to be $(T_1 + T_2) / 2$.

Thus the two governments can minimize the approximate deadweight loss by: (i) harmonizing tax policies so that $T_1 = T_2$ and $t^1 = t^2 = \tau^1 = \tau^2 = 0$ or (ii) setting $w_1 = w_2 = w^*$ as the optimal regulated transfer price defined by (12).

Of course governments in the two jurisdictions may not care what happens to world output; they may care only about the value-added produced in their jurisdictions. Thus we define the value-added produced in jurisdiction i as a function of the distortion parameter ξ as follows:

$$Y_1(\xi) \equiv \pi^1(p^1, -x(\xi)) \; ; \; Y_2(\xi) \equiv \pi^2(p^2, x(\xi)). \tag{42}$$

$$\therefore \; Y_1'(0) = \lambda^* x'(0) \text{ and } Y_2'(0) = -\lambda^* x'(0) \text{ using (4).} \tag{43}$$

Thus to the first order, what one jurisdiction gains by manipulating its tax and transfer price policies, the other jurisdiction loses. However, to the second order, such manipulations on the part of either government can only result in a loss of world output.

In order to give the reader an indication of the magnitude of the approximate loss L_A defined by (41), it is useful to put the formula into an elasticity format. We consider the special case where all trade taxes are zero but where the rates of income taxation are different, leaving the general case to the reader. Define $Y^* \equiv \pi^1(p^1, x^{1*}) + \pi^2(p^2, x^{2*}) > 0$ to be the socially efficient amount of value-added produced by the firm. Recall that the σ_i^* parameters in (41) were defined as rates of change of the intermediate good shadow prices in the two sectors with respect to a marginal change in the intermediate good allocation; i.e. $\sigma_i^* \equiv \partial \lambda_i(x^{i*})/\partial x^i = - \partial^2 \pi^i(p^i, x^{i*})/\partial x^i \partial x^i$ for i=1,2. Let us convert these σ_i into elasticities; i.e. define

$$\eta_i \equiv x^* \sigma_i^* / \lambda^* \; ; \qquad i = 1,2. \tag{44}$$

Define also the optimal share of the intermediate good as $s^* \equiv \lambda^* x^* / Y^*$, the ratio of the efficient value of the intermediate good to firm value-added. Finally, we need to convert the difference between the profit-maximizing transfer price w_0 and the efficient transfer price λ^* into a percentage. Thus we define

$$\varrho \equiv (w_0 - \lambda^*) / \lambda^*. \tag{45}$$

Substitution of the above definitions into (41) yields the following formula for the approximate loss of output as a fraction of firm value added (we defined $T^* = T_1$ in this case):

$$L_A/Y^* = (T_2 - T_1)^2 \, \varrho^2 s^* / 2(\eta_1 + \eta_2)T_1^2. \tag{46}$$

If the η_i are around one, the right-hand side of (46) will be minuscule for reasonable values of T_1, T_2, ϱ and s^*. However, if at the efficient solution, x^{1*}, x^{2*}, the two plants exhibit almost constant returns to scale with respect to variable inputs, outputs and the intermediate good so that the variable profit functions $\pi^i(p^i, x^{i*})$ are almost linear with respect to the x^i, then the η_i could be very small numbers and the approximate loss defined by (46) could become very large. For example, if $T_1 = .5$, $T_2 = .6$, $\varrho = (w_2 - \lambda^*)/\lambda^* = .2$, $s^* = 1$ and $\eta_i = .01$ for $i = 1,2$, then $L_A/Y^* = 4\%$. If $T_1 = .4$, $T_2 = .6$, $\varrho = .4$ and $\eta_i = .01$ for $i = 1,2$, then $L_A/Y^* = 100\%$. Hence the magnitude of the approximate loss defined by (46) is to a large extent an empirical matter.

The above analysis applied to a firm that maximized profits in a centralized fashion. What happens if the divisions maximize profits independently using the arm's-length transfer price $\tilde{w}$ defined in section IV? The firm value-added function can again be defined by (37) but now $x(\xi)$ is defined as the solution to (30) rather than to (21), and $x'(0)$ is defined by (31) instead of (22). Making these changes, we find that a second order approximation to the loss of output induced by arm's-length transfer pricing behaviour is:

$$L_a \equiv [(\tau^2 - \tau^1)\lambda^* + (1+\tau^1)t^2 - (1+\tau^2)t^1]^2 / 2[\sigma_1^* + \sigma_2^*] \geq 0. \tag{47}$$

The two governments can minimize the approximate deadweight loss in this situation by: (i) eliminating trade distortions (i.e. set $t^1 = t^2 = \tau^1 = \tau^2 = 0$) or (ii) imposing offsetting trade distortions (i.e. set $t^1 = t^2$ and $\tau^1 = \tau^2$). Note that the loss is unaffected by different rates of business taxation when the divisions engage in arm's-length transfer pricing.

VII. A More General Model

We now assume that there are $K \geq 2$ plants or divisions that can produce or utilize a common intermediate good. We assume that the production possibilities set for division i is S^i and we define the division i variable profit function $\pi^i(p^i, x^i)$ by (1) except i = 1,2, . . . ,K.

We assume that division k is in the jurisdiction k and the relevant tax rate is $1 - T_k > 0$ for k = 1, . . . ,K.

We also assume that the different governments levy indirect taxes, tariffs and/or subsidies on the intermediate good transactions of the firm. Let t^k be the specific tax or subsidy on x^k and let τ^k be an *ad valorem* tax or subsidy on x^k. Let $0 < w_1$ be the smallest transfer price that all tax authorities will agree to accept and let $w_2 \geq w_1$ be the largest transfer price that all jurisdictions will accept. The firm's tax distorted profit maximization problem may be defined as (48) below:[23]

$$\max_{x^1, \ldots, x^K, w} \{\Sigma_{k=1}^{K} T_k[\pi^k(p^k, x^k) + w(1 + \tau^k)x^k + t^k x^k]:$$
$$\Sigma_{k=1}^{K} x^k = 0, w_1 \leq w \leq w_2\}. \tag{48}$$

Theorem 4. Assume that a solution $x^{1\circ}, x^{2\circ}, \ldots, x^{K\circ}, w_0$ to (48) exists. Then w_0 can be chosen to be w_1 or w_2.

Proof. Let $x^1, x^2, \ldots, x^K$ be feasible for (48) so that $\Sigma_{k=1}^{K} x^k = 0$. Let $w_1 \leq w \leq w_2$. Then

$$\Sigma_{k=1}^{K} T_k[\pi^k(p^k, x^k) + w(1 + \tau^k)x^k + t^k x^k]$$
$$= \Sigma_{k=1}^{K} T_k[\pi^k(p^k, x^k) + t^k x^k] + w[\Sigma_{k=1}^{K} T_k(1 + \tau^k)x^k]$$
$$\leq \Sigma_k T_k[\pi^k(p^k, x^k) + t^k x^k] + w_2[\Sigma_k T_k(1 + \tau^k)x^k]$$
$$\text{if } \Sigma_k T_k(1 + \tau^k)x^k \geq 0$$

$$\text{or} \leq \Sigma_k T_k[\pi^k(p^k, x^k) + t^k x^k] + w_1[\Sigma_k T_k(1 + \tau^k)x^k]$$
$$\text{if } \Sigma_k T_k(1 + \tau^k)x^k \leq 0.$$

Hence in order to maximize (48) with respect to w, we may chose w to be w_1 or w_2. (QED)

Theorem 4 tells us that the money or *profit-maximizing transfer price* w_0 will be w_1 (if $\Sigma_k T_k(1 + \tau^k)x^{k\circ} < 0$) or w_2 (if $\Sigma_k T_k(1 + \tau^k)x^{k\circ} > 0$) or any price between w_1 and w_2 if $\Sigma_k T_k(1 + \tau^k)x^{k\circ} = 0$.

We now turn our attention to efficient transfer prices.

If all $T_k = T > 0$ and all $\tau^k = 0$, $t^k = 0$, then the distorted profit maximization problem (48) is equivalent to the following (efficient) profit maximization problem:

$$\max{}_{x^1, \ldots, x^K} \left\{ \Sigma_{k=1}^K \pi^k(p^k, x^k) : \Sigma_{k=1}^K x^k = 0 \right\}. \tag{49}$$

If the production possibilities sets S^k are convex, then the functions $\pi^k(p^k, x^k)$ are concave in x^k and we can apply the Karlin-Uzawa Saddle Point Theorem to (49). This theorem guarantees the existence of at least one efficient transfer price λ^* which is an optimal Lagrange multiplier for the constraint in (49). If the functions π^k are not differentiable, then there may exist a set of efficient transfer prices.[24]

However, the case where the S^k are not necessarily convex is more interesting. Assume that $x^{1*}, \ldots, x^{K*}$ solves (49) and there exists $\lambda^* \geq 0$ such that the following first order conditions are satisfied:

$$\nabla_{x^k} \pi^k(p^k, x^{k*}) + \lambda^* = 0, \qquad k = 1, \ldots, K, \tag{50}$$
$$\Sigma_{k=1}^K x^{k*} = 0.$$

Define $\sigma_k^* \equiv -\nabla^2_{x^k x^k} \pi^k(p^k, x^{k*})$ for $k = 1, \ldots, K$. We assume that the following strong second order sufficiency conditions are also satisfied:

$$\Sigma_{k=1}^K \sigma_k^* v_k^2 > 0, \qquad \Sigma_{k=1}^K v_k = 1, \qquad \Sigma_{k=1}^K v_k^2 = 1.$$

Hence at most one of the σ_k^* can be 0 or negative, and if say $\sigma_1^* \leq 0$, then $\sigma_1^* > -\sigma_1^*$ for $k = 2, \ldots, K$. If say $\sigma_1^* < 0$, then division 1 corresponds to Copithorne's (1976, p. 344) non-conformist division.

The λ^* defined in (50) is the common efficient transfer price that all divisions should use in order to maximize world output when there are no tax distortions.

Thus we have characterized efficient transfer prices in the convex technology case and in the smooth technology cases. We turn now to the possibility of defining decentralized transfer prices.

Assume that $T_k > 0$ and that the $\pi^k(p^k, x^k)$ are concave functions of x^k. Then set $w = w_0$ (w_1 or w_2) in (48) and (48) reduces to the following concave programming problem:

$$\max\nolimits_{x^1, \ldots, x^K} \{ \Sigma_{k=1}^K T_k[\pi^k(p^k, x^k) + w_0(1 + \tau^k)x^k + t^k x^k] : \Sigma_{k=1}^K x^k = 0 \}$$
$$= \max\nolimits_{x^1, \ldots, x^K} \min\nolimits_u \{ \Sigma_{k=1}^K T_k[\pi^k(p^k, x^k) + w_0(1 + \tau^k)x^k + t^k x^k] + u\Sigma_{k=1}^K x^k \}$$

by the Karlin-Uzawa Theorem, where u is unrestricted

$$= \max\nolimits_{x^1, \ldots, x^K} \{ \Sigma_k T_k[\pi^k(p^k, x^k) + [w_0(1 + \tau^k) + t^k + T_k^{-1}u^*]x^k] \} \tag{51}$$

for any $u^* \ \varepsilon \ U$ where U is a nonempty closed convex set of multipliers for the constraint in (51)

$$= \Sigma_{k=1}^K T_k \max\nolimits_{x^k} \{ \pi^k(p^k, x^k) + [w_0(1 + \tau^k) + t^k + T_k^{-1}u^*]x^k \}. \tag{52}$$

From (52), we see that division k can correctly solve its divisional profit maximization problem in a decentralized fashion if it uses the division k transfer price $w_k^* \equiv w_0(1 + \tau^k) + t^k + T_k^{-1}u^*$ where $u^* \ \varepsilon \ U$. Hence just as in section V, the centre can theoretically achieve an optimal allocation of resources (from its profit-maximizing perspective) in a decentralized manner.

Our final task is to measure the loss of output (from the perspective of the world) due to the inefficient tax and transfer price system. We use the same loss concept as in section VI. The reader should have no difficulty in proving a new version of Theorem 3, but some difficulty may be encountered in deriving a new version of the approximate loss measure defined by (41). Therefore we shall indicate how this may be done.

Our starting point is the distorted equilibrium situation represented by (51). Assume that $x^{1o}, \ldots, x^{Ko}$ solves (51) and there exists a Lagrange multiplier λ^o such that the following first order conditions are satisfied:

$$T_k[\nabla_{x^k} \pi^k(p^k, x^{ko}) + w_0(1 + \tau^k) + t^k] + \lambda^o = 0,$$
$$k = 1, \ldots, K \tag{53}$$

$$\Sigma_{k=1}^{K} x^{ko} \qquad\qquad = 0 \qquad\qquad (54)$$

Rewrite (53) as follows:

$$\nabla_{x^k}\pi^k(p^k,x^{ko}) + w_0(1 + \tau^k) + t^k + T_k^{-1}\lambda^o = 0,$$
$$k = 1, \ldots, K. \qquad (55)$$

Now consider the following system of first order conditions that implicitly defines a distorted equilibrium allocation $x^1(\xi), \ldots, x^K(\xi)$ and the corresponding Lagrange multiplier $\lambda(\xi)$ for $0 \le \xi \le 1$:

$$\nabla_{x^k}\pi^k(p^k,x^k(\xi)) + \lambda(\xi)[1 + (T_k^{-1} - 1)\xi] + [w_0(1 + \tau^k)$$
$$+ t^k]\xi = 0 \quad k = 1, \ldots, K,$$
$$(56)$$

$$\Sigma_{k=1}^{K} x^k(\xi) = 0 \qquad (57)$$

Define $x^k(0) = x^{k*}$ and $\lambda(0) = \lambda^*$. Then (56) and (57) with $\xi = 0$ reduce to (50), the efficient equilibrium first order conditions. Define $x^k(1) = x^{ko}$ and $\lambda(1) = \lambda^o$. Then (56) and (57) reduce to (55) and (54), the distorted equilibrium first order conditions. We conclude that (56) and (57) map the efficient equilibrium into the distorted equilibrium as ξ goes from 0 to 1.

Differentiate (56) and (57) with respect to ξ and evaluate the resulting derivatives at $\xi = 0$. We obtain

$$\begin{bmatrix} -\hat{\sigma}, 1_K \\ 1_K^T, 0 \end{bmatrix} \begin{bmatrix} x'(0) \\ \lambda'(0) \end{bmatrix} = \begin{bmatrix} \lambda^*1_K - \delta \\ 0 \end{bmatrix} \qquad (58)$$

where $\hat{\sigma}$ is a diagonal K by K matrix with element kk equal to $\sigma_k^* \equiv -\nabla_{x^kx^k}^2\pi^k(p^k,x^{k*})$, 1_K is a vector of ones of dimension K, $x'(0) \equiv dx(0)/d\xi$ where $x(\xi) \equiv [x^1(\xi),x^2(\xi), \ldots, x^K(\xi)]^T$, $\lambda'(0) \equiv d\lambda(0)/d\xi$, λ^* is the efficient transfer price characterized by (50) and $\delta \equiv [\delta_1,\delta_2, \ldots, \delta_K]^T$ is a distortions vector whose kth component is defined as

$$\delta_k \equiv w_0(1 + \tau^k) + t^k + T_k^{-1}\lambda^*, \quad k = 1,2, \ldots, K. \qquad (59)$$

The second order conditions for the efficient allocation imply that the matrix $-\hat{\sigma}$ is negative definite in the subspace orthogonal to 1_K. This in turn is sufficient to imply the existence of the inverse of the matrix which appears on the left-hand side of (58) (e.g. see Diewert and Woodland, 1977, p. 396). Thus we have

$$
\begin{bmatrix} -\hat{\sigma}, 1_K \\ 1_K^T, 0 \end{bmatrix}^{-1} \equiv \begin{bmatrix} D, e \\ e^T, f \end{bmatrix}
\tag{60}
$$

and from Samuelson (1947, p. 379) or Diewert and Woodland (1977, p. 396), it can be shown that D is a negative definite matrix in the subspace orthogonal to 1_K; i.e.

$$
v^T D\ v < 0,\ v \neq k1_K \text{ for any k.}
\tag{61}
$$

It can also be shown that

$$
D1_K = 0_K.
\tag{62}
$$

Hence (58), (60) and (62) yield the following result:

$$
x'(0) = D[\lambda^* 1_K - \delta] = -D\delta.
\tag{63}
$$

Define the world value-added function $Y(\xi)$ by

$$
Y(\xi) \equiv \Sigma_{k=1}^K \pi^k(p^k, x^k(\xi))
\tag{64}
$$

$$
= \Sigma_{k=1}^K \pi^k(p^k, x^k(\xi)) + \lambda(\xi)\Sigma_{k=1}^K x^k(\xi) \text{ using (57).}
\tag{65}
$$

$$
\begin{aligned}
Y'(\xi) = &\ \Sigma_{k=1}^K [\nabla_{x^k} \pi^k(p^k, x^k(\xi)) + \lambda(\xi)]\nabla_\xi x^k(\xi) + \\
&\ \lambda'(\xi)\Sigma_{k=1}^K x^k(\xi)
\end{aligned}
$$

$$
\begin{aligned}
= &\ - \Sigma_{k=1}^K [\lambda(\xi)(T_k^{-1} - 1)\ \xi + (w_0(1 + \tau^k) + \\
&\ t^k)\xi]\nabla_\xi x^k(\xi) + 0 \text{ using (56) and (57).}
\end{aligned}
\tag{66}
$$

Using (66) and (59), we find that

$$Y'(0) = 0;$$
$$Y''(0) = -\Sigma_{k=1}^{K}[-\lambda^* + \delta_k]\nabla_\xi x^k(0)$$

$$= [\lambda^* 1_K - \delta]^T x'(0)$$

$$= -[\lambda^* 1_K - \delta]^T D\delta \quad \text{using (63)} \tag{67}$$

$$= \delta^T D\delta \quad \text{using (62)}$$
$$< 0 \quad \text{unless } \delta = k1_K \text{ using (61).} \tag{68}$$

Thus our second order approximation to the loss of output induced by profit-maximizing transfer pricing is:

$$L_A \equiv Y(0) - [Y(0) + Y'(0) + (1/2)Y''(0)]$$

$$= -(1/2)\delta^T D\delta$$
$$\geq 0. \tag{69}$$

Hence the magnitude of the approximate loss hinges on the magnitude of the elements of the matrix D (see (60)) and the magnitude of the elements of the distortions vector δ (see (59)). Remember that w_0 is either w_1 or w_2.

When there were only two divisions, recall that the efficiency loss could be reduced to zero by either tax harmonization or optimal transfer price regulation. In the K division case, tax harmonization will still work. If all trade taxes are abolished so that $t^1 = \ldots = t^K = 0 = \tau^1 = \ldots = \tau^K$, and each jurisdiction has the same rate of income taxation so that $T^* = T_1 = \ldots = T_K$, then $\delta_k = w_0 + T^{*-1}\lambda^*$ for $k = 1, \ldots, K$ using formula (59); i.e. $\delta = (w_0+T^{*-1}\lambda^*)1_K$. Hence using (62) and (69), it can be verified that $L_A = 0$ so that tax harmonization and the abolition of trade barriers will still lead to an efficient solution in the case of K divisions. The same conclusion holds under complete tax harmonization where $T_1 = \ldots = T_K$, $t^1 = t^2 = \ldots = t^K$ and $\tau^1 = \ldots = \tau^K$, since in this case, the components of δ are again all equal. However, it no longer seems possible to attain an efficient allocation in the K division case if $K > 2$ by transfer price regulation.

We leave to the reader the nontrivial task of generalizing our two-division deadweight loss model when the divisions engage in arm's-length transfer pricing to the case of K divisions.

VIII. Conclusion

We have found that it was necessary to consider five different types of transfer price in this paper:

(i). The *efficient transfer price*. This price arose when solving the firm's global profit maximization problem when there were no tax distortions. This price is the value to society of the intermediate good that is being traded between the various divisions of the firm. An intermediate good is one where no adequate market price exists. The efficient transfer price is the optimal Lagrange multiplier for the intermediate good constraint in the undistorted profit maximization problem. It may be used to evaluate divisional performance if there are no tax distortions.

(ii). The *profit-maximizing transfer price*. This is the transfer price the profit-maximizing firm will use as its official transfer price in its dealings with the tax and customs authorities. It will be set either as high as possible or as low as possible if there are tax distortions.

(iii). *Decentralized profit-maximizing transfer prices*. If the divisional technology sets do not exhibit increasing returns to scale (more generally, they are convex sets), then the divisions can be induced to produce the profit-maximizing inputs and outputs in a decentralized manner if the centre tells the divisions to use these transfer prices in order to value their production (or utilization) of the intermediate good. These transfer prices will usually differ across divisions if there are tax distortions. These prices should be used in order to evaluate divisional performance in the tax distorted case.

(iv). The *arm's-length transfer price*. Each division is assumed to maximize profits independently, taking the arm's-length transfer price as given. An equilibrium arm's-length transfer price is one which makes the net supply of the intermediate good across all divisions equal to zero. Firms using this type of transfer price should make lower profits than firms who use the profit-maximizing transfer price. The same conclusion applies even if there are no tax distortions but one of the divisions exhibits increasing returns to scale (or more generally, the divisional technology sets are nonconvex).

(v). The *optimal regulated transfer price*. If there are only two divisions, then governments could induce the firm to produce in an efficient manner by forcing the firm to use this transfer price w* defined by (12). Unfortunately, this result does not appear to generalize to the case of three or more divisions producing or utilizing the same intermediate good.

A major contribution of the present paper is the recognition and comparison of the above five types of transfer price in a unified framework.

A second contribution of the paper is the development of a methodology for measuring the amount of world output that is wasted due to different methods of transfer pricing. We also developed a second order approximation to this loss which exhibits more clearly how the loss depends on the size of the tax distortions and various production elasticities (see formulae (41), (46), (47) and (69)).

There appear to be a number of implications of our analysis. Independent profit-maximizing firms trading in an intermediate good will probably use something which approximates arm's-length transfer pricing. Hence if there are tax distortions, there will be an incentive for the firms to merge, since joint profit-maximizing behaviour will generate higher profits. Alternatively, there will be an incentive for a multinational enterprise to engage in direct foreign investment if there are (i) trade taxes between the home and foreign country or (ii) different rates of business income taxation in the two countries.

Rugman and Eden (Introduction, this volume) ask the following question: does transfer pricing by multinational enterprises in a world of government regulation improve or worsen global resource allocation; i.e. is unregulated transfer pricing efficient? Using Theorem 2 and the comparative statics results in (18), we noted that in the case of two divisions, a relaxation of optimal regulation will always worsen global resource allocation (too much intermediate good will be produced), provided that the firm is using profit-maximizing transfer pricing.

There appear to be at least three strategies for achieving an efficient global allocation of resources: (i) optimal transfer price regulation; (ii) an anti-monopoly strategy; i.e. the elimination of all trade taxes plus the forced break-up of the firm into independent divisions; and (iii) a global tax harmonization strategy; i.e. the elimination of all trade taxes (or trade tax harmonization so the $t^1 = \ldots = t^K$ and $\tau^1 = \ldots = \tau^K$), plus the adoption of a uniform rate of business income tax across jurisdictions.

There are a number of difficulties with each of the above strategies. With respect to (i), difficulties are that it will only work if there are only two divisions and even in the case of two divisions, it is necessary to know the efficient transfer price λ^* in order to define the optimal regulated transfer price w^* defined by (12). In general, governments will have no way of determining λ^* accurately. With respect to (ii), if the divisions are located within separate states of the same country, it may be legally impossible to force the firm to break up. Moreover, strategy (ii) will not work if any division exhibits increasing returns to scale. Strategy (iii) suffers from the obvious defect that it is difficult to get governments to agree on anything. Another difficulty can arise in the context of multinational enterprises which have the head office and most of the shareholders residing in one country (the home country) but branches are located abroad. Suppose the tax harmonization strategy is implemented. The multinational enterprise may choose to manipulate transfer prices so that *all* of the firm's profits show up in the home country, thus depriving the foreign countries of their share of the profits. The multinational may find it advantageous to do this for a variety of reasons, such as the circumvention of present or potential future foreign exchange controls.[25] However, strategy (iii) still appears to be the most attractive to me. The last difficulty with it mentioned above could be circumvented by an international tax sharing agreement; i.e. the imposition of a common world business income tax.

Another implication of our analysis is that governments in the different jurisdictions will have incentives to set official transfer price bounds in opposite directions.[26]

It should be noted that our loss of output measures are biased downwards. The models developed in this paper are essentially static; they hold capital fixed throughout the analysis. In a dynamic intertemporal model, the capital stocks of the firm become endogenous. The existence of the static tax and transfer price distortions tend to induce the profit-maximizing firm to alter plant capital stocks in an inefficient manner. Diewert (1983b) shows in a similar model that the overall approximate discounted loss of output due to tax distortions within the production sector is equal to a discounted sum of static output losses (that hold capital accumulation decisions fixed at their socially optimal levels) plus an additional dynamic loss term that reflects the additional loss of output due to the investment misallocation.

The research presented in this paper could be extended in a number of directions: (i) the comparative statics properties of the more general model presented in section VII should be worked out; (ii) the model should be extended to many intermediate goods; (iii) the multidivisional firm model should be imbedded in a complete multicountry general equilibrium model;[27] (iv) the model should be dynamized so that firm investment decisions become endogenous variables; (v) the complexities of existing systems of business taxation should be modelled more precisely;[28] and (vi) future modelling should focus on the effects on the welfare of the different jurisdictions of changes in policy parameters as well as the effect on world welfare.

The main point of the paper is that the existence of trade taxes and different rates of business income taxation induces firms to behave in an inefficient manner from the viewpoint of world welfare.[29] This loss of efficiency will persist in more complex models with, say, many intermediate goods or, say, in a complete general equilibrium model. To deal with the general equilibrium model, one could adapt the theory of customs unions[30] to show that the tax distorted system of taxation could be replaced by an efficient tax scheme to achieve any Pareto optimal allocation of resources. However, in order for each tax jurisdiction to preserve its distorted equilibrium level of welfare, lump sum transfer payments (i.e. tax sharing arrangements) will usually be necessary. These optimal fiscal sharing arrangements are usually difficult to achieve due to the usual game theoretic bargaining considerations. However, it seems useful to strive for world productive efficiency even though it may be difficult to achieve such a state in practice.

Notes

This research has been supported by the SSHRC of Canada. The author thanks L. Eden for very helpful and detailed comments.
   1. Comparative statics results in alternative models are available in a host of papers; for some results and further references to the literature, see Horst (1971), Eden (1978, 1983a, this volume) and Itagaki (1979).
   2. See Diewert (1974, 1982) or Varian (1978) for expositions.
   3. So $y^i \equiv (y_1^i, y_2^i, \ldots, y_{N_i}^i)^T$, $i = 1,2$. Notation: $p^T y = p \cdot y \equiv \Sigma_i p_i y_i$ is the inner product of the vectors p and y of the same dimension, $p \geq 0_N$ means each component of the N dimensional vector p is nonnegative, $p \gg 0_N$ means each component is positive and $p > 0_N$ means $p \geq 0_N$ and $p \neq 0_N$.

4. Regularity conditions on S^i and the resulting properties of π^i are developed in Gorman (1968), McFadden (1978) and Diewert (1973). In particular, if S^i is a closed convex set, then $\pi^i(p^i,x^i)$ is a concave function of x^i. A set S is convex if $z^1 \varepsilon$ S, $z^2 \varepsilon$ S, $0 \leq \lambda \leq 1$ implies $\lambda z^1 + (1 - \lambda)z^2 \varepsilon$ S. A function f(u) is concave over a convex set D if $u^1 \varepsilon$ D, $u^2 \varepsilon$ D, $0 \leq \lambda \leq 1$ implies $f(\lambda u^1 + (1 - \lambda)u^2) \geq \lambda f(u^1) + (1 - \lambda)f(u^2)$. In definitions (1), if there is no y such that $(y,x^i) \varepsilon$ S^i, then define $\pi^i(p^i,x^i) = -\infty$. This situation can occur if the intermediate good can only be used as an input in division 1. Then for $x^1 > 0$ (so that we are trying to produce the intermediate good as an output in division 1), $\pi^1(p^1,x^1) = -\infty$.

5. $\nabla_x\pi(p,x) \equiv \partial\pi(p,x)/\partial x$; $\nabla_p\pi(p,x) \equiv [\partial\pi(p,x)/\partial p_1, \ldots ,\partial\pi(p,x)/\partial p_N]^T$ is the gradient vector of π with respect to the components of p.

6. See Samuelson (1947).

7. Samuelson's (ibid., pp. 376-8) strong second order sufficient conditions for the constrained maximization problem (3) reduce to (4) and (5) with a strict inequality. $\nabla_{xx}^2f(x)$ denotes the matrix of second order partial derivatives of f; in (5) x^1 and x^2 are scalars so $\nabla_{x^1y^1}^2\pi^1 = \partial^2\pi^1/\partial x^1\partial x^1$.

8. A function f is convex if $-f$ is a concave function.

9. Actually the two divisions could be located in the same country and still face different tax rates since state and local governments also tend to impose different tax rates.

10. Verlage (1975) outlines various criteria that tax authorities use in order to define admissible transfer prices. These criteria are often incredibly complex.

11. Horst (1971, p. 1061) and Copithorne (1976, p. 351) stated the first results of this type. In their models, $t^1=t^2=\tau^2=0$. If we set $t^1=t^2=\tau^2=\tau^1=0$, then the last part of the theorem may be found in Copithorne (1971, p. 339).

12. For proofs, see Gorman (1968) or Diewert (1973).

13. In order to harmonize tax policies, the authorities need only choose $T_1=T_2$, $t^1=t^2$, and $\tau^1=\tau^2$; i.e. equal income tax rates, and subsidy rates in jurisdiction 2 equal to tax rates in jurisdiction 1 on the intermediate good. With these assumptions, the tax distorted maximization problem (6) becomes equal to T_1 times the undistorted problem (3).

14. See Rugman and Eden (this volume) and Eden (this volume) for discussion and further references.

15. A similar result has been obtained by Eden (this volume).

16. Similar results have been obtained by Horst (1971, p. 1064) and Eden (1983a).

17. See Eden (1983a, p. 674) for similar results.

18. Under these hypotheses, (31) becomes $x'(0)=0$. In this case, our methodology breaks down. The first order approximation to the discrete change in x yields no information about the actual direction of change in x.

19. If the two divisions are independent firms, then under the above hypotheses, there would be a financial incentive for the two firms to merge into a single firm and jointly profit maximize as in Theorem 1, thus destroying the original efficient allocation of resources achieved under arm's-length transfer pricing.

20. Convexity of S^1 and S^2 implies these concavity properties.

21. The conclusion of the theorem also holds if the firm is behaving as a mark-up monopolist or monopsonist in any of its y^1 or y^2 markets. In this case, the reference prices p^1 and p^2 are defined to be market prices minus the mark-ups on input markets.

22. This value-added differs from the usual concept of value-added, which is equal to the value of outputs minus the value of intermediate (raw material) inputs, excluding labour and capital. Our value-added is equal to the value of outputs minus the value of raw materials minus the value of variable labour inputs.

23. The firm's profit maximization problem may be more complicated than (48) if: (i) some plants can produce the intermediate good or use it as an input and (ii) the tax rates τ^k and t^k change as x^k changes from plus to minus. Under these circumstances, we have to consider a separate problem of the type (48) for each tax regime. We assume that (48) represents the tax regime and plant utilization scheme that leads to the maximum profits of the firm. We are implicitly assuming that any nonnegativity restrictions on the x^k are not binding at the solution to (48).

24. In the undistorted case (63), we may replace the constraint $\Sigma_k x^k = 0$ by $\Sigma_k x^k \geq 0$. This will ensure the nonnegativity of the efficient transfer prices. We also need to assume that the Slater constraint qualification holds; i.e. there exist $\bar{x}^k$ such that $\Sigma_k \bar{x}^k > 0$.

25. Another reason may have to do with the provision of local public goods; i.e. if the multinational 'contributes' its profits to the home government, a part of this 'contribution' will show up as increased (or cheaper) services provided by the government to the shareholders and officers of the company.

26. Thus for the model developed in section VI where $T_2(1+\tau^2) > T_1(1+\tau^1)$ and plant 2 produces the intermediate good, using (18) and (43), it can be seen that the jurisdiction 1 transfer price authorities will want to make w_2 (the highest possible transfer price) as large as possible, while the jurisdiction 2 authorities will want to make w_2 as low as possible (from the viewpoint of maximizing their jurisdiction value-added). This point is also made in Eden (this volume).

27. The deadweight loss models developed in Diewert (1983a, 1984) could be adapted to this problem.

28. See Horst (1977), Itagaki (1979), Caves (1982, ch. 8) and Eden (1983a, this volume).

29. This waste of resources due to inefficient schemes of taxation and transfer pricing is not confined to multinational enterprises. In Canada, it seems likely that the relatively high rates of business taxation in the Province of Quebec induce multiprovincial enterprises to manipulate their interprovincial transfer prices in a manner that will lead to zero or negative taxable income in the Province of Quebec.

30. See Ohyama (1972), Dixit and Norman (1980, pp. 191-3) and Woodland (1982, pp. 348-51).

Editors' Comment

Copithorne (1976) uses the terms *money transfer price* and *profit-maximizing transfer price* interchangeably, as do Diewert (this volume, pp. 48, 54) and Eden (1983a). We believe this usage is unfortunate and have deliberately distinguished between the two terms in the Introduction (see pp. 6, 7). We define the profit-maximizing transfer price as the transfer price, discussed in the economics literature, which maximizes global net MNE profits and influences MNE resource allocation decisions. The money transfer price is defined as the external transfer price, discussed in the business school literature, which minimizes MNE tax payments but does not influence resource allocation. Diewert does not discuss this latter kind of transfer price (although he distinguishes among five types of economic transfer prices, one of which is the profit-maximizing price).

4 TRANSFER PRICING: A TAXONOMY OF IMPACTS ON ECONOMIC WELFARE

Robert Z. Aliber

I. Introduction

Two types of propositions dominate the transfer pricing literature — one is that firms shift income from high-tax jurisdictions to low-tax jurisdictions to reduce their effective tax payments, or funds from currency areas subject to exchange controls to other currency areas; both shifts usually occur by overinvoicing payments on imports from related affiliates abroad or by underinvoicing export proceeds.

> The multinational enterprise uses transfer pricing as a means of withdrawing funds from subsidiaries by raising prices on goods and services sold to an affiliate by other units in the system. . . The most widespread use of transfer pricing is to locate profits in an appropriate affiliate in order to reduce the system's total tax burden. (Robbins and Stobaugh, 1973a, p. 91)

The second type of proposition in this literature is that transfer pricing reduces economic welfare — that private gains are achieved at social cost. Vaitsos (1974) found overpricing in the pharmaceutical, rubber, chemical and electronics industries, especially in Colombia.

Transfer pricing occurs when several units of one firm are involved in non-market transactions or exchange of goods or factor services. Petroleum companies transfer price when they ship crude oil from the field production units to the refineries; they transfer price again when the gasoline is shipped to their wholly-owned stations. Universities transfer price when the various schools and divisions 'buy' electricity, heat, computer time and cleaning services from the central administration. The US Government sets transfer prices for the travel of White House Staff on Air Force jets. The US Post Office transfers prices when its service bureau repairs the vehicles of the mail delivery units. Ford Motor transfers price when power-trains produced in its factories in Indiana are shipped to assembly plants in Michigan.

The *need* for a transfer price arises wherever the firm has several profit or cost centres that exchange goods or services with each other. Such transfer prices are shadow prices chosen to facilitate optimization of production and sales decisions across profit centres, almost always in the context of uniform tax rates, interest rates and wage rates. The objective of the firm in setting transfer prices should be to maximize the value of the firm. If the usual competitive assumptions hold, the classic result is that the firm should choose the level of output 'such that the sum of the divisional marginal costs equals the marginal revenue in the final market' (Hirshleifer, 1956, p. 183). 'If the market for the intermediate commodity is imperfectly competitive, transfer price should be at the marginal costs of the selling division' (ibid., p. 183).

Transfer pricing that occurs between divisions of a firm operating within one country usually does not generate much question. Some state or local tax authorities may be concerned that their tax revenues are smaller because firms shift income to other states, even those with identical tax rates. The charge that transfer pricing is antisocial is heard infrequently in the domestic context.

Transfer pricing is inevitable if the firm has several profit centres in different countries. The international economy differs from the domestic economies in that there is much more extensive segmentation of markets by tax rates, currencies, tariffs and quotas. These distinctions among countries are both more extensive and significantly sharper than the distinctions among the several regional areas of one country. Many — not all — reflect or are a result of efforts by national authorities to segment markets, perhaps for the conduct of monetary policy or industrial policy or welfare policy.

Within the international economy, firms can manage transfer prices to arbitrage national differences in tax rates, interest rates, tariff and exchange controls. If transfer pricing is viewed as a productive activity, they should continue to manage transfer price until the costs of doing so equal the incremental return.

That firms manage transfer prices to enhance their own market value within the international economy is understandable. The key question is whether these efforts to enhance private gain enhance or reduce social welfare on a global basis and in each country. The segmentation of the world economy by national tax rates, national currencies, national tariffs and national social and labour policies almost always causes a reduction in world welfare, since resource allocation becomes less optimal. These measures introduce wedges between prices, costs, wages and interest rates in the various countries and thus distort margins. Within some countries, national welfare may increase as a result of the adoption of these measures since the thrust of the policy may be to attract a larger share of capital, exports, production, employment and income from other countries. However, even if such protective measures increase local production and employment, production and employment in other countries may decline; the optimal tariff argument provides an analogy. Thus if a tax haven is established to attract taxable income from abroad, the taxable income available in other countries almost certainly declines.

The effectiveness of an individual nation state in segmenting its own economy from the world economy depends on the scope of its monopoly power. The costs of shipping products or factors or income across the borders between national economies is low, and so firms — both national firms and multinational firms — arbitrage national differentials in interest rates, prices and tax rates. Some domestic factors may move abroad in response to domestic efforts at segmentation. Some foreign factors may not be attracted to the countries that exercise — or attempt to exercise — monopoly power. The more extensive the measures of national states to use their monopoly power to segment markets, the greater the scope for transfer pricing by firms.

This paper analyzes the impact of transfer pricing by multinational firms. The analysis examines the changes in economic welfare through a series of stages — initially domestic policies are identical with those abroad, then one country alters its tax rate or its tariff or adopts exchange controls or some other measure that segments its own economy from those abroad. Thus in the first stage, the world market is fully integrated; no segmentation can be attributed to national differences in tax rates or to possible changes in exchange rates or to exchange controls. The rates of return to firms in the several countries are identical.

Moreover there are no multinational firms in this stage; indeed since all countries are essentially identical in the key parameters, the significance of the term multinational is questionable. But even if there were multinational firms, they would have no incentive to transfer price. The national measures that segment the economies — differential tax rates, exchange rates, tariffs — in the second stage lead to a disequilibrium, which in turn induces some adjustments to equalize rates of return at home and abroad. The welfare consequences of the adjustments of economic agents to these fences or barriers are reviewed; however, there are no multinational firms in this stage.[1] Multinational firms are introduced and manage transfer prices to enhance their own income; the welfare consequences of their transfer pricing decisions are discussed.

The key question involves the welfare implications of the transfer pricing, and the comparison with the economic welfare following the segmentation of the world economy in the second stage. The multinational firms are considered transparent and any gains achieved through their ability to transfer price are passed on to their customers or shareholders or workers or some other group; the rates of return achieved by these firms are assumed competitive.

The scope and impacts of transfer pricing in response to changes in the corporate tax rate in one country are analyzed in section II; changes in the corporate tax rates alter the relative spread between pre-tax and after-tax rates of return in several countries. Capital flows are induced as national firms seek to equalize the after-tax returns in the several countries. The impacts of transfer pricing in response to price controls are examined in section III. The scope and impacts of transfer pricing in response to tariffs and quotas are considered in section IV. The role of transfer pricing in currency market segmentation is considered in section V.

II. Transfer Pricing and Tax Market Segmentation

Consider the possible array of tax arrangements in a world of three countries, Alpha, Beta and Omega, where Omega is a tax haven without any production or consumption.

— Alpha and Beta have identical corporate tax rates and identical definitions of taxable income.

— Alpha and Beta have different corporate tax rates and identical definitions of taxable income.

— Alpha and Beta have identical corporate tax rates but define corporate taxable income differently.

— Alpha and Beta have different corporate tax rates; moreover, the domestic tax rate applied in each country to foreign income differs from the domestic tax rate applied to domestic income. Hence each country has a foreign tax rate on corporate income as well as a domestic tax rate on corporate income. Note that the foreign tax rate may be higher (double taxation) or lower than the tax rate on domestic income, depending on both the recognition given the tax payment abroad in the calculation of domestic taxable income or of domestic tax liability. There may be many more foreign tax rates than there are countries.

— Omega acts as a tax haven, when the foreign tax rates for each country (or for each pair of domestic and foreign countries) may differ.

Differences in the national corporate tax rates affect both where the firms generate income and how the firms are organized. Analysis of the impact of differences in national tax rates, of differences between foreign and domestic tax rates and of changes in these rates vary with the assumptions about the incidence of the corporate tax and of changes in the incidence as tax rates change. One 'corner solution' is full forward shifting, so the full burden of changes in the corporate tax is passed on to the firm's customers in the form of higher selling prices. Another is full backward shifting; the full burden of changes in the corporate tax is passed backward to the firm's owners and may be capitalized by an increase or decrease in the value of their ownership claims. In addition, there may be partial forward and partial backward shifting. Conceivably there might be magnified forward shifting; then the increase in corporate revenue would exceed the increase in the corporate tax bill, so the corporate profits would increase as the corporate tax rate increases, at least for modest changes in tax rates. Each set of assumptions about shifting implicitly reflects both a set of assumptions about the scope of competition in the goods market and in the factor markets, and about whether the firm had set the optimal price prior to the change in the effective corporate tax rate.

Both investors and firms arbitrage both activities and differences in effective tax rates so that there are no effective differences in the after-tax rates of return at home and abroad adjusted for risk, at least in equilibrium. If two firms — either two domestic firms or a domestic firm and a foreign firm — may produce in the same jurisdiction with different after-tax rates of return, the implication is that the market share of the firm with the lower after-tax rate of return must decline. If after-tax returns decline in one country, then capital will tend to flow abroad.

Consider initially that the tax rates are identical in both Alpha and Beta; before-tax rates of return and after-tax rates of return in Alpha and Beta are not significantly different. Definitions of income are identical. The allocation of capital is optimal between Alpha and Beta, in that the profit rate in Alpha is equal to the profit rate in Beta.

$$r_A = r_B$$

where

r_A is the before-tax return in Alpha and r_B is the before-tax return in Beta,
Since

$$t_A = t_B$$

where

t_A is the tax rate in Alpha,

t_B is the tax rate in Beta,

$$r_A^* = r_B^*$$

where the asterisks refer to the after-tax returns. The capital-labour rates are identical in both countries.

There are no multinational firms.

Then Beta increases the tax rate on corporate income, which causes the after-tax profit rate to decline relative to the before-tax profit. Some firms within Beta raise their selling price to capture from their customers part of the proceeds to pay the tax; their market share declines. The size of the corporate sector in Beta declines; fewer firms are able to earn the cost of capital. Capital leaves the corporate sector in Beta, both for the unincorporated sector in Beta and for the corporate sector in Alpha. As capital leaves the corporate sector in Beta, the pre-tax and post-tax profit rates in Beta increase. The pre-tax profit rate in Alpha falls as a result of the increase in the supply of capital. The unincorporated sector in Alpha becomes larger. The redistribution of capital between Alpha and Beta continues until after-tax profit rates in both Alpha and Beta are not significantly different. This shift in the allocation of capital leads to a decline in economic welfare, since the capital-labour ratio in Alpha is now higher than in Beta. In the new equilibrium the capital stock is larger in Alpha and smaller in Beta, while the corporate sector is larger in Alpha and smaller in Beta. The price of corporate output is higher in Beta and lower in Alpha. Nominal wages are higher in Alpha and lower in Beta, and real wages are higher in Alpha and lower in Beta.

Several of the consequences of the introduction of the corporate tax are unambiguous. Economic welfare has declined on a global basis, since the allocation of capital between Alpha and Beta now is suboptimal. Economic welfare in Alpha has increased, however, while economic welfare in Beta has declined — although within Beta some residents may gain more from the increase in expenditures financed by the increase in government revenues or from the reduction in other taxes.

Now assume there are multinationals headquartered in both Alpha and Beta who produce both at home and abroad. These firms recognize that because of the reallocation of capital towards Alpha, attributable to the increase in the Beta tax on profits, the pre-tax rate of return on capital in Beta exceeds the pre-tax rate of return in Alpha. On the margin, the 'best of both worlds' is to employ capital in Beta to achieve the high rates of return and to shift income on this capital to Alpha to avoid Beta's higher tax rate. Firms headquartered in Alpha will transfer price to shift income from Beta. Firms headquartered in Beta will transfer price to park relatively more income in their Alpha subsidiaries (unless Beta taxes income on a world-wide basis concurrently). Because of transfer pricing, the effective corporate tax rate in Beta is lower than the posted rate, since the impact of transfer pricing is to reduce the size of the corporate tax base.

Indeed in the extreme case, the multinationals will shift capital to Beta until the after-tax returns in Alpha and Beta are identical. As a result of this shift in capital, Beta is better off, because relatively more production occurs in Beta, although the tax collector in Beta collects no revenue on the income produced in Beta by the multinationals; the presumption is that the welfare gain associated with the increased level of corporate production in Beta is larger than the welfare loss associated with the decline in corporate profits tax collections. The greater the opportunity to transfer price, the smaller the shift towards a suboptimal allocation of capital between Alpha and Beta; thus transfer pricing mitigates the distortions introduced by the increase in Beta's corporate tax rate. Because of transfer pricing, the distortion from the optimal conditions for allocation of capital introduced by the increase in the tax rates is partially offset or undone.

The cause of the capital outflow from Beta is the increase in its high tax rate; because of the capital outflow the corporate tax base in Beta is reduced. To the extent that firms in Beta engage in transfer pricing to offset the decline in the after-tax profit resulting from the increase in the corporate tax rate, then the corporate tax base in Beta is larger than it otherwise would have been. To fault or blame transfer pricing for the reduction in the tax base and tax collections in Beta is to fall into the trap of the fallacy of misplaced concreteness — the source of the welfare loss in Beta is the increase in its tax rate rather than transfer pricing.

If firms in Alpha and Beta are involved in competitive industries, then any tax saving realized as a result of transfer pricing will be passed forward to their consumers in the form of lower prices. If the industry is less than perfectly competitive, then the increase in profits that results from transfer pricing will be capitalized in the market value of Alpha and Beta firms.

Can transfer pricing introduce its own distortions? If corporate tax rates are identical, either at low levels or high levels, firms have no incentive to transfer price. The necessary condition for transfer pricing is that corporate tax rates differ. If transfer pricing introduces or increases an economic distortion in a world with different corporate tax rates, transfer pricing widens the wedge between the before-tax profit rates in Alpha and Beta. Assume that the corporate profits rate pre-tax in Beta exceeds that in Alpha and that the tax rates are identical; pre-tax corporate profits in Beta exceed pre-tax corporate profits in Alpha.

Now Beta increases its corporate tax rate. One response to the reduction in the after-tax returns in Beta is a shift of capital to Alpha. If multinational firms are introduced and shift profits to Alpha, there is no loss in economic welfare. Assume instead that Beta had reduced its corporate profits tax rate, so that the spread between the pre-tax corporate profits and after-tax profits will be greater in Beta than in Alpha. The reduction in Beta's tax rate will induce a shift in capital to Beta, even in the absence of multinationals. If multinationals are introduced, they may transfer price to induce a shift of income from Alpha to Beta. Alpha will incur a revenue loss; the volume of economic activity in Alpha is likely to change.

III. Price Controls and Transfer Pricing

From time to time, many countries have adopted price controls, either on a comprehensive basis or on a selective industry-specific basis. The rationale for comprehensive price controls is to limit the rate of increase in the price level. The purpose of industry-specific controls is to limit the 'windfalls' that producers or owners receive when there is a sudden increase in demand for a product or service believed to have a low supply elasticity in the short run.

Assume Beta adopts price controls to limit increases in its inflation rate while Alpha relies on market prices. Assume that Alpha and Beta are part of the same currency area, and there are no multinational firms. Beta's price controls reduce the profit attached to the production of particular goods, so the volume of goods which are produced in Beta will decline. As a result, excess demand in Beta will appear in Alpha. Several responses will occur. Non-price rationing mechanisms will develop. Some goods and services will be sold at black market prices. Queues will develop. Goods and services will be sold at the legal price plus a side payment. The production of 'old' products subject to the price ceilings will decline, and the production of new products not subject to the price ceilings (or subject to the price ceilings with a higher cost basis) will increase. A larger share of current production in Beta will be allocated to exports since exports are not likely to be subject to price controls. Similarly imports may increase if importers are able to pass on their cost increases as higher prices. Beta firms will tend to overinvoice import payments as a way to establish a higher-cost basis, and hence increase the profit rate above the level they can secure in Beta; transfer pricing is not a monopoly of multinational firms. And some of Beta's domestic products will be relabelled with phony 'certificates of origin' to suggest these products are imported, and hence not subject to price controls.

Beta's price controls reduce the profit rate, for profits are squeezed between the fixed selling prices and the costs which are likely to rise. The consequence of the decline in the profit rate in Beta is that capital will shift to Alpha. Capital will continue to move from Beta to Alpha as long as the after-tax and pre-tax returns in Beta are below those in Alpha. Beta's price controls lead to a decline in economic efficiency on a global basis and to a decline in economic welfare within Beta.

Now assume there are both Alpha and Beta multinationals; Beta still has its price controls. Both Alpha and Beta firms will seek to minimize or avoid the profit squeeze initiated by Beta's price ceilings. So both will export more of their Beta production to Alpha. Both will overinvoice imports as a way to increase profits. Transfer pricing is a back door way to maintain a competitive profit rate.

Whether these multinational firms are more likely to over-invoice import payments than domestic firms is an empirical issue. To the extent that national firms or multinationals engage in transfer pricing, the implicit profit rate in Beta is likely to exceed the profit rate permitted by the price controls; the more extensive transfer pricing, the smaller the welfare loss associated with the price controls.

IV. Tariffs, Quotas and Transfer Pricing

From time to time, individual countries have adopted tariffs to segment their domestic goods market from the world goods market. Numerous rationales are provided for tariffs and quotas, including the infant-industry argument, national defence, increasing employment and income. Similar justifications are provided for subsidizing exports.

Assume Beta increases its tariffs on one or several goods to achieve one of these several objectives. As Beta's imports decline, either its currency appreciates in the exchange market or its price level increases in response to its payments surpluses. In either case exports from Beta of particular goods will decline because of a loss of price competitiveness. Beta's decision to segment its goods market is likely to reduce its economic welfare, unless Beta has market power or unless production in Beta is subject to declining costs.

The impact of the tariff is to increase the return to capital in Beta in those firms that produce behind tariff walls since the price that these firms can charge will be higher while their costs will be unchanged. However, the appreciation of Beta's currency or the increase in its price level will reduce the return to capital to those firms that export, since the local currency equivalent of their export price is lower while their costs are unchanged.

One consequence of the import tariff is that importers in Beta may underinvoice as a way to reduce their tariff payments. As a result, their profits will be higher, and so the corporate tax will be higher. If the tariff rate is below the effective corporate tax paid by the firm, underinvoicing imports will reduce after-tax profits. The incentive to underinvoice exists only as long as the tariff rate is higher than the effective corporate tax rate paid by these firms.

Assume Alpha firms had exported intermediate products to their subsidiaries in Beta prior to the increase in Beta's tariff. Alpha firms have an incentive to underinvoice exports as a way to minimize the bite of Beta's tariff; they may seek to divert income from Beta to Alpha to reduce the corporate tax paid in Beta. As long as the Beta tax rates are not higher than the Alpha tax rates, Alpha firms should have no incentive to underinvoice.

The incentive to underinvoice exists only as long as the tariff rate exceeds the lower of the corporate tax rates in Alpha or Beta. Both national firms and multinational firms may have an incentive to underinvoice. The potential for underinvoicing may be greater for multinationals to the extent they can more readily transfer income to an affiliate in Alpha.

The loss in welfare occurs because the introduction of the tariff weakens the firm link between prices and costs. To the extent transfer pricing reduces the bite of the tariff, the welfare loss is diminished. To argue that transfer pricing reduces global welfare under tariff barriers must mean that one is implicitly assuming that tariffs are an appropriate response to market failure.

V. Transfer Pricing and Currency Market Segmentation

Consider now the use of transfer pricing in response to the adoption of exchange controls by Beta. In most cases exchange controls are adopted because currency parities are misaligned; countries with overvalued currencies adopt controls to limit the downward pressure on their currencies in the foreign exchange market. Similarly, exchange controls enable the countries to maintain undervalued currencies by limiting capital inflows. At best these controls might enable countries to delay changes in the foreign exchange value of their currencies that are otherwise inevitable. Moreover, if controls persist even as the foreign exchange value of a country's currency is changing, the controls are used to ration foreign exchange among various buyers. Thus importers of raw materials and spare parts may be favoured relative to importers of luxury goods and importers of goods may be favoured relative to those who wish to import foreign securities.

In most cases — probably 80-90 per cent — currency overvaluation results from a more rapid increase in the domestic price level than of the world price level, with the consequence that the domestic demand for imports increases and the domestic supply of exports declines. The usual cause of the more rapid increase in the price level is a more rapid increase in the domestic money supply.

Assume Beta's currency is becoming increasingly overvalued as a result of an excessive rate of monetary expansion; Beta's price level is increasing relative to those of its trading partners. One consequence of the increase in the Beta price level is that the real interest rates are likely to fall in Beta if the price level increases more rapidly than nominal interest rates, so the demand for financial assets denominated in Beta's currency will decline; capital will flow from Beta to Alpha. Moreover, as the probability of an increase in the Beta price of Alpha's currency increases, the demand for Alpha assets by Beta residents also rises.

A second consequence of increasing overvaluation of Beta's currency is that the profit rate falls in Beta because the wages and other costs which are set in the domestic market will increase with the increase in the price level, although prices which are set in the world market may be constant. If Beta firms raise selling prices to reduce the profit squeeze, their market share will decline relative to the market share of Alpha firms both in Alpha and Beta. To some extent Beta producers of goods that require extensive imported components may realize increased profits on their domestic sales (as long as they can continue to obtain imported components) since the increase in their selling prices may exceed the increase in their costs. The consequence of the reduction in profit rate is that relatively less capital is invested in Beta, and relatively more capital is invested in Alpha. While the increasing overvaluation of Beta's currency means the Alpha currency equivalent of Beta profits tends to increase, the percentage decline in profits in Beta is almost certain to exceed the percentage overvaluation of Beta's currency, since profits are small relative to total revenues.

The increasing overvaluation of Beta's currency leads to a decline in the foreign exchange holdings of Beta's central bank, and for two reasons. One is that Beta's current export earnings will decline relative to current import payments. The second is that investors — both lenders and borrowers — alter the currency mix of their assets and liabilities in response to the combination of changes in the interest rates in both Alpha and Beta, and the anticipated increase in the price of Alpha's currency in terms of Beta's currency. Thus the 'leads and lags' will turn against Beta; firms will borrow more in Beta and invest more in Alpha.

Each differential in the real returns between Alpha and Beta implies a particular rate of loss of holdings of foreign exchange by Beta's central bank. As the differential in real returns increases, the rate of loss of Beta's central bank's holdings of foreign exchange increases — even if the anticipated price of Alpha currency in terms of Beta currency remains unchanged. As investors attach a higher probability to the increase in terms of currency, Beta's central bank's holdings of foreign exchange will decline at an even more rapid rate.

Assume Beta adopts exchange controls to limit the rate of decline in its central bank's holdings of foreign exchange. Such controls may enable Beta to prolong the period of overvaluation, and overvaluation as measured by the deviation between the nominal exchange rate and the real or price-level adjusted exchange rate may increase. As a result, the decline in the profit rate in Beta will be even larger.

The reaction of firms to the overvaluation of Beta's currency should be distinguished from their reaction to Beta's exchange controls. As the profit rate in Beta declines in Beta, capital will flow from Beta to Alpha. Production and employment in Beta will decline while production and employment in Alpha will increase. Exports from Beta will decline, exports from Alpha will increase. Beta firms will acquire assets denominated in Alpha's currency, while Alpha firms will issue liabilities denominated in Beta's currency. Exchange controls may retard the capital flows. National firms will respond to these controls by underinvoicing export receipts and overinvoicing import payments.

Now introduce Alpha and Beta multinational firms. These firms have incentives to increase production in Alpha and to reduce production in Beta for both the Alpha and the Beta markets. The economic pressures on the multinational firms are identical with those on the national firms. The multinationals may find it easier to shift production from low-profit sources in Beta to high-profit sources in Alpha.

Multinationals might respond to the exchange controls in several ways. They might underinvoice exports and overinvoice imports as a way to shift funds from Beta to Alpha, much like the national firms. This pattern might enable them to achieve a higher profit rate in Beta than the posted profit rate.

The impact of the increasing overvaluation in reducing the profit rate in Beta domestic currency should be distinguished from the impact of the exchange controls in reducing the parent company's valuation of this lower profit rate. To the extent that multinational firms and national firms can transfer price, they can reduce the severity of the decline in the profit rate because of the overvaluation. The source of the disequilibrium is the growing overvaluation of Beta's currency; transfer pricing simply reflects the desire of firms to minimize the erosion of their profit rates.

Summary and Conclusion

This paper has evaluated some of the traditional claims about the welfare loss to particular countries associated with transfer pricing by multinational firms. The paper evaluated the impacts of transfer pricing in response to differentials in tax rates, price ceilings, tariffs and exchange controls.

The necessary condition for transfer pricing is that a firm have two or more cost or profit centres that engage in transactions in goods, services and factors. Within the international economy, multinational firms manage their transfer prices to arbitrage differences in tax rates, price levels and interest rates. National firms will have as much of an incentive to arbitrage these price spreads as multinational firms.

If corporate tax rates are identical across countries, no incentive exists to manage transfer pricing to shift income among tax jurisdictions; after-tax rates of return are identical. If tax rates are raised or lowered in one country, a wedge is driven between before-tax rates of return in the several countries, and capital flows towards the country with the lower tax rates. The consequence of this shift adjustment is that economic welfare declines on both a global basis and in the higher tax country. The impact of transfer pricing by the multinational firm to shift income from the high tax jurisdiction to the low tax jurisdiction is to undo partially or reverse the welfare-reducing impact of the increase in the tax rate, so less production is diverted from this jurisdiction. Transfer pricing also reduces the reserves of the tax collector in the high-tax jurisdiction while increasing economic welfare. The distribution of the gains realized from the tax savings attributable to transfer pricing depends on the competitiveness of goods markets and of factor markets; if taxes are shifted forward, the gains will be realized by the consumers in the form of lower prices.

This result appears pervasive across the various measures that segment national markets. Measures that segment national markets for goods or factors raise economic welfare in the country adopting these measures but at the expense of global welfare. Transfer pricing tends to lessen the global welfare-reducing impact of these measures, and thus undercuts the efforts of the state to exercise its monopoly power. Criticisms of transfer pricing as a welfare-decreasing activity are exercises in misplaced concreteness.

Note

1. National firms will arrange their transactions to circumvent these efforts to segment national markets. Thus the importers in the countries with exchange controls may arrange with the exporters to overinvoice as a way to shift funds to areas less extensively subject to exchange controls. Similarly, they may arrange to shift income to a lower tax jurisdiction.

Editors' Comment

To clarify the statements by Aliber on page 92, note that the MNE's incentive to under(over) invoice depends on a comparison between the tariff rate and the international tax differential. For example, assuming Alpha firms export to their subsidiaries in Beta, a tariff τ_B is levied by Beta, and t_A and t_B are the corporate tax rates, then Alpha firms will under(over) invoice if $\tau_B - (t_B - t_A)/(1 - t_B)$ is positive (negative). Note also that a negative tax differential (i.e. $t_B < t_A$) reinforces the incentive to underinvoice due to the tariff. (See Horst, 1971, p. 1061.)

5 TRANSFER PRICING IN EXHAUSTIBLE RESOURCE MARKETS

Larry Samuelson

I. Introduction

The markets for many exhaustible resources are characterized by multinational enterprises.[1] This paper constructs a model of a multinational which extracts an exhaustible resource in two countries. The enterprise may transfer resource from one country to the other, and uses the resource in the production of a processed good in each country. We are especially interested in the internal transfer pricing policies of the firm. Section II demonstrates that under plausible tax and tariff schemes, the enterprise will adopt a transfer price equal to a government-imposed lower limit. Attention is accordingly directed to the implications of varying transfer price limits.

Section III examines the multinational's optimal extraction strategy and its dependence upon transfer price limits. The standard exhaustible resources result, that the marginal profitability of extraction should grow at the interest rate, is obtained. In order for this to occur, the enterprise will only coincidentally extract simultaneously from both countries, with the preferred order of extraction depending upon the rate of growth of the transfer price limit. Section IV develops comparative static properties of government transfer pricing limitations. An increase in the minimum allowed transfer price reduces the amount of resource transferred between countries.

These results allow us to address (in the context of a resource-extracting multinational) some central questions in the transfer pricing literature. Under what conditions are the transfer prices adopted by the firm efficient? How do these conditions depend upon the transfer price limitations imposed on the firm? What equity considerations arise in setting such limits? Section V examines an equity issue: the implications of the multinational for host-country revenues. Comparative static transfer pricing results are derived and the outcomes of various market structures compared. Section VI examines the efficiency implications of various transfer pricing policies. Section VII concludes.

II. The Model

Consider an enterprise which costlessly extracts an exhaustible resource in two countries, called countries 1 and 2, using the resource to produce (possibly different) outputs in each country. If, for example, the resource is petroleum, the outputs might consist of refined products such as gasoline and kerosene. We are interested in cases in which the enterprise finds it optimal to transfer resource from one country to another, and choose to name the countries so that the resource importer is country 1.[2] Intuitively, we shall think of country 1 as a developed nation with relatively limited resource stocks, with country 2 being a less developed but resource-rich nation. We shall refer to country 1 as the home country. There is no trade in produced goods. Profits (under the above naming convention) are given by

$$\int_0^\infty \left\{ (1 - z_1(t))[\Phi_1(R_1(t) + R_{21}(t)) - (1 + \tau(t))pR_{21}(t)] \right.$$
$$\left. + (1 - \bar{z}_2(t))[\Phi_2(R_{22}(t)) + p(t)R_{21}(t)] \right\} e^{-rt}dt \qquad (1)$$

where $\Phi_1(R_1(t) + R_{21}(t))$ and $\Phi_2(R_2(t))$ are increasing, strictly concave functions identifying for resource input $R_1(t) + R_{21}(t)$ and $R_{22}(t)$ the profit gained from selling the resulting final product, and where:

t	=	time index, hereafter often suppressed
R_1	=	resource extracted in country 1
R_{2i}	=	resource extracted in country 2 and used in production in country i
r	=	interest rate
z_i	=	country i tax rate
τ	=	tariff rate
p	=	transfer price
$\bar{z}_2(t)$	=	$\max[z_1(t), z_2(t)]$

Country 1 taxes the profits earned in country 1 at rate z_1.[3] Profits earned in country 2 are assumed to be immediately and completely repatriated to country 1 and taxed by country 1 at rate max$[0, z_1 - z_2]$, thus allowing a credit for foreign tax payments (cf. Itagaki, 1979). As indicated by the presence of $\bar{z}_2(t)$ in (1), the total tax on profits earned in country 2 is then the higher of z_1 and z_2.

Profits are maximized subject to

$$\int_0^\infty R_1(t)dt = S_1(0)$$

$$\int_0^\infty (R_{21}(t) + R_{22}(t))dt = S_2(0) \tag{2}$$

$$0 \le R_1(t) \qquad 0 \le R_{21}(t) \tag{3}$$

where $S_i(t)$ is country i resource stock at time t. The variables at the enterprise's discretion include R_1, R_{21}, R_{22}, and the transfer price.

The transfer price is easily determined. Collecting the terms from (1) which include the transfer price yields:

$$\int_0^\infty [(1 - \bar{z}_2(t)) - (1 - z_1(t))(1 + \tau(t))]p(t)R_{21}(t)e^{-rt}dt \tag{4}$$

Since $\bar{z}_2 \ge z_1$, (4) is the integral of a negative term (if $R_{21} > 0$) multiplied by $p(t)$, and can be increased by decreasing $p(t)$ for any t. Hence, the enterprise finds it profitable to lower its transfer price, transferring profits to the relatively favourable country 1 tax environment and avoiding tariff payments, and will set the transfer price as low as is allowed. Since lowering the transfer price has the apparent effect of avoiding country 2 tax payments and country 1 tariff payments, a lower bound on allowable transfer prices is likely to be set by country 2 and country 1 customs authorities.[4]

The enterprise maximizes (1) by forming the Hamiltonian, which is, with time indices suppressed:

$$\begin{aligned} H = &[(1 - z_1)(\Phi_1(R_1 + R_{21}) - (1 + \tau)pR_{21}) + (1 - \bar{z}_2) \\ &(\Phi_2(R_{22}) + pR_{21})]e^{-rt} - x_1R_1 - x_2(R_{21} + R_{22}) \\ &+ \lambda_1R_1 + \lambda_2R_{21} \end{aligned}$$

where controls are R_1, R_{21} and R_{22}; state variables are S_1 and S_2, with costate variables x_1 and x_2; λ_1 and λ_2 are Kuhn-Tucker multipliers attached to the constraints given in (3); and the transfer price is set equal to the exogenous lower limit. Let $\Phi_1(R_1 + R_{21}) \equiv$

$\partial\Phi_1(R_1 + R_{21})/\partial R_1 = \partial\Phi_1(R_1 + R_{21})/\partial R_{21}$ and $\Phi_2(R_{22}) \equiv \partial\Phi_2(R_{22})/\partial R_{22}$. We assume $\lim_{x\to 0} \Phi_1(x) = \lim_{x\to 0} \Phi_2(x) = \infty$ (which obviates the need for a nonnegativity restriction on R_{22}). First order conditions are (2) and:

$$(1 - z_1)\Phi_1(R_1 + R_{21})e^{-rt} - x_1 + \lambda_1 = 0 \tag{5}$$

$$[(1 - z_1)\Phi_1(R_1 + R_{21}) + ((1 - \bar{z}_2) - (1 - z_1)(1 + \tau))p]e^{-rt} - x_2 + \lambda_2 = 0 \tag{6}$$

$$(1 - \bar{z}_2)\Phi_2(R_{22})e^{-rt} - x_2 = 0 \tag{7}$$

$$\dot{x}_1 = 0 \qquad \dot{x}_2 = 0 \tag{8}$$

$$\dot{S}_1 = -R_1 \qquad \dot{S}_2 = -R_{21} - R_{22} \tag{9}$$

$$\lambda_1 R_1 = 0 \qquad \lambda_2 R_{21} = 0 \tag{10}$$

where a $\cdot$ denotes a time derivative. These combine with (2) to describe the profit-maximizing solution.

III. Equilibrium

The equilibrium described by (5)-(10) embodies the basic exhaustible resources result that, in an optimal extraction programme, marginal profits increase at the rate of interest, though in this case these profits are earned by selling the processed goods rather than the resource itself. Consider country 1. If the solution is interior in R_1, so that $\lambda_1 = 0$, (5) and (8) imply that the marginal profit of the resource in the production of country 1 output grows at the rate of interest. If instead the solution is interior in R_{21}, so that (6) holds with $\lambda_2 = 0$, the marginal profit of the resource in country 1 minus the net cost of transferring a unit of resource from country 2 to country 1 (given by $-[(1 - \bar{z}_2) - (1 - z_1)(1 + \tau)]p \equiv -\psi)$ grows at the rate of interest. In such a case, the growth rate of marginal profit depends upon that of the cost of transfer. For example, if tax and tariff rates are constant, marginal profit grows faster (slower) than the rate of interest as the lower transfer price boundary grows faster (slower) than the rate of interest. Finally, from (7), the marginal profit of the resource in country 2 production grows at the rate of interest.

Whether the solution is interior in the various extraction rates depends upon the time path of ψ. In particular:

Lemma 1. Let $\dot{\psi}(t)/\psi(t) \equiv n(t)$ be constant in t (denoted n). Then:

If $n < r$, then $\exists t \ \varepsilon \ (0,\infty)$ such that $\lambda_2(t) > 0$ and $\lambda_1(t) = 0$ for $t < t$; $\lambda_2(t) = 0$, $\lambda_1(t) > 0$, and $S_1(t) = 0$ for $t > t$.　　(11)

If $n > r$, then $\exists t \ \varepsilon \ (0,\infty)$ such that $\lambda_2(t) = 0$ and $\lambda_1(t) > 0$ for $t < t$; $\lambda_2(t) > 0$ and $\lambda_1(t) = 0$ for $t > t$.　　(12)

Proof. We prove (11); (12) is analogous. Since $n < r$ and $\psi < 0$, ψe^{-rt} increases in t. Combining (5) and (6) gives $\psi e^{-rt} = x_2 - x_1 + \lambda_1 - \lambda_2$, so that $\lambda_1 - \lambda_2$ must increase in t (since $\dot{x}_1 = \dot{x}_2 = 0$, from (8)). Furthermore, only one of λ_1 and λ_2 can be nonzero at any t (since $\lim_{x \to o} \phi_1(x) = \infty$), and both are non-negative. Finally, λ_1 must be positive for some t or no country 1 resource is extracted, which is not optimal. Then it must be that $\lambda_2 > 0$ for some interval $(0,t)$ and $\lambda_1 > 0$ for (t,∞). If $S_1(t) \neq 0$ for $t \ \varepsilon \ (t,\infty)$, all of country 1 resource has not been extracted, which is again nonoptimal. This establishes (11). ∎

We interpret (11). If the net cost of transfer is growing at a rate slower than the interest rate ($n < r$), it is cost-reducing to delay any transfer of country 2 resource to country 1, since the present value cost of such a transfer is falling. Hence, the enterprise will initially use only country 1 resource in country 1 ($\lambda_1(t) = 0$ and $\lambda_2(t) > 0$). This pattern will continue until country 1 resource is exhausted ($S_1(t) = 0$), at which time imports from country 2 will occur.[5] Statement (12) describes a converse situation. If $n = r$, we have the border line case in which the enterprise is indifferent as to which stock it depletes.

It is clear that the nature of the profit-maximizing strategy depends upon the transfer price, and hence upon the lower transfer price boundary. For analytic convenience, we hereafter restrict attention to the case of a transfer price boundary which is set so that the net cost of transfer grows at the rate of interest.[6]

Implications of other transfer price boundaries are derived via analysis analogous to that employed below.

Assumption 1. The transfer price boundary is set so as to ensure $\dot{\psi}/\psi = r$.

An implication of Assumption 1 is that $\lambda_1(t) = \lambda_2(t) = 0$ for all t.

Some comments on transfer pricing in this model are in order. If $\psi = 0$, we could characterise the tax and tariff scheme as neutral. In this case, the enterprise is indifferent as to the distribution of its profits between the two countries, and hence as to the levels of its transfer prices. Transfer price limitations affect the location in which the enterprise earns its profits, but not its production plans.

If $\psi < 0$, the tax and tariff scheme is not neutral. The enterprise prefers to earn the profits on transferred resource in country 1. If allowed, the enterprise will reduce the transfer price until its profits in country 2 equal zero. Some regulation of the enterprise, in the form of a minimum permissible transfer price, is then required if country 2 is to collect its 'fair' share of tax revenues (and if country 1 is to collect 'fair' tariff revenues). The determination of this minimum is likely to be particularly difficult in exhaustible resource markets. The arm's-length lower limit on transfer prices is often taken to be some cost-related measure. Such measures may be inappropriate in resource markets, since exhaustible resource prices are determined by scarcity rents and not costs. Notice also that the choice of a lower transfer price boundary is not completely arbitrary, as country 1 tax authorities will presumably not tolerate a lower boundary which allows the enterprise to avoid 'unfairly' country 1 taxes.

IV. Transfer Pricing Policies

This section develops the implications of varying government transfer pricing policies. In order to isolate the effects of transfer prices, we assume:

Assumption 2. $\dot{z}_1 = \dot{z}_2 = \dot{\tau} = 0$.

Notice that the lower transfer price boundary must then grow at the rate of interest if Assumption 1 is to hold. The government's transfer pricing policy can accordingly be entirely characterized by the initial transfer price boundary, which we denote p(0). Notice also that the optimal extraction pattern is completely described by $\Phi_1(0)$ ($\equiv \Phi_1(R_1(0) + R_{21}(0))$) and $\Phi_2(0)$ ($\equiv \Phi_2(R_{22}(0))$), since under Assumption 1 the marginal profit of resource use in each country grows exponentially from these values.

Remark 1. A higher (lower) $\Phi_i(0)$ implies that in each time period less (more) resource will be used in country i.

Given Assumptions 1 and 2, the equilibrium conditions in (5)-(10) can be summarized by, in abbreviated notation:

$$\frac{\dot{\Phi}_1}{\Phi_1} = r = \frac{\dot{\Phi}_2}{\Phi_2} = \frac{\dot{\Phi}_1 + \dot{\Gamma}}{\Phi_1 + \Gamma} \tag{13}$$

$$\Phi_1 + \Gamma = \Phi_2 \left[\frac{1 - \bar{z}_2}{1 - z_1} \right] \tag{14}$$

where

$$\Gamma = \left[\frac{1 - \bar{z}_2}{1 - z_1} - (1 + \tau) \right] p$$

Condition (13) is obtained by differentiating the natural log of equations (5), (6) and (7), given that $\dot{z}_1 = \dot{z}_2 = 0$; and (14) is obtained from (6) and (7).

Proposition 1. Given Assumptions 1 and 2, we have, for all $t \geq 0$:

$$\frac{\partial(R_1(t) + R_{21}(t))}{\partial p(0)} < 0 \tag{15}$$

$$\frac{\partial R_{22}(t)}{\partial p(0)} > 0 \tag{16}$$

Proof. Follows from differentiation of (14) and Remark 1.

An increase in $p(0)$ increases the transfer price in each period. This renders the transfer of resource from country 2 to 1 less profitable, and reduces the amount transferred. The result is decreased resource use in country 1 and increased use in country 2. A decrease in the transfer price has the opposite effect.

Remark 2. From (15)-(16), we see that there is a unique initial transfer price, say p^*, which yields $\Phi_2(0) = p^*$. Furthermore, from (15)-(16):

$$p(0) \gtreqless \Phi_2(0) \text{ as } p(0) \gtreqless p^* \tag{17}$$

V. Tax Revenues

Multinational enterprises have often been criticized for not acting in the best interests of the host country, primarily by manipulating transfer prices to avoid tax payments. This issue is especially important in the case of a multinational which extracts an exhaustible resource from a less developed country, since the revenues generated by such extraction may be a primary source of economic growth. This section first establishes the effects of government transfer pricing policies on country 2 tax revenues, and then examines the contention that the multinational unfairly avoids such payments.

The present value of country 2 tax revenue is given by:

$$z_2 \int_0^\infty (\Phi_2(R_{22}(t)) + p(t)R_{21}(t))e^{-rt}dt \equiv Z_2 \tag{18}$$

We then have:

Proposition 2. Under Assumptions 1 and 2, there exists a (lower boundary on the initial transfer price) $\bar{p} > p^*$ such that

$$\frac{\partial Z_2}{\partial p(0)} > 0 \text{ if } p(0) < \bar{p} \tag{19}$$

Proof. Differentiating (18) gives:

$$\frac{\partial Z_2}{\partial p(0)} = z_2 \int_0^\infty \left[\Phi_2(t) \frac{\partial R_{22}(t)}{\partial p(0)} + p(t) \frac{\partial R_{21}(t)}{\partial p(0)} \right] e^{-rt} dt$$
$$+ z_2 \int_0^\infty R_{21}(t) dt$$

It is known that $p(t)$ and $\Phi_2(t)$ grow at rate r. Furthermore, from (2) and (16) we have $-\int_0^\infty \frac{\partial R_{21}(t)}{\partial p(0)} dt = \int_0^\infty \frac{\partial R_{22}(t)}{\partial p(0)} dt > 0$. Hence,

$$\frac{\partial Z_2}{\partial p(0)} = z_2(\Phi_2(0) - p(0)) \int_0^\infty \frac{\partial R_{22}(t)}{\partial p(0)} dt + z_2 \int_0^\infty R_{21}(t) dt$$

From (16) and (17), the first term takes the sign of $p^* - p(0)$, and (19) follows.

We conclude that a revenue-maximizing country 2 would prefer an initial transfer price above p^*. As long as the transfer price is not too high, the government of country 2 prefers higher to lower transfer prices.

We now investigate whether the multinational unfairly avoids country 2 tax payments. There are several ways to formulate this issue more precisely, and we choose the following. We examine whether country 2 would be better off, in terms of revenue collection, with the multinational or with two independent firms, one in each country.[7] The answer to this question depends upon the transfer price imposed on the multinational and the market structure which prevails in the absence of the multinational. We consider three alternatives for the second specification: the two firms trade as perfect competitors; the country 1 firm (firm one) buys resource from the country 2 firm as a monopsony; and the country 2 firm (firm two) sells resource to the country 1 firm as a monopoly. We make the following assumption, which not only simplifies the analysis, but sharpens the results (cf. note 8):

Assumption 3.

$$(-1, 0)_3 \frac{\partial \Phi_1(R_1 + R_{21})}{\partial (R_1 + R_{21})} \frac{R_1 + R_{21}}{\Phi_1(R_1 + R_{21})} \bigg| \text{ is constant}$$

Let $p(0,\cdot)$ be the initial price under monopoly ($\cdot = mp$), monopsony ($\cdot = ms$), or competition ($\cdot = c$). Let $Z_2(\cdot)$ be the corresponding revenue collected by country 2 in each structure, and let $Z_2(p(0,\cdot),mn)$ be the revenue colected given that a multinational exists and $p(0,\cdot)$ is the initial transfer price boundary.

Proposition 3. Given Assumptions 1-3, each of the monopoly, monopsony and competitive outcomes gives $\dot{p}/p = r$ (if trade occurs in the monopoly and monopsony outcomes). In addition:[8]

$$p(0,ms) < p(0,c) = p^* < p(0,mp) \tag{20}$$

$$Z_2(p^*,mn) = Z_2(c) \tag{21}$$

$$Z_2(p^*,mn) > Z_2(ms) > Z_2(p(0,ms),mn) \tag{22}$$

$$Z_2(p^*,mn) < Z_2(mp) < Z_2(p(0,mp),mn) \tag{23}$$

Proof. Consider first the case of a competitively organized market. It is well known that the price of the resource must grow at the rate of interest in such a market. The first order conditions for the country 1 firm in such a case are the appropriate parts of (2), (8), (9), and:

$$(1 - z_1)\Phi_1 e^{-rt} - x_1 = 0 \tag{24}$$

$$(1 - z_1)(\Phi_1 - (1 + \tau)p)e^{-rt} = 0 \tag{25}$$

while those of the country 2 firm are (2), (8), (9), and:

$$(1 - \bar{z}_2)\Phi_2 e^{-rt} - x_2 = 0 \tag{26}$$

$$(1 - \bar{z}_2)pe^{-rt} - x_2 = 0 \tag{27}$$

Conditions (26) and (27) require $p(0,c) = \Phi_2(0)$, which is compatible with (25), (2), and with $\Phi_1(t)$ and $\Phi_2(t)$ growing at rate r if $p(0,c) = p^*$ (cf. (14)-(17)). A comparison with (5)-(10) indicates that the competitive extraction profiles in such a case match those of a multinational with an initial transfer price of p^*. Hence $Z_2(p^*,mn) = Z_2(c)$, completing the perfect competition results. Proof of the remaining results are available from the author.

To attain an intuitive account of these results, we compare the monopoly case with a multinational whose transfer price equals the monopoly price (see especially the second inequality in (23)). In the former structure, the country 1 firm takes the price of resource as given, and imports that quantity of resource which renders the marginal profitability of imports equal to zero (cf. (25)). Given this behaviour, firm 2 follows the standard monopoly rule of setting the price of exports so as to equate their marginal revenue with the marginal profit of the resource in country 2 (Φ_2), which is the marginal opportunity cost of such exports. As a result, the equilibrium price exceeds Φ_2 (and hence the competitive price, cf. (20)). The multinational can then increase the profit earned in country 2 by increasing exports at the existing price. Moreover, the effect of marginal export increases on the sum of country 1 and country 2 profits is positive, being zero in country 1 and positive in country 2. The multinational accordingly increases exports over the monopoly level (and hence increases country 2 profits and tax revenues), with decreases in country 1 profits more than offset by increasing country 2 profits. In the monopsony case, the multinational again exercises its ability to increase exports without altering the export price. In this case increases in country 1 profits more than offset decreases in country 2 profits, with the latter inducing decreases in country 2 tax revenues.

The extent to which country 2 is better or worse off with the multinational then depends upon the transfer price boundary. If the country can set high transfer prices, the multinational is more desirable than a country 2 monopoly, in the sense that a transfer price boundary can be set which induces the multinational to yield higher tax revenues than the monopoly. This price need not be as high as the actual monopoly .price, so that a monopoly country should be willing to lower its price in return for allowing a multinational to enter. Conversely, at low prices the country is better off selling to a monopsony than with the multinational. If the initial transfer price is p*, the multinational extraction path and tax payments duplicate those of a competitive market, so that the multinational is preferred to a competitive market if p(0) ε (p*,p̄] (see Proposition 2 for p̄).

VI. Efficiency

The analysis of the previous sections allows us to offer some comments on the existence and efficiency of a multinational enterprise. The multinational internalizes the international resource market, allowing the firm to avoid the transactions costs or uncertainty inherent in the market. Such factors may be particularly important in resource markets. Petroleum markets, for example, are often thought to be characterized by the uncertain availability of resource supplies.

If a perfectly competitive market would prevail in the absence of a multinational, these types of considerations may provide the primary incentives for the existence of a multinational. Another incentive arises if the market would be characterized by imperfect competition in the absence of a multinational. Consider the monopoly market. As long as the initial lower transfer price limit placed on a multinational is not too much higher than the initial price adopted by a monopoly seller, the multinational earns higher profits than the sum of the profits earned by the two firms in the absence of the multinational. Hence, the formation of a multinational enterprise, by internalizing an imperfectly competitive market, allows higher profits than those earned by the independent firms together. An analogous result holds for a monopsony market. These potential profit gains may provide powerful incentives for the formation of a multinational.

It is interesting to note that the formation of a multinational may allow some efficiency gains. For example, the monopoly seller arrangement is characterized by a deadweight loss, caused by insufficient transfer of the resource to country 1. A multinational faced with a transfer price limit equal to the monopoly price transfers more resource to country 1 than the monopoly, allowing some efficiency gains.

This directs attention to whether the multinational's resource allocation decisions are efficient. To examine this question, it is useful to introduce the concept of a shadow price. Suppose that the firm was subjected to no tax or tariff payments. Its objective would be to maximize:

$$\int_0^\infty [\Phi_1(R_1(t) + R_{21}^i(t)) + \Phi_2(R_{22}(t))]e^{-rt}\,dt \tag{28}$$

$$\text{s.t}\quad R_{21}^e(t) - R_{21}^i(t) \geq 0 \tag{29}$$

$$\int_0^\infty (R_{21}^e(t) + R_{22}(t))dt = S_2$$
$$\int_0^\infty R_1(t)dt = S_1 \tag{30}$$

$$0 \leq R_1(t) \qquad 0 \leq R_{21}^i(t)$$

where $R_{21}^i(t)$ is the amount of resource imported by country 1 in time t, and $R_{21}^e(t)$ is the amount exported by country 2. The inclusion of both of these may appear redundant, since $R_{21}^e(t) - R_{21}^i(t) = 0$ will obviously characterize the solution. However, explicitly including both allows a convenient shadow price representation of the result. First order conditions for the maximization are (suppressing the nonnegativity conditions):

$$\Phi_1(R_1 + R_{21}^i)e^{-rt} - x_1 = 0 \tag{31}$$

$$\Phi_1(R_1 + R_{21}^i)e^{-rt} - y = 0 \tag{32}$$

$$\Phi_2(R_{22})e^{-rt} - x_2 = 0 \tag{33}$$

$$y - x_2 = 0 \tag{34}$$

$$\dot{x}_1 = \dot{x}_2 = 0 \ (=\dot{y}) \tag{35}$$

$$\dot{S}_1 = -R_1 \qquad \dot{S}_2 = -R_{21}^c - R_{22} \tag{36}$$

$$R_{21}^e - R_{21}^i = 0 \tag{37}$$

where y is the multiplier attached to (29). We now follow standard practice and define the shadow price y^* which solves (31)-(37) as the efficient transfer price, and the solution to (31)-(37) as the efficient solution (cf. Diewert, this volume). If the output markets in countries 1 and 2 are perfectly competitive, an issue about which we have yet to comment, we might interpret this efficiency as the Pareto efficient allocation of resources.

Consider now the relationship between the transfer price and the shadow price. A question of interest is whether a proper government policy can induce the efficient solution. We immediately see that if the tax and tariff scheme is neutral ($\psi = 0$), the transfer price does not appear in the profit maximization conditions (5)-(10), and the solution to these conditions duplicates the solution to (31)-(37). Hence, a neutral tax and tariff scheme yields the efficient market outcome. Transfer prices do not affect the market outcome in this case, and do not have efficiency implications. They do, of course, affect the amounts of taxes and tariffs paid in the two countries.

If the tax and tariff scheme is not neutral ($\psi < 0$), complications arise. If $\tau = 0$, then choosing $p(0) = y^*$ prompts the multinational to adopt the efficient solution; while if the initial transfer price limit is higher (lower) than the efficient shadow price, too little (too much) resource will be transferred. If a tariff exists ($\tau > 0$), however, the issue is more complicated. In this case, setting the initial transfer price equal to the efficient shadow price does not yield the efficient outcome. Instead, too little resource is transferred, reflecting the presence of the tariff. Hence, constraining the initial transfer price to equal the efficient shadow price may not be justified on efficiency grounds if tariffs are nonzero. Notice, however, that in such a case a multinational allows the possibility of avoiding the inefficiency of a tariff by appropriately setting the transfer price ($p(0) < y^*$).

To make these comments more precise, define $p^e(z_1, z_2, \tau)$ to be the initial transfer price limit which must be imposed on the multinational to achieve the efficient outcome; i.e. to prompt the multinational to adopt a resource allocation path which solves (31)-(37), given tax rates z_1 and z_2 and tariff rate τ. Recall that if $\psi = 0$, $p^e(z_1, z_2, \tau)$ is arbitrary.

Proposition 4. Let $\psi < 0$ and Assumption 1 holds. For any z_1, z_2 and τ, $p^e(z_1, z_2, \tau)$ exists and is nonnegative. In addition,

$$p^e(z_1, z_2, \tau) > (=) 0 <=> z_1 < (\geq) z_2 \tag{38}$$

Proof. The multinational solves (5)-(10). Comparison of these conditions with (31)-(37) indicates that the multinational will yield an efficient outcome if the transfer price can be set so as to induce

$$\Phi_1(0) = \Phi_2(0) \tag{39}$$

Combining (39) with (5)-(7), setting t = 0, and solving for $p^c(z_1, z_2, \tau)$ gives

$$p^c(z_2, z_2, \tau) = \frac{x_2(z_1 - \bar{z}_2)}{(1 - \bar{z}_2)[(1 - \bar{z}_2) - (1 - z_1)(1 + \tau)]} \tag{40}$$

Since $(1 - \bar{z}_2) - (1 - z_1)(1 + \tau) = \psi/p < 0$ and $\bar{z}_2 \geq z_1$, we have $p^c(z_1, z_2, \tau) \geq 0$ ($x_2 > 0$ is obvious); and (38) is then immediate.

This proposition gives incomplete information about the efficient transfer price, since (40) presents an expression for $p^c(z_1, z_2, \tau)$ which involves x_2, an endogenous variable. It is known that $x_2 > 0$, but the magnitude of x_2 depends upon z_1, z_2 and τ. Hence, we offer:

Proposition 5. Let $\psi < 0$. Then

$$\frac{\partial p^c(z_1, z_2, \tau)}{\partial \tau} < 0 \tag{41}$$

If $\tau = 0$, then

$$p^c(z_1, z_2, 0) = y^* = p(0, c) = p^* \tag{42}$$

If $\tau > 0$, then

$$p^c(z_1, z_2, \tau) < p^* = p(0, c) < y^* \tag{43}$$

Proof. Condition (41) follows from (15)-(16) and the observation that an argument similar to that of Proposition 1 gives

$$\frac{\partial(R_1(t) + R_{22}(t))}{\partial \tau} < 0 \qquad \frac{\partial R_{22}(t)}{\partial \tau} > 0$$

Conditions (42) and (43) follow from (5)-(10), (31)-(37), (20) and (24)-(27).

We can interpret these results as follows. If the tax and tariff scheme is neutral, the multinational will adopt an efficient resource allocation pattern, regardless of transfer price limitations. If the tax and tariff scheme is not neutral, the enterprise can be induced to adopt an efficient allocation by appropriate transfer price limitations. When the tariff rate is zero, this is accomplished by setting an initial transfer price equal to the efficient shadow price. However, this limitation does not give the efficient outcome if the tariff rate is positive, as a positive tariff prompts a reduction in the amount of resource transferred. Efficiency is then restored by decreasing the transfer price limit, prompting the firm to increase the amount of resource transferred, with the latter restored to the efficient level by an appropriately chosen transfer price limit. These results are analogous to those found in static models. Diewert (this volume) demonstrates the efficiency in the no-tariff case of a transfer price which equals the efficient shadow price, while the Horst model (see Horst, 1971, and Eden, this volume) can be easily manipulated to give an expression analogous to (40) for the efficient transfer price in the presence of a positive tariff.

In summary, we note that a multinational may allow some efficiency gains over an imperfectly competitive market, but does not produce an efficient outcome if transfer price limitations are not properly set. To achieve efficiency, the latter should be set at the competitive level if the tariff is zero, and must otherwise be set below the competitive level.

Why do the governments involved not set the transfer price limitation equal to the efficient level, and hence achieve the efficient market outcome? An obvious difficulty arises in computing this level. A second potential difficulty is that distributional, or equity, issues arise. Decreasing a transfer price below the monopoly level may allow potential efficiency gains, but this potential may be irrelevant if the distribution of these gains does not allow Pareto improvements. Notice that both countries may welcome the replacement of a monopoly by a multinational. Country 2 receives higher tax revenue, and country 1 receives additional resource as well as higher tariff revenue.[9] However, unanimity is not likely to exist when considering a reduction of the transfer price. Country 1 may welcome such a reduction, as it promises additional resource use; while country 2 is likely to be antagonistic to the attendant reduction in its tax revenues. Hence, efficiency does not produce a compelling argument for adopting a particular transfer price limit. How transfer price limits are determined in such cases is a subject for further research.

VII. Conclusion

The results are summarized in Propositions 1-5 and need not be repeated. A factor pervading the results is their dependence upon the level of the transfer price. Even if we assume that transfer price regulations will enforce the knife edge case of a net cost of transfer which grows at the rate of interest, no clues are readily available as to the level of the transfer price. This level has implications for the optimal extraction strategy of the multi-national, the equity considerations of the multinational and other market arrangements, and the efficiency of the multinational.

Since the enterprise will desire a low transfer price, and since a low transfer price is often perceived to be inimical to country 2, lower limits on acceptable transfer prices are likely to be set by country 2 tax officials and country 1 customs authorities. These, however, are not completely arbitrary. The limits must be acceptable to country 1 tax authorities. If observable arm's-length prices (prices for the same good traded in an ordinary market between unrelated traders) are available, they may set the bounds on allowable transfer price limitations. If not, no obvious notion presents itself as to what might be a fair range of transfer prices. It is often assumed in the transfer pricing literature that in the absence of arm's-length prices, the (government-set) lower bound on transfer prices should be related to the cost of production (cf. note 4), presumably on the grounds that this provides a lower bound on likely values for the arm's-length price. In the case of an exhaustible resource, this is clearly inappropriate, since the price at which such a resource is traded is set not by the cost of production but by its scarcity rent. Obvious limitations are accordingly not available. The determination of transfer price limitations for exhaustible resources warrants further study.

Additional topics for further research include the examination of tax and tariff policies, which can be accommodated within the context of the present model, and extensions of the model to approximate more clearly actual experience in resource markets. We observe that many resource prices have not been growing at the rate of interest in recent years. A possible explanation is that such growth would be observed if market conditions were sufficiently stable, but that revisions in estimates of resource stocks and future demand have frequently altered this path. Inclusion of such factors in the model might provide further interesting insights.

Notes

I am grateful to Lorraine Eden who, in addition to offering several sets of helpful comments on this paper, suggested that I pursue the issues developed in section VI. Helpful comments from the conference participants and my discussant Abe Hollander are also gratefully acknowledged. I alone am responsible for errors.

1. Basic multinational references include Vernon (1971), Horst (1971) and Itagaki (1979). Exhaustible resources are studied in Dasgupta and Heal (1979) and Kemp and Long (1980), the latter examining resources and international trade. Chudson (1981) and Helleiner (1981) present data on multinational trade. While trade in exhaustible resources is not a majority of multinational transactions, it is important. For example, petroleum constituted 84 per cent of US multinational imports from developing countries in 1974 (68 per cent in 1973) (cf. Chudson, note 9; Helleiner, p. 37).

2. For simplicity, we then assume that resource cannot be transferred from country 1 to country 2, though no important results depend upon this assumption. Introducing these conventions at this point allows a more compact presentation of the model, at the cost of some generality. Postponing these considerations and initially presenting the model in its full generality requires additional, tedious notation.

3. We assume that tax variations do not affect the interest rate. This will occur if taxes on interest earnings and profits are independent, so that changes in the former do not affect after-tax interest yields. Alternatively, the interest rate might be set in a world capital market in which the two countries are perfect competitors, so that variations in their tax rates cannot affect the world after-tax interest rate. A brief discussion of the effect of taxes on interest earnings is given by Dasgupta and Heal (1979, p. 366). In order to isolate the issues connected with exhaustible resources, we also make the simplifying assumptions that all profits are repatriated, and that extraction costs are zero. Inclusion of additional taxes (such as royalties on resource extraction), extraction costs or partial repatriation yields analogous but more complex results.

4. Restrictions on transfer prices are modelled by Horst (1971) and Itagaki (1979). For a discussion of transfer pricing, see Robin Murray (1981) and Verlage (1975). Analogous conditions for determining whether a high or low transfer price is desired appear in static models of multinational enterprises. See Eden (this volume) for a discussion and summary of these issues.

5. Limitations on the rate at which the resource can be extracted from either country may yield simultaneous extraction with $n < r$, with one country then initially experiencing extraction at the maximum possible rate. Notice that the country 2 resource stock is never depleted in finite time. The country 1 stock will be depleted in finite time if $n < r$; will not be finitely depleted if $n > r$; and may or may not be if $n = r$.

6. While this assumption is analytically convenient, my discussant, Abe Hollander, has observed that it may well fail to hold. In particular, it may be unreasonable to expect two countries to agree on a set of transfer pricing limitations complex enough to include boundaries which grow at the rate of

interest, or to be able to enact such a knife edge agreement. Given these difficulties, countries may instead turn to taxes and tariffs to regulate multinationals, perhaps leaving transfer prices to be governed by some arm's-length concept. An interesting question for further study is then the effect of various tax and tariff policies on the multinational, and the corresponding implications for government policy. The present model is easily applied to such questions.

7. The desirability of an extractor of an exhaustible resource will depend upon the tax revenues it generates; the benefits generated by resource directed into the domestic market; the amount of profit income retained domestically; and the rate of depletion of the resource stock. We concentrate in this section on tax revenues because the primary criticism of multinationals has been that they surreptitiously avoid tax payments, and because tax payments (perhaps including royalties) are likely to be of importance to a less developed resource exporter. We assume either that $z_2 \geq z_1$ or that in the absence of a multinational, the firm extracting the country 2 resource is still owned by country 1 (it is not termed a multinational because it is concerned with profits earned in a single country). This causes effective tax rates to be independent of market structure. If both assumptions fail, $\bar{z}_2$ must be replaced by z_2 in (26) and (27), and obvious modifications made in the results.

8. Notice that under the constant elasticity assumption, the monopoly and perfect competitor choose identical rates of growth for price, as is well known (cf. Dasgupta and Heal, 1979). However, they do not yield identical solutions, unlike many other extraction problems, because they choose different boundary values for the price path (cf. Stiglitz and Dasgupta, 1982, p. 137). My discussant has noted that some (though not all) of the results established in this Proposition have counterparts in the literature on vertically integrated firms, and presents an extremely helpful intuitive account of those counterparts.

9. The two countries may have much more complex objectives than this simple example suggests.

Editors' Comment

In practice, the transfer price acceptable to country 1 tax authorities need not be acceptable to (or even known by) either country 1 or 2 officials. (See Samuelson's comments on the acceptable transfer price on page 114.) Valuation for customs purposes occurs at different dates and uses different methods (e.g. the GATT transfer value method) than valuation for income tax purposes (e.g. US Section 482 or the Canadian 'fair and reasonable' standard). In most cases tax and tariff officials, even in the same country, work independently and do not exchange information. Given that the authorities, interested in maximizing their own revenues, are likely to set quite different 'official' transfer prices, the possibility of several external transfer prices existing for the same intra-firm transaction is very high. As a result, double taxation can occur, and is used by Shoup (this volume) as a rationale for voluntary arbitration of transfer pricing disputes. In the microeconomic models in this volume (e.g. Eden, Diewert, Samuelson, Itagaki), the authors assume only one transfer price applies to each intra-firm transaction. This simplification should not blind the reader to the fact that there may be as many official transfer prices as there are authorities regulating intra-firm trade.

6 THE EQUIVALENCE OF TARIFFS AND QUOTAS IN THE MULTINATIONAL ENTERPRISE

Takao Itagaki

I. Introduction

Whether or not tariffs and quotas yield equivalent effects has been important at both theoretical and empirical levels. The study of the equivalence of tariffs and quotas was developed by Bhagwati (1965). Since then the study has been extended principally in two ways. One way is to relax the assumptions of perfect competition in production, export, import and quota-holding, and/or to extend the definition of equivalence (Bhagwati 1965, 1968; Shibata 1968; Yadav 1968; McCulloch, 1973). Another way is to introduce uncertainty about demand and supply in two trading countries, and to compare the welfare implications of tariffs and quotas (for example, Fishelson and Flatters, 1975; Pelcovits, 1976; Dasgupta and Stiglitz, 1977; Young 1979, 1980).

Nowadays multinational enterprises (henceforth MNEs) occupy a substantial portion of world trade. They have features distinctive from the traditional framework of the analysis of the equivalence. That is, (i) a typical MNE monopolizes its production and trade in a global scale, and (ii) also internalises its international trade within the MNE using transfer prices. The implications of these characteristics for the equivalence of tariffs and quotas are an open question, since in most cases previous studies take up monopoly in domestic production, foreign supply, import or quota-holding separately, and assume that international trade takes place between independent economic units.

Another common feature in previous analyses of the comparison of tariffs and quotas under uncertainty is the assumption that policy makers face uncertainty about market demand and supply. While this approach produced important results for policy making, the problem of the equivalence of tariffs and quotas in cases where producers and traders face uncertainty has been entirely neglected.

This paper investigates the equivalence of tariffs and quotas from the new aspect of international trade and production, that is, in the framework of the MNE operating under certainty and uncertainty. A tariff and a quota are market imperfections faced by MNEs: the former belongs to price control while the latter belongs to quantity control.[1] In the light of this distinction, the purpose of this paper is considered to clarify whether the two kinds of market imperfections produce identical consequences for the behaviour of the MNE and for communities. The paper demonstrates that under certainty, depending on the relative magnitude of the price of unit import licence to the tariff payments per unit of import and on cost conditions, the equivalence may or may not hold in the sense that a tariff will give rise to a level of importable production and of imports which, if alternatively set as a quota, will generate the same level of price of importable good or the same level of importable production (Shibata, 1968; Bhagwati, 1968). It is also shown that the equivalence does not generally hold in terms of Bhagwati's original sense that a tariff rate will produce an import level which, if alternatively set as a quota, will produce an identical discrepancy between price in the importing country and foreign price or cif price in the exporting country, i.e. an implicit tariff rate (Bhagwati (1965)). Furthermore, it is shown that once we introduce uncertainty about domestic and foreign demand and costs, the equivalence in the sense of Shibata (1968) and Bhagwati (1968) holds in even more limited cases, and the equivalence in Bhagwati's original sense breaks down in general. Moreover, we show some new implications of the MNE for the problem of equivalence. In section II we assume certainty, while in section III we consider the case of uncertainty. In section IV a summary is given.

II. The Certainty Case

In the following we shall use the Horst model (1971) with international price discrimination possible. That model seems sufficient to highlight the implications of the MNE for the present problem of the (non)equivalence of tariffs and quotas. The model is briefly sketched as follows. The monopolistic MNE produces identical final goods in the two countries, and also exports some of the goods produced in the home country to the foreign subsidiary. Let x_i ($i=1, 2$) denote the amounts of production in country 1 (home country) and country 2 (foreign country), and z denote the amount of export. We write total revenue functions in the home and the foreign country as $h_1(x_1-z)$ and $h_2(x_2+z)$, and total cost functions as $f_i(x_i)$ ($i=1, 2$). Furthermore, denoting the transfer price and the *ad valorem* tariff by p and τ, respectively, the global profit function under the tariff, which is assumed to be the objective function of the MNE, is written as

$$\pi_t = \{h_1(x_1-z) - f_1(x_1) + pz\} + \{h_2(x_2+z) - f_2(x_2) - p(1+\tau)z\}, \tag{1}$$

where the first and the second term represent the profit of the parent firm in the home country and that of the subsidiary in the foreign country, respectively.

A. The Increasing Marginal Costs Case

When marginal costs of production in the two countries are increasing, the first order conditions for the maximization of the global profit under the tariff are

$$\frac{\partial \pi_t}{\partial x_1} = h_1'(x_1-z) - f_1'(x_1) = 0, \tag{2}$$

$$\frac{\partial \pi_t}{\partial x_2} = h_2'(x_2+z) - f_2'(x_2) = 0, \tag{3}$$

$$\frac{\partial \pi_t}{\partial z} = h_2'(x_2+z) - h_1'(x_1-z) - p\tau = 0, \tag{4}$$

where the primes denote derivatives. Here and in the remainder of this paper it is assumed that the second order conditions are satisfied.

Equations (2) and (3) indicate that the marginal revenues are equated to the marginal costs of production in the two countries, while equation (4) indicates that the marginal revenues (and hence the marginal costs) in the two countries differ by the tariff payments per unit of import.

On the other hand, when the quota equal to $\bar{z}$, which is the solution for z in (2)-(4), is imposed, that is, $z \leq \bar{z}$, the optimal decisions of the MNE are obtained by maximizing the following expression:[2]

$$L = \Pi_q + \lambda(\bar{z} - z)$$

$$= \{ h_1(x_1 - z) - f_1(x_1) + pz \} + \{ h_2(x_2 + z) - f_2(x_2) - pz - qz \} + \lambda(\bar{z} - z), \tag{5}$$

where q is the price paid for purchase of the licence per unit of import and λ is the Lagrange multiplier. Assuming the existence of an interior solution and also that the quota is not redundant ($z = \bar{z}$), we have the following Kuhn-Tucker first order conditions:

$$\frac{\partial L}{\partial x_1} = h_1'(x_1 - z) - f_1'(x_1) = 0, \tag{6}$$

$$\frac{\partial L}{\partial x_2} = h_2'(x_2 + z) - f_2'(x_2) = 0, \tag{7}$$

$$\frac{\partial L}{\partial z} = h_2'(x_2 + z) - h_1'(x_1 - z) - q - \lambda = 0, \tag{8}$$

$$\frac{\partial L}{\partial \lambda} = \bar{z} - z = 0. \tag{9}$$

Comparing the system of equations (2)-(4) and that of (6)-(9) with the amount of import z equal to the level of $\bar{z}$ and common in the two systems, we see from (2) and (6), and (3) and (7) that the amounts of x_1 and x_2 are also identical. Thus the tariff and the quota are equivalent in the sense of Shibata (1968) and Bhagwati (1968). But, here it is important to note that from (4) and (8) we have $p\tau = q + \lambda$ or $\lambda = p\tau - q$. Since λ is nonnegative, the solution $z = \bar{z}$ under the quota requires that $q \leq p\tau$. This in turn implies that for the above equivalence to hold the price of unit import licence should not exceed the tariff payments per unit of import. Otherwise, the cost of unit import licence under the quota is greater than the tariff payments per unit of import, and hence it is not profitable for the MNE to expand the volume of trade up to the level of $\bar{z}$. This means that for $q > p\tau$, x_1 and x_2 are not identical under the tariff and the quota. Therefore, the equivalence does not hold in the sense of Shibata and Bhagwati.

λ represents the increase in profit when the quota is relaxed. That increase is zero when the price of unit import licence is equal to the tariff payments per unit of import, that is, $q = p\tau$, while the increase in profit is equal to the tariff wedge $p\tau$ when $q = 0$. From the point of view of the foreign government, if the import licence is sold to the MNE at the price of $p\tau$, the revenue effect is the same under the tariff and the quota. Since the decisions on production and sales in the two countries under the two circumstances are the same for $q = p\tau$, in this case the welfare effects are also equivalent in the two countries.[3]

In order to make it easy to understand the above results, following Horst (1973) we shall use the marginal cost of exporting schedule and the marginal revenue from importing schedule as in Figure 6.1. The marginal cost of exporting schedule (CD) is derived as the horizontal distance from the marginal revenue curve ($h_1'(x_1-z)$) to the curve of marginal cost of production ($f_1'(x_1)$) in the home country. The marginal revenue from importing schedule (AB), on the other hand, is derived as the horizontal distance from the curve of marginal cost of production ($f_2'(x_2)$) to the marginal revenue curve ($h_2'(x_2+z)$) in the foreign country. $p_1(x_1-z)$ and $p_2(x_2+z)$ are the domestic and the foreign demand curve, respectively. The marginal cost of exporting schedule is upward-sloping under increasing marginal costs in the home country.

Without a tariff the MNE expands the volume of trade until the marginal cost of exporting and the marginal revenue from importing schedule intersect each other, where profits from trade (AGC) are maximized. When the *ad valorem* tariff is imposed by the foreign country, either the net marginal revenue from importing declines or the marginal cost of exporting rises by the amount of tariff payments, $p\tau$. Figure 6.1 depicts the former case. Then the volume of trade shrinks from the level of OH to OK. If instead the quota OK is imposed, the net marginal

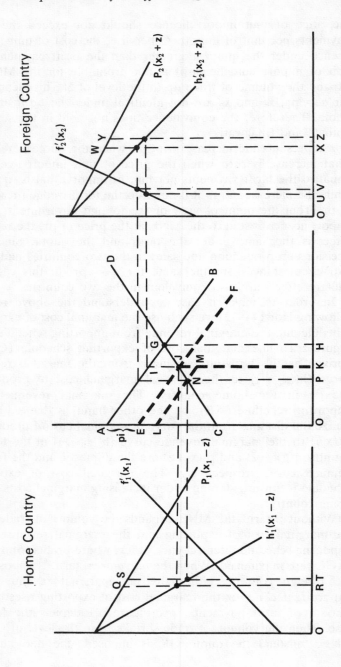

Figure 6.1: The Equivalence of a Tariff and Quota Under Increasing Marginal Costs

revenue from importing schedule not only shifts down by the purchasing cost of unit import licence, q, but also kinks at the level of OK. When $q = p\tau$, the net marginal revenue from importing schedule become EJK, and trade occurs at point J, where EJK intersects the marginal cost of exporting schedule. We see that the tariff and the quota produce identical levels of price in the importing country (YZ) and of importable production (OU). This illustrates the equivalence in the modified sense by Shibata and Bhagwati.[4] When $q < p\tau$, the net marginal revenue from importing schedule lies above EJ, and kinks at the import level of OK (not drawn). But, trade occurs at J. Therefore, also in this case the equivalence holds. Suppose that q $> p\tau$. Then the net marginal revenue from importing schedule takes a shape such as LMK, and trade occurs at point N. Thus, the profit-maximizing import level falls short of the quota OK. The corresponding price and production in the foreign country are WX and OV, respectively. Therefore, the equivalence does not hold.

Next, we consider the equivalence in terms of Bhagwati's original definition. A problem is what prices we should use to define an implicit tariff rate in the case of the MNE. The cif export price in the case of the MNE is given by the transfer price.[5] Therefore, the corresponding implicit tariff rate is defined by the ratio of the difference between the market price in the importing country and the transfer price to the latter. Since the transfer price may be considered to be determined arbitrarily by the MNE, the implicit tariff rate under the quota deviates from the explicit tariff rate τ in general. Thus, the equivalence does not generally hold in Bhagwati's original sense.[6]

B. The Decreasing Marginal Costs Case

Let us consider the case in which marginal costs in the two countries are decreasing. In this case, as Horst (1971, 1973) points out, the MNE chooses one of three different supply strategies: (i) produce all its output in the home country and serve the foreign market entirely with exports; (ii) produce in both countries, but refrain from exporting between the two; and (iii) produce all its output in the foreign country and serve the home market entirely with imports. In considering the present problem of equivalence, it suffices to take up strategy (i). For this strategy x_2 is deleted from the profit functions (1) and (5). Under the tariff we have the following first order conditions with respect to x_1 and z:

$$\frac{\partial \pi_t}{\partial x_1} = h_1'(x_1-z) - f_1'(x_1) = 0, \tag{10}$$

$$\frac{\partial \pi_t}{\partial z} = h_2'(x) - h_1'(x_1-z) - p\tau = 0. \tag{11}$$

On the other hand, when the quota $\bar{z}$, which is the solution to (10) and (11), is imposed, and the quota is assumed to be not redundant, the first-order conditions are given by

$$\frac{\partial L}{\partial x_1} = h_1'(x_1-z) - f_1'(x_1) = 0, \tag{12}$$

$$\frac{\partial L}{\partial z} = h_2'(z) - h_1'(x_1-z) - q - \lambda = 0, \tag{13}$$

$$\frac{\partial L}{\partial \lambda} = \bar{z} - z = 0. \tag{14}$$

Similarly to the case of increasing marginal costs, we see from (10) and (12) that when z is common, which occurs for $q \leq p\tau$, x_1 takes a common value. Thus, the tariff and the quota are equivalent in the sense of Shibata (1968) and Bhagwati (1968), although importable production in this case is zero so long as the MNE does not switch its supply strategy.

Under decreasing marginal costs of production the marginal cost of exporting schedule is downward-sloping like CD in Figure 6.2.[7] On the other hand, the marginal revenue from importing schedule coincides with the marginal revenue curve in the foreign country, and is depicted as AB in Figure 6.2. The optimum under free trade is obtained at point G where CD intersects AB. When the tariff is imposed, the net marginal revenue from importing schedule shifts down to EF, and trade

Figure 6.2 : The Decreasing Marginal Cost Case

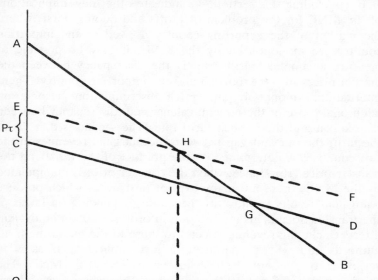

occurs at the level of OI. When the quota OI is imposed and q is equal to pτ, the net marginal revenue from importing schedule takes the shape EJI, and trade occurs at point J. This illustrates the equivalence in the modified sense of Shibata and Bhagwati. For q < pτ or q > pτ, the net marginal revenue from importing schedule is located above or below EJI, respectively (not drawn). Then, similarly to the case of increasing marginal costs, we can easily show that for q < pτ the equivalence holds, but for q > pτ it does not hold. However, there is a qualification for the results in the case of q ⋛ pτ. Suppose that q < pτ. Then the profit of the MNE is less under the tariff than under the quota. This may lead the MNE to undertake foreign production (strategy (ii) or (iii)) under the tariff, while adopting strategy (i) under the quota. For q > pτ the reverse may happen. Thus, the tariff and the quota may not be equivalent even for q < pτ. As for the equivalence in Bhagwati's original sense, the implicit tariff rate deviates from the explicit tariff rate τ in general, and therefore the equivalence does not generally hold in Bhagwati's original sense regardless of whether $q \lessgtr p\tau$.

In concluding this section, we indicate other new implications of the MNE for the problem of tariffs and quotas. First, where the market of the exporting country as well as the importing country are monopolized by the MNE, it may be possible to measure an implicit tariff rate by the discrepancy between the market prices in the exporting and the importing country. Then, international monopoly and price discrimination become an additional cause of the nonequivalence, i.e. discrepancy between the explicit and the implicit tariff rate. The second is that under the tariff the relevant gap between the marginal revenues in the two countries is determined by the product of the tariff and the transfer price, τp. Hence, when the transfer price is manipulated by the MNE, there are many explicit tariff rates which produce equivalent results to those of the quota, depending on levels of the transfer price. This implies that in order to obtain equivalent effects (including revenue effects) to those of the quota the tariff authority must be prepared to adjust explicit tariff rates in response to levels of the transfer price set by the MNE. The third, which is related to the second, is that while levels of the transfer price for given τ affect also the decisions on production, trade and sales, the quota nullifies the manipulation of the transfer price by the MNE. Hence we can say that for the purpose of restriction of the MNE a quota is preferred to a tariff.

III. The Uncertainty Case

Suppose that the prices and the cost functions in the two countries are random, and that randomness takes multiplicative forms:[8] that is, $\tilde{h}_i = \tilde{\alpha}_i h_i$ and $\tilde{f}_i = \tilde{\beta}_i f_i$ (i=1, 2), where $\tilde{\alpha}_i$ and $\tilde{\beta}_i$ are the random variables and assumed to be pair-wise independent. The MNE is assumed to maximize the expected utility from the global profits, $Eu(\pi_t)$ or $Eu(\pi_q)$.

A. The Increasing Marginal Costs Case

When marginal costs of production in the two countries are increasing, the first order conditions for the expected utility maximization under the tariff are given by

$$\frac{\partial Eu(\pi_t)}{\partial x_1} = Eu'(\pi_t)\{\tilde{\alpha}_1 h_1'(x_1-z) - \tilde{\beta}_1 f_1'(x_1)\} = 0, \qquad (15)$$

$$\frac{\partial Eu(\pi_t)}{\partial x_2} = Eu'(\pi_t)\{\tilde{\alpha}_2 h_2'(x_2+z) - \tilde{\beta}_2 f_2'(x_2)\} = 0, \qquad (16)$$

$$\frac{\partial Eu(\pi_t)}{\partial z} = Eu'(\pi_t)\{\tilde{\alpha}_2 h_2'(x_2+z) - \tilde{\alpha}_1 h_1'(x_1-z) \qquad (17)$$
$$- p\tau\} = 0.$$

Using the definition of covariance, cov $(u'(\pi_t),\tilde{\alpha}_i) = Eu'(\pi_t)\tilde{\alpha}_i - Eu'(\pi_t)E\tilde{\alpha}_i$ and cov $(u'(\pi_t),\tilde{\beta}) = Eu'(\pi_t)\tilde{\beta}_i - Eu'(\pi_t)E\tilde{\beta}_i$, and dividing (15), (16) and (17) by $Eu'(\pi_t)$, we get

$$\alpha_{1t}^s h_1'(x_1-z) - \beta_{1t}^s f_1'(x_1) = 0, \qquad (18)$$

$$\alpha_{2t}^s h_2'(x_2+z) - \beta_{2t}^s f_2'(x_2) = 0, \qquad (19)$$

$$\alpha_{2t}^s h_2'(x_2+z) - \alpha_{1t}^s h_1'(x_1-z) - p\tau = 0, \qquad (20)$$

Where $\alpha_{it}^s = E\tilde{\alpha}_i + \{\text{cov } (u'(\pi_t),\tilde{\alpha}_i)/Eu'(\pi_t)\}$ and $\beta_{it}^s = E\tilde{\beta}_i + \{\text{cov } (u'(\pi_t),\tilde{\beta}_i)/Eu'(\pi_t)\}$. It is important to notice that these are functions of π_t and, therefore, of x_i, z and $p\tau$. Noting that the optimal values of x_i and z can be written as functions of parameters $p\tau$, we have $\alpha_{it}^s = \phi_{it}\{x_1(p\tau), x_2(p\tau), z(p\tau); p\tau\}$ and $\beta_{it}^s = \psi_{it}\{x_1(p\tau), x_2(p\tau), z(p\tau); p\tau\}$.

On the other hand, the optimal solutions under the quota $\bar{z}$, which is the solution for z in (18)-(20), are obtained by maximizing

$$L = Eu (\pi_q) + \lambda (\bar{z} - z). \qquad (21)$$

Letting $z = \bar{z}$, and following a similar procedure to the derivation of (18)-(20), we get the first order conditions under the quota:

$$\alpha_{1q}^s h_1'(x_1-z) - \beta_{1q}^s f_1'(x_1) = 0, \qquad (22)$$

$$\alpha_{2q}^s h_2'(x_2+z) - \beta_{2q}^s f_2'(x_2) = 0, \qquad (23)$$

$$\alpha_{2q}^s h_2'(x_2+z) - \alpha_{1q}^s h_1'(x_1-z) - q - \frac{\lambda}{Eu'} = 0. \qquad (24)$$

Here $\alpha_{iq}^s = E\tilde{\alpha}_i + \{\text{cov } (u'(\pi_q),\tilde{\alpha}_i)/Eu'(\pi_q)\}$ and $\beta_{iq}^s = E\tilde{\beta}_i + \{\text{cov } (u'(\pi_q),\tilde{\beta}_i)/Eu'(\pi_q)\}$ are functions of x_i, z and q : $\alpha_{iq}^s = \phi_{iq}\{x_1(q), x_2(q), z (q); q\}$ and $\beta_{iq}^s = \psi_{iq}\{x_1(q), x_2(q); q\}$.

Since α_{it}^s, β_{it}^s, α_{iq}^s and β_{iq}^s in general depend on values of the parameters $p\tau$ and q, we must examine the two systems of equations in a way different from the certainty case. Suppose that $q = p\tau$. Then the profit function under the tariff takes the same form as that under the quota: $\pi_t = \pi_q = \tilde{\alpha}_1 h_1(x_1-z) - \tilde{\beta}_1 f_1(x_1) + \tilde{\alpha}_2 h_2(x_2+z) - \tilde{\beta}_s f_s(x_2) - p\tau z$. Then under the quota the MNE chooses the same (maximum permissible) import level as the quota $\bar{z}$. With $\bar{z}$ common, the two systems of equations, (18) and (19), and (22) and (23), include only the two variables, $x_1(p\tau)$ and $x_2(p\tau)$, or $x_1(q)$ and $x_2(q)$. With the profit function identical it immediately follows that the two systems of equations produce identical values of x_1 and x_2. This means that the tariff and the quota are equivalent in the sense of Shibata (1968) and Bhagwati (1968) even when the MNE operates under uncertainty. Furthermore, the above result is seen independent of MNE's attitudes towards risk. With x_i and z common, it follows from (20) and (24) that $p\tau = q + \lambda/Eu'$. This implies that $\lambda = 0$ for $q = p\tau$, that is, the expected utility is invariant when the quota is relaxed.

Suppose that $q \neq p\tau$. Then the actual level of import under the quota is equal to or less than $\bar{z}$, i.e., $z \leq \bar{z}$. In either case for $q \neq p\tau$ the profit under the tariff is not equal to the profit under the quota. If the attitude of the MNE towards risk is risk aversion or risk preference ($u''(\cdot) < 0$ or $u''(\cdot) > 0$), then α_{it}^s and β_{it}^s are not identical to α_{iq}^s and β_{iq}^s, respectively. This means that the two systems of equations do not produce identical values of x_1 and x_2. The reason is as follows. Levels of $p\tau$ and q affect the marginal utilities through changes in the profits. The marginal utilities are random variables, and are correlated with random prices and costs. Hence different values between $p\tau$ and q yield different levels of x_1 and x_2 under the two regimes. Thus the equivalence does not hold in the modified sense of Shibata and Bhagwati. If, on the other hand, the MNE is risk neutral, $u'(\cdot)$ is constant, and this ensures cov $(u',\tilde{\alpha}_i) = $ cov $(u',\tilde{\beta}_i) = 0$ and hence $\alpha_{it}^s = \alpha_{iq}^s = E\tilde{\alpha}_i$ and $\beta_{it}^s = \beta_{iq}^s = E\tilde{\beta}_i$. Then, if q is less than $p\tau$, and the import level under the quota is equal to $\bar{z}$, the two systems of equations, (18) and (19), and (22) and (23), yield identical levels of x_1 and x_2. Thus, the equivalence holds in the modified sense. In this context, under certainty there is no correlation in the stochastic sense between profits and prices and costs, and hence between profits and x_1 and x_2. Therefore, as was shown in the previous section, the difference between q and $p\tau (q < p\tau)$ does not affect levels of x_1 and x_2.

While the revenue effects are known before the resolution of uncertainty, the welfare effects are known only after the actual home and foreign prices are realized. For these effects, only when $q = p\tau$ or unit import licence is sold to the MNE at the price of $p\tau$, they become identical under the tariff and the quota. Otherwise, the equivalence in the revenue and the *ex post* welfare effects break down.

Since we cannot define the actual implicit tariff rate until the resolution of uncertainty, we can consider the equivalence in Bhagwati's original sense only *ex post*. But, even *ex post* there is no guarantee that the realized implicit tariff rate equals the explicit tariff rate τ. Therefore, regardless of $q = p\tau$ or $q \neq p\tau$ the equivalence in Bhagwati's original sense breaks down in general.

B. The Decreasing Marginal Costs Case

Let $x_2 = 0$. Following a similar procedure to the increasing marginal costs case, we have the following first order conditions under the tariff:

$$\alpha_{1t}^s h_1'(x_1-z) - \beta_{1t}^s f_1'(x_1) = 0, \tag{25}$$

$$\alpha_{2t}^s h_2'(z) - \alpha_{1t}^s h_1'(x_1-z) - p\tau = 0. \tag{26}$$

In this case α_{it}^s and β_{1t}^s are functions of x_1, z and $p\tau$: $\alpha_{it}^s = \theta_{it}\{x_1(p\tau), z(p\tau); p\tau\}$ and $\beta_{1t}^s = \omega_{1t}\{x_1(p\tau), z(p\tau); p\tau\}$.

Under the quota $\bar{z}$, which is the solution for z in (25) and (26), the first order conditions are

$$\alpha_{1q}^s h_1'(x_1-z) - \beta_{1q}^s f_1'(x_1) = 0, \tag{27}$$

$$\alpha_{2q}^s h_2'(z) - \alpha_{1q}^s h_1'(x_1-z) - q - \frac{\lambda}{Eu'} = 0. \tag{28}$$

Here $\alpha_{iq}^s = \theta_{iq}\{x_1(q), z(q); q\}$ and $\beta_{1q}^s = \omega_{1q}\{x_1(q), z(q); q\}$. Suppose that $q = p\tau$, and hence z takes the common value $\bar{z}$ in

(25) and (27). Then the two equations include the only one variable, $x_1(q)$. Noting also that the profit function under the tariff takes the same form as that under the quota, we see that (25) and (27) produce an identical value of x_1. Thus, in this case the tariff and the quota are equivalent in the modified sense, although it is defined in terms of the identical expected foreign price, and importable production in the foreign country is zero. The revenue and the *ex post* welfare effects are also equivalent.

When $q \neq p\tau$, $z \leq \bar{z}$ and, moreover, the profits are not identical under the tariff and the quota. Therefore, (25) and (27) do not produce an identical value of z_1 even for $z = \bar{z}$ unless the MNE is risk neutral, as under certainty it is also possible that the MNE takes different supply strategies under the tariff and the quota. Thus, the equivalence may break down in the modified sense of Shibata and Bhagwati. It is easy to see that the equivalence does not hold in terms of Bhagwati's original sense in general both for $q = p\tau$ and $q \neq p\tau$.

IV. A Summary

In this section we summarize new findings obtained from the analyses in the previous sections.

Under certainty and increasing marginal costs of production the equivalence in the modified sense of Shibata and Bhagwati holds when the price of unit import licence does not exceed the tariff payments per unit of import. Otherwise the equivalence does not hold. When the price of unit import licence is equal to the tariff payments per unit of import, the revenue and the welfare effects are identical under the tariff and the quota. When marginal costs of production in the two countries are decreasing, not only the same conclusions as those under increasing marginal costs are obtained, but the possibility of switchover of supply strategy in the case of inequality between the price of unit import licence and the tariff payments per unit of import also becomes a cause of the nonequivalence. Under uncertainty and increasing marginal costs the equivalence in the modified sense holds only when the price of unit import licence is set equal to the tariff payments per unit of import, if the MNE's attitude towards risk is risk-aversion or risk-preference. Also only in this case the equivalence in the revenue and the *ex post* welfare effects hold. When marginal costs of production are decreasing under uncertainty, the case for the equivalence in the modified sense is limited to the case in which the price of unit import licence is equal to the tariff payments per unit of import, unless the MNE is risk neutral, and moreover, as in the certainty case, there is also the possibility that the MNE switches its supply strategy. The equivalence in Bhagwati's original sense generally breaks down in any case, as mentioned above. Furthermore, we found new implications for the MNE in the problem of tariffs and quotas: (i) international monopoly and price discrimination may become an additional cause of nonequivalence, i.e. discrepancy between explicit and implicit tariff rates; (ii) discretional transfer pricing by the MNE yields many explicit tariff rates which produce equivalent effects to those of the quota; and (iii) for the purpose of restriction of the MNE a quota is preferred to a tariff by nullifying the manipulation of transfer price by the MNE.

Notes

The author is grateful to Lorraine Eden for comments.

1. Tariffs are well-known measures applied to MNEs as well as nonMNEs. Quotas are also often used for both nonMNEs and MNEs. For MNEs' great concern about quotas in Colombia, India, Argentina, Thailand and Brazil, see Robbins and Stobaugh (1973a, p. 113).

2. This is the kind of problem for the firm facing regulatory constraints.

3. The welfare effects are, as usual, measured by consumers' and producers' surplus, and revenues from the tariff or revenues from the sale of the import licence.

4. Although the equivalence holds in the modified sense, one result which differs from the result in Bhagwati's paper (1965) is that while in the case of monopoly only in domestic production the quota generates a higher domestic price than the tariff (p. 60), in the case of global monopoly by the MNE the two trade barriers produce the identical level of domestic price (QR in Figure 6.1).

5. In this context it is important to point out that the transfer price is not relevant to the true export supply price, which is appropriately given by the marginal cost of production in the exporting country. The divergence between the transfer price and the true export supply price is one of the distinctive features of MNEs.

6. It is noted that in the case of monopoly in quota-holding in Bhagwati (1965) the equivalence holds when the quota is fully utilized (pp. 61, 63), whereas in our case the equivalence may not hold even when the quota is fully used.

7. See Horst (1973, p. 78).

8. It does not matter in the following analysis what forms the random variables may take, so long as they are pair-wise independent.

7 FISCAL TRANSFER PRICING: ACCOUNTING FOR REALITY

G. David Quirin

Introduction

Transfer prices are purely accounting prices used in accounting for transactions between different entities which are part of the same organization, usually between divisions of the same corporation or between corporate affiliates. Such prices perform a number of functions. One set of functions might best be described as motivation and control. Transfer prices used for this purpose help to administer a decentralized organization by conveying information. They enter divisional profit or contribution objectives, and provide the basis for calculating and reporting divisional performance. The second set of functions relates to the outside world rather than the world within the corporation. Here the role of the transfer price is to allocate group income among the constituent units, in order to determine the proper share of such income attributable to tax authorities, to minority interests and to the parent company and its shareholders.

These two types of purpose are not closely related, and there is no particular reason to believe that a set of transfer prices designed with one of these objectives in mind will be satisfactory for the other, in fact the presumption is that they will not. Internal transfer prices, established for control purposes, are intended to produce goal congruence between different parts of the organization and encourage economic efficiency. Where the purpose is to allocate income between different interests, either different classes of shareholders or different tax jurisdictions, considerations of fairness or equity assume a primary role. Equity is seldom the handmaiden of efficiency, and 'fair' systems may be inefficient, while efficient systems will be perceived by some as unfair. Economists are more comfortable with efficiency than with fairness, as papers elsewhere in these proceedings will attest. Indeed most of the literature on the subject, (Dean, 1951;

Hirshleifer, 1956, 1957; Gould, 1964; Goetz, 1967; Horngren, 1967, 1982; Ronen and McKinney, 1970; Anthony and Dearden, 1980; Benke and Edwards, 1980) has focused on the efficiency issues involved in internal motivation and control. Economic analyses of the use of transfer prices in the tax-liability context may be found in Shulman (1966), Horst (1971), Copithorne (1971) and in Mathewson and Quirin (1979). The last-mentioned use the term 'fiscal transfer prices' to refer to transfer prices established for purposes of allocating tax liability. Tax minimization and other considerations enter the establishment of such prices; such manipulation and its impacts are the major focus of the works cited. These impacts are twofold. The most obvious impact is on the revenues of some governments. Less obviously, efforts to avoid taxes involve relocating activity and restructuring transactions in ways which have clear implications for efficiency, as these contributions show.

Fiscal transfer prices are set within a framework of rules and constraints established by tax legislation and administration. This paper examines some of those rules in two jurisdictions (Canada and the USA); the degrees of freedom remaining within the conflicting rules established by the two jurisdictions; and suggests an accounting model which appears to be consistent with existing legislation, and which is less open to the charge of being one-sided — charges that can be levied against existing rules — and which, since it gives greater recognition to economic reality, is less likely to result in efficiency-distorting tax-avoidance behaviour.

Existing Rules

Where the majority of a business unit's transactions involve arm's-length dealings with unrelated parties, the market prices at which these transactions take place provide a reasonably reliable basis for equitable pricing of incidental transfers. In these circumstances, such market prices are usually accepted in both jurisdictions. Where there are few or no dealings at arm's-length, or where such dealings involve distinct differences in function between the affiliated buyer (seller) and arm's-length buyers (sellers), market prices, even if available, tend to lose credibility. In many cases the product made for the affiliate may differ from that sold to others, or may be sold under different warranty conditions, etc.

In such circumstances some other estimation-validation process is required, and the cost-accounting system often provides the most suitable alternative available. In the USA, the Internal Revenue Code establishes, in Section 482, a hierarchy of valuation methods to be used if market prices are unavailable. The preferred substitute is the 'resale price method' in which a transfer price is obtained by working back from the resale price, deducting an appropriate mark-up to reflect the functions performed by the buyer. Where this is unsuitable, resort is had to the 'cost-plus method' in which an appropriate margin is added to accounting costs. No specific method is required under the Canadian Income Tax Act, which merely requires (S.S.69(2),69(3)) that prices be 'reasonable in the circumstances'. Similar methodologies to Section 482 are in fact employed in Canada, with the critical difference that, at least for some types of transfers, any amount in excess of accounting cost is simply disallowed by the authorities (O'Keefe, 1975).

Thus there is conflict between the apparent positions of the taxing authorities in the two countries with respect to the extent and even the appropriateness of the mark-up to be added to costs when the cost-plus method is used, and perhaps with respect to the mark-up to be deducted when the resale price method is used. These conflicts can lead to double taxation with respect to certain activities or to relocation of the activities in question in order to avoid double taxation. They thus involve efficiency effects as well as considerations of fairness.

Both positions can be, as is usual in disputes over fairness, based on principle, in this case accounting principle. The US position is based on the accrual principle, implicitly holding that profit, when it emerges at the point of sale, is the result of all of the activities leading up to the sale, and ought, therefore, to be imputed to those activities in some appropriate manner. The Canadian position is equally based on the conflicting recognition rule which decrees that no profits should be recognized until sale to a third party takes place. This rule is introduced to prevent the manipulative creation of 'profits' by transfers back and forth within an organization, and is hardly relevant in the taxation context. A more likely reason for the popularity of the rule in some jurisdictions, including Canada, is its impact on the share of profits accruing at the point of final sale. The attraction of such a rule to a jurisdiction which more often than not is the recipient of transferred commodities is obvious, as is the attraction of the opposite rule for a country such as the USA which is most frequently a supplier.

The basic assumption of the paper is that transfer prices are necessary and will continue to have to be constructed from accounting records because market prices are often unavailable or unsatisfactory. It should be noted that this is not the only solution to the problem of inter-jurisdictional income allocation. Available alternatives include the use of arbitrary 'top reference prices' set by the taxing authorities and the use of unitary taxes, in which each jurisdiction taxes the parent on its world-wide income. Either of these cases appears to have the potential of being worse than the transfer-pricing disease. A forum for the arbitration of transfer pricing disputes, as suggested by Professor Shoup, is desirable; use of the allocation rules suggested here should reduce the need to resort to such a body.

Problems Arising in Practice

The available evidence, cited in Mathewson and Quirin (1979), suggests that authorities in both countries tend to use 'fully-distributed costs', as computed by conventional cost-accounting practice, as the basis for determining whether or not a given transfer price is reasonable. In most cases, some sort of profit margin will be required or permitted, although Canadian authorities have refused to allow the inclusion of any mark-up in transfer prices established for management services provided by foreign parents (O'Keefe, 1975), and Ontario prohibits even the reimbursement of costs.

Where used, such margins are applied as a kind of secondary overhead, charged at a uniform rate against all expenses involving transactions with parties outside the group. This accrual approach does have the advantage of implicitly recognizing that much of accounting 'profit' is really nothing more than the opportunity cost of the capital employed. The procedure, applying the uniform profit margin against all recorded expenses, is analogous to procedures used in handling many other overhead items, including such capital cost items as depreciation, by a uniform load applied to direct material, to direct labour, to their sum, or to such costs plus previously allocated overheads. Again there is a root in existing accounting practice, and again there are obvious attractions from the point of view of taxing authorities, this time to those of the jurisdiction in which the bulk of the expenses are incurred. This procedure is exemplified, e.g. in the US transfer pricing rule laid down in *Eli Lilly and Co.* v. *U.S.* [372 F. 2d 520 (9th Cir.)]. In *Lilly*, the margin actually applied to US costs for the transferred merchandise was half that normally obtained in domestic transactions, thus increasing the profits of the subsidiary above the level which would have resulted if an equal margin had been applied. The subsidiary was, however, a Western Hemisphere Trade Corporation (WHTRC), a class of subsidiary enjoying preferential treatment under the Internal Revenue Code. The lower margin was expressly indicated to have been allowed to reflect the incentives intended by Congress to apply in the case of WHTCs. Similarly, generous treatment was also made available for Domestic International Sales Corporations (DISCs). Where such creatures are not involved, the general rate is that mark-ups over domestic costs must be at least as great as those earned on other domestic business, where the 'cost-plus method' is used, or that the margin on sales in the foreign country be no greater on transferred goods than on comparable arm's-length goods, where the 'resale price method' is used.[1]

Margin rules are at least superficially fair, in that they do not claim all of the taxes from an operation which involves some production stages in one jurisdiction and further stages, plus sales in a second. Further, they give at least some recognition to the opportunity cost of capital employed, in that they effect a division of the available margin between the jurisdictions in which capital is invested. Since, however, it is this opportunity cost (net of certain interest expenses) which constitutes the implicit tax base of the income tax system, it should be accounted for rather carefully in establishing the transfer prices which determine ultimate tax liability. Systems which apply uniform profit margins on possibly disparate activities do not do so; their basic failure is that they do not consider the time dimension of economic activity explicitly. Profit margins are only apparently dimensionless. They represent the profit which accrues on the capital employed once per operating cycle, and vary between industries primarily because of differences in the length of the respective operating cycles. There is much less variation in return on investment, which is expressed on a uniform (usually annual) time base, adjusted for difference in asset turnover (Weston and Brigham, 1969, pp. 77-9). Applying a common profit margin to two operations which account for different fractions of the operating cycle makes the simple but usually-unwarranted assumption that capital costs accumulate at the same rate as the direct labour, direct materials and explicit overhead which constitute costs as ordinarily measured. Typically, they do not. While direct material costs are incurred at the time of purchase, most labour costs and factory overheads are incurred during the short period the product is in work-in-process inventory. In contrast, a significant fraction of capital costs are incurred while (and because) the product is just sitting around, either in materials or finished goods inventories, or after it has gone out the door but before receivables have been collected.[2]

On the financial side, the operating cycle may be viewed as a process in which various sums are advanced from time to time to cover costs as they accrue, to be recovered from the proceeds after the product is sold. The average period of production concept, defined as the average time a dollar so advanced is outstanding before it is collected, has played a central role, as a measure of capital use, in the development of capital theory in economics (Bohm-Bawerk, 1891), and as 'duration' in modern financial economics (Macaulay, 1938). Fractional periods of production provide an appropriate basis on which opportunity costs of capital may be allocated to fractional parts of the operating cycle when it is necessary to establish transfer prices at their boundaries.

Accounting systems which make explicit provision for the opportunity cost of capital in computing product costs remain a rarity. While the practice has been endorsed by the Cost Accounting Standards Board (in CASB Standard 414), it remains in the words of Horngren (1982, p. 512) 'not a generally accepted accounting principle for reports to stockholders'. Since the provision of inventory values for such reports remains a primary purpose of most cost-accounting systems, the practice has not been widely adopted. There have been a number of proposals to reform accounting to make appropriate provision for the implicit interest on shareholders' equity, most notably those of Anthony

(1973, 1975, 1982), but they have fallen on stony ground.

Most such schemes incorporate a cost determined by multiplying a cost rate by an assets-invested base. The CASB proposes the use of a rate based on the commercial loan rate, others have advocated using the rate of interest at which the company borrows money. None have recommended the use of the company's 'cost of capital' as that has come to be defined in the finance literature (Quirin, 1967; Llewellen, 1969; Quirin and Wiginton, 1981), although that rate, in its before-tax version, is clearly the theoretically-correct rate.

An analogous procedure is widely used by regulatory bodies in determining the 'cost of service' for required public utilities under their jurisdiction. The usual calculation involves the use of a rate base, which is a measure of capital employed, which is multiplied by a rate of return, usually an approximation to the 'cost of capital' of the finance literature, to determine an allowed-return component which is added to operating expenses to determine allowed revenues or 'cost of service'.

A Suggested Procedure

Unlike these approaches, the procedure proposed here does not involve the use of an explicitly-determined rate of return, although approaches using such a rate remain as obvious alternatives. The procedure proposed does not seek to determine 'costs', as such, but rather to develop a method for allocating the excess of revenues over the usually-defined accounting costs, in a manner which takes account of the *relative* opportunity costs incurred in the different jurisdictions. The method is best illustrated by considering the following example. For the sake of computational convenience, it is assumed that opening and closing inventory balances in the parent company are identical, as are those in the Canadian branch plant. For similar reasons, no provision is made for the compounding of imputed rates of return during the fiscal period. A constant exchange rate of $1.25 Can. = $1.00 US is assumed, and it is further assumed that this rate is applicable to all book values and to income statement items alike.

AB Corp. manufactures and sells a small consumer durable. US sales are 100,000 units at a price of $100.00 (US); a Canadian

Figure 7.1: Materials and Intermediate Product Flows

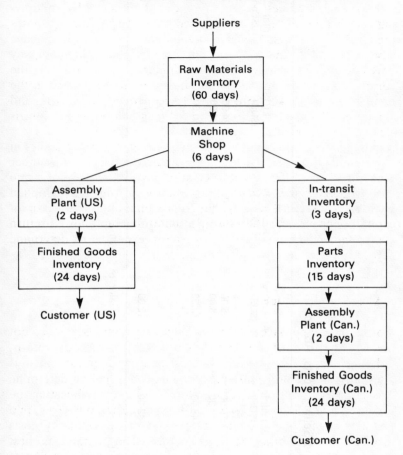

branch plant sells 10,000 units per year at a price of $140.00 (Can.). Manufacturing operations include the machining of parts, carried out at the main US plant only, and assembly. Products destined for the US market are assembled at the main US plant; the Canadian plant assembles units intended for the Canadian market from parts imported from the USA and was originally established to qualify for the lower rate of customs duty applied to parts as opposed to finished products. The flow of goods is as shown in Figure 7.1. In the USA, raw materials are purchased and held in inventory an average of 60 days. Payment is made,

Table 7.1: Manufacturing and Selling Costs, AB Corp.

	Machining ($US)	US Assembly ($US)	Can. Assembly ($Can.)	Total (US) ($US)	Total (Can.) ($Can.)
Direct materials	12.00	–	–	12.00	15.00
Direct labour	18.00	6.00	9.00	24.00	31.50
Manufacturing overhead	18.00	6.00	7.50	24.00	30.00
Subtotal — Manufacturing	48.00	12.00	16.50	60.00	76.50
Duty on parts	–	–	–	–	12.00[a]
Freight on parts	–	–	–	–	1.00
Selling costs	–	–	–	10.00	12.50
Total	48.00	12.00	16.50	70.00	102.00

Note: a. At an assumed rate of 15 per cent on an estimated value of $80.00.

again on average, 30 days afer receipt of the goods.

Production operations are well-integrated. Machining is completed in six days. Assembly of those parts destined for the US market follows immediately and is completed in another two days. Parts destined for the Canadian operation are shipped immediately after machining. They spend three days in transit and a further 15 days in parts inventory before assembly, which takes two days as it does in the USA. Both plants keep finished goods inventories equal to 24 days' sales, and carry receivables totalling 45 days' sales.

Denoting the date when machining is completed as time T, we can construct a calendar for the production/sales process as it is carried out in Canada and the USA. Such a calendar appears in Figure 7.2.

Figure 7.2: Production and Financing Calendar, AB Corp.

	US	Canada
Raw material inventory received	T−65	−
Raw material inventory paid for	T−35	−
Production process started	T−5	−
Machining of parts completed	T	−
Parts shipped and duty paid	−	T
Parts inventory received	T	T+3
Assembly starts	T+1	T+19
Assembly completed	T+2	T+20
Goods sold	T+26	T+44
Payment received	T+71	T+89

Manufacturing and selling costs, exclusive of depreciation and imputed capital costs, are as shown in Table 7.1. In addition to the costs identified in Table 7.1, administrative and general expenses are incurred by the parent and cannot be identified with either the US or Canadian operations as such, in an amount totalling $10.00 (US) per unit. This is allocated to the manufacturing operation (both parts) in proportion to direct labour hours, resulting in a per-unit charge of $6.66 (US) to machining and $3.34 (US) to assembly respectively.

In addition to the working capital requirements associated with the production process, net plant investment is $3 million (US) in the USA and $150,000 ($Can.) in Canada, invested in facilities as follows (average values during year):

US Plant ($US '000)		Canadian Subsidiary ($Can. '000)	
Raw material storage	250	Parts storage	37.5
Machinery and shop	2,000	Assembly plant	75.0
Assembly plant	500	Finished goods storage	37.5
Finished goods storage	250		

Depreciation on these facilities is charged at an annual rate of 12 per cent to the appropriate stage of the production process.

In the proposed procedure, transfer prices are based on the time-weighted investment up to the point of transfer, equating the before-tax rate of return on such investment in the transferred goods to that earned on goods which are not transferred but completed and sold in the domestic market, as is implied in the margin rule associated with the cost-plus method. This investment has two components. One is investment in fixed assets, which is computed on a time-weighted basis for standard volumes in Table 7.2. The other is investment in working capital, representing amounts advanced at various stages in the production cycle as shown in Table 7.3 (US operations) and Table 7.4 (Canadian operations). Figure 7.3 shows how these costs accrue through time and shows dramatically the much larger time-weighted investment in the product sold by the Canadian subsidiary. Table 7.5 presents estimates of the time-weighted investment incurred in US operations.

Table 7.2: Fixed Investment per Unit Output (dollars x days, '000 omitted except last column)

	Investment	Dollar/ Days	Units	Dollar/ Days per Unit
Raw material storage	250	91,250	110	829.55
Machinery and shop	1,000	365,000	110	3,318.18
Assembly plant (US)	500	182,500	100	1,825.00
Finished goods storage (US)	250	91,250	100	912.00
Parts storage (Can.)	30	10,950	10	1,095.00[a]
Assembly plant (Can.)	60	21,900	10	2,190.00[a]
Finished goods storage (Can.)	30	10,950	10	1,095.00[a]

Note: a. US funds.

Table 7.3: Cost Accrual Schedule - US Operations ($US)

Stage and Date / Materials Acquired	Direct Materials	Direct Labour	Manufacturing Overhead	Sales and Administration	Depreciation	Duty	Total — Period	Total — to Date
Materials Acquired								
T–35	12.00	—	—	—	—	—	12.00	12.00
T–34 to T–6	—	—	—	—	.27	—	.27	12.27
Machining								
T–5	—	3.00	3.00	1.11	.36	—	7.47	19.74
T–4	—	3.00	3.00	1.11	.36	—	7.47	27.21
T–3	—	3.00	3.00	1.11	.36	—	7.47	34.68
T–2	—	3.00	3.00	1.11	.36	—	7.47	42.15
T–1	—	3.00	3.00	1.11	.36	—	7.47	49.22
T	—	3.00	3.00	1.11	.36	—	7.48	57.09
Assembly								
T+1	—	3.00	3.00	1.67	.30	—	7.97	65.06
T+2	—	3.00	3.00	1.67	.30	—	7.97	73.03
Storage — Finished goods								
T+3 to T+26	—	—	—	—	.30	—	.30	73.33
Sale								
T+26	—	—	—	10.00	—	—	10.00	83.33
Cost Incurred Totals	12.00	24.00	24.00	20.00	3.33	—		

Table 7.4: Cost Accrual Schedule - Canadian Operations ($Can)

Stage and Date	Costs Incurred						Total — Period	Total — to Date
	Direct Materials	Direct Labour	Manufacturing Overhead	Sales and Administration	Depreciation	Duty and Freight		
Materials acquired								
T−35	15.00	–	–	–	–	–	15.00	15.00
T−34 to T−6	–	–	–	–	.34	–	.34	15.34
Machining								
T−5	–	3.75	3.75	1.39	.45	–	9.34	24.68
T−4	–	3.75	3.75	1.39	.45	–	9.34	34.02
T−3	–	3.75	3.75	1.39	.45	–	9.34	43.36
T−2	–	3.75	3.75	1.39	.45	–	9.34	52.70
T−1	–	3.75	3.75	1.39	.45	–	9.34	62.04
T	–	3.75	3.75	1.39	.45	–	9.34	71.38
Transit								
T+1 to T+3	–	–	–	–	–	13.00	12.00	84.38
Parts storage								
T+4 to T+18	–	–	–	–	.45	–	.45	84.83
Assembly								
T+19	–	4.50	3.75	1.67	.45	–	10.37	95.20
T+20	–	4.50	3.75	1.67	.45	–	10.37	105.57
Storage – Finished goods								
T+21 to T+44	–	–	–	–	.45	–	.45	106.02
Sale								
T+44	–	–	–	12.50	–	–	12.50	118.52
Cost Incurred Totals	15.00	31.50	30.00	24.18	4.84	13.00		

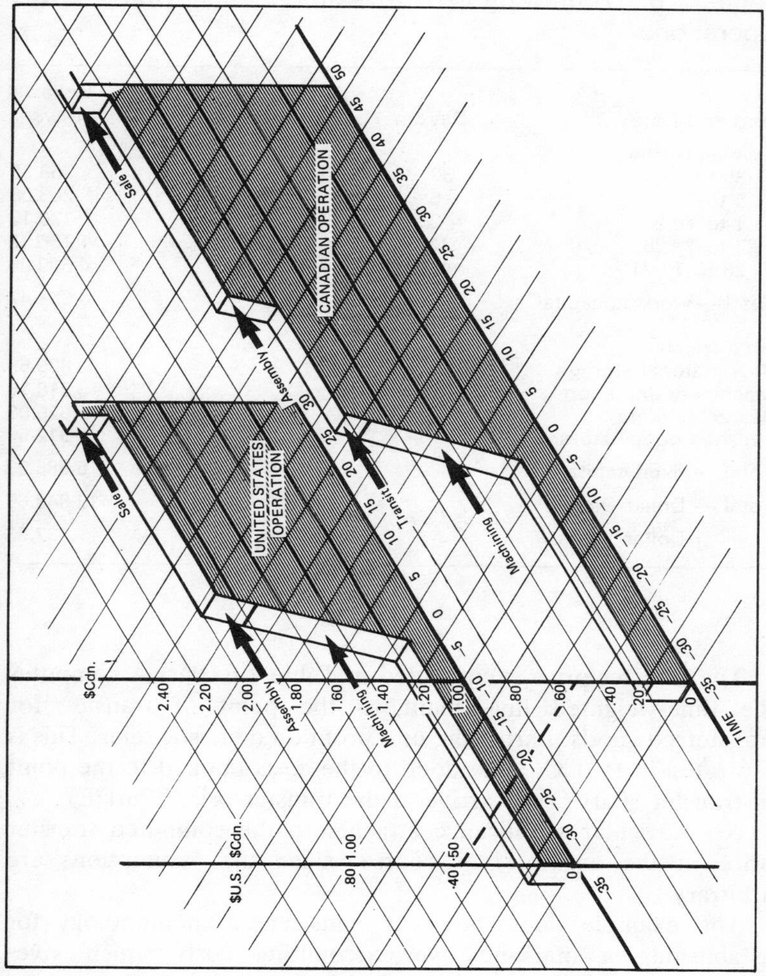

Figure 7.3: Accrual of Costs to Point of Sale

Table 7.5: Time-weighted Investment per Unit — US Operations

Item and Date	Days	Average Amount Invested	Dollar/ Days
WORKING CAPITAL			
T−35 to T−6	30	12.13	363.90
T−5 to T	6	34.68	208.08
T+1 to T+2	2	65.06	130.12
T+3 to T+26	24	73.18	1,756.32
T+26 to T+71	45	100.00	4,500.00
Total — working capital			6,958.42
FIXED CAPITAL			
Raw material storage			829.55
Machinery and shop			3,318.18
Assembly plant			1,825.00
Finished goods storage			912.50
Total — fixed capital			6,885.23
Total — Dollar/Days			13,843.65
Dollar/Years			37.93

The transfer price is computed in Table 7.6. Part A computes the time-weighted investment to the point of transfer for transferred goods, Part B the unit profit on domestic sales. This is pro-rated in Part C, and added to the costs booked to the point of transfer (Part D) to arrive at the transfer price (Part E).

No particular significance attaches to the computed transfer price in the example, of course, since the assumptions are arbitrary.

The example does, however, illustrate a methodology for establishing a mark-up over accounting costs which gives appropriate weight to the opportunity cost of the capital employed in making them, treating further processing and sale in the USA as the implicit foregone opportunity. As such it is superior to mark-ups based on sales/cost comparisons which do not consider investment requirements.

This is, of course, not the only investment-sensitive allocation procedure available. Rates of return could, for example, be equalized over global operations instead of adopting US operations as the base. Alternatively, risk premia could be explicitly

Table 7.6: Transfer Price Computations Basis : Equal ROR on all US Operations

A. Investment Component of Goods Transferred as a Percentage of Total Investment Component on Goods Retained	
Working capital, T−35 to T−6	363.90
T−5 to T	208.08
Fixed: R.M. storage	829.55
Machinery and shop	3,318.18
Investment on goods transferred:	4,719.71
Ratio: $\dfrac{4,719.71}{13,843.65}$ = .3409	
B. Profit per Unit on Domestic Sales	
Selling price	100.00
Costs booked	83.33
Unit profit	16.67
C. Pro-rata Profit on Units Transferred 16.67 X .3409	5.68
D. Production Costs Booked to Point of Transfer (Table 7.3)	57.09
E. Transfer Price	62.77

introduced into the computation while continuing to use time-weighted investment on a global basis as the allocation base. A final alternative would use an absolute rate of return requirement to allocate costs to time-weighted investments, showing opportunity profits or losses for individual operations depending on whether sales revenues exceeded those costs or did not. Such complexity will seldom be called for where the purpose is the relatively simple one of allocating tax liability fairly; the other alternatives may be useful in specific instances.

Some Concluding Observations

This paper has outlined an allocation procedure which uses time-weighted investment measures to establish transfer prices to allocate global income. This and similar procedures provide a basis on which to establish and support profit margins which are applied to accounting costs.

These procedures may not be as attractive in the short run to corporate taxpayers as more abritrary techniques which allocate larger shares of income to low-tax-rate jurisdictions. On the other hand, they provide a degree of credibility that should reduce compliance costs and the risk of a dispute with tax authorities, and may be attractive on that score.

From the tax administrator's point of view, they may again be less attractive than rules which impute a larger share of global income to their jurisdiction. However, they provide a basis of allocation which should minimize risks of double taxation, and one which should be neutral in its location effects, unlike share-maximizing rules. In this context neutrality means that while firms may be attracted or repelled by tax rates, the attraction or repulsion is not accentuated by the income allocation method employed. As such, models of this kind should form the basis for the international agreement on income-allocation rules which will ultimately be required in this area.

One unresolved issue which this paper does not address concerns the fair allocation of economic rents derived from access to low cost resources, from the monopoly power which results from patents or simply successful innovation. Cost-based rules, such as those adopted here, will tend to make such profits accrue at the point of sale; where this is inappropriate an explicit charge for the use of the resource, the patent or the technology will shift the income back to the parent's home jurisdiction or elsewhere. What is really needed here is agreement between countries as to who should have priority in taxing such rents.

Notes

1. In Mathewson and Quirin (1979) formulations of the margin rule based on *Lilly* in equations A.13 (p.104) and A.20 (p. 106) derive from the resale price method, and thus differ from those used here, where the 'cost-plus' method is assumed to apply. I am grateful to Lorraine Eden for pointing out this discrepancy.

2. Parenthetically, it should be noted that the costs avoided in the much discussed Japanese 'just-in-time' inventory system are in this category, which goes unrecognized in most conventional cost-accounting systems.

8 FINANCIAL DIMENSIONS OF TRANSFER PRICING

Donald J.S. Brean

Introduction

The transfer price issue first emerged in the context of intra-firm trade in tangible intermediate goods or intangible services. In such cases transfer prices — if properly set — provide internal signals for the efficient allocation of production among the divisions of the firm. In the process, net revenues are appropriated among the various divisions according to their respective contributions to overall profits and rents.

It is only in the international arena where intra-firm trade is international trade that transfer pricing takes on a shadowy connotation involving a game without rules played between corporations and nations. Transfer prices can be set to dupe customs agents and tax authorities thereby saving money for the corporation. The corporation can handle the efficiency problem noted above separately from international tax/tariff minimization problems. If a nation feels its sovereign right to tax is at risk in this game, the defensive challenge — in keeping with the established accounting basis of taxation — is to impute transfer prices for intermediate goods or services. However, as much of the recent discussion of transfer pricing has revealed, this exercise is highly arbitrary. Since the integrity of national tax bases is at stake, however, the threat of the tax base erosion is frequently considered sufficient reason to justify strict limitations on values attached to intermediate goods.

As rules for pricing intermediate goods and services become more restrictive or as the relevant bases for imputation — comparable products, marginal costs, profit margins, etc. — are better understood and recognized by tax authorities, corporations find that tinkering with transfer prices is simply not worth the candle, especially since so many factors in addition to taxes and tariffs enter the 'optimal' transfer price decision. Indeed, it appears that the big fishes of intermediate goods and services are becoming red herrings. Recent developments in the theory of multinational corporate finance indicate that a firm has much more scope for minimizing the global tax bill (and achieving other corporate objectives as well) through international, intra-corporate financial manoeuvring. Of course, the exercise is cloaked in corporate secrecy and, therefore, evidence is harder to uncover, but there are some consistencies.

This paper discusses how financial strategy of multinational enterprises can achieve virtually all that traditional transfer pricing can and perhaps more. We demonstrate that several long-standing principles of corporate taxation are simply inappropriate in the context of multinational enterprises. For example, the tight links between tax, cost of capital and capital structure that provide the conventional basis (e.g. the Jorgenson model) for analysing corporate tax cannot be assumed to constrain similarly the response of multinationals to tax. Indeed, the main purpose of this paper is to demonstrate how the absence of comparable constraints on the multinational corporation provides scope for strategic international financial manoeuvring — the financial counterpart of transfer pricing.

Fiscal Transfer Prices, Internal Shadow Prices and Connections Between Them

The argument — that an MNE can pursue a strategic financial policy which minimizes its global tax bill, mitigates the effects of barriers to capital flows and has potential allocative and distributive consequences — follows from several well established points concerning transfer pricing and so-called international tax planning. A brief summary of those points will sharpen the contrast between the conventional transfer pricing problem and the financial dimension which is the focus of our discussion.

The first point concerns the connection between transfer prices, tariffs and taxes. Transfer prices of intermediate goods which cross an international border determine the tariff bill and the international division of the corporate income tax base. Consequently, one dimension of the transfer pricing problem facing MNEs is to report prices which minimize the overall tax-plus-tariff bill in the light of prevailing tax and tariff rates. Horst (1971) and Copithorne (1971) were first to address this issue.

They present fundamentally similar solutions wherein strategically set profit-maximizing transfer prices take on extreme values — depending on the tariff rate relative to the corporate income tax differential. More elaborate operational models have since been developed in the business and accounting literature, for example by Nieckels (1976) and Elam and Henaidy (1980).

The second general point regarding transfer prices concerns their function as internal signals — sometimes called shadow prices — in integrated production processes. This long-standing issue in the theory of the firm had a revival following the evolution of the management accounting procedure known as *responsibility accounting*, essentially the system of decentralized profit centres. Copithorne (1982) offers a fine review of the literature. Joel Dean (1955), in the spirit of Walras (tr. 1954), Lange (1937) and Coase (1937), depicted the modern multidivisional firm as a miniature economy wherein efficiency is subject to the same allocative criteria as a market economy. Hirshleifer formalized the problem of internal signals for optimal allocation of resources within the corporation for the purposes of management and control. Optimal internal prices ensure the pursuit of divisional profit maximization contributes to, and does not detract from, overall corporate profit maximization. Hirshleifer's work shows that among various candidates that could be considered for the transfer price, only one — marginal production cost of the 'selling' division — provides the correct signal regardless of the degree of competition in the market for the intermediate good or service. This rule follows directly from the first order optimality conditions for a multidivisional firm.

Thus there are two categories of transfer prices. There are those set to minimize the global tax-tariff bill à la Horst and Copithorne, later dubbed *fiscal transfer prices* by Mathewson and Quirin (1979), and those which provide optimal internal allocative signals à la Hirshleifer, termed *shadow prices*. This distinction in fact leads to the third general point about transfer prices: in principle, optimal fiscal transfer prices and correct shadow prices are determined in the light of fundamentally different objectives and constraints. Copithorne (1982) dramatically emphasises this point while noting the implication for who does what within the MNE: '[T]his logical dichotomy between shadow and [fiscal] transfer prices allows an important division of labour in setting them: shadow prices are the normal concern of the corporation's Walrasian auctioneer (or at least its manager of operations); [fiscal] transfer prices upon which the actual financial transactions are based are the natural concern of the corporation's financiers. It is the job of the current operations department to make profits; it is the job of the finance department to hang onto them; these two functions can be completely separate' (p. 16).

Only in special cases, for example if an MNE faces different tax rates in two countries plus *ad valorem* duties on intermediate goods which cross the border — the situation described by Horst (1971) — is there any relevant link between fiscal and shadow transfer prices. Indeed, analytical models which derive allocative consequences of fiscal transfer pricing — for example, involving investment location and/or international trade patterns — generally take off from the stylized Horst position. Eden (1978) presents a rigorous extended treatment of the interaction of taxes and tariffs while others, such as Itagaki (1979, 1981) and Katrak (1981) retain the essence of such interaction in analyses of the allocative effects of exchange rate risk and commercial policy, effects which in that context can be mitigated by manipulation of fiscal transfer prices.

Despite their elegance, the relevance of such analyses appears to be fading as a result of various structural changes in the international economy. Above all, we are experiencing general reductions in both tariff rates and international tax differentials. Furthermore, tax administrators are systematically narrowing the permissible range of transfer prices of intermediate goods and services. In addition to such changes in external conditions, internal constraints also limit the conventional transfer pricing exercise (Booth and Jensen, 1977), not to mention that tax and tariff systems provide incentives for fiscal transfer price manipulation which tend to be offsetting (Mathewson and Quirin, 1979). In practice, then, strategic fiscal transfer pricing in the traditional vein appears to be of questionable relevance for the task of maximizing global pre-tax profit, primarily because it is constrained by numerous factors and considerations in addition to taxation. That also rules out allocative repercussions. In short, the *conventional* case of transfer prices of intermediate goods and services — at least in the industrialised world — seems to pose no continuing threat to the integrity of national tax systems nor is it likely substantially to affect the international division of the corporate tax base.

However, there is a counterpart to the transfer pricing issue which involves the internal finance function of an MNE which by its nature is subject to fewer constraints than apply to the more tangible inputs or intangible transfers such as management fees and royalties. The financial structure of an MNE unquestionably influences the international division of the corporate tax base and has potential allocative consequences for international investment. The following sections deal with finance-based international tax planning. The purpose is to outline objectives and constraints and to present examples which indicate the tax dimension of MNE financial strategy as an effective — indeed *more* effective — substitute for conventional fiscal transfer pricing.

Theory of Finance: Multinational Models

In its purest form, the theory of multinational corporate finance assumes exchange controls and other strict barriers to international capital flows do not effectively separate the international capital market into distinct national segments. With this assumption, the decision rules developed for corporate finance in the single country are simply extensible internationally. The multinational firm becomes a case analogous to the domestic multidivisional firm.[1]

To the extent that international capital markets are segmented, capital which flows through such markets cannot act to reduce international differences in capital costs. However, if the inefficiencies and/or restrictions cause only decentralized markets to be segmented, then a multinational enterprise with potential sources and uses of funds in several countries could devise internal centrally-directed schemes to finance efficiently *its* world-set of operations quite independently of conventional international financial markets. In this sense, the multinational enterprise is potentially an international conduit of finance in lieu of markets and *pari passu* capable of achieving internal allocative efficiency in respect of its own global investment and finance objectives despite market inefficiencies.[2] Allocative efficiency in finance is achieved by equating the marginal costs of finance in its various forms and from various sources. Efficiency in (real) investment is achieved when marginal returns on capital used in production are equated internationally. When the common real return equals the marginal corporate cost of capital, i.e. the simultaneous solution of both the investment and financial problems, the value of the multinational corporation is maximized.

Clearly, a global optimum requires the perspective of a central planning function with respect to both investment and finance. With no constraints on international intra-corporate financial flows, foreign subsidiaries are in effect simply operating divisions of the parent just as they would be if international financial markets were efficient. All new equity may be assumed to enter the corporate consolidated capital structure. Finance is then reallocated to subsidiaries as required. Accordingly, any accounting rendition of a separate financial structure for a subsidiary is wholly illusory. In general, subsidiaries in different countries are financed differently and, contrary to any suggestion of irrelevance, there are specific reasons for the observed financial structure of each subsidiary. However, as we shall see, the basis for financial decisions *within* the MNE is *not* the same as that for the uninational firm, where capital *structure*, capital *costs* and the capital *budget* are inextricably linked through the complex interaction of finance and risk. Instead, for the MNE, market imperfections, non-financial risks, national restrictions and, above all, the international structure of taxation are the major determinants of financial policy.

Consider, for example, the fundamental financial decision regarding the relative proportions of debt and equity, the capital structure decision. In a strictly national firm, the ratio of debt to equity is judiciously set to minimize the firm's weighted average cost of capital. Lower-cost, interest deductible debt is added to capital structure to the point where the incremental financial risk from debt pushes up its marginal cost equal to the cost of equity.[3] On the other hand, *within* a firm — in our case, within an MNE — no comparable connection exists between a *divisional* (i.e. a subsidiary's) debt:equity ratio and its cost of capital. The relevant factor determining the opportunity cost of capital placed in a foreign subsidiary is the *consolidated* leverage position of the MNE (Shapiro, 1975). The link between consolidated leverage and capital costs gives rise to two corollaries: (1) the opportunity cost of corporate funds is the same for all parts of the multinational, wherever situated, however financed; and (2) for a given subsidiary, average and marginal costs of corporate funds employed are equal (Shapiro, 1978a, b).

Optimal Financial Positioning

The tax-minimizing rule of thumb for a corporation with operations and sales in two countries is to maximize reported costs in the high-tax country (H) and maximize reported revenues in the low-tax country (L). A dollar of cost incurred in L but reported in H saves the company $\$(t_H - t_L)$ in tax. Similarly, a dollar of revenue shifted from H to L adds $\$(t_H - t_L0$ to consolidated after-tax income. The conventional transfer pricing strategy, then, is to *overprice* intra-firm *exports* from and *underprice* intra-firm *imports* to the *low* tax country, and vice versa for the high tax country.

MNE financial costs, like operating costs, also have a tax-minimizing international allocation. For example, an interest deduction taken in H instead of L adds $i(t_H - t_L)$ to consolidated after-tax income. Furthermore, interest deductions are easily reallocated without disturbing the MNE consolidated debt-to-assets ratio; a dollar more of debt here is simply offset by a dollar less debt there.[4]

The fundamental difference between the problems of allocating operating costs versus financial costs is that the former are directly linked to production functions whereas the latter, at least in the first round, are not. A cost imbedded in a production function has a relevant shadow price — even if that shadow price is zero over some range, e.g. research and development or management services. The conventional transfer pricing problem is thus made interesting only in so far as *reported* price — which enter tax and tariff calculations — differ from shadow prices. On the other hand, regarding financial costs, once it is established that relevant ratios are calculated from consoldiated financial figures, no (financial) shadow can be specified in the conventional sense, i.e. as directly linked to internal resource use. An MNE financial shadow price is related strictly to tax savings.

Thus the MNE's global tax liability is sensitive to the international allocation of financial costs although, aside from the tax angle, the allocation of finance itself is inconsequential (Senbet, 1979). However, second order effects on the internal allocation of real investment within the MNE arise because in so far as strategic allocation of finance reduces the global tax liability it also reduces international effective tax rate differentials (Errunza and Senbet, 1981; Adler, 1979; Horst, 1977). In other words, within the MNE the effective tax rate on each subsidiary's net operating income — the source of distortion of real investment — is a function of the MNE's internal allocation of finance. As a result, the efficiency conditions for the allocation of real capital and financial capital are derived simultaneously such that, in equilibrium, the after-tax marginal return on assets placed in the high-tax country *plus the implicit return in the form of tax savings via financial adjustments* equals the after-tax marginal return on assets in the low tax country.

A numerical example will demonstrate the effect of intra-firm financial strategy on the international allocation of real capital of the MNE. Assume the tax rate in the high-tax country, t_H, is 0.50 while the tax rate in the low-tax country, t_L, is 0.40. Assume also the marginal return on assets in H is 0.20. The shadow price of financial adjustments is $(t_H - t_L)i$, or 0.01 if i is assumed to be 0.10. An indication of the effect of strategic intra-firm financing on real asset allocation results from comparing the efficiency conditions where the shadow price of financial adjustments is not considered versus the situation where it is:

Situation A: financial adjustments are not considered. In this case the criterion for asset allocation is the equality of marginal returns net of tax. Let G' be the marginal pre-tax return on assets in L. Then in equilibrium:

$$(1-0.50)\ (0.2) = (1-0.40)\ G'$$
$$G' = 0.167$$

The pre-tax marginal return in the high tax country H, 0.20, is greater than that in country L, 0.167. The tax differential creates a bias towards the country of relatively lower tax.

Situation B: financial adjustments considered. In this case the MNE allocates real capital internationally such that the marginal return on assets in H plus the shadow price of financial adjustments equals the marginal rate of return on assets in L:

$$(1-0.50)\ (0.20) + (0.50-0.40)\ (0.10) = (1-0.40)\ G'$$
$$G' = 0.183$$

The pre-tax marginal return in H, (0.2) is still higher than in L, (0.183). That is, a tax-created bias of capital allocation towards the low-tax country still exists but the size of the bias has been reduced, i.e. 0.183 is greater than 0.167. It is in this sense that financial adjustments are capable of reducing international effective tax rate differentials. This result requires that the marginal investment in the high-tax country is financed entirely with tax deductible debt.

Reallocation of debt within an MNE does not necessarily involve *intra-firm* debt. Indeed, we are addressing a somewhat different question from optimal intra-firm capital transfers (Horst, 1977) or the optimal mix of repatriation flows — among dividends, royalties or intra-firm interest — examined by Mutti (1981). Financial economists might recognize what amount to international analogues of the theorems of Miller and Modigliani. These classic axioms maintain that corporate financial decisions — involving, for example, capital structure or dividends — are irrelevant in a world of no taxation and, in turn, finance has no bearing on investment decisions. On the other hand, when tax is introduced, optimal financial decisions are characterized by corner solutions which call for maximization or minimization of particular ratios in order to minimize the after-tax cost of capital. That essentially depicts the problem of optimal internal allocation of finance within the MNE.

Tax administrators responsible for the integrity of national tax systems may feel like unsophisticated countrymen somehow involved in an international shell game. To curtail any potential adverse impact of such strategy on fiscal revenue, explicit restrictions on the financial structure of foreign subsidiaries have typically been introduced by countries involved.[5] The irrelevance of corporate finance, of course, means such restrictions are arbitrary. Although some rules are quite aggressive, the large number of options for structuring multinational corporate finance invariably gives the edge to the corporation. Indeed, as a matter of tax administration in the international setting, Mathewson and Quirin (1979) suggest that there is 'serious difficulty in even determining when income-shifting via intra-corporate debt financing is taking place, and almost insuperable difficulty in showing that it is illegal, as long as the amounts involved are modest. Nor, given the availability of financial intermediaries as substitutes for the parent company, does there appear to be very much that could be done to stop it without interferring with perfectly proper transactions' (p. 76).

In the following section we discuss three widely used MNE internal financial tactics which typify the financial dimension of transfer pricing.

MNE Financial Strategy in Practice

In practice — under the rubric of international tax planning — MNEs employ various tactics in line with a tax-minimizing financial strategy. Like conventional transfer pricing, the objective of internally co-ordinated financial manoeuvres is to lower the MNE's tax bill. But, unlike transfer prices of intermediate goods and services, no allocatively relevant shadow prices or market price approximations can be defined for most of these transactions. There are no arm's-length counterparts to the following examples.

The three cases to be outlined deal with: (1) MNE financial policy to take full advantage of the deferral provision with respect to taxing foreign source income; (2) a triangular arrangement involving a tax haven enabling an MNE to take the same interest deduction twice; and (3) a timing exercise for repatriating foreign source income which virtually eliminates the tax liability at home.[6]

Getting the Most Out of Deferral

The feature of international tax arrangements with the greatest influence on the structure of multinational corporate finance is the deferral provision pertaining to the tax liability in the home country of the parent company. The provision itself is a vestige of the accounting 'realization' principle whereby income is not realized until all relevant transactions are complete; foreign source income, therefore, does not enter the residence tax base until it is repatriated.

When the source tax rate is less than the residence rate, the deferral provision creates an incentive to reinvest subsidiary earnings in order to avoid the immediate impact of an incremental tax imposed at home. In effect, from the point of view of the multinational corporation a dollar not paid in taxes is a dollar reduction in borrowing requirement: deferred taxes thus amount to interest-free loans from the treasury of the residence country. Viewed in this way, they are particularly valuable 'loans' because they are available without security and are repayable entirely at the option of the borrower. Therefore multinationals correctly ascribe a lower cost of capital to earnings reinvested in the source country than to alternate forms of capital.[7] The magnitude of the effect of residence tax deferral on subsidiary capital costs depends primarily on the size of the differential between the source and residence rates of tax.

Since unremitted foreign earnings are shielded from any net residence tax liability, the cost of equity relative to debt is lower than it would be if retentions did not receive the implicit subsidy through deferral. As a result foreign subsidiaries tend to have lower financial leverage than domestic firms, i.e. each dollar of foreign investment is financed with relatively more equity than domestic investment. Shapiro (1980) surveyed the finance of American subsidiaries in Canada and found that compared to domestic corporations, American subsidiaries have substantially lower financial leverage. For example, in 1975 the debt to assets ratio was 0.32 for US-owned subsidiaries while the ratio was 0.55 for the average Canadian corporation. Furthermore, empirical evidence on relative capital intensity and profitability of foreign subsidiaries versus domestic industry is consistent with the view that deferral of residence tax reduces the opportunity cost of reinvested earnings, ultimately with allocative consequences.[8]

MNE Financial Manoeuvres Through Tax Havens

This next example — a surefire manoeuvre to exploit the interaction of host and home tax systems — has been refined by Canadian-based multinationals. It is typical of an internal MNE tactic in lieu of conventional transfer pricing. The financial arrangement, dubbed 'the double dip', reveals the difficulty in international taxation of defining complete but non-overlapping *source rules*, i.e. rules which allocate the corporate tax base among countries involved.

The double dip is a two-stage loan from a division in Canada to a foreign operating division in, say, the United States. The loan is channelled through a financial subsidiary in a tax haven.[9] The initial corporate borrowing is done in Canada, creating a tax deductible interest expense in Canada. The funds are transferred at zero interest to the financial subsidiary — typically in the

Netherlands Antilles — and the funds are then on-loaned at commercial rates to the operating subsidiary in the United States. Thus a second interest deduction — on the same borrowed capital — is taken in the United States; the intra-firm 'interest' accumulates tax free in the tax haven, perhaps to return eventually to Canada. The net effect of this triangular intra-firm financial arrangement is that Canadian debt capital exported by multinational enterprise is virtually costless (on an after-tax basis) to the corporation.

Another example of the use of a tax haven indicates how an MNE internal financial arrangement can mitigate the effects of an impediment to international capital flows. We refer specifically to the above-average level of withholding taxes Canada and the USA reciprocally levy on dividends flowing across the border. Because of this tax cost on direct transfers between the USA and Canada, it is to the advantage of an MNE — again say a Canadian company with an operating subsidiary in the USA — to channel its foreign investment through a holding company in a tax haven.[10] For example, under the terms of the US: Netherlands tax treaty, dividends paid from the USA to the Netherlands bear only a 5 per cent US withholding tax. As noted earlier, normally no additional tax is incurred on the second leg of the financial transfer to Canada. This is in contrast to a US withholding tax of 15 per cent charged on dividends flowing directly to Canada.

Strategic Timing of MNE Financial Transfers

Our final example of the use of internal financial markets within the multinational enterprise to reduce the after-tax cost of capital is a further indication of the greater effectiveness of the *financial* dimension of transfer pricing as opposed to the conventional focus on intermediate goods and services. Again, the specific context involves Canada and the United States — a Canadian subsidiary of an American MNE — although the structure of the manoeuvre has its counterparts in various other contexts.[11]

The United States taxes Canadian source income on a 'deferral basis with foreign tax credit'. This means such income is taxed by the USA only when it is repatriated; Canadian taxes paid — corporate income tax as well as the 15 per cent withholding tax on dividends — are credited against the US liability. In some circumstances credits created by Canadian taxes are sufficient to eliminate completely the US tax liability. Indeed, that is the thrust of the 'rhythm method', a dividend-timing tactic wherein repatriations from Canada to the United States are co-ordinated with the Canadian capital cost allowance to minimize the MNE's (time-cumulative) international tax bill.

Essentially, to adopt the rhythm method the subsidiary pays a maximum amount of Canadian income tax and remits 100 per cent of its earnings in some years, and it minimizes its Canadian income tax and pays no dividends in others. In years dividends are paid, sufficient credits accompany remittances to cancel any effective tax liability in the United States. As a result, in all years the corporation pays tax only in Canada at the lower (than US) Canadian tax rate.

The feature of Canadian tax law that facilitates the rhythm method is the optional timing provision of the capital cost allowance and the investment tax credit. Canadian firms (including foreign-owned subsidiaries in Canada) may choose the year in which the allowance and credit are taken. In effect, by compounding two years' allowance and credits every second year, as far as the corporation is concerned Canada becomes alternately a 'high' and then a 'low' tax country *vis-à-vis* the USA. In remittance years, Canada is a high-tax country and no residence liability is incurred; in non-remittance years, Canada is a low-tax country and the corporation takes advantage of deferral of residence tax.

Deferral is permanent if the funds are reinvested in Canada. In fact, the benefit from the rhythm method of timing repatriation depends directly on the availability of worthwhile investment opportunities in Canada.

Summary and Conclusions

The purpose of this paper was to demonstrate that the financial strategy of the multinational enterprise can achieve virtually all that traditional transfer pricing can and perhaps more. Because financial manoeuvring involves the *right-hand side* of the balance sheet and the *non-operating section* of the income statement, MNE financial strategy can concern itself with tax planning and hedging currency risks. To assign such tasks to less subtle forms of transfer pricing directly linked to operations and production risks unnecessary complexity, interferes with internal control systems and inevitably creates the accounting (not to mention legal!) problem of keeping two sets of books.

The financial dimension of transfer pricing, like its conventional counterpart, is co-ordinated from the centre. Indeed, MNEs usually do maintain strong central finance functions. There are two fundamental reasons, each a facet of the special nature of a firm that operates successfully internationally. First, a central finance function provides the necessary vantage point to consider the relative worth of various international opportunities for investment. It enables the MNE to control information about international capital market conditions, foreign exchange risks and opportunities for arbitrage. Such conditions, risks and opportunities are relevant for the international firm as a whole although, in contrast, they are relatively unimportant for individual divisions of the firm. Second, consistent with the view that the multinational enterprise is a set of non-market contractual arrangements which emerge in lieu of markets which fail, the centralisation of finance within the firm overcomes barriers and inefficiencies of segmented international capital markets. In a sense the multinational corporation establishes its finance function as a surrogate integrated international capital market. Tactics within this function encompass what we have termed the financial dimension of MNE transfer pricing.

Whereas central administration is the *sine qua non* of effective transfer pricing, the contention that the financial variant is more relevant than the conventional form must be rejected if MNEs do not, in fact, centralize financial decisions to a greater extent than operation/production decisions. To determine first what type of decisions are the responsibility of the parent and subsidiaries respectively, Yunker (1982) put the following question to 52 large American MNEs:

> From the point of view of the overall corporation, relatively how independent are the managers of foreign and domestic subsidiaries engaged in *international* transfers with respect to each of the following business policy variables?

The range of answers consists of 'Subsidiary determines entirely', 'Subsidiary determines mostly', 'Parent determines mostly' and 'Parent determines entirely'. Thirteen categories of corporate decision variables are suggested. One is the 'Price of sales to subsidiaries in other countries', an obvious reference to what we have termed the conventional transfer pricing problem. On the other hand, two answer categories are strictly financial, dealing with intra-firm dividends and borrowings. The replies reveal a striking difference in the degree of centralization: 45.2 per cent of the respondents report that parents mostly or entirely determine the price of intra-firm sales while almost twice as many (87.1 per cent) consider intra-firm financial decisions to be (mostly or entirely) the parent's prerogative. These survey statistics are an indication of the greater relevance of financial transfer pricing strategy *vis-à-vis* the other.

To conclude our discussion of MNE tactics to minimize the global tax bill, we must emphasize that international tax planning is a very sophisticated business. We have presented only sketches of the strategy. In practice, a good international tax adviser, well worth his weight in tax credits, is unlikely to suggest an MNE overprice unfinished gizmos or underprice intermediate widgets. Such tactics are clumsy, they interfere with internal control and may run afoul the law. But to allocate strategically otherwise amorphous financial capital — manoeuvres which involve virtually nothing but the global tax bill — is quite another matter.

Notes

1. See Adler (1974), Shapiro (1978a,b), and Mehra (1978).
2. For general discussion of internal markets within MNEs see Rugman (1981) and with specific reference to internal financial markets, see Rugman (1980a) and Lessard (1979). It is important to note that if international financial markets are inefficient and multinational enterprise is unable to circumvent the inefficiencies with internal transactions, the concept of global efficiency in multinational corporate finance is vacuous. For example, international corporate financial adjustments would be stymied in the absence of an efficient, costless mechanism for hedging exchange risks or if exchange controls or limits on foreign finance are binding. As a consequence, subsidiaries resort to local optimization — the parent and its subsidiaries pursue different valuation objectives and employ different investment-acceptance criteria.
3. The literature on this topic is voluminous. For an excellent overview, see Copeland and Weston (1983), especially Chapter 12, 'Capital Structure and the Cost of Capital: Theory' and Chapter 13, 'Capital Structure: Empirical Evidence and Applications'.
4. Although typically *not* via an intra-firm transaction. Intra-firm debt reallocation generally involves the services of a multinational bank. To illustrate: if a foreign subsidiary borrows a dollar from its local branch of the bank while the parent simultaneously reduces its borrowings from its branch by a dollar, the

consolidated debt position of the MNE does not change.

5. For instance, Canada's Thin Capitalization Rule disallows interest deductions on intra-firm debt in excess of 75 per cent of total finance of a subsidiary in Canada. France has a similar rule and so does Taiwan. Most countries further stipulate that interest payments are not automatically deducted but must be incurred for the purpose of earning business income.

6. The institutional detail in these examples draws heavily on Brean (1983b).

7. The preferential use of internal sources of funds to finance the growth of foreign subsidiaries was recognized, although not fully explained, in early studies of foreign direct investment. See, for example, Penrose (1956) and Barlow and Wender (1955). Later contributions to the theory of finance of foreign investment established a theoretical basis for the observed preference for reinvestment versus capital transfers. See Richardson (1971), Bilsborrow (1977) and Shapiro (1978a, b). Recently the role of tax (including implicit taxes such as foreign exchange risk) has been shown to have important implications for the finance of foreign investment and, in particular, to be the principal determinant of the financial mix of foreign subsidiaries. See Brean (1983b), Mehra (1978) and Hartman (1980, 1981).

8. D. Murray (1981) estimates that Canada has accumulated more foreign capital than it otherwise would in the absence of an explicit US incentive to reinvest there. Also, see Horst (1977) and Hartman (1981). Caves (1980) analyses structural differences between foreign subsidiaries and Canadian-controlled companies and his results indicate Canadian subsidiaries of US MNEs tend to be more capital intensive than their Canadian rivals, a phenomenon which could be attributed in part to the implicit tax subsidy to foreign capital.

9. Tax havens have an integral role in MNE tax planning. However, empirical estimates of such involvement is difficult for two of the very reasons — secrecy and the hands-off attitude of tax havens — that tax havens are used for in the first place. The US Treasury reports that in 1981 $7 billion (US) of corporate income was paid from US sources to nonresident aliens, i.e. corporations outside the USA. Of this, $2.5 billion or approximately 36 per cent was delivered to the Netherlands and the Netherlands Antilles (more than half went to the latter). If we bring in the Bahamas, Bermuda, Panama and Switzerland, i.e. four additional tax havens, the share of US corporate income paid from US sources flowing to these countries is 49 per cent of the total. See Carson (1983). Such revealed preference confirms the relevance of tax havens for international business and likewise for tax authorities.

10. For more technical detail, see McCart (1982).

11. More detailed discussion of relevant tax principles, practice and laws is found in Brean (1983b), Chapter 8, from which this example is drawn.

* * *

COMMENTS ON UNRESOLVED ISSUES IN TRANSFER PRICING MODELS
Harry Grubert

The theoretical models of transfer pricing often raise issues they do not resolve. I want to comment on three of these issues: how large are the possible benefits to the MNE from manipulating transfer prices; do MNEs keep more than one set of books; and whether the arm's-length principle is efficient.

I. How Large are the Benefits to the MNE from Transfer Price Manipulations?

Let me put the transfer pricing issue in perspective. How big is the problem?: How much could multinational corporations possibly be benefiting from opportunities for transfer price manipulations? One way of making a first approximation of the upper bound for US-based multinationals, from the US tax point of view, is to look at the cost of ending the deferral of taxation on unrepatriated earnings of US affiliates abroad. Presumably, if all foreign income were currently taxed at US rates, there would be no benefits to distorting transfer prices. The benefits of manipulating transfer prices appear, at most, equal to the benefits of deferral. The last time this was calculated, when President Carter proposed ending deferral, it was estimated that net taxes on US multinationals would increase by $800 million for 1981. Now this is not quite the true absolute upper bound that we are looking for because of the way the US overall foreign tax credit limitation works. A firm that may not appear to gain much from deferral, because it has enough overall credits, may still have found it profitable to shift income to low-tax countries because it can use credits from high-tax countries. The correct maximum upper bound from the US point of view is, therefore, the cost to firms of ending deferral with a per-country limitation on foreign tax credits. This is harder to estimate but it appears to be no more than twice the $800 million estimate for ending deferral only but keeping the present limitation provision. The upper bound for the benefits that could possibly be attributed to transfer price distortions is, therefore, less than 2 per cent of world-wide after-tax profits of US multinational corporations. Furthermore, since deferral was ended in 1982 for the downstream profits of oil companies, the absolute upper bound is probably now closer to 1 per cent of world-wide after-tax profits.[1]

In interpreting this rough upper bound for how much US-based multinationals could conceivably be gaining from transfer price distortions, several things should be kept in mind. One is that the US Treasury could lose more than the multinational gains because a change in transfer prices can transfer tax revenues to a foreign government. In addition, the estimate does not reflect income transferred *to* the United States from very high-tax countries. However, this is not likely to be significant because there are not many countries with substantially higher marginal corporate tax rates than the United States. Finally, any potential gains to the companies may be competed away so that consumers or other factors of production are the ones who end up ahead.

It is also worth pointing out that governments are not always innocent victims of transfer price distortions. Many governments like to offer export subsidies. Granting *ad hoc* favourable transfer price deals in return for establishing export industries is not unheard of, and has the added advantage of being not very transparent from a GATT point of view.

II. Do Multinationals Keep Two Sets of Books?

One issue that keeps coming up in the Horst-Eden type of transfer pricing models is whether multinationals keep two sets of books. The usual assumption is that they don't. Where this belief comes from, apart from an assertion by Richard Caves, is not clear. It does not seem to be based on any empirical, legal or theoretical analysis. Because of differences in tax accounting in various countries, there will be several sets of books to start with and the corporation may have great difficulty producing a single consistent set.

There are several kinds of two-sets-of-books issues. One is tax books versus accounts based on transfer prices used for internal incentive and signaling systems in the decentralized firm. Some interesting court cases have indicated that major corporations can manage to separate them without getting confused. (See for example, *E.I. du Pont* v. *U.S.*, 1979, in the US Court of Claims.) In addition, firms may legitimately use an internal incentive system inconsistent with tax accounting, e.g. they may wish to capitalize rather than expense R&D. We are also all aware of multidimensional scorekeeping systems with various handicaps and bonus points. There is no reason why a complex incentive system, even with the best of intentions, should be consistent with tax books. This is a subject we will return to in discussing the efficiency of arm's-length prices.

I am also skeptical about the single-set-of-books assumption in the question of customs and tax valuations. As any of you who have tried to reconcile trade data derived from customs and financial sources know, tax and trade accounts arise from different concepts. One is related to physical shipments and the other is based on charges and credits to various accounts. The rules for customs valuation and tax transfer pricing may be different, although the new 1980 Customs Valuation Code does seem much more consistent with the Internal Reveue Code Section 482 regulations. In the United States, the courts have sometimes rejected the attempt by the Internal Revenue Service to make 482 prices conform to customs valuations.[2]

III. Is the Arm's-length Principle Inefficient?

A third interesting issue raised by transfer pricing models is the validity of the arm's-length principle, which is by now an almost universal international standard. Does the insistence on arm's-length prices interfere with economic efficiency (as Eden seems to suggest near the end of her paper)? The issue arises in the context of the Hirshleifer optimum transfer pricing rule in decentralized firms. If a US manufacturing firm with some market power sells to a foreign affiliate, the Hirshleifer rule requires marginal cost pricing, but the arm's-length rule may recognize the monopoly profit that would be earned on the product if the sale were to a third party in the foreign market. Does that mean that the arm's-length rule leads to economic inefficiency? The short answer is no, because, as noted above, there is no reason why the firm should use tax prices for internal decision making.

In addition, I'm not sure that the arm's-length principle necessarily leads to significant departures from efficient transfer prices. The appropriate question from a tax policy point of view is: what is the *world-wide* marginal product of inputs in a given location? The arm's-length principle seems to be in accord with this inquiry. The answer would also seem to generate efficient shadow prices. If a company produces goods of high value to foreigners, this presumably should be to the credit of the producing country. In this area, as in other areas of economics, there may be reasons why it is conceptually difficult to measure shadow prices, e.g. because of indivisibilities, but it is not clear that these exceptions are more prevalent here than elsewhere.

In the cases where arm's-length pricing and efficient transfer prices appear to be in conflict, the multinational corporation may have ways of resolving this conflict by using pricing schemes outside the usual simple framework. The parent in the monopoly case, for example, might offset the 'inefficiency' of a transfer price above marginal cost by forcing the affiliate to take minimum quantities.

How the affiliate's market power arises must also be introduced into the analysis. If, as is frequently the case, it is because of valuable R&D by the parent, it would be efficient for the affiliate to help finance the R&D, perhaps with overhead charges. If the market power exists because of an exclusive franchise granted by the host government, the arm's-length rule would recognize that a similarly situated independent distributor could claim the monopoly return.

Always insisting on marginal cost pricing may also be inefficient because it biases the firm's choice between affiliates and independent distributors as ways of selling in a foreign market. If the firm could always price at marginal cost when selling to affiliates in low-tax countries, it would never choose independent distributors.

The case of internalization economies may appear to cause more of a problem. The arm's-length principle as practised may assign the benefits of internalization in an arbitrary way. However, internalization economies presumably occur because the firm doesn't have to use prices as internal incentive devices. The effect on efficiency may, therefore, be modest. In addition, it appears that a conceptually correct arm's-length price (and shadow price) is at least theoretically possible. If there are internalization economies, presumably they have been discovered by someone, to whom the increase in productivity should be attributed.

Notes

The views expressed are my own and do not necessarily represent the position of the US Treasury Department.

1. The estimates of the effect of ending deferral depend to some extent on the particular legal form chosen, but this consideration would not alter the rough orders of magnitude used in the text.

2. See the cases cited in Singer and Karlin (1983).

PART TWO
EMPIRICAL EVIDENCE ON TRANSFER PRICING

9 TRANSFER PRICING IN THE CANADIAN PETROLEUM INDUSTRY

Alan M. Rugman

I. Introduction

The Canadian susbsidiaries of foreign-owned petroleum multi-national enterprises dominate the petroleum industry in Canada. The recent expansion of the state-owned Petro Canada has added a new presence to the industry but Imperial Oil (the Exxon subsidiary) is still the largest firm in the industry, with the other major foreign firms being Gulf, Texaco and Shell. Smaller firm participants are Mobil, Sun and British Petroleum while Irving Oil and Dome are Canadian-owned. Each foreign-owned subsidiary is part of a vertically integrated multinational enterprise (MNE).

The key benefits of this multinational association are:

(a) Security of oil supply, which reduces the risks of interruptions in refining operations.
(b) Marketing brand name advantages, which reduce buyer uncertainty and help ensure stable distribution.
(c) Information and research transfers through the internal market of the multinational, which reduce the costs of knowledge acquisition.

In this paper the modern theory of the MNE (internalization) is applied to the petroleum industry. It is shown that vertical integration is an efficient process for overcoming transaction costs, especially in avoiding supply and marketing uncertainties. The research, refining and distributional functions of the MNE are determined in conjunction with its access to crude oil supplies and other aspects of the supply function. These involve the use of an internal market to minimize logistics and inventory costs. It is also necessary to overcome buyer uncertainty and other such costs by the provision of a brand name product. An affiliate benefits from access to the internal market of the MNE and the process of vertical integration generates a valuable firm-specific advantage shared by both parent and subsidiary.

The reason for the firm-specific advantage of a multinational oil firm is its degree of vertical integration. Oil firms need to have secure supplies of crude oil from uncertain foreign sources of supply. They also need to have internal markets for the refining and distribution of oil products. The managerial, technological and general knowledge skills of the MNE are intertwined and are not separable components of multinational activity.

It is also known that the transfer prices of an MNE are merely the internal (shadow) prices required to lubricate the engine of the internal market.[1] Transfer prices should not be examined as separate items since they are instruments of internalization for the MNE and have no independent life of their own. Transfer pricing is not a distributional issue but an efficiency issue as such prices arise naturally within the organization when a firm establishes production facilities in one or more foreign nations, each of which has its own tax system.

In a domestic context, as first noted by Hirshleifer (1956), transfer pricing also occurs within nations between the divisionalized operations of a multi-plant firm. This may present some difficulty in allocating income for tax purposes between state or provincial jurisdictions since the multi-plant firm is not a series of separate entities, but an integrated organization with common ownership and control. The primary use of transfer prices is by the firm itself to co-ordinate activities of its divisions and to help evaluate the performance of the various operations.

In an international context, the focus of this paper, Section 482 of the US Internal Revenue Code, gives the US federal authorities the right to treat the divisions (or subsidiaries) of the MNE as separate entities. Yet they are really integrated units and only the parent company should have its performance examined. Transfer pricing is a device used by MNEs to help solve horrendous difficulties of making a market in the face of transaction costs which have denied the existence of a regular market, see Rugman (1981). As such, the use of transfer pricing cannot be separated from the related issue of the reasons for multinational activity (as opposed to other methods of servicing foreign markets, such as exporting or licensing).

The basic premise of this paper is that transfer pricing is an integrated part of the theory of the MNE. This theory, internalization theory, is concerned with efficiency aspects of the organization and administration of internal markets, so the focus of this paper is not on distribution (or accounting) aspects of money transfer prices, just with the real, shadow, transfer price.

The nature of multinational activity is complex but not incomprehensible. In economic terms MNEs are efficient business organizations. It is only on non-efficiency grounds that questions of money transfer prices and foreign control arise to become troublesome. In such circumstances, the issue of transfer pricing is analysed usually from the viewpoint of the nation state. For example, Vaitsos (1974), Lall (1980) and several authors in the Murray (1981) volume consider the potential adverse impact on the economies of developing nations when transfer pricing is practised by multinational enterprises.[2]

In particular, they are concerned that transfer prices are not the same as 'arm's-length', or market prices. Similarly, the Bertrand Report (1981) adopts the perspective of the nation state alone. It attempts to evaluate the extra cost paid by Canadians for alleged higher priced imports of crude oil acquired by Canadian affiliates from their parent MNEs or other non-Canadian affiliates. The accuracy and methodology used in the estimates of the Bertrand Report (as an illustrative case) will be examined later, but at this stage it is necessary to question their premise which considers transfer pricing solely from the viewpoint of the nation state. Clearly transfer pricing must also be examined from the viewpoint of the MNE.

Once this is done it will become apparent that 'arm's-length' prices simply do not exist except in the imagination of some economists and that the transfer prices used by the MNEs are the only true prices. This insight from the theory of internalization has many implications, not the least of which is that the conceptual basis of the Bertrand Report is flawed since there are no 'arm's-length' prices to use as a yardstick to evaluate the alleged overcharge to Canadians.

II. Theoretical Background of Multinational Activity

It is now established in the literature on international business that the MNE exists under conditions of market imperfections. The seminal work of Coase (1937), Hymer (1976) and

Kindleberger (1969) has recently been integrated into a single explanation of multinationality: namely, the theory of internalization. Clear explanations of internalization theory appear in Buckley and Casson (1976), Dunning (1977, 1979, 1981) and Rugman (1980b, 1981). On a parallel track, work by Williamson (1975) identifies the transaction costs which make it efficient for a firm to do what a regular market fails to do. This transactional model has been applied internationally by Caves (1982).

Both of these approaches identify conditions under which the MNE makes an internal market. Such internal markets are required when the costs of using a regular market are excessive (such as when buyer uncertainty leads to high transaction costs) or when a market fails to price intermediate goods, or intangibles (such as knowledge). The MNE uses the internal market to establish relevant property rights over its firm-specific advantage. These advantages are generally in the areas of knowledge and information, broadly defined to include technological, research and managerial skills specific to the firm.

In the case of petroleum companies the type of firm-specific advantage that may be controlled within the MNE is usually one determined by external market imperfections. Aliber (1970) puts it this way:

> Efficiencies may be realized by co-ordinating activities that occur in several different countries within the firm. Thus an international oil company co-ordinates the production, transport, refining, and the distribution of petroleum at lower costs than individual firms at each stage might be able to by using the market. The economies of vertical integration involve reduction in transactions costs, the costs of search, and the costs of holding inventories. (pp. 19-20)

Petroleum MNEs engage in vertical integration in response to both natural and government induced market imperfections. Their control over sources of supply and over markets is justified when a firm-specific advantage needs to be protected. The rate of development of an oil field requires co-ordination of the production and marketing function in a dynamic sense; and is best achieved within a firm, where accurate information about all the functions can be assembled. If such knowledge is made freely available, the firm will not recover its initial outlays, so it is entitled to overcome the classic externality of knowledge as a public good by the assignment of property rights which permit it to protect its firm-specific information. This gives the MNE a knowledge advantage; no problems of economic inefficiency arise so long as there are existing or potential rival firms with the same ability to internalize markets.

Figure 9.1 illustrates this process. There are four stages of vertical integration; extraction, transportation, refining and distribution. Control of the supplies and markets is needed to allow the crucial capital-intensive refining stage to operate at full capacity. An oil MNE can put together this package at lower costs than the market. The MNEs have managed to continue this process even after OPEC disrupted the extraction stage in 1973 and 1979. The oil MNEs retained control over distribution, so they were able to pass on to consumers the higher costs of crude oil. In return, the oil MNEs only required stable supplies of oil. Of course, over the last ten years the bargaining over crude oil prices has moved away from firms and now resides with governments. Yet the oil MNEs still retain the ability to overcome the set of transaction costs identified in Figure 9.1, so their role as internalizers will continue in the future.

It can be argued that one of the key benefits of a subsidiary's multinational association involves access to the large set of crude oil supplies owned by its multinational parent. If there is a disruption to part of the supply, action can be taken by the parent to minimize the effect on any one affiliate. Also, an affiliate can always renew its contracts for supplies of crude oil. During times of crisis a firm with no on-going relationship with a supplier of crude oil may have difficulty in obtaining adequate supplies of crude oil at any price.

Another benefit for the subsidiary is access to new research and technology produced within the multinational; activities which are controlled and centralized in the parent firm but used optimally by all affiliates. While there are no theoretical problems with the concept of making internal markets, practical issues may arise when it is applied internationally. The key problem is that of sovereignty. The host nation (Canada) often has a different viewpoint from that of a US-based multinational parent firm. The host nation may look at the same picture as the MNE firm and its subsidiary but interpret it differently.

Figure 9.1: Vertical Integration of Oil MNEs

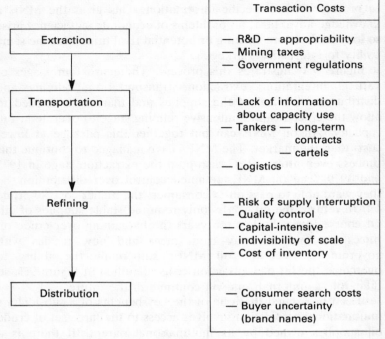

	Transaction Costs
Extraction	— R&D — appropriability — Mining taxes — Government regulations
Transportation	— Lack of information about capacity use — Tankers — long-term contracts — cartels — Logistics
Refining	— Risk of supply interruption — Quality control — Capital-intensive indivisibility of scale — Cost of inventory
Distribution	— Consumer search costs — Buyer uncertainty (brand names)

Why can MNEs decrease the transaction costs?
By: (1) secure supply (extraction and transportation).
(2) secure demand (marketing).
This permits refining at capacity.

III. Conflicts Between Multinationals and Host Governments

The problem of conflict between the perceptions of the host nation and those of the MNE is a basic one, well recognized in the field of international business. The MNE is a legal entity with control vested in the parent firm but with operations in several nations. It produces goods abroad as well as at home and markets them in many nations. It seeks to secure stable supplies of raw materials and, whenever possible, sets up distributional networks to market its products. This vertical integration is particularly appropriate in resource-processing sectors where capital costs are high and scale economies need to be realized.

The presence of multinationals in host nations such as Canada raises no problems on strictly economic grounds. Multinationals serve to increase the stock of investment and capital in Canada, provide employment opportunities and tax revenues, increase national output and raise welfare. They also transfer technology by the simple process of establishing factories to produce goods using new technology. All of these beneficial activities are experienced in Canada by the very presence of multinational oil companies. The Bertrand Report (1981) unfortunately fails to recognize these benefits for the Canadian economy.

The conflicts which arise between MNEs and host nations are on non-economic grounds. For example, many nation states feel that the size and power of MNEs in the economic sphere spill over into the political arena. The ability of multinational oil firms to constrain the activities of nation states has been alleged by Penrose (1968). It is felt at times that MNEs do not contribute enough to the development of the host nation, or at least that they manage to avoid paying their full share of taxes.

There is relatively little evidence to support such claims; indeed, it has been shown in Rugman (1980b), following Grubel (1974), that MNEs provide a social benefit to the host nation, as taxes are paid there, rather than in the home nation which allows tax credits on foreign taxes. These taxation issues are basically equity arguments, rather than efficiency ones. If, indeed, multinationals are not contributing enough to the host nation, it remains up to the host government to correct the situation. The sovereign power of the nation state is ultimately greater than that of any corporation, since only the state can impose taxes and regulations, while the corporation is in a passive role responding to such measures.

Transfer pricing is an example of a response by MNEs to such government regulations. If there are effective tax rate differentials, currency exchange controls or other regulations restricting the remittance of profits to the parent firm, then the MNE has an incentive to develop an internal transfer pricing system to respond to such government imposed market imperfections. The reason for transfer pricing can usually be traced to some such regulation or distortion in the international price system by a government.

For example, one of the classic reasons for transfer pricing is international tax rate differentials. It is the fault of governments that tax rates are not harmonized; the multinationals merely respond to such exogenous market imperfections. Multinationals are clever at adjusting their internal markets to respond to environmental changes, this flexibility being a key factor in their continued success. Indeed, MNEs which fail to adapt dynamically eventually pass away. The list of large corporations in the annual Fortune directory exhibits a continuous movement over time, as new corporations enter and the less successful drop off the list.

The conflict between MNEs and host nations such as Canada need not exist. It is due to a mix-up in the understanding of efficiency and equity issues. Multinationals are interested in business efficiency alone. Nation states will place efficiency as only one of many of their economic, social and political objectives. The trade-off between efficiency and equity is understood in business but not in government. Unfortunately in an investigation such as the Bertrand Report, which is concerned with the role of multinationals in the economy, many of these issues are confused.

Much of the Bertrand Report is concerned with equity questions, but throughout it attempts to use economic efficiency arguments. This leads to basic mistakes in economic analysis; for example in the failure to recognize that transfer pricing is related to tax rate differentials or other exogenous government-determined factors. Similarly the basic structure-performance-conduct model of industrial organization is misused in the Report. The efficiency of the petroleum industry is not seriously tested; for example, there are no conclusive tests of profits of the oil firms relative to all manufacturing industry. Similarly, the economic benefits of this industry to Canada are not even considered.

IV. Concentration, Monopoly and Profitability

The petroleum industry is not highly concentrated relative to other sectors. Thus it is not uncompetitive, so it is difficult to support the allegation of collusion made in the Bertrand Report. Readily available data on concentration ratios supports this point which is reviewed in Part XIII of Imperial Oil's *Third Submission . . . on the State of Competition in the Canadian Petroleum Industry* (1983). There is additional evidence on competitive activity since normal profits are observed for the petroleum industry as a whole, and for its component sectors, see Rugman (1980b). There are no indications of collusion; indeed, the prices for petroleum inputs and outputs are determined in as competitive a manner as in most industrial sectors in Canada.

The Bertrand Report criticizes the 'monopolistic situation which developed through the small group of firms with closely linked interests (which) governed the performance of the Eastern Canadian market through control over imports' (vol. I, p. 62). On the same page the Report refers to the 'practical monopoly' of the four majors in the imports of Canadian crude oil, which accounted for 61 per cent of imports into Quebec in 1973. The model implicit in the Report is that of a dominant firm, yet it is clear that this model is used in a very loose manner throughout the Report, as these quotations illustrate. Somehow the dominant firm always becomes a monopoly.

The use of 'monopoly' is incorrect. Monopoly is defined in economic theory as a single producer and seller. Instead, the Canadian oil industry has several firms; it is an oligopoly. Yet an oligopoly is not a monopoly; indeed, its economic structure is just as likely to be dominated by price rivalry as price collusion, as the theory of games demonstrates. Yet the Report consistently argues that there is effective collusion in the oil monopoly and that there is a lack of competition.

The major evidence produced by the Report to support this is a selective use of company documents seized by the Commission. The documents were generally prepared by the oil companies to discuss crude oil prices, either internally or with their parents. The documents are worthless in terms of economics. They are simply administrative observations about common oil prices. As such, the documents may just as easily be describing a market price as any other price. The Report presents no economic model which tests for causality in oil pricing. It is necessary to demonstrate that oil firms set uncompetitive prices *ex ante*, yet all the Report does is to recite quotations about observed prices, *ex post*. Finally, there is little objective evidence to support transfer pricing activities, so the uncompetitive nature of the petroleum industry is not evident.

V. The Bertrand Report's Estimation of a Transfer Pricing Overcharge: a Critique

The Bertrand Report, completed in March 1981, contained this conclusion about transfer pricing:

> the higher prices paid by Canadians . . . are the result of artificial transfer prices Canadian subsidiaries of multinational oil companies paid for imports of crude oil. This amounted to $3.2 billion in 1980 terms over the period 1958 to 1973

To remedy this situation, Bertrand recommends legislation against high transfer prices, regulation of multinational oil companies and increased Canadian ownership of the petroleum industry.

The Canadian government had commissioned the study in 1973 during a period of concern over rising world oil prices and foreign ownership of the Canadian economy. Volume III of the Bertrand Report deals with transfer pricing in the Eastern Canadian petroleum industry. The area to the west of the Ottawa valley (i.e. all of Canada to the west of Montreal) was supplied by domestic oil (from the Alberta oil fields). The American oil companies — Exxon, Gulf and Texaco, along with Shell and British Petroleum — controlled over 90 per cent of the Eastern Canadian market during the period studied (1958 to 1973). These firms, charges Bertrand, used transfer prices in excess of arm's-length prices on oil imports and passed these costs on to Canadian consumers.

In calculating this overcharge, Bertrand first adjusted the actual delivered price of each MNE's Venezuelan crude by his own estimated freight rates less his own estimated 'arm's-length' price. Bertrand adjusted the prices of other crudes for different sulphur contents. He also reasoned that higher prices might be concealed in freight rates, so he estimated these on his own. The arm's-length price was based on selected third party sales as opposed to the intra-firm sales of the vertically integrated MNEs. The arm's-length price, chosen in an apparently arbitrary manner, averaged $1.66/bbl. for Venezuelan crude and $1.32/bbl. for Middle Eastern crude from 1962 to 1970.

There are three areas in Bertrand's overcharge calculation where serious problems of methodology occur: base crude selected, freight rates and arm's-length price.

A. Base Crude

In Imperial's case, Bertrand calculated his 'excess price' for Guanipa crude imports only. This 'excess' was then applied to all imports — Venezuelan, African and Middle Eastern — by multiplying the 'excess price' by Imperial's share of the total crude oil imports into Quebec. However, Imperial's actual imports of Guanipa crude into Quebec only comprised 17-50 per cent of the total imported crude during the time period studied.

The same methodology (using a Venezuelan base crude) was applied to the other four majors (Texaco, Gulf, Shell and Sun) for which Bertrand calculated an 'excess price'. Some of these firms had negligible imports of Venezuelan crudes during this time period.

A comparison of the Venezuelan crudes selected as base crudes and a few Middle Eastern crudes is reported in Exhibit 9.1. It is apparent that the Venezuelan crudes are significantly more expensive than Middle Eastern crudes. Although Bertrand did make an attempt to adjust non-Venezuelan crudes for varying sulphur contents, the different gravities and resultant process yield differentials and changeover costs at the refinery are ignored.

The Venezuelan crudes employed as a base are of the highest quality and, consequently, are of the highest prices. By applying these crudes across the board to all imports, Bertrand has grossly overstated his 'overcharge' calculations.

The prices shown in Exhibit 9.1 are Bertrand's 'implicit' (transfer) prices. All these prices have been adjusted upwards by the difference between actual freight rates and Bertrand's calculated freight rates. The latter are now examined.

B. Freight Rates

The methodology used by Bertrand in calculating freight rates underestimates the actual shipping costs since he assumes that all oil is transported by efficient new ships, while in practice the oil firms chartered many older ships from third parties. Bertrand ignores the actual weighted average of ships owned by affiliates and vessels term-chartered for specific terms and voyages.

An example of this bias can be found by examining the actual composition of Imperial's fleet, as revealed in the Bertrand Report's document 88558.

Exhibit 9.1: Implicit Prices for Imperial, Gulf, Shell and Texaco

Year	Imperial Venezuelan Guanipa (30°-31°)	Gulf Venezuelan (31°)	Shell Venezuelan	Texaco Venezuelan Mata (31°)	Imperial Arabian Lt. (32°-34°)	Texaco Arabian Lt. (34°-35°)	Gulf Kuwait (31°)
1960		2.86	2.56	2.64		2.01	1.82
1961	2.31		2.24	2.66		1.95	
1962	2.36	2.61	2.18	2.58		1.88	1.71
1963	2.38	2.60	2.16	2.37		1.76	1.54
1964	2.33	2.60	2.09	2.36	1.64	1.86	1.62
1965	2.25	2.31	2.09	2.29	1.64	1.76	1.39
1966	2.27		2.08	2.28	1.71	1.77	1.39
1967	2.19	1.96	2.05	2.31	1.63	1.78	1.42
1968	2.22	1.93	1.98	2.28		1.82	1.36
1969	2.21	1.82	1.97	2.26	1.91	1.78	1.42
1970	2.35	1.83	1.97	2.03		1.67	1.65
1971	2.63	2.21	2.34-2.36	2.58		2.32	
1972	2.90	2.33	2.59-2.62	2.65		2.31	1.78

Note: The Shell figure is for its average crude slate of Venezuela. The Gulf figures for 1960-7 are for 31° East Venezuelan; for 1968-72 they are for 31° Ceuta. The Sun estimate relates to 32° Lagomar, Lagomedio type crudes.

Source: Bertrand Report (1981), Vol. III, pp. 98-100.

Per Cent	Type	Rate
30.8	owned by B&B	I–55½%
40.5	term charter	I–33½%
28.7	affiliate	I–35¾%

The average overall cost was Intascale minus 37 per cent, I–37. However, Bertrand's assumed freight rate for Imperial oil is I–55. Bertrand also does not make a distinction between affiliate and independently-owned tankers. As only 29 per cent of shipments can be made using an affiliate-owned tanker, only this amount is available to conceal higher prices.

Document 88543 was used by Bertrand to confirm his estimates of I–55 freight costs. The same document gives Imperial's average fleet costs as I–34½ with a range of I–13 to I–55. Bertrand makes selective use of the data to support his position by assuming that each company had the fleet with the lowest after-the-fact cost. Where hindsight is available this would not guarantee that the capacity required could be obtained. In reality, hindsight is not possible so estimates and forecasts must be used.

A comparison of Bertrand's estimated freight rates and those actually in existence is given in Exhibit 9.2. Bertrand's estimates are consistently below actual observed prices from this variety of sources. His estimates also demonstrate much less variability over time than the figures. In doing so he has added anywhere from 0.019 $US/bbl. (1965) to 0.81 $US/bbl. (1973) to the cost of the 'overcharge'. Bertrand also ignores environmental events. The 1967 closure of the Suez Canal resulted in an increase in freight rates yet Bertrand finds freight rates to be in a decline from 1967 to 1970. It is apparent that Betrand, in attempting to find 'concealed' higher prices in freight rates, has underestimated the actual freight rates and thereby overestimated the 'overcharge' to Canadians from transfer pricing over the 1958 to 1973 period.

C. Arm's-length Prices

Finally, the arm's-length price, as calculated by Bertrand, is inappropriately based and the interpretation of his own data is in error. The arm's-length price is based on a very small and thin third party market where prices are lower than intra-firm sales. Such third party sales were made on the basis of marginal

Exhibit 9.2: Comparison of Calculated Average Freight Rates ($US/bbl.)

	AFRA	Model Fleet	IOL Rates	Director's Estimate
Peurto La Cruz to Portland 31° API Guanipa Crude Oil				
1960	0.293		N/A	0.182
1961	0.279		0.208	0.182
1962	0.268		0.228	0.176
1963	0.254		0.226	0.176
1964	0.227		0.203	0.155
1965	0.198	0.174	0.225	0.155
1966	0.192	0.164	0.222	0.148
1967	0.212	0.196	0.215	0.150
1968	0.219	0.179	0.184	0.153
1969	0.190	0.170	0.189	0.149
1970	0.246	0.238	0.289	0.150
1971	0.291	0.212	0.268	0.163
1972	0.246	0.227	0.270	0.173
1973	0.343	0.334	0.403	0.186
1974	0.373	0.325	0.360	
1975	0.354			
1980	0.711			
Ras Tanura to Portland 34° API Arab Light Crude Oil				
1960	1.091		N/A	0.716
1961	1.045		N/A	0.716
1962	1.009		N/A	0.690
1963	0.964		N/A	0.690
1964	0.876		N/A	0.599
1965	0.776	0.694	0.697	0.599
1966	0.756	0.662	N/A	0.586
1967	0.924	0.842	0.721	0.560
1968	1.007	0.959	N/A	0.560
1969	0.874	0.892	N/A	0.563
1970	1.073	1.421	N/A	0.555
1971	1.280	1.003	N/A	0.603
1972	1.095	1.007	N/A	0.629
1973	1.530	1.976	N/A	0.720
1974	1.665	1.615	1.600	
1975	1.629			
1980	2.732			

Note: N/A — not available.
Source: Imperial Oil Limited (1982), Vol. A, pp. IV-21, IV-22.

production which ignored other costs facing an oil-based MNE. Intra-firm sales by MNEs actually include additional costs for the overhead on production facilities and the costs of drilling dry holes. Intra-firm sales also include costs related to the security of supply and flexibility of contractual obligations afforded by the MNE's international network. Finally, the premise that *lower* prices can be obtained in the third party market is no longer valid today. Since the 1973 formation of OPEC, the third party market prices have been generally above the prices observed in intra-firm sales.

The assumption made by Bertrand is that the MNE's subsidiaries could purchase their crude requirements in the third party market at a lower rate than is obtainable from affiliates. However, it is unlikely that the quantities required could be consistently purchased in such a small market. This is not something that should be assumed, but must be explained, indicating why the Canadian subsidiaries should be expected to do better than others.

The type of sale and the contractual characteristics of a sale can also result in variations in price for the same type of crudes. Exhibit 9.3 outlines some of the factors that contribute to the variability in price for a single type of crude.

Exhibit 9.3: Factors Accounting for the Variability in Sale Prices For a Single Crude Type

Type of Sale	Contractual Characteristics
(1) Intra-firm	(1) Flexibility allowed in volume
(2) Long-term contract with escalation and/or renegotiation features	(2) Flexibility allowed in delivery and receipt
(3) Short-term contracts or specific volume contracts with little flexibility	(3) Substitutability of crude types
(4) Government tenders	(4) Size of the shipment and the advance notice required
(5) Spot sales	(5) Performance guarantees and/ or penalties
	(6) (De)escalation clauses to reflect changing market conditions
	(7) Back-haul shipments on return freight

Exhibit 9.4: Estimates of Third Party or Arm's-length Prices ($US/bbl.)

(i) Light Arabian (32°-34°)

Year	Director's Statement A	Alternative Sales to Latin America B	Alternative Sales to Japan C
1958			
1959	1.60*		
1960		1.59	
1961		1.66	
1962			
1963	1.40*	1.58	1.58-1.65
1964	1.42	1.39	
1965	1.31-1.35	1.35-1.58	
1966	1.30*	1.46	
1967		1.335-1.43	1.55
1968	1.28-1.35		
1969	1.30		
1970	1.20*		
1971	1.30		
1972	1.70		

(ii) Medium Kuwait (31°)

Year	Director's Statement A	Alternative Sales to Latin America B	Alternative Sales to Japan C
1958	1.65*		1.42-1.44
1959	1.47*		1.43-1.45
1960	1.34*		1.41-1.45
1961	1.34*	1.39	1.38-1.43
1962	1.29-1.34*		1.39-1.40
1963	1.29*		
1964	1.24-1.29* 1.25	1.23-1.40	
1965	1.24-1.29* 1.25	1.31-1.35	
1966	1.24-1.29* 1.20		
1967	1.24-1.29*		
1968	1.15* 1.18-1.24*	1.155-1.37	
1969			
1970			
1971			
1972			

(iii) Light Iranian (Agha Jari 34°)

Year	Director's Statement A	Alternative Sales to Latin America B	Japan C
1958	1.79*		
1959	1.56*		
1960	1.43*; 1.45	1.56	
1961	1.43*		
1962	1.38-1.43*		
1963	1.38*		1.47-1.52
1964	1.29-1.34*		1.37-1.53
1965	1.29-1.34*	1.27-1.50	1.47-1.55
1966	1.29-1.34*; 1.20-1.35	1.26-1.46	1.28-1.50
1967	1.29-1.34*; 1.10	1.30-1.48	1.29-1.54
1968	1.28-1.35*; 1.20	1.184-1.25	1.41-1.43
1969	1.15-1.20		
1970			
1971			
1972	1.697		

(iv) Heavy Iranian (Gach Saran 31°)

Year	Director's Statement A	Alternative Sales to Latin America B	Japan C
1958			
1959			
1960			
1961			
1962			
1963			1.42-1.48
1964			1.35-1.48
1965		1.23-1.30	1.34-1.47
1966		1.18-1.23	1.35-1.44
1967			1.28-1.44
1968			1.33
1969		1.15	
1970			
1971			
1972			

Notes: A. Director's Table C-1, Vol. III, p. 148; B,C. US Senate Hearing, pp. 49-56; * Director's Source: US Senate Hearing.
Source: Imperial Oil Limited (1982), Vol. B, p. I. 67.

Exhibit 9.5: Variation in Crude Oil Price ($US/bbl.)

Type of Crude Oil	Year	Number of Observations	Mean	One Standard Deviation	Range Encompassing Two-thirds Observations	Director's Reported Price Range, Vol. III, Table C-1
Light Arabian	1965	8	1.48	0.07	1.41-1.55	1.31-1.35
Medium Kuwait	1965	4	1.33	0.08	1.25-1.41	1.24-1.29
	1968	5	1.24	0.08	1.16-1.32	1.15-1.24
Light Iranian	1965	11	1.35	0.08	1.27-1.43	1.29-1.34
	1966	7	1.35	0.06	1.29-1.41	1.29-1.34
	1967	8	1.36	0.07	1.29-1.43	1.29-1.34

Source: Imperial Oil Limited (1982), Vol. B, p. I. 67.

For these reasons, a single price for crude does not exist; rather there is a range of prices.

Exhibit 9.4 shows Bertrand's reported arm's-length price and Walter S. Newton's (columns B and C) estimates of third party prices for four types of Middle Eastern crude from a well-known Senate document on oil prices. Here again, it is apparent that Bertrand has selected only the lower end of the actual price range.

Exhibit 9.5 shows the range of prices reported by Bertrand and Imperial Oil for selected crudes and years, using the same data. It is apparent that Bertrand has used only the lower end of the range, in effect his range is the mean less one standard deviation from the mean itself. Fully half of the range is ignored.

In one case, Light Arabian crude, Bertrand's entire range is below Imperial's. Bertrand's source for this crude price is page 68 of the Senate document which acknowledges that these prices are 'the lowest arm's-length prices'. This important qualification, however, is ignored by Bertrand.

VI. Conclusion

It is clear from the points raised in this paper that the Bertrand Report makes selective use of the data available, misinterprets data and makes incorrect implications without any basis in (efficiency based) economics. Unfortunately, the unscientific nature of this work is representative of the Bertrand Report. In this specific case, Bertrand's analysis of an alleged overcharge due to transfer pricing in the Canadian oil industry is meaningless and without any basis in fact on either theoretical or empirical grounds.

Here it has been shown that the conceptual basis for the Bertrand analysis was flawed since it did not relate the use of transfer pricing to the need for internal prices by multinationals. On the basis of the evidence presented by Bertrand it was shown, that, on his own terms, there is no significant difference between the transfer prices actually observed and the 'arm's-length' prices hypothesized.

Notes

The author wishes to acknowledge the research assistance of David Komus and John McIlveen. Helpful comments were provided by Lorraine Eden.

1. The distinction between shadow transfer prices and money prices was first made by Copithorne (1976) and has been used effectively by Eden (1983a).

2. Jenkins and Wright (1975) also employ the nation state approach by attempting to calculate 'lost' tax revenues incurred by individual nations. They found that in 1970 Canada incurred a 'loss' of $147.7 million in foregone potential tax revenues due to transfer pricing by multinational oil firms. This estimate can be adjusted downwards due to the different risk level (with a lack of scale economies and high distribution costs) of Canada compared to the United States and due to the recent change in Canada's status from a consuming to a producing nation.

10 AN EMPIRICAL INVESTIGATION OF INTERNATIONAL TRANSFER PRICING BY US MANUFACTURING FIRMS

Anita M. Benvignati

A distinctive and decisive attribute of multinational firms is the presence of intra-corporate transfers of goods and services across national boundaries. While precisely such flows have tended to make government officials uneasy — because corporate profits, and hence, various forms of government revenues or competitive objectives can be affected — there has been relatively little documentation of their magnitude, uniqueness, method of pricing, and associated firm and/or industry characteristics.[1] Furthermore, there has been a tendency to assume, without empirical support, that 'foreign' intra-corporate transfers are more problematic from a government standpoint than 'domestic' intra-corporate transfers (Shulman, 1969). This paper attempts to address these voids by examining transfer pricing data filed with the US Federal Trade Commission (FTC) for a large sample of US manufacturing firms. The findings are among the relatively few which document patterns of behaviour in the transfer pricing area.

In section I, the strengths and weaknesses of the data are addressed, as well as methods adopted to cope with the weaknesses in this study. In section II, a variety of descriptive statistics are presented emphasizing a comparison between domestic and foreign transfers. And, in section III, the rules governing the pricing of foreign transfers under Regulation 482(e) of the US Internal Revenue Code are reviewed and then evaluated in terms of their apparent application as indicated by FTC sample responses. Finally, in section IV, an attempt is made to relate statistically some firm and industry characteristics to the transfer pricing decision, using both the FTC data and information filed in the Standard Enterprise Classification SEC 10-K reports.

I. Data

The data used in this study come from a confidential series filed by leading US manufacturing firms with the Line of Business Program of the US Federal Trade Commission.[2] Data for the year 1975 were selected from the four years of data compiled by the FTC (1974 to 1977) because, to date, they are the most thoroughly processed and the most extensively matched to 'outside' data series.

The FTC series has several features which make it unique and exciting for research purposes. First, it is more disaggregated than most comparable manufacturing series. Each company reports its financial data by each 'line of business' (LB) in which it operates.[3] Lines of business are formally defined by the FTC and correspond with the Standard Industrial Classification System (SIC) defined by the US Census Department. This correspondence occurs at roughly the three- to four-digit level.[4] A second advantage of the data is that profit components are greatly detailed and include values of intra-corporate transfers of goods and services as well as the methods of intra-corporate pricing used. Third, there is a considerably large number of observations to examine at the LB level, which for this study covers 466 companies and 3,186 LBs.

The data are not without their deficiencies, however, particularly when a narrowly defined topic is imposed upon them. For instance, the FTC report form does not treat non-manufacturing business activities as systematically, or in as great detail, as it does manufacturing activities, making it difficult to conduct a comparable analysis of all sectors.[5] A further problem arises, even for manufacturing LBs, due to asymmetric reporting requirements of intra-corporate transfers. Where applicable, firms are required to divide their operations into three groups — an LB section, a domestic regulated section (DRS) and a foreign section (FS).[6] Only three types of intra-corporate transfers then get reported: (1) transfers from one domestic, unregulated LB to another; (2) transfers from each domestic, unregulated LB to the FS; and (3) transfers from each domestic, unregulated LB to the DRS. This procedure results in two important omissions for a study of international transfers — transfers from the firm's foreign section to each of its LBs and DRS, i.e. transfers *into* the United States; and transfers from the firm's DRS to its foreign section. In addition to these omissions, the reported method of pricing used for a firm's intra-corporate transfers applies to *all* three types of transfers reported, not just to the LB to FS transfers; hence, pricing data are not uniquely determined where more than one type of transfer is made by a firm in a particular LB. Finally, the 1975 sample of LBs includes LBs which did not appear on either a firm's 1974 or 1976 report form. Due to the likely aberrant behaviour of firms newly entering or recently dropping out of particular industries, such observations are of questionable value.

We address these data deficiencies by limiting this empirical study in the following ways:

— omit non-manufacturing observations;
— analyze LB to FS transfers only;
— split LB sample observations into four groups: (1) no intra-corporate transfers reported, (2) predominantly foreign transfers reported, (3) predominantly domestic transfers reported and (4) combined domestic/foreign transfers reported;
— omit observations where no reports were filed in either 1974 or 1976 despite existence of a 1975 report.

Effectively this study is then one of intra-corporate transfers of manufactured goods *to* a firm's foreign operations. The transfer of services is regrettably not part of the study. The exclusion of regulated domestic business activities, on the other hand, has its advantages since it should enable a clearer interpretation of pricing patterns.

Table 10.1: Sample Breakdown by Type of Transfer

	Number of LB Observations
No transfers	875
Foreign-transfers group	674
Domestic-transfers group	1,380
Combined-transfers group	257
Total	3,186

A breakdown of the sample that forms the basis of our analysis appears in Table 10.1. Once non-manufacturing LBs and entry and exit observations are eliminated, we are left with a total of 3,186 observations, of which a little over one-quarter are LBs with no transfers of the type specified in the FTC report form. By assigning arbitrary cut-off points, the remaining LB observations can be grouped into 'domestic', 'foreign' and 'combined' transfer categories. Where the ratio of LB to FS transfers to total LB transfers (i.e. LB to FS, LB to DRS and LB to other LBs) exceeds 0.7, the observations became part of a foreign-transfers group; where they were less than 0.3, they became part of a domestic-transfers group; and, where they were between 0.3 and 0.7, they became part of a combined-transfers group. On this basis, 30 per cent of the sample observations (where intra-corporate transfers existed) fell into the foreign-transfers group.

In terms of dollar value, roughly 8 per cent of total revenues are domestic transfers and roughly 4 per cent of total revenues are foreign transfers *out* of the United States. If foreign transfers *in* were known, it seems likely that domestic and foreign transfers would be roughly equal in magnitude in US manufacturing. As a fraction of total US manufacturing exports in 1975, our sample of intra-corporate exports constitutes a little over 25 per cent,[7] a figure which represents a substantial fraction of the population estimate made by Lall (1973, p. 183) for the year 1970.[8]

II. A Comparison of Transfer Pricing Methods

Four categories of pricing methods are offered in schedule III(A) of the FTC report form. They are: market, cost-plus, cost and other (which firms must specify).[9] For a particular LB, companies must indicate what fraction of their total transfers (i.e. intra-corporate exports to their foreign section, other domestic LBs and domestic regulated section), were made using each of the indicated methods. Responses for 1975 are summarized in Table 10.2 for two groups of observations — domestic-transfers group and foreign-transfers group, as we have now specified them.

It is clear that there is substantially more non-market pricing applied to the foreign-transfers group than to the domestic-transfers group. Whereas on average 24 per cent of the former are made using market prices, an average of as much as 50 per cent of the latter are similarly made. A 2-tail test of the

Table 10.2: Method of Intra-corporate Pricing: Comparison of Foreign and Domestic Transfers

| | Mean % of Transfers | | Mean Difference Test: Ho: $\mu_F = \mu_D$ | |
	Foreign-Transfers Group (n=674 LBs)	Domestic-Transfers Group (n=1,380 LBs)	t Statistic	2-tail Probability
Market	24.04	49.44	−12.36	0.001
Non-market:	75.96	50.56	12.36	0.001
Cost-plus	57.24	29.27	12.84	0.001
Cost	14.48	18.83	−2.64	0.008
Other	4.25	2.46	2.11	0.035

difference in these means indicates there is a statistically significant difference at the 0.001 level.[10]

A comparison of the distribution of non-market pricing methods reveals further distinctive patterns. Much greater emphasis is placed on cost-plus pricing for the foreign-transfers group than for the domestic-transfers group. And, despite the general tendency for the domestic-transfers group to be market-priced, they are much more reliant on cost pricing. For both categories of transfers, relatively little use was made of other pricing methods.[11]

Industry breakdowns reveal some further interesting patterns. In Table 10.3 we have listed for both the foreign and domestic groups of transfers the mean value of transfers, the mean percentage valued at market prices and the number of LB observations — all broken down by 20 broad industry categories.[12] We first notice the top-four industries according to dollar value for the foreign-transfers groups are very different from the top-four in the domestic-transfers group.[13] For the foreign-transfers group they are: transportation equipment, non-electrical machinery, instrumentation, and chemicals and allied products. And, for the domestic-transfers group they are: electrical machinery, petroleum refining, leather and leather products, and primary metal industries. Whereas 52 per cent of the LB observations in the foreign transfers-group fall into their top-four industries, only 24 per cent of LB observations in the

Table 10.3: Industry Patterns

Major Industry*	Foreign-transfers Group			Domestic-transfers Group		
	Mean Value ($000)	Mean % at Market	# Obs.	Mean Value ($000)	Mean % at Market	# Obs.
Food and kindred products	7,354	25	49	17,370	30	134
Tobacco manufacturing	**	**	**	**	**	**
Textile mill products	2,098	23	13	9,711	38	47
Apparel and other fabric products	**	**	**	3,171	24	34
Lumber and wood products, except furniture	**	**	**	27,788	67	57
Furniture and fixtures	619	11	7	1,859	22	21
Paper and allied products	2,672	24	16	19,794	66	104
Printing, publishing and allied industries	2,030	15	13	2,200	43	45
Chemicals and allied products	12,663	30	99	27,522	62	161
Petroleum refining and related industries	**	**	**	51,385	60	31
Rubber and miscellaneous plastic products	4,079	37	24	19,689	47	64
Leather and leather products	0	0	0	38,015	30	8
Stone, clay, glass and concrete products	3,996	25	27	8,857	59	72
Primary metal industries	8,167	62	13	35,367	64	120
Fabricated metal products, except machinery and transportation equipment	2,300	22	61	7,434	51	113
Machinery, except electric	27,559	21	164	11,600	44	136
Electrical, electric machinery, equipment and supplies	6,560	25	72	64,338	44	123
Transportation equipment	107,843	16	40	12,297	35	67

Table 10.3 cont'd

Major Industry	Foreign-transfers Group			Domestic-transfers Group		
	Mean Value ($000)	Mean % at Market	# Obs.	Mean Value ($000)	Mean % at Market	# Obs.
Instruments; photographic, medical and optical goods; watches and clocks	22,847	24	47	16,169	45	22
Miscellaneous manufacturing industries	6,430	10	20	2,216	53	19
Entire sample	19,096	24	674	22,252	49	1,380

Notes: *   Approximately the 2-digit SIC level.
      ** Fewer than four observations in the category; hence, disclosure rules do not permit reporting.

domestic-transfers group fall into their top-four industries. Hence, it would appear foreign transfers are much more industry concentrated than domestic transfers.

The extent to which variations in the tendency to use market pricing for intra-corporate transfers are due to inter-industry differences versus inter-firm differences is suggested in Table 10.4 where analysis of variance calculations on a MKT variable, defined as the percentage of transfers made using market prices, are presented for both the foreign-transfers and domestic-transfers groups. Total variation in the MKT variable is decomposed into 'industry effects', 'firm effects' and 'residual effects'. From two-way analysis of variance calculations, it is clear that inter-firm differences are far more important than inter-industry differences in accounting for the source of MKT variations — once industry effects are taken into account (contributing 3.5 per cent and 7.2 per cent to total MKT variations for the foreign and domestic groups, respectively), firm effects account for an *additional* 78.9 per cent and 64.8 per cent of MKT variations in these same two samples. This is indeed a very interesting finding. It is also interesting to note that industry effects in the domestic-transfers case are statistically significant while they are not in the foreign-transfers case.

Table 10.4: Analysis of Variance: MKT Variable*

Source of Variation	Sum of Squares	d.f.	Mean Square	F Statistic	Sig.	ETA Sq.**
Foreign-transfers Group						
Industry effects	40,190	18	2,233	1.33*	0.16	0.035
Firm effects	898,356	237	3,791	7.95	0.001	0.789
Residual	199,429	418	477			
Total	1,137,975					
Domestic-transfers Group						
Industry effects	234,902	19	12,363	5.55*	0.001	0.072
Firm effects	2,114,715	327	6,467	7.30	0.001	0.648
Residual	915,392	1,033	886			
Total	3,265,009					

Notes: * Note that the importance of industry effects is diminished further when firm effects are entered first and industry effects are left to account for remaining variations; then the F-statistics on the industry-effects variables are 0.66 and 2.20 for foreign-transfers and domestic-transfers groups, respectively, with the latter still statistically significant but at the 0.002 level.
** ETA sq. is the ratio of the sum of squares for a particular effect to the total sum of squares.

III. US Tax Regulation 1.482-2(e)

While there are many reasons why a firm might want to alter the prices it charges for goods and services transferred within its own corporate system, US tax law poses something of a constraint. As we shall see, however, there remains a considerable degree of pricing flexibiity that is legally acceptable, reflected in not only the rules themselves but also in apparent practices.

Section 482 of the US Internal Revenue Code governs the allocation of income and deductions between related parties for purposes of recording taxable income. Where intra-corporate sales of tangible property occur, the US Treasury Department requires that pricing be at 'arm's-length'. What effectively constitutes legally acceptable pricing behaviour under this rule is detailed in Regulation 1.482-2, section (e). In general an 'arm's-length' price is defined as:

> the price that an unrelated party would have paid under the same circumstances for the property involved in the controlled sale . . . normally involves a profit to the seller.

In practice, of course, the establishment of an 'arm's-length' price is not a simple matter. In recognition of this, the US Treasury permits the taxpayer a certain amount of flexibility, where circumstances warrant. Ideally they want intra-corporate transfers to be priced using what they term the 'comparable uncontrolled price' (CUP). However, where it is not possible to ascertain a CUP, using specific Treasury guidelines, the taxpayer may use the 'resale price (RP) method'. And, where RP standards do not apply, the taxpayer may use the 'cost-plus' (CP) method. Finally, where all else fails, and where *facts and circumstances* justify, any other pricing method may be used.[14]

While the US regulation is really quite detailed in specifying the conditions and standards to be met in each successive stage in the selection process, it is clear that different corporate taxpayers can still end up with a fairly wide range of pricing methods. Indeed, our sample FTC data suggests this is the case. If we assume FTC respondents provided the same transfer pricing information to the FTC that they did to US tax authorities,[15] then the pricing statistics provided in Table 10.2 may also reveal something about the way US Regulation 482 is practically applied. Before any conclusions can be drawn, however, the data in Table 10.2 must be regrouped to correspond more closely to IRS pricing categories. To do this we first assume the FTC market category includes both the CUP and RP methods specified by IRS. When the reseller (i.e. the foreign subsidiary) adds little additional value to the property purchased from the parent company, the RP method should approximate a market-based method. We also assume the FTC cost category is part of IRS's 'other' category.

On this basis, it appears that in 1975 US manufacturing firms in filing their income taxes probably valued (on average across LBs) foreign intra-corporate transfers *out* of the United States in the following manner: 24 per cent using CUP or RP; 57 per cent using CP; and 19 per cent using other. No single pricing method clearly dominates the pattern. And, more surprisingly, the most preferred methods from Treasury's standpoint (i.e. CUP and RP) were the least frequently used by US firms. One possibility is that foreign intra-corporate transfers, typically made by large multi-national firms, involve highly differentiated products (either high-technology or highly advertised), which may lead to greater difficulty in meeting the comparability test of the CUP method; such products are most likely to be unrepresented in open-market transactions. Similarly, finding an applicable resale price for the RP methods may be especially difficult even when the value-added by foreign subsidiaries is not substantial (as in the case of simple sales or warehousing subsidiaries) since handling a specialized product usually entails specialized support services which are also not easily priced on the open-market.

IV. Correspondence Between Transfer Pricing Method Used and Firm and Industry Characteristics

The transfer pricing literature implies much about the nature of firms and/or industries that is likely to give rise to the use, or non-use, of market-based intra-corporate pricing. From our analysis of MKT variance, we have already concluded that firm differences are likely to be much more important than industry differences in that decision. Hence, in this section we will examine some of the features of firms and, to a lesser degree, industries that are likely to influence internal pricing decisions in favour of, or against, market transfer pricing for our foreign-transfer group. We will then use regression analysis to measure the statistical significance of implied relationships.

Where no conflicts exist between managers heading different divisional units, the profit-maximizing multi-divisional firm with perfect information, centralized decision making and adequate computer facilities, will essentially price its internal transfers of goods and services at marginal cost (Hirshleifer, 1956). Where perfectly competitive outside markets exist for all intermediate and final goods produced by the firm, marginal cost will be equated with market price. However, many of these conditions do not always hold, and the method of pricing of transfers becomes a decision variable.

First, where the market for the transferred good is *not*

perfectly competitive, market prices are less likely to be used for internal transfers. Market price exceeds marginal cost for monopolistic firms; and hence a market transfer price would result in a suboptimal allocation of the firm's resources. In addition, even when the monopolistic firm is faced with other pressures to use market prices (e.g. from divisional managers, or national tax authorities) establishing such a price may prove difficult. For instance, a monopolistic advantage based on product differentiation, technological know-how or vertical integration advantages, is not likely to produce situations where either 'comparable' products or sufficient outside market activity exist to establish a reliable open-market price (Rugman, 1981). These same set of circumstances can, of course, also afford firms an easy cover for hiding actual profits.

Secondly, government interventions may also encourage the firm to not use market-based pricing. The optimal internal transfer price may become altered by effective corporate income tax differentials, tariff rate differentials, and a variety of other regional or national policies which can alter the ability of firms to realize actual profit earned in a particular location. The profit-maximizing response to these measures may be either to underprice or overprice internal transfers to minimize costs of government interferences (Horst, 1971).

Finally, the larger the organization and the more diversified its product markets, the more likely it is firms will move towards market-pricing, despite any monopolistic advantages, for the following reasons: (1) they are more visible to government authorities who do routine audits, and hence market-pricing becomes a safer alternative; (2) they face greater difficulties in reconciling managerial objectives where they conflict with overall corporate profit-maximizing goals, and hence it is likely that market-pricing will be more acceptable to various divisional managers as, at least, a 'fair' indication of their division's performance; and (3) the administrative costs of keeping 'two sets' of accounting books are too great (Caves, 1982).

Taking these forces into account, and acknowledging two specifics with regard to this case — namely, the USA is generally considered a high-tax area, *and* use of market-based pricing by our sample firms generally resulted in the highest profits for internal transfers *out* of the USA[16] — we would predict that companies priced a smaller percentage of their LB transfers *out* of the United States at market prices when: (1) the firm had monopolistic advantages (such as those stemming from technological advances and/or product differentiation); (2) the firm operated in a concentrated and/or vertically integrated industry; (3) the firm had substantial incentives to minimize the effect of government interventions. These incentives may be indicated by any one of a number of circumstances, for example, (i) a large absolute value of foreign intra-corporate transfers, which indicate the extent to which profit flows could be altered by government policies, in particular, by US tax policies; (ii) a large number of distinctly different countries where the firm has foreign affiliates, potentially giving rise to greater government interferences as well as greater opportunities to shuffle profits; and (iii) whether or not the firm has a foreign subsidiary located in a 'tax haven' country, giving it a convenient mechanism to minimize global taxes.

Features which would encourage firms to price a greater percentage of their foreign transfers at market price include: the amount of foreign intra-corporate transfers made to branch affiliates as an indication of the inability to escape high US taxes;[17] the fraction of its foreign affiliates located in less developed countries (LDCs) which may indicate the extent to which its profits are exposed to national instabilities (e.g. foreign exchange controls, nationalizations, profit-remittance policies, etc.); a large corporate size (both in terms of domestic headquarters and number of foreign affiliates controlled by the parent); and the number of different product lines the firm handles.

To test these relationships we used our sample of 674 LB observations in the foreign-transfers group and ran multiple regressions on the MKT variable using both ordinary least squares (OLS) and maximum likelihood estimation (MLE) procedures. The MLE regressions were run to correct for any biases that may occur using OLS when the dependent variable is limited in range — in this instance, from 0 per cent to 100 per cent. Very similar results were obtained using both methods.

The linear equation estimated is:

$$\begin{aligned} MKT = a_0 &+ a_1 RD + A_2 ADV + a_3 CR4 + \\ &a_4 FVI + a_5 LBFS + a_6(LBFS*BRANCH) + \\ &a_7 COUNTRY + a_8 LDC + a_9 HAVEN + \\ &a_{10} SIZE + a_{11} DIV + a_{12} SUBY + e, \end{aligned}$$

where the dependent variable is:

MKT: the percentage of a firm's transfers to its foreign section which were priced at 'market' for each LB in which it operated in 1975 ($0\% \leqslant$ MKT $\leqslant 100\%$),

and where the independent variables are:

RD: Company R&D Intensity — the ratio of private, domestic applied research and development expenditures by a firm (across all its manufacturing LBs) to its total domestic revenues in those LBs, for 1975

ADV: is Company Advertising Intensity — the ratio of domestic expenditures on media advertising by a firm (across all its manufacturing LBs) to its total domestic revenues in those LBs, for 1975

CR4: the Four-Firm Industry Concentration Ratio, for 1972, using Weiss-Pascoe adjusted series (Weiss and Pascoe, 1980)

FVI: Ravenscraft's Domestic Forward Vertical Integration Measure, calculated at the industry level — weighted average of a firm's ratio of transfers out of one domestic LB to another domestic LB *to* revenues of the transferring LB[18]

LBFS: Magnitude of Company Foreign Transfers Out — summation of a firm's transfers from all its manufacturing LBs to its foreign section ($ billion), for 1975

(LBFS*BRANCH): Foreign Branch Activity — interaction between BRANCH, a dummy variable which takes a value of 'one' when a firm's 1975 SEC 10-K form showed no foreign subsidiaries listed, and COLBFS (i.e. at the same time foreign transfers out of the USA existed)

COUNTRY: Company Country Locations — the number of unique foreign countries in which a firm had majority-owned subsidiaries listed on their 1975 SEC 10-K form

LDC: Company LDC Intensity — ratio of number of foreign subsidiaries listed on a firm's SEC 10-K form in 1975 located in LDCs[19] *to* the total number of foreign subsidiaries listed in that same source

HAVEN: the Tax Haven Dummy — takes a value of 'one' where a firm has listed at least one foreign subsidiary in a 'tax haven' country on its 1975 SEC 10-K form[20]

SIZE: Domestic Company Size — total domestic revenues for a firm in its manufacturing LBs ($ billion) for 1975

DIV: Domestic Company Product Diversification — the number of manufacturing LBs a firm has listed on its FTC form in 1975

SUBY: Foreign Subsidiary Number — the number of majority-owned, foreign subsidiaries the firm has listed on its 1975 SEC 10-K form

It is expected that:

$$a_1, a_2, a_3, a_4, a_5, a_7, a_9 < 0$$

and

$$a_6, a_8, a_{10}, a_{11}, a_{12} > 0.$$

Regression results are presented in Table 10.5. They generally support the hypotheses although there are some notable contradictions. Among the imperfect competition variables, only a firm's advertising intensity (used as an indication of product differentiation advantages) is strongly related to the use of non-market pricing alternatives. The R&D intensity variable is suprisingly insignificant.[21] The other two market imperfection variables — CR4 and FVI — are both statistically insignificant as well; the behaviour of these variables, however, is consistent with our earlier findings that industry-level effects are not an important component of market-pricing variation (see Table 10.4).

The second set of variables, intended to reflect various aspects of effects of government interferences at the international level (e.g. tax, tariff, foreign exchange controls, etc.) reveal some interesting patterns. As expected, the larger the volume of a firm's intra-corporate exports, *ceteris paribus*, the greater the tendency for it to use non-market pricing. Once the

Table 10.5: Regression Results For MKT Variable

Independent Variable	OLS		MLE	
	Est. Coeff.	t-value	Est. Coeff.	t-value
Constant	27.10	4.61[d]	−45.13	−2.43[c]
RD	−44.01	−0.55	83.28	0.33
ADV	−299.92	−4.57[d]	−1,295.95	−4.68[d]
CR4	−3.96	−0.41	−15.98	−0.52
FVI	30.25	0.92	69.44	0.70
LBFS	−39.54	−3.08[d]	−176.95	−3.07[d]
LBFS* BRANCH	124.24	3.35[d]	244.51	2.46[c]
COUNTRY	−0.63	−1.08	−1.93	−1.74[a]
LDC	1.36	0.12	7.69	0.23
HAVEN	5.34	1.23	26.97	1.91[a]
SIZE	3.50	2.80[d]	15.53	3.49[d]
SUBY	0.27	2.37[c]	0.69	1.96[b]
DIV	−0.23	−0.93	−0.73	−0.96
# obs.	674		674	
R^2	0.0774			
F	4.62[d]			

a. Statistically significant at 0.10 level
b. Statistically significant at 0.05 level
c. Statistically significant at 0.02 level
d. Statistically significant at 0.01 level.

COUNTRY and LDC variables are taken into account to reflect the firm's exposure to both numbers of different national policies, and proportion affiliate activity in potentially less stable (economic or otherwise) nations, respectively, the remaining variables — LBFS, LBFS*BRANCH and HAVEN — should more specifically, reflect the effects of tax and/or tariff policies. Since our analysis of variance suggested inter-industry effects are not important, we might further conclude the tariff effect is minimal, insomuch as tariffs are usually industry-specific levies. This leaves us to explain the LBFS, LBFS*BRANCH and HAVEN variables exclusively from a tax standpoint. Hence, it would appear that the negative coefficient on the LBFS variable, which is statistically significant at the 0.01 per cent level, suggests that firms with large volumes of intracorporate exports try to avoid market-based pricing to shift profits out of the high-tax US area. Further supporting our tax interpretation of the LBFS variable, is the sign and significance of the interaction of this variable with BRANCH. Where firms have their foreign investments completely in the form of branches rather than subsidiaries (such that the US tax deferral does not apply and, therefore, branch income is taxed as it is earned), larger volumes of intra-corporate exports tend to be significantly related to the use of market-based pricing — indicating no benefits to shifting profits out of the USA. The behaviour of the HAVEN variable, however, fully contradicts our expectations. Where firms have at least one subsidiary located in a 'tax haven' country, transfer prices of intra-corporate exports tend to be market-based rather than not. It may be that the proposed and eventual tightening of the restrictions on use of tax havens in the US Tax Reduction Act of 1975[22] made US-based corporations with 'tax haven' subsidiaries especially careful of their pricing behaviour. The COUNTRY variable behaves as expected; firms operating in more foreign countries appeared significantly to avoid the market-pricing method. However, the LDC variable reveals no statistically significant patterns whatsoever.[23]

The final set of variables, which were intended to reflect organizational factors, reveal somewhat mixed findings. As we expected, the domestic firm-size variable, SIZE, and the foreign firm-size variable, SUBY, are both statistically significant and positively related to the MKT variable in the OLS and MLE regressions. However, the final organizational variable, DIV, is negative, but statistically insignificant, in both regression equations. Hence, product diversification does not tend to lead firms to use market pricing, once other features of the firm are accounted for.

V. Conclusions

In terms of money flows, it would appear that domestic and foreign intra-corporate transfers are roughly equal in overall magnitude in US manufacturing industries. However, as many have suspected but never documented, foreign transfers are potentially much more problematic for government officials insomuch as they are more frequently priced on a non-market basis. Even in the United States, where foreign transfer practices are regulated, there is a substantial amount of pricing flexibility permitted and actually adopted. US multinationals appear to have difficulties in meeting the standards of the preferred pricing methods (namely, CUP and RP) outlined by US Treasury officials.

An especially interesting finding in this study came from an examination of variations in pricing behaviour of firms as they operate across different industries. As much as 65 per cent to 85 per cent of variations in use of market-pricing originated with firm-to-firm differences and, at most, 4 per cent to 7 per cent originated with industry-to-industry differences. By itself, this finding strongly implies that tariff policy, which is usually an industry-related phenomenon, is *not* likely to be an important factor in the pricing of foreign intra-corporate transfers. This contradicts conclusions drawn by Horst (1971), as well as those who have claimed 'mutually-offsetting' effects from tariffs and taxes in the transfer pricing decision (Mathewson and Quirin, 1979, p. 87).

In our regression analysis firm characteristics found to be strongly related to non-market pricing behaviour (once other factors were taken into account) include: advertising intensity, volume of foreign transfers and number of different countries where firms operate. The first characteristic suggests that market imperfections based on product differentiation make it inefficient as well as difficult for firms to use open-market prices. The latter two factors suggest (once firm-size and number of foreign subsidiaries are taken into account) government interferences, perhaps most notably in the tax policy area, induce firms to underprice foreign transfers (except when investments are in branch form). On the other hand, large corporations and those with a large number of foreign subsidiaries tend to be strongly associated with market-based pricing, perhaps because of their greater visibility to government tax officials, their greater propensity to have difficulties with conflicting management objectives and/or their greater administrative costs in keeping 'two sets' of accounting books.

Notes

The representations and conclusions presented herein are those of the author and have not been adopted in whole or in part by the Federal Trade Commission or its Bureau of Economics. The Manager of the Line of Business Program has certified that he has reviewed and approved the disclosure avoidance procedures used by the staff of the Line of Business Program to ensure that the data included in this paper do not identify individual company line of business data.

The author is very much indebted to Joseph Cholka and William Long for their programming assistance. The paper has also benefited from comments by Tom Horst, John Kwoka, William Long, David Ravenscraft and participants at the conference, in particular Lorraine Eden, Bruce Kogut and Don Lecraw.

    1. See Business International (1965), Greene and Duerr (1970), Arpan (1972a,b), and Tang (1979).

    2. For a complete description of the sample selection process, see US Federal Trade Commission, *Statistical Report: Annual Line of Business Report, 1974*, Bureau of Economics, September 1981, pp. 340-1.

    3. Lines of business where the firm has less than $10 million in revenues are grouped together in a 99.99 category.

    4. See Appendix D of US Federal Trade Commission's 1975 report for a listing of the FTC categories and corresponding SICs.

    5. Non-manufacturing activities include: agricultural production and services, forestry and fishing, mining, oil and gas extraction, construction, transportation and public utilities, wholesale trade, retail trade, finance, insurance, real estate, and services.

    6. The DRS section essentially includes all the firm's activities which are regulated in some important respect by the US government: i.e. banking, finance, insurance and any other activity for which the firm is required to file an annual financial statement with a US regulatory commission. The FS section covers all the firm's foreign entities (corporate and non-corporate), foreign branches and domestic corporations primarily engaged in foreign operations, when the parent has at least 51 per cent ownership in each.

    7. US Department of Commerce, Bureau of Census, *U.S. Commodity Exports and Imports as Related to Output 1976 & 1975*, issued November 1979.

    8. On p. 183, Lall estimates that 35.1 per cent of total US manufacturing exports were exports to foreign (majority-owned) affiliates.

    9. Marginal cost pricing, while a theoretically important concept, is generally not used by corporate accountants who prerpare forms for the FTC.

    10. In every pairwise comparison, the hypothesis that the variances are equal was rejected at the 5 per cent level using F-tests. Hence, mean-difference tests do not assume homogeneous variances; and t-statistics and degrees of freedom are 'estimated' using separate sample variances.

    11. The 'other' category had a positive value for 38 LBs in the foreign-transfers group and 49 LBs in the domestic-transfers group. The total number of companies involved were 15 and 24, respectively, suggesting roughly comparable company-concentration in the use of Other methods for both types of transfers.

    12. Industry categories here are at approximately the 2-digit SIC level.

    13. These industry rankings do not include any industries where data could not be provided for disclosure reasons.

    14. See Reg. 1.482-2(e) for conditions needed to meet the standards of each pricing method.

    15. It can be argued that this assumption is realistic. IRS is the only other US government agency requiring any documentation of transfer pricing, if only for audit purposes. Hence, in the interest of minimizing reporting costs, firms are likely to have offered the same information to both FTC and IRS.

    16. After taking into account traditional industrial organization variables, Ravenscraft (1981) estimated that sample firms' profits were, on average, 4.8 per

cent, 5.8 per cent and 17.2 per cent lower using 'cost-plus', 'cost' and 'other' transfer pricing methods, respectively, compared to using 'market' pricing.

17. Branch forms of foreign direct investment do not benefit from the 'deferral' feature of the US tax system; hence, it is not possible to take advantage of any lower foreign tax rates.

18. See Ravenscraft (1982), pp. 7-8, where the measure is described as 'a measure of the degree to which a firm substitutes through vertical forward integration internal control for market exchange'.

19. We define an LDC country as one which appeared among the World Bank's 1976 list of 'low income countries' or 'middle income countries', as well as those listed among 'capital surplus oil exporters' or 'centrally planned economies' when 1976 *per capita* GNP fell below $6,200. See The World Bank, *World Development Report, 1978*, Table 1: Basic Indicators, pp. 76-7.

20. Included among 'tax haven' areas were: Bahamas, Bermuda, Cayman Islands, Netherlands and Netherlands Antilles, Panama, Costa Rica, Bahrain, Hong Kong, Luxembourg, Singapore, Switzerland, Liberia, Lichenstein, Barbados, Cyprus and Virgin Islands. All but the three final areas were identified in a study by the US Treasury Department: *Estimates of Level of Tax Haven Use*, Report to Assistant Secretary (Tax Policy), Assistant Attorney General (Tax Division), and Commissioner of Internal Revenue Service, Tax Haven Study Group, May 1981, Table 5, p. 32.

21. Estimates of the RD coefficient may be unreliable because of a possible multicollinearity problem; the simple correlation coefficient between RD and COUNTRY is 0.37.

22. The US Tax Reduction Act of 1975 lowered the acceptable level of 'passive' income permitted a foreign subsidiary before deferral privileges would be partially or completely withdrawn.

23. Multicollinearity may also be the source of this insignificant relationship. Simple correlation coefficients between the LDC variable and the COUNTRY, HAVEN and SIZE variables are, respectively, 0.54, 0.33 and 0.40.

11 A COMPARISON OF IMPORT PRICING BY FOREIGN AND DOMESTIC FIRMS IN BRAZIL

Paul A. Natke

Introduction

One recent development in the analysis of multinational enterprises (MNE) focuses attention on their ability to overcome market imperfections through the internalization of transactions. This allows MNEs to set the prices on intra-firm transactions and, theoretically, to maximize global profits. Incentives to alter transfer prices arise from market imperfections caused by government regulations or 'natural' externalities in the transfer of knowledge and information. Government regulations have received the greatest attention in the literature on transfer pricing: Aliber (this volume), Bond (1980), Booth and Jensen (1977), Brean (1979a), Copithorne (1971), Diewert (this volume), Eden (this volume), Horst (1971), Plasschaert (1979, this volume), Rugman (1981) and UNCTAD (1978b). These market imperfections include tariffs, profit repatriation, tax rate differentials, exchange controls, intervention in currency markets, multiple exchange rates, price controls, investment barriers and perceived political instability.

Corporate policy may also influence the setting of transfer prices and which subsidiaries' profits are affected (Vaitsos, 1974). Corporations might be inclined to declare their returns in nations where their affiliates have high expenditure requirements relative to their inter-firm sales; where the declaration of returns will not likely be reported (Arpan, 1972b; Lall, 1973; UNCTAD, 1978b); or where a subsidiary might require access to non-company funds.

However, altering transfer prices on commodities is only one method MNEs could use to move funds among their subsidiary operations (Brean this volume; Vaitsos, 1974). Direct inter-company loans, purchases or sale of equity, royalty fees for the use of licensed technology or branded products (Kopits, 1976a), contributions towards overhead costs such as research and

212

development (Lall, 1978a) and specific fees related to management consultation also affect the global distribution of funds
within the MNE.

These alternative methods of moving funds highlight a major
problem in the analysis of transfer pricing: separating those intra-
firm transactions which can be valued in external markets from
those which are purely internal to the firm. If an external market
does not exist there is no consensus on how to value the
transaction (Quirin, this volume; Business International 1983).
Transfers of intangibles such as information and management
skills fall into this category. For tangible goods, it is possible,
with varying degrees of precision, to compare prices paid on
intra-firm transactions with those paid between unrelated firms.

Some analysts argue that it is meaningless to examine transfer
prices on their own or to attempt to compare them to non-
existent arm's-length prices (Rugman, 1981). Instead, consumers
and governments should concern themselves with the firm's
performance in producing goods and services. This efficiency
issue can best be addressed by examining the overall profits of
MNEs. If transfer prices are set at inefficient levels, the firm may
earn lower profits and be forced into bankruptcy by its
competitors.

Policy makers, however, concern themselves not with the
long-run impacts of efficiency but with the short-run distributional consequences of transfer pricing. Government revenue can
be adversely affected if transfer pricing alters invoice prices on
imports or exports and affects reported profits. When profits are
understated, local stockholders receive lower dividends and
workers may moderate wage demands. Consumers might lose by
paying higher prices particularly if MNEs are able to increase the
level of tariff protection. Other producers could be hurt if
transfer pricing behaviour reduces the earning of foreign
exchange and causes a shortage of essential imports. Finally, an
international redistribution of income may occur if funds are
transferred from developing countries to developed nations
through transfer pricing practices.

Transfer pricing may have long-run effects which alter the
pattern of economic development. Two studies suggest that
transfer pricing behaviour may be partially responsible for
lowering the profits earned by MNE subsidiaries below that of
their Brazilian competitors (Mooney, 1982; Newfarmer and

Marsh, 1984). Low profit levels reported by MNEs could discourage domestic investment in industries dominated by MNEs, reduce local competition, increase the prices paid by consumers and perpetuate dependence on MNE activities. If MNEs declare low profits and are effective in arguing for increased trade protection, domestic investment in inefficient industries, or those not dominated by MNEs, will be encouraged.

Brazil is appropriate for this analysis for several reasons. First, the Brazilian government has actively encouraged foreign direct investment as a part of its import-substitution development policy. Another reason is the importance of trade in the Brazilian economy: it ranked 13th and 15th in the world as an importer and exporter respectively, in 1977. Third, Brazil's status as an emerging economic power in the Third World and its reliance on a capitalistic method of development make it a model for other developing nations.

The major reason for studying Brazil, however, is the existence of prominent market imperfections caused by government regulation. There are five major, and sometimes conflicting, influences on transfer pricing behaviour. Government price control may have encouraged the overpricing of intermediate good imports so that MNEs could argue that rising costs of production entitled them to price increases. Similarly, limits on the official repatriation of profits and a desire to reduce profits taxes are incentives to overprice imports. On the other hand, a desire to reduce tariff payments and avoid credit control should have encouraged MNEs to underprice imported goods in those industries where tariffs were not already prohibitive (e.g. most consumer goods).

Methodology and Data

Data on imports were collected for 141 manufacturing firms, both privately-owned domestic firms and MNEs, operating in Brazil during 1979. Two measures of import pricing are used. TPRICE is a unit price per kilo of weight. The TPRICE which Brazilian firms pay are assumed to reflect world market prices while the TPRICE for MNEs are likely to be transfer prices on intra-firm trade.[1] These assumptions are used to calculate an index price INDEX which compares actual prices paid on imports to a proxy for those available on world markets. INDEX is the ratio of TPRICE to the mean Brazilian TPRICE for the product category expressed as a percentage.

It is important to note that these variables deviate in several ways from an ideal measure of transaction prices. First, the basic measure (TPRICE) is not a true unit price but is an average over the course of the year. This measure should exhibit stability since it irons out short-term fluctuations. Second, differences in unit prices across firms may be due to quality differences rather than price manipulation by MNEs. These differences are limited by the narrow definition of products (eight-digit code) and by careful sampling procedures. Third, the unit price is a price per unit of weight. This may be misleading for intermediate goods which are sold by piece rather than weight and whose composition may vary due to substitution (e.g. cast iron, steel and aluminium). Above all, neither the quality nor non-competing sub-product differences would appear to exert a systematic bias up or down on prices by ownership group.

The sample was restricted to firms operating in 18 industries (four-digit level) as defined by Brazil's Ministry of Finance. All sample industries include several of the leading firms as defined by market share. Additional criteria limited the number of products chosen for study. Product categories which were too general to control for quality differences (e.g. 'all other pumps') and most capital goods were excluded. Capital goods are often highly differentiated to fit the needs of unique production processes and relatively minor modifications may result in large price differences.

These criteria resulted in the selection of 127 product categories at the eight-digit level of the Brazilian trade codes. A few outlying observations were discarded. An observation whose price was $2\frac{1}{2}$ times greater or smaller than the mean price for the category was discarded. There were 29 such observations: 20 representing MNE transactions and nine those of Brazilian firms. There are 975 observations in the final sample of which 644 represent MNE prices and 331 those of Brazilian firms.

The basic hypothesis is that import prices paid by MNEs will be higher than those of Brazilian firms for the same products because of transfer pricing behaviour. Two factors bias the predicted relationship downwards. First, some limited portion of MNE trade is not intra-firm so the transaction price may be the price paid on the open market. Earlier studies have shown, however, that a high proportion of subsidiary trade comes from the parent organization.[2] Second, the transfer price may be understated to achieve goals other than transfering funds abroad.

For similar reasons, the import prices of MNEs should exhibit greater variability. If some MNEs consistently overprice imports while others underprice imports the variance of MNE prices should be higher than Brazilian firms which pay, in theory, the competitive world market price.

The existence and strength of market imperfections should also influence the degree of transfer price manipulation. If the market imperfection is exogenous to the firm the MNE should react by internalizing the market transaction. As the level of intra-firm trade (market imperfections) rises, transfer prices should exhibit greater variation for two reasons. First, price alterations are more difficult for governments to detect when there are fewer external market transactions as appropriate arm's-length prices are harder to determine. Secondly, if the imperfections can be influenced by MNEs themselves (endogenous) these firms may enhance their profitability by manipulation of transfer prices.

In summary, the major hypotheses are: (1) MNEs pay higher import prices than Brazilian-owned firms; (2) MNEs exhibit greater variability of import prices in accordance with their internal financial requirements; and (3) the degree of transfer price variation is positively related to the degree of market imperfection.

Empirical Results

A direct comparison of mean import prices across ownership groups for each product category in the sample reveals some overpricing by MNEs. The mean price of MNEs was greater in 76 of the 127 product categories (60 per cent of the sample), Brazilian firms paid higher prices for 47 products (37 per cent), and in four product categories (3 per cent) the prices paid by both ownership groups were identical.

However, these comparisons may be misleading since over half of the product categories had only one firm in either of the ownership groups. For these products, the comparison of means is essentially a comparison of the mean price for a number of firms in one ownership group with one firm's price in the other ownership group. Another sample was selected by eliminating all product categories which had only one MNE or Brazilian firm. This resulted in a sample of 611 observations over 48 product categories. To help identify if there was any bias in the sampling procedure, a third sample was selected which included only those products with a minimum of three observations in each ownership group. This sample consists of 439 observations spread over 26 products.

A direct comparison of mean import prices in these samples yielded similar results as the full sample: MNEs paid higher prices than Brazilian firms in 67 per cent (65 per cent) of the product categories and lower prices in the remainder (33 and 35 per cent) of the 48-product and 26-product samples respectively. Only 12 price differentials in the 48-product sample and six in the 26-product sample are statistically significant at the 10 per cent level.

A simple comparison of prices in each product line may not reveal an underlying statistically significant relationship which would appear when the sample is considered as a whole. This is appropriately tested through a differences of means test applied to all products in the sample using an index to produce an unweighted, standardized average.

The average price paid by Brazilian firms in each product category was taken as the base for the transaction price index. It was calculated as $INDEX = (TPRICE_{ij}/mean\ Brazilian\ TPRICE_i) \times 100$ where the subscript 'i' refers to each product category and 'j' refers to each firm. The meaning of the index number is clear — a value of 150 would indicate that the price paid on that transaction was 50 per cent greater than the average price paid by Brazilian firms for the same product. The strength of the index lies in allowing direct comparisons across products, aggregation, and measuring the degree of over- and underpricing.

A paired means test was performed for each of the three samples. In these tests, the mean index price for Brazilian firms and MNEs for each product category are aggregated and tested. The test results will indicate whether MNEs in aggregate pay higher or lower prices than domestic firms on imported goods.

The results, presented in Table 11.1, reveal that for all samples MNEs paid higher prices than Brazilian firms with the degree of overpricing ranging from a high of 39 per cent in the full sample to 21 per cent in the narrow sample. The paired mean differences tests for the two largest samples are significant at the 10 per cent level.

Table 11.1: Comparison of Mean Index Prices by Ownership Group

Ownership Group	N	Mean	Standard Deviation	t-statistic	Probability of Equal Means
Full sample[1]					
MNE	643	138.68	232.22	3.90	0.0001
Brazilian	332	100.00	38.69		
Middle sample[2]					
MNE	379	132.20	259.64	2.36	0.019
Brazilian	232	100.00	44.81		
Narrow sample[3]					
MNE	265	121.23	296.34	1.14	0.254
Brazilian	174	100.00	48.55		

Notes:
1. All observations (127 products).
2. A minimum of two observations in each ownership group (MNE or Brazilian) for each product category (48 products).
3. A minimum of three observations in each ownership group (MNE or Brazilian) for each product category (26 products).

These results, however, could also be explained by considerations other than price manipulation. MNEs may pay higher prices than Brazilian firms because they import higher quality goods. Alternatively, MNEs may sell premium products at premium prices both to their subsidiaries and non-affiliated firms while Brazilian firms are more likely to shop around to find the lowest price. Additional support for the non-manipulation hypothesis comes from the data. The INDEX price means for MNEs and Brazilian firms in the narrow sample are not significantly different. Possible explanations for this are that MNEs under- and overprice imports, there are problems in the sampling process, or there is no systematic overpricing by MNEs.

The prices paid by MNEs, however, also exhibited greater variability. When import prices were tested for equality of variances within product categories, MNEs were more likely to have greater variances in all samples. In the middle sample (48 products), the variance of MNE prices was significantly greater (10 per cent level) in eight product categories while for only three products was the variance of Brazilian firm prices greater. In 77 per cent of the product categories there was no significant difference in variances. The narrow sample produced similar results: MNE price variances were greater in six products and lower in two while 69 per cent exhibited no difference.

The use of INDEX prices allows a test of equality of variances across all product groups in Table 11.2. MNE prices exhibit greater variability than Brazilian firms in all samples which suggests that MNEs under- or overprice their imports. All tests are highly significant.

Table 11.2: Test of Equality of Variances Across Ownership Groups

Ownership Group	Mean	Variance	F-statistic	Probability of F
Full sample[1]				
MNE	138.68	53,923.62	794.93	0.0001
Brazilian	100.00	1,497.09		
Middle sample[2]				
MNE	132.30	67,411.89	531.58	0.0001
Brazilian	100.00	2,007.79		
Narrow sample[3]				
MNE	121.23	87,818.46	412.62	0.0001
Brazilian	100.00	2,356.80		

Notes:
1. All observations (127 products).
2. A minimum of two observations in each ownership group (MNE or Brazilian) for each product category (48 products).
3. A minimum of three observations in each ownership group (MNE or Brazilian) for each product category (26 products).

If MNEs are faced with market imperfections their efficient response is to internalize trade transactions. They may then manipulate transfer prices to redistribute the gains from increased efficiency. The exact nature of this linkage between prices and measures of imperfection in empirical work is not fully developed. Several alternative regression models have attempted to describe this linkage but with little success. A regression of the independent variables, tariffs, market concentration, a crude

proxy for intra-firm trade, and a variable reflecting the importance of MNEs in the Brazilian market, against the dependent
variable INDEX yielded poor results. The goodness of fit
measures and the individual coefficients were generally insignificant.

Several reasons for this result can be offered. There may be
considerable variation in quality within the eight-digit product
categories. Another factor may be the choice of independent
variables with low variances across products. Many of these
represent industry characteristics rather than firm characteristics.
At a more fundamental level, the variables chosen may be
inappropriate proxies for market imperfections or the model may
not accurately represent the economic theory.

Future work in this area might further delineate the influence
of firm characteristics (e.g. corporate organization, R&D expenditures) and those of industries (e.g. market concentration and
industry advertising) on transfer pricing behaviour. Lecraw (this
volume) and Benvignati (this volume) have made valuable
contributions in this direction.

Summary and Conclusions

The empirical work showed that, in the aggregate, MNEs paid
higher prices on imports than Brazilian firms. This is born out in
the comparison of raw prices within each category as the mean
MNE price was higher than the mean Brazilian price in 60 per
cent of the 127 product categories. For an aggregate analysis
across all product categories, a set of indexed prices was
computed using the mean Brazilian price as the base. With this
set of indexed prices, MNEs paid higher import prices in all
samples used and the degree of overpricing was significant at the
2 per cent level in two samples. The extent of overpricing ranged
from 21 to 39 per cent.

MNE prices were not only higher on average but they also
exhibited greater variability. In those product categories where a
test of equal variances was possible, MNE prices were more than
twice as likely to have greater variances than domestic firms. This
result held for both samples and the raw and indexed prices. A
test of equality of variances also showed MNE prices were more
variable at the 1 per cent level of significance for all samples.

This result supports the hypothesis that MNEs set transfer prices in accordance with their internal financial requirements. Other explanations are possible. Different management control systems imply different transfer pricing policies by MNEs, for example cost-plus and market prices (Lecraw, this volume, and Benvignati, this volume). Costs may vary in the home nations which leads to different market prices for MNEs. Also, MNEs may import goods with greater quality variation within each product category.

Despite the alternative explanations for the empirical results (both overpricing and variability), the extent of the MNE overpricing may be understated for two reasons. First, all highly differentiated goods were ignored because the price differential across firms may be due to differentiation (quality) or different pricing policies. However, manipulation is more likely to be practised using these differentiated products because it is more difficult to detect. The second explanation assumes that MNEs do manipulate prices on imports but not in a consistent direction. Some firms may overprice imports while others may underprice.

The conclusions reached in this study support other research on transfer pricing behaviour. At least three other studies have used a sample of firms and directly compared import prices paid by MNEs with prices found on world markets (Lall, 1973; UNCTAD, 1978a; Vaitsos, 1974). Each found the overpricing on individual products ranged from 19 to 300 per cent. The greatest overpricing by MNEs was found in the pharmaceutical industry where assumptions regarding the allocation of R&D expenditures are crucial to the conclusions.

The appropriateness of using the arm's-length criterion is crucial in assessing the strength of the conclusions. Government customs and tax officials, without access to full information available to corporate executives, must make their decisions based on the prices they see. Market prices provide information about opportunity costs associated with government decisions on importing, domestic production and development. From the viewpoint of society, the world market prices paid by domestic firms are the efficient prices, not those set by MNEs to maximize firm efficiency (global profits). Furthermore, governments in developing nations are keenly aware of the potential redistribution impact of transfer pricing behaviour and may choose to act on that basis alone.

Notes

1. Earlier studies have estimated the extent of intra-firm trade. Helleiner (1981) estimated that intra-firm trade accounts for 25-33 per cent of all international trade. Helleiner and Lavergne (1979) noted that 54 per cent of manufactured goods imported to the United States in 1977 were intra-firm transactions. Newfarmer and Mueller (1975) estimated from a sample of 197 MNEs in Brazil that 74 per cent of their exports were with firms related by ownership.

2. See note 1 for estimates of the extent of intra-firm trade among all nations, US trade and a sample of MNEs in Brazil.

12 SOME EVIDENCE ON TRANSFER PRICING BY MULTINATIONAL CORPORATIONS

Donald J. Lecraw

Transfer pricing by multinational enterprises (MNEs) has received considerable attention from academics, host-country governments and international organizations. This research has taken essentially four forms: (1) theoretical analyses of the conditions under which MNEs might find it to their advantage to charge transfer prices that do not reflect market, arm's-length prices (Mathewson and Quirin, 1979, Chapters 4-6; Abdel-Khalik and Lusk, 1974); (2) studies that focus on the transfer pricing practices of one or a small number of MNEs (Tang, 1979, 1980; Arpan, 1972a); (3) studies that use large-sample, often highly aggregate data to draw inferences on the extent of manipulation of transfer prices by MNEs (Vaitsos, 1974); and (4) studies that examine the implications of transfer pricing for management in accounting, marketing, finance, control, personnel evaluation, etc. (Barrett, 1977; Benke and Edwards, 1980; Finnie, 1978; and Merville and Petty, 1978). This paper helps to link the theoretical and the descriptive analyses of the determinants of the *level* at which MNEs set transfer prices. It uses data collected in 1978 on the import and export pricing practices of 111 MNEs that operated 153 subsidiaries in six light manufacturing industries in the five countries of the ASEAN region: Thailand, Malaysia, Singapore, Indonesia and the Philippines.[1] It uses these data to test hypotheses concerning the determinants of the transfer price policies and the extent by which non-market transfer prices differed from market-based prices for imports and exports by the MNEs in the sample.

Whenever an MNE engages in transactions across national boundaries between related units of the firm, the price at which the good or service is transferred may be set such that it does not equal the value that would prevail if the units were independent of each other, i.e. the market price for the good or service. Intra-firm sales of goods and services include exports and imports of final and intermediate products and capital equipment, licencing, technical service and management fees, and intra-firm loans or credit. An MNE determines the price at which a good or service was transferred between related units of the firm based on many factors: reductions of taxes at home or in one of the host countries in which it operates, reduction of tariff fees, allocation of funds from one unit of the firm to another, avoidance of import or export restrictions, meeting local value-added requirements, and reduction of profits accruing to joint-venture partners. In short MNEs determine transfer prices to maximize the risk-adjusted discounted profits accruing to the firm.[2]

The prices that firms set for intra-firm exports and imports across national boundaries are the subject of continual controversy between MNEs and the governments in the countries in which they operate — for three reasons. First, the prices of intra-firm exports and imports directly affect the impact of MNEs on host and home economies — tax and tariff payments, balance of payments, price levels, etc. — as well as affecting the profitability of MNEs and their ability to allocate resources within the firm. Both MNEs and governments have a high stake in the level at which transfer prices are set. Second, there is often considerable latitude between the transfer price that is optimal for the MNE, the price that is optimal for government, and the market price. Third, an arm's-length, competitive market price often does not exist for the product or service, and hence there is often no benchmark against which transfer prices can be evaluated.

The next section presents some data on the extent of intra-firm trade by the MNEs in the sample to serve as a background for the study and give an indication of the scope of the transfer pricing problem faced by the MNEs in the sample and the host countries in which they operated. Section III reviews the theory of the determinants of an MNE's transfer pricing strategy and Section IV tests the hypotheses that arise from this theory. Section V summarizes the results and draws some of their implications for host-country governments and MNEs.

II

The potential scope and latitude for an MNE to set transfer prices outside the market depends in part on the quantity of goods and services transferred between related units of the MNE across national boundaries. This study focuses on intra-firm exports and imports, often the most important component of intra-firm transfers. The extent of these exports and imports has a direct bearing on the importance of transfer pricing for the firms in the sample and the potential impact of nonmarket-based transfer prices on the host countries. A brief description of intra-firm trade of the firms in the sample is, therefore, useful.

All the countries in the ASEAN region have had policies to encourage firms to increase their exports of manufactured products. Until the mid-1970s, however, only Singapore had much success in its efforts. Prior to 1970, with the exception of Singapore, most of the foreign direct investment (FDI) in the manufacturing sector in the countries in the ASEAN region was made to serve the domestic market. The firms in the sample followed this pattern according to the data collected in 1978. In aggregate they exported only 7.1 per cent of their output

Table 12.1: Export and Import Intensities Normalized by Host Country and Industry (USA = 100)

Home Country	Exports	Imports
United States	100	100
Europe	80	125
Japan	39	235
LDC	13	74

Note: All data for all tables based on 1978 questionnaire.

Table 12.2: Export Destination by MNE Home Country

Export Destination (% of Exports)	MNE Home Country			
	USA	Europe	Japan	LDC
USA	63	21	47	62
Europe	21	54	32	15
Japan	10	11	14	12
LDC	6	14	7	11
	100	100	100	100

although there was a wide variation about this average depending on the MNE, the industry and the host country. Normalizing for industry and country effects, export intensities were highest for US-based MNEs, followed by European, Japanese and MNEs based in other LDCs (Table 12.1).[3] Table 12.2 displays the destination of exports by home-country group. In general, US- and Europe-based MNEs exported mostly to their home countries; Japan- and LDC-based MNEs tended to export to the United States and Europe rather than to their home-country markets. Per cent intra-firm exports were highest for Japanese MNEs and lowest for MNEs based in other LDCs (Table 12.4).

The imported inputs of the MNEs in the sample represented 40.8 per cent of their total inputs in their final products. Normalized import intensity was highest for Japanese MNEs and lowest for MNEs based in other LDCs (Table 12.1). All the MNEs in the sample tended to source their imported inputs in their home countries rather than from other countries. Japanese

Table 12.3: Import Source by MNE Home Country

Import Source (% of imports)	MNE Home Country			
	USA	Europe	Japan	LDC
USA	53	12	2	8
Europe	12	47	11	3
Japan	28	30	73	17
LDC	7	11	14	72
	100	100	100	100

Table 12.4: Per cent of Exports to and Imports from Related Units of the MNE

Home Country of the MNE	Exports	Imports
USA	68	53
Europe	65	57
Japan	79	84
LDC	23	37

MNEs tended to source most at home, US-based MNEs the least (Table 12.3). Japanese MNEs tended to source their imports from related units of their firm to a greater extent than did the other MNEs in the sample (Table 12.4). Charging nonmarket transfer prices on imported inputs and exports can only occur when these transactions are between units of the same MNE. Some MNEs in the sample internalized their import and export transactions even when the ultimate source or destination of the product was not related to them by routing the transaction through a wholly-owned sales subsidiary either in a third country or in the country of origin or destination. The extent of intra-firm exports and imports of the MNEs in the sample indicates that there was considerable scope for transfer pricing at nonmarket-based prices.

III

Several factors have been suggested in the literature that could influence the type and level of transfer prices used by MNEs between related units for their exports and imports.[4] The model of the MNE presented here is one of constrained optimization at the firm level. The MNE is viewed as optimizing firm-wide, risk-adjusted profits given its opportunity set and internal (managerial) and external constraints (Robbins and Stobaugh, 1974). In general, tax and tariff revenues that accrue to the governments of the host and home countries in which an MNE operates and profits which accrue to unrelated joint-venture partners reduce the profits of an MNE. All else equal, an MNE will determine transfer prices to minimize payments to those outside the firm. An MNE's latitude for determining transfer prices is constrained by the goals, power and expertise of the external agents which have a claim on its resources.

Ceteris paribus, as tariffs on imports increase in the host country, the MNE has an incentive to charge lower transfer prices on its imported inputs in order to reduce the amount of duty it pays. Similarly, as the tariffs facing an MNE's exports increase in the country of destination, it may lower its export prices to reduce tariff payments. The higher the profit taxes in the host country relative to the home country of the MNE, the greater is the incentive to reduce reported profits in the host country to avoid profit taxes. An MNE can reduce profits in the host country by increasing the transfer price of imported inputs and reducing the transfer price of exports.[5] An MNE may also use transfer prices to reduce the risk of its operations and increase its flexibility in moving funds from one country to another. A high perceived risk by the MNE for its operations in the host country might increase its propensity to transfer money out of the country via high prices for imported inputs and low export prices.[6] The existence of price controls in the local market might also affect transfer pricing policies. Regulatory agencies often control prices in an industry in relation to the costs and profits of firms in the industry. High prices for imported inputs would reduce profits and increase costs and could be used as a justification for increased prices. Reduced export prices would also lower profits reported in the host country. If the government imposed capital or profit repatriation restrictions on MNEs, these might be avoided by setting transfer prices at a low level for intra-firm exports or a high level for intra-firm imports.

Management control considerations may also influence the use of transfer prices that do not reflect market prices. If the MNE's accounting, control and reward system is decentralized by country, manipulation of transfer prices can wreak havoc with the evaluation, control and reward systems (Barrett, 1977; Petty and Walker, 1972; Robbins and Stobaugh, 1973b). In another article (Lecraw, 1983) a variable was constructed to measure the extent of the centralization of corporate control of the MNEs in the sample. This variable essentially measures the locus of control between the headquarters of the MNE and the subsidiary, i.e. whether control over a set of decision variables rests with the parent or with the subsidiary. An MNE's transfer pricing strategy may be influenced by the degree it centralizes control over decision making, evaluation and rewards. The US-based MNEs in the sample tended to be run on a more decentralized basis than the MNEs based in other home countries (especially Japanese MNEs), so, *ceteris paribus*, US-based MNEs might be expected to use transfer prices that approached market prices to a greater extent than did other MNEs, especially the more centralized Japanese MNEs, in the sample.

If an MNE's subsidiary in the host country is a joint venture with a partner outside the MNE's system, the latitude of its transfer price strategy may be limited. If profits in the host country are affected by its transfer price strategy and profits accruing to the joint venture are raised, the MNE will earn a lower return on its total operations; if profits in the host country are reduced, the MNE's local partner may object. The presence of a local partner might, therefore, increase the use of market-based transfer prices. On the other hand, the presence of a joint venture partner might motivate the MNE to set transfer prices to reduce reported profits in the subsidiary, profits which would partially accrue to the joint venture partner. The influence of a joint venture partner on transfer prices is uncertain.

Finally, in the ASEAN countries there have been charges from time to time that Japanese MNEs have a greater tendency to use nonmarket-based transfer prices to avoid host-country controls and as competitive weapons than do other MNEs. If this were true, then ownership (Japanese-other MNEs) would be a factor in explaining the use of nonmarket-based transfer prices.

IV

The potential influences on the transfer pricing strategy of MNEs described in the previous section have been well developed in the literature. The actual extent to which they influence transfer pricing strategy is not known, however, since data on transfer prices (compared to market price) are scarce. The unique feature of this study is that it uses data on actual prices and methods of determining transfer prices obtained from the MNEs in the sample to test the effects of these potential determinants of transfer pricing strategy. The data were obtained by the author in 1978 during structured interviews with several top managers of the 153 subsidiaries of the 111 MNEs in the sample in response to a questionnaire.

Tables 12.5 and 12.6 display the responses to questions concerning the pricing practices of the MNEs in the sample for imports and exports from the host country. Striking differences emerge in the pricing practices of the MNEs when selling to other units of the MNE (intra-firm sales) and to unrelated firms. Four pricing practices (at world market price, at the market price in the country of destination for exports from the host country, at the market price in the host country for imports into the host country and at full cost of production plus profit) might serve as

Table 12.5: Export Pricing Practices

Question: In general exports were priced:

Pricing Practices	Type of Buyer	
	Intra-firm	Unrelated Firm[a]
A. By the subsidiary at:		
1. World price	15	16
2. Price in country of destination	17	31
3. Price in host country (exporting country)	8	4
4. Full cost of production (plus profit)	17	12
B. At the direction of parent:	45	31
5. At prices in (1-4)	8	24
6. At another price than in (5)	44	7
Number of firms responding	82	94

Note: a. The numbers in the columns do not add to the number of exporting firms (82) due to multiple responses since the categories of pricing practices are not mutually exclusive.

Table 12.6: Import Pricing Practices

Question: In general, imports were priced:

Pricing Practices	Type of Seller	
	Intra-firm	Unrelated Firm[a]
A. By the subsidiary at:		
1. World price	20	67
2. Price in the host country (importing country)	8	28
3. Price in the source country (exporting country)	10	40
4. Full cost of production, plus profit	28	2
B. At the direction of the parent:	112	71
5. At price (1-4)	31	58
6. At another price	81	13
Total number of firms	142	152

Note: a. The numbers in these columns do not add to 130, the number of importing firms, due to multiple responses.

reasonable proxies for arm's-length prices.[7] Pricing at a price determined on another basis besides these four such as marginal cost pricing, penetration pricing, etc., would seem to reflect the use of nonmarket-based transfer prices. The data in Table 12.5 show that intra-firm exports tended to be at prices that were generally nonmarket based, while prices for transactions with unrelated firms were generally priced in relation to market prices or full costs.

Data on the pricing practices of the MNEs in the sample for their imports are displayed in Table 12.6. Again the same pattern as for exports emerges: there would seem to have been widespread use of nonmarket-based transfer prices when imported inputs were purchased from other units of the MNE.

Classifying pricing practices #1-#4 in Tables 12.5 and 12.6 as market-based and #5 as a nonmarket-based transfer price, then, as shown in Table 12.7, Japanese MNEs tended to use nonmarket-based transfer prices for both intra-firm imports and exports to a greater extent than did US or European MNEs.[8] This tendency may be due to the more centralized control system employed by Japanese MNEs (See Lecraw, 1983).

Table 12.7: Intra-firm Export and Import Prices (all figures in per cent)

Home country	Market-based	Nonmarket-based
USA	68	32
Europe	65	35
Japan	25	75
Other LDC	45	55
Total	42	58

In order to test the hypotheses concerning the determinants of the firms' transfer pricing practices, the export pricing behaviour of the MNEs in the sample were classified as 'market based' (MB) or 'nonmarket based' (NMB) as defined above. Multiple discriminant analysis was used to uncover the relationships between the characteristics of the MNEs in the sample, the environment in which they operated and the transfer pricing practices they followed. The use of multiple discriminant analysis allows tests for the relative significance of the effects of these variables on transfer pricing and determination of the linear combinations of independent variables that best discriminate among firms that used 'market-based' or 'nonmarket-based' transfer prices. Essentially the multiple discriminant analysis assigned the pricing behaviour of each firm to one of the two classifications so as to minimize the probability that the firm's pricing practice was assigned to the class in which it did not in fact belong.[9]

A discriminant function using the variables tariff level, the relative rates of profits taxes, the existence of price controls and capital-profit repatriation controls, perceived risk of operations in the host country, the degree of centralization of the MNE, the existence of a joint-venture partner, and Japanese-other MNE, was estimated to classify the MNEs in the sample into those using market-based and nonmarket-based transfer prices for their exports. (The same type of analysis was done for pricing strategies for imports as described below.)

The discriminant function was of the form:

$$Z = \sum_{i=1}^{8} \alpha_i X_i$$

where Z is the score of the discriminant function, the a_i's are the weighting coefficients, and the x_i's are the standardized values of the eight discriminating variables used in the analysis. The x_i's are defined as:

X_1 = nominal tariff rate in country of destination
X_2 = tax rate for the MNE in the host country relative to the home country tax rate
X_3 = 1 if price controls, 0 if not
X_4 = 1 if restrictions on capital and dividend repatriation were in effect, 0 otherwise
X_5 = country risk as perceived by the managers of the subsidiary of the MNE (1 = low, 10 = high)
X_6 = 1 if the subsidiary had Japanese-ownership, 0 otherwise
X_7 = per cent ownership of the subsidiary held outside the MNE
X_8 = degree of centralization of management control
X_9 = nominal host country tariff rate.

The results of the discriminant analysis are shown in Table 12.9.
Data to construct these eight variables were obtained from the

questionnaire administered during interviews with managers of the 153 subsidiaries in the sample. The variable X_5 is the rating of country risk as perceived by the manager of the subsidiary interviewed ranked 1 (low) to 10 (high). Variable X_8 was a composite variable constructed from responses to questions relating to the locus of control (parent MNE or subsidiary) for 21 decision variables of each subsidiary weighted by their perceived importance to the subsidiary's success. (This variable and its construction are discussed at more length in Lecraw, 1983.)

Table 12.8: Confusion Matrix of the Discriminant Functions for Market Based and Nonmarket Based Import and Export Pricing on Intra-firm Transactions

Actual	Exports	Predicted	
	Market Based	Nonmarket Based	Total
Market based	30	7	37
Nonmarket based	10	35	45
Total	40	42	82

Correct classification = 79%

Actual	Imports	Predicted	
	Market Based	Nonmarket Based	Total
Market based	55	8	63
Nonmarket based	9	70	79
Total	64	78	142

Correct classification = 88%

The discriminant function correctly classified the export pricing behaviour of 30 of the 37 MNEs whose export pricing was classified as 'market based'. It classified 35 of the 45 firms that used nonmarket-based export prices correctly (Table 12.8).[10] These success rates were significantly above the level for random classification. As can be seen in Table 12.9, the F statistic was significant for the variables: degree of centralization of control over the subsidiary, perceived risk, price controls, capital-profit repatriation restrictions, the degree of centralization of the MNE,

Table 12.9: The Discriminant Functions for Market-based and Nonmarket-based Export-Import Pricing

	Exports $\bar{Z}_1$	Imports $\bar{Z}_2$
Nominal tariff in country of destination, X_1	+0.22 (3.75)	N.A.
Host country tax rate relative to home country tax rate, X_2	+0.17 (4.32)	+0.22 (3.54)
Price controls, X_3	+0.20 (2.75)	+0.15 (3.10)
Dividend and capital repatriation restriction, X_4	+0.12 (2.95)	+0.093 (3.15)
Perceived country risk, X_5	+0.032 (5.71)	+0.043 (6.75)
Japanese subsidiary, X_6	+0.021 (0.67)	+0.052 (0.34)
Per cent local ownership, X_7	−0.0035 (4.75)	−0.0047 (6.30)
Degree of centralization, X_8	+0.23 (4.15)	+0.19 (7.10)
Nominal host country tariff rate, X_9	N.A.	0.037 (5.42)

Notes: 1. The numbers in parenthesis are the F statistics. For exports, at the 5 per cent level, the critical value for $F_{(8,73)}$ is 2.10; for imports the critical $F_{(8,133)}$ is 2.02. At the 1 per cent level the critical Fs are 2.78 and 2.63 respectively.
2. Firms with $\bar{Z}_1 > 2.03$ or $\bar{Z}_2 > 1.85$ were classified as using nonmarket-based transfer prices on intra-firm exports or imports.

tariffs in the country of destination and relative profit taxes. In the discriminant analysis of pricing strategies for exports the nationality of the MNE (Japanese and non-Japanese) was not a significant discriminating variable when the variable representing the degree of centralization of control of the MNE was included. When the centralization variable was dropped, however, nationality was significant: Japanese MNEs tended to use nonmarket-based transfer prices to a greater extent than did other MNEs. This finding is similar to that of Tang (1979).[11] These statistical results support the hypotheses concerning the determinants of the use of transfer prices not based on market prices for exports.

A similar analysis was carried out for the determinants of prices for intra-firm and inter-firm imports. A discriminant function was estimated to classify the import pricing on intra-firm imports as 'nonmarket based' and 'market based' using variables X_2 through X_8 and the height of the tariff in the host country, X_9. This discriminant classified 88 per cent of the firms to the correct category, 55 of 63 firms that used market-based import prices and 70 of 79 firms that used corporate-based prices. (The confusion matrix and the discriminant function are in Tables 12.8 and 12.9.) As indicated by the F statistic, the significant variables were the nominal tariff in the host country, relative tax rates, price controls and the presence of dividend and capital repatriation restrictions, perceived country risk, per cent local ownership and the degree of centralization of the parent MNE. Japanese ownership was not significant.

To test the determinants of the *extent* by which export prices on inter-firm and intra-firm sales differed, multiple regression analysis was used with

$$ \text{PDX} = \frac{|P_T^x - P_M^x|}{P_M^x} $$

the per cent deviation of prices for intra-firm (P_T^X) from inter-firm (P_M^X) sales of the same product as the dependent variable, using data from the 35 MNEs that exported the same product to related firms and to unrelated firms, and that followed nonmarket-based transfer pricing practices. The price of exports to unaffiliated firms, P_M^x, was used as the baseline for the competitive arm's-length value of the product on the export market. The relationship between this baseline price and the intra-firm transfer price may depend on conditions in the local market (profits taxes, price controls, country risk, etc.) and on export markets (tariffs).

A priori we predict the following signs of the coefficients of the independent variables.

1. The higher are tariffs in the country of destination, the greater the incentive to price intra-firm exports low relative to inter-firm exports to avoid paying tariffs in the country of destination. The coefficient of X_1 should be positive.

2. The greater the difference between local profits taxes and home country taxes, the greater the incentive to under- or overprice intra-firm exports to reduce reported local profits and

the greater the absolute value of the per cent deviation of intra-firm and inter-firm export prices for the same product. The value $|X_2-1|$ was used as the independent variable where X_2 is the ratio of the profits tax rate in the host and home countries.[12] The sign of $|X_2-1|$ should be positive.

3. If price controls are in effect in the host country ($X_3 = 1$) the MNE may reduce the price of its intra-firm exports to show low profits in the host country in order to increase its bargaining power in trying to have price increases approved in the host country. The sign of X_3 should be positive.

4. Similarly, if capital or dividend repatriation controls were in effect ($X_4 = 1$) or, 5., country risk, X_5, were perceived as high, the firm may reduce intra-firm export prices in order to transfer money out of the country. The signs of X_4 and X_5 should be positive.

6. Japanese MNEs ($X_6 = 1$) are thought to engage in more widespread use of nonmarket-based transfer prices than other MNEs (Tang, 1979). The sign of X_6 should be positive.

7. The presence of a local joint venture partner, X_7, may reduce the ability of MNEs to set nonmarket-based transfer prices that deviate from market prices. The sign of X_7 should be negative.

8. Finally, the more decentralized the decision, evaluation and control system of the MNE, the greater the problems caused by deviations of the transfer price from the market price and the greater the incentive to use market-based transfer prices. The sign of X_8 should be positive.

The signs of the independent variables and the regression results are displayed in Table 12.10. All the variables had the predicted sign, but the variable for Japanese MNE (X_6) was not significant when X_8 was included in the regression equation. The regression equation explained 55 per cent of the variation of PDX. The average value for PDX was 7.8 with a standard deviation of 5.3.[13]

A similar regression analysis of the determinants of the transfer prices for intra-firm imports was performed. The dependent variable was the absolute value of the percentage difference between the price for intra-firm imports, P_T^I, and inter-firm imports P_M^I for products from 65 firms in the sample which used nonmarket-based transfer prices on intra-firm imports and imported the same input from both related and unrelated firms,

Table 12.10: Regression Results for PDX and PDI

	PDX		PDI	
	Predicted Sign	Coefficient	Predicted Sign	Coefficient
Constant	+	1.3[a] (2.71)	+	2.5[a] (3.25)
Nominal tariff in country of destination, X_1	+	0.032[a] (3.52)		N.A
Absolute value of relative host-country tax rate -1, $\lvert X_2 - 1\rvert$	+	3.57[a] (3.05)	+	2.34[b] (2.51)
Price controls, X_3	+	2.32[b] (2.34)	+	3.26[b] (2.11)
Dividend and capital repatriation restrictions, X_4	+	3.25[b] (2.17)	+	4.2[b] (2.10)
Perceived country risk, X_5	+	0.20[b] (2.25)	+	0.37[b] (1.90)
Japanese subsidiary, X_6	+	1.5 (0.63)	+	2.3 (0.34)
Per cent local ownership, X_7	−	0.22[b] (2.40)	−	0.19[a] (2.73)
Centralization of control, X_8	+	0.32[a] (3.15)	+	0.17 (2.96)[b]
Nominal host-country tariff, X_9		N.A.	+	0.056[b] (3.15)
$\bar{R}^2$		0.63		0.72
N		35		65

Notes: Numbers in parenthesis are the t values.
a = significant at the 99 per cent level.
b = significant at the 95 per cent level.

i.e. $\text{PDI} = \lvert\ P_T^I - P_M^m\rvert/P_M^I$. The independent variables were the same as those for the regression analysis of export prices, with the exception that the nominal tariff in the host country replaced the nominal tariff in the country of destination. PDI should increase as the tariff in the host country (X_9) increases, as the differences between relative tax rate, $|X_2-1|$, increases, if there are price controls ($X_3=1$), if there are restrictions on dividend and capital repatriation ($X_4=1$), as the perceived country risk (X_5) increases, as the degree of centralization of control (X_8) increases and if the subsidiary has Japanese ownership. PDM should decrease as the extent of local equity increases.

The signs of the coefficients of the independent variables and the actual regression results are in Table 12.10. All the coefficients except Japanese ownership had the predicted sign and were significant at the 95 per cent level. Taken together these variables accounted for 74 per cent of the variance in PDI.[14] The average value of PDI was 12.2.

A similar analysis was performed for the prices of imports and exports for the firms that followed a market-based pricing practice for intra-firm trade. None of the variables was significant. The average values of PDX and PDI were 1.2 per cent and 2.4 per cent respectively. Only 5 per cent of the variance of PDX and 8 per cent of the variance of PDI was accounted for by the independent variables.

In summary, the MNEs in the sample charged nonmarket-based transfer prices for intra-firm imports and exports to reduce duties and profit taxes, allocate capital between countries, reduce risk, and to circumvent government price and capital-profit remittance controls. Local joint venture partners decreased the use and extent of nonmarket-based transfer prices.

V

The results of the analysis in this paper support the position often taken by host governments in LDCs and industrialized countries alike that MNEs engage in a widespread and systematic use of transfer prices that differ from market prices to increase their global profits, reduce risk, move funds across national boundaries and allocate them between subsidiaries.[15] The presence of a local partner tended to reduce both the magnitude and the pervasiveness of the use of nonmarket-based transfer prices. The ability of local joint venture partners in the ASEAN region to influence the transfer pricing practices of the MNE partners, however, may exceed that of firms in most other LDCs. To this extent these conclusions may not be applicable in other LDCs.

Governments in both host and home countries of MNEs are certainly aware of the potential problem of the use of nonmarket-based transfer prices on intra-firm transactions of goods and services. This study indicates that charging nonmarket-based transfer prices is not confined to MNEs based in one country, or operating in one industry, or producing in one host country, but is a general practice used by MNEs.

When government imposes high tariffs on imports, relatively high taxes on profits, price controls and controls on profit and capital movements, it should expect MNEs which are affected by these policies to charge transfer prices to avoid their incidence. Government might direct its attention towards these MNEs in its efforts to bring transfer prices towards the arm's-length, market level. The presence of a local partner also might decrease the incidence and extent of the use of corporate-based transfer prices that differ from market prices. A local partner both may have access to intra-firm data that would allow the assessment of the basis of transfer prices of goods and services and may have the incentive to ensure that intra-firm prices approach the arm's-length level.

Notes

The research of this study was partially funded by the United Nations Centre on Transnational Corporations and the Centre for International Business Studies, the University of Western Ontario.

1. See Lecraw (1981) for a description of the firms in the sample and the industries in which they operated.
2. The risk associated with these cash flows must be incorporated into their valuation in the discounting process.
3. See Lecraw (1981) for a description of the normalization procedure.
4. This section draws heavily on the work of Mathewson and Quirin (1979). See Vernon and Wells (1981, chapters 3 and 4) for a broader discussion of the relationship between transfer pricing and accounting, control and taxation of MNEs.
5. Mathewson and Quirin (1979) concluded that, in the case of Canada, the effects on transfer prices of host-country profits taxes and import duties largely offset each other.
6. Burns (1980) in a survey of corporate executives found that the internal foreign environment was perceived as the most important determinant of transfer pricing strategy. This variable may subsume risk and government price controls and profit and capital repatriation controls.
7. When this paper was originally presented there was disagreement over whether 'cost-plus profit' should be classified as a 'market-based price'. The point

is well taken since this price is one set internally by the firm. During the interviews, however, many managers stated that they regarded such a price as a fair market price which the firm had to receive in order to trade. This price is also used by several governments in anti-dumping and tariff regulations as an approximation of market price.

8. Those firms which followed a mixed strategy, i.e. set prices in both categories 1-5 *and* #6 were excluded from the analysis. This reduced the sample size from 82 to 63 for exports and from 130 to 118 for importing firms.

9. Discriminant analysis is a well-developed and often-used technique particularly in marketing and the behavioral sciences. Its use is gradually increasing in economic analysis. Green (1978, chapters 4 and 7) gives a thorough review of discriminant analysis.

10. If 'cost-plus profit' were shifted to the 'nonmarket based' classification, the power of the discriminant function declined.

11. Tang (1979) found that the transfer pricing strategies followed by US and Japanese MNEs differed in extent and type.

12. The strength of this relationship may be reduced by the provision for foreign tax credits in the tax laws.

13. Tests were run to determine if there were problems of heteroscedasticity of the residuals or multicollinearity of the variables. Regression of the residuals on the estimated values of PDX yielded no significant relationship. The hypothesis of heteroscedasticity was rejected. The only significant collinearity was between Japanese ownership and centralization of control. Despite this problem, there was sufficient variation in the data to break the deadlock, to the extent that the centralization variable was significant although the ownership variable was not.

14. The same tests for heteroscedasticity and multicollinearity were performed for this regression with similar results (see note 13).

15. The study did not cover the transfer prices of intra-firm debt, management and technical service fees, licencing, etc.

*   *   *

COMMENTS ON EFFICIENCY, EQUITY AND TRANSFER PRICING IN LDCs
Gerald K. Helleiner

The concept of 'efficiency' that has been employed throughout this conference is a rather narrow and value-loaded one. Usage at this meeting has been no sloppier than is normal for discussions among mainstream economists, but sloppy it has nevertheless been. 'Efficiency' as employed here has meant Pareto efficiency — efficiency in the sense that by assuming income distributional objectives away or assuming that they can be dealt with 'after', or by other specialized investigators, or both, it is logically possible to concentrate on output maximization. But in the real world lump-sum transfers to achieve appropriate 'desired' income redistribution are few and far between. At the same time, global disparities in *per capita* income are enormous. While distributional effects of government policies and corporate practices within the industrialized world, and those affecting relations between industrialized countries, *may* frequently 'cancel out' and, in any case, not be of primary significance, there can be no such presumption in the case of relations between the poorest nations and the rest of the world. World output maximization is, therefore, by no means the only sensible objective to which theoretical analysis should be directed.

Theoreticians concerned with welfare — in the traditional textbook sense in which social objective functions incorporate distributional objectives — might equally (indeed, most development economists would say, more profitably) devote their analytical effort to the exploration of the effects of alternative institutional and policy scenarios upon the incomes of the global poor. The recent literature of project evaluation and growth accounting, not least within such bastions of orthodoxy as the World Bank, has featured many such theoretical investigations. Failure of theoreticians to address these issues must reflect either dubious value judgements, professional inertia or sheer intellectual provincialism. The professional colleagues with whom I usually interact rejected Pareto efficiency as a sensible objective in the consideration of international economic issues years ago.

The intellectual puzzles associated with distributional objectives are many. What *are* the redistributive poverty-alleviating *as well as* global output maximization effects of multinational corporate behaviour, of various governmental policies, of corporate response to government policies? What are the trade-offs, if any, between global output maximization and distributional objectives in this sphere? (On the basis of the debate between Aliber and Diewert earlier today it seems there may still be theoretical disagreement even as to the *direction* of change in total output associated with a firm's response to government policies, let alone distributional effects, so there appears work enough to be done!)

There are other major intellectual issues that require far more exploration than they have received. For example, how important is static allocative efficiency in the overall scheme of things anyway? The Schumpeterian revival of recent years has fuelled widespread previous doubts as to the capacity of conventional static efficiency analysis to tell us what we really want to know — about growth and 'dynamic' efficiency. It is quite possible, after all, to stagnate in a highly efficient fashion! Again, do we have a useful positive theory of how the complex relationship between governments, multinational corporations and other actors actually works? The transfer pricing issue is obviously only one dimension — probably a relatively minor one — in total relationships in which bargaining, rent-seeking and 'games' play greater roles than competitive markets. And what are the possible trade-offs among objectives faced by the governments of developing countries, whose aims and constraints are objectively just as interesting and deserving of analytical exploration as those of firms, still endlessly modelled in schools of international business? Where is there rent or quasi-rent that may be relatively costlessly bargained away?

Some of the disagreements among those at this conference undoubtedly stem from disagreements as to objectives. The analytical discussion here has also been bedevilled, however, by lack of clarity as to what the analysts' counterfactual worlds are. On the one hand, there are those who analyse multinational firm behaviour and its effects against the counterfactual of a world without borders — either without *national* governments or without Government entirely. They tend to focus on the 'segmentation' of world markets and its pernicious effects upon overall efficiency. (Some go on to assess the efforts of firms to overcome these effects.) As an exasperated Brazilian economist friend has commented — with reference to American policy analysts of similar orientation — 'they seem to see national sovereignty as just another nontariff barrier'.

On the other hand, it is possible to consider a counterfactual world in which there *are* national borders but there are *no* multinational corporations. Those, like Rugman and Diewert, who pursue this line of argument ask whether, given market segmentation, multinationals are 'efficient' in the sense that output would be less without them. If they are, Rugman suggests, then multinationals should be left to get on with their output-increasing task. We are invited to 'take them or leave them', warts and all. Rugman and Aliber argue that multinationals are efficient, Diewert that they are not, relative to a multinational-less but segmented world.

The debate in developing countries has never been concerned with such abstract and academic counterfactuals. Rather, it has centred on analysis of alternative outcomes in a world in which there are *both* governments (borders) *and* multinationals. *Granting* that, for one reason or another, in particular sectors and at particular times, internalization is an appropriate (perhaps the globally most efficient) means for transacting international activity — all parties agree that multinationals are a superior alternative to markets — what then? The counterfactual world is one in which the multinational is still there, 'doing its thing', but the distribution of the gains from its activity differs in consequence of host governmental action from that which would result from its 'free' activity. Debates and disputes over transfer pricing typically arise *after* governments, multinationals and others have already agreed to deal with one another. (There are some exceptions to this generalization, as for instance when firms try to induce subsidies and protection by overstating their costs upon start-up.) Granting the frequent importance or even inevitability of internalization, there remains an adversarial relationship between firms and governments (and sometimes others), and there frequently exists a variety of possible outcomes. The 'price' of direct foreign investment is rarely fixed as if supplied from a perfectly competitive market.

What most distinguishes developing country governments from those of industrialized countries as they interact with multinational corporations is their limited capacity to bargain, police agreements, impose penalties, or even gather data. There are obviously great differences among developing countries in this respect, and it can be dangerous to attempt to generalize across the entire Third World. There certainly are 40 or more countries, however, in which virtually the only taxation power of the government *vis-à-vis* multinational corporations is that of moral suasion. In these cases MNEs' generation of appropriate transfer prices and the payment of legally required taxes are essentially voluntary acts of 'good corporate citizenship'.

The importance of transfer pricing in developing countries has increased in the years since the original Sussex conference — for a number of reasons. First, recent US Department of Commerce benchmark data show a significant increase in the proportion of US imports of manufactures from developing countries that originate with majority-owned foreign affiliates of US firms. (Most of this is intra-firm trade.) This proportion doubled between 1966 and 1977, and is now substantially higher than that for developed countries other than the special Canadian case.

Secondly, disillusion with arm's-length interest-bearing financial instruments has led both borrowers and lenders to call for a new relative emphasis upon direct foreign investment in developing countries. One can confidently predict that the relative share of direct investment in development finance will rise during the next decade, and that of commercial bank and bond finance will fall. Thirdly, multinational corporations based in the developing countries have begun to appear in larger numbers, and presumably they will have some impact upon developing country policies. It will be interesting to see whether and how governmental policies may alter as developing countries, like Canada, become important homes as well as hosts for multinationals. Finally, it is worth noting — since Harry Grubert brought it up — that while the taxes involved in transfer pricing abuse are probably a very small proportion of US Treasury total revenue, they can be a highly significant proportion of the government revenue of a small poor country.

In recent years increased exchange rate instabilities and uncertainties have greatly increased incentives for care with intra-corporate financing and transfer pricing in developing countries. The emergence of the international debt problem has underlined how little factual information there still is on unguaranteed private and international intra-corporate debt. (As special exchange rates are introduced to protect debtors against the full impact of major devaluations some of these private debts are coming out of the woodwork!) On the basis of experience to date, if Plasschaert is correct about the growth of LDC manufactured exports in the coming years, there will also be an increasing need to grapple with the issues surrounding the 'management' of international trade, growing proportions of which have been and will be undertaken on an intra-firm basis. The choice of protectionist policy instruments, and the precise manner of their use — the rents to which they give rise and the preferences of the major rent-seekers and of governments, the issues addressed in Itagaki's paper — will be of increasing importance.

PART THREE
REGULATION OF TRANSFER PRICING

13 TRANSFER PRICING PROBLEMS IN DEVELOPING COUNTRIES

Sylvain R.F. Plasschaert

I. Introduction

It is often claimed that transfer price manipulation (TPM) is more widespread in less developed countries (LDCs) than in more developed ones (MDCs). This could be due to one or both of the following factors. First, LDCs, as compared to MDCs, may have enacted a wider array of regulations in which the recourse to TPM would allow multinational enterprises (MNEs) to soften the adverse impact of these regulations. Second, LDC governments are poorly equipped, relative to MDCs, to thwart the attempts of MNEs to TPM.

As illustrated in this paper, the first explanation can be readily observed in the real world. Usually LDCs do impose more constraints on the operations of multinationals than is the case in MDCs (as documented in UN, 1978b). In fact, the stricter regulatory stance in LDCs is a symptom of the usually rather strained overall relationship between LDC governments and MNEs. (An interesting and related question is whether the more lukewarm attitude of LDCs *vis-à-vis* MNEs, as reflected in a wider array of restrictions and regulations, is predicated upon ideological and political considerations or upon objective, 'structural' features of the economies of LDCs.) The second explanation also is a plausible one. For example, in the corporate tax area, only a few MDCs, foremost the United States, have equipped themselves with detailed regulations against TPM.

The purpose of this paper is to explore whether policies and regulations in LDCs are such that the temptations for the MNE to practise TPM must be expected to be stronger — relative to the amount of intra-MNE payment flows — than is the case in MDCs. However, this approach does not imply that MNEs actually exploit all theoretical opportunities to benefit from TPM. (In other words, temptations must not be construed as actually committed sins.) Both government measures, and the difficulties

247

in reconciling TPM with the autonomy of foreign subsidiaries, dampen the propensity to take advantage of TPM.

Unfortunately, little reliable evidence about the extent of TPM is available. The deductive line of reasoning adopted in this paper, however, allows us to clarify the question whether *a priori* the scope for TPM is larger in LDCs than in MDCs. The findings are also useful for the interpretation of the meagre data on actual TPM practices.

Several limitations of this paper must be noted at the outset:

(a) In order to preserve a high degree of generality, 'the' LDC under consideration tends to be highly stylized. Obviously, such approach hides significant differences amongst LDCs.

(b) The analysis refers basically to MNEs which manufacture for sale in the domestic markets of LDC host countries. Such host countries typically adhere to import-substitution strategies. The findings of this paper may not be applicable to foreign direct investments geared to exports for world markets.

(c) A list of conceivable inducements for TPM appears in Appendix I.[1] This list may not be exhaustive, and space does not allow us to cover all the inducements that are listed.

(d) The subject matter and approach adopted in this paper imply an incursion into the field of development economics. In order to keep the discussion within reasonable bounds, several topics must be treated in their bare essentials and references to the relevant literature are also quite laconic.

II. Major Motivations for Transfer Pricing Manoeuvres in LDCs

A. *Corporate Taxation*

Discussions about transfer pricing rules and practices tend overwhelmingly to focus on corporate taxation. This is also the field in which governments are likely first to enact measures against TPM. And yet, paradoxically, various factors point to the conclusion that corporate tax differentials are less likely to tempt the MNE into TPM than has generally been believed. The reasons why considerations about corporate taxes should not be overrated are rather straightforward:

(a) Nominal corporate rates are typically lower in LDCs than in MDCs. In such cases the MNE would not derive any benefit from artificially siphoning taxable profits from the LDC host country to the MDC home country if TPM were inspired only by overall corporate tax-burden considerations.

(b) The assessment of taxable profits is almost certainly less severe in LDCs than in MDCs: a high degree of 'underadministration' is usually a major complaint in analyses of LDC tax systems.

(c) Although tax gratifications appear to be granted to foreign direct investment as frequently in MDCs as in LDCs (Zakour, 1981), the benefits from tax incentives are likely, on the whole, to be more generous in LDCs, e.g. tax holidays are more readily accorded.

(d) Due to the two factors (b) and (c), the differences between typical LDC and MDC tax rates are likely to be even larger in terms of effective rates than when only nominal rates are considered.

(e) By definition TPM affects the tax bases of the two countries involved in a given international intra-firm transaction. The gain which the MNE reaps from under- or overinvoicing in the jurisdiction with the higher effective rate is partially offset by higher tax liability in the country with more lenient corporate taxation.

(f) The MNE must not only heed the taxes due in the host country on the profits generated by its subsidiary, but also claims of tax authorities in the home country. However, claims of the latter are largely alleviated by way of bilateral double taxation agreements and by the unilateral measures which the home countries have taken in order to reduce international double taxation. Thus major capital-exporting countries, such as the United States, apply the 'foreign tax credit' mechanism, i.e. corporate taxes paid in the host country on the profits of the subsidiary can be deducted from the corporate tax which the home country levies on such profits when remitted. Withholding taxes in the host country on dividends, interests and royalties usually also qualify for the foreign tax credit in the home country. It follows, under the assumption that the burden of creditable taxes in the host country does not exceed the corporate tax in the home country, that the tax variable would be neutral as between foreign and domestic investments by the MNE (Plasschaert, 1979).

(g) The 'deferral rule', another mainstay of international tax arrangements, is also likely to dampen the temptation to reduce taxable profits in LDCs by way of TPM. According to this principle, the claim of the home country only bears on profits and other returns from investments that are actually repatriated. This deferral rule contains a built-in incentive for the MNE to plough back profits into the foreign subsidiary, as the application of the withholding tax on remittances is thereby avoided. This incentive is often reinforced by tax gratifications which are specifically attached to the reinvestment of profits.

Thus, if differences in corporate tax burdens are viewed in isolation from other conceivable motivations for TPM, one would expect that TPM would turn rather to the benefit of LDCs than to their detriment. This general finding, however, requires some further qualifications, such is the complexity of international tax matters:

(i) In some LDCs, nominal corporate tax rates exceed those commonly found in MDCs. As shown in Appendix II, India and Pakistan belong to that category.

(ii) Not only the rates on corporate profits proper, but also the withholding taxes on repatriated dividends, interests and royalties, must be taken into account when figuring out the total tax burden in the country. As shown in Appendix I, such withholding taxes are often high in LDCs, and particularly in Latin American countries, with the result that a proportion of the host-country tax burden may no longer be creditable against the corporate tax in the home country. In fact the foreign tax credit is a one-way mechanism in the sense that any excess of host-country over home-country tax is not refunded.

(iii) Taxable profits may be artificially rerouted over tax-haven jurisdictions. The zero or minimal tax rates which apply in such jurisdictions contain an inducement to underinvoice sales made by operating subsidiaries in LDCs (and for that matter also in MDCs) to tax-haven subsidiaries. Few LDCs appear as yet to be equipped against TPM-moves that involve tax havens. However, action taken by a number of MDCs, such as the subpart F provisions in the USA, also serve the legitimate concerns of LDCs.

(iv) Finally, as already mentioned, specific measures against TPM are rare in LDCs but are implemented in a number of MDCs (see Peat, Marwick, Mitchell and Co., 1980). Co-ordinated action by tax officials of the countries involved in given intra-firm deals has been scheduled in a few bilateral tax agreements amongst MDCs. International co-ordination within the EEC has also been ordered by a 1977 directive (Burns and Ross, 1981).

It would be utterly wrong to state that corporate tax considerations do not play any role in seducing the MNEs into TPM. The large number of subsidiaries that have been established in some tax havens, the sophistication of tax planning seminars and the cases litigated between MNE and tax authorities testify to the contrary. But the conclusion appears warranted that, as far as LDCs are concerned, corporate tax variables proper are likely to be less relevant than in MDCs, since the MNE would most often reap little or no advantage from artificially reducing taxable profits in LDCs through TPM. This statement, however, does not deny that in specialized segments of tax law, TPM may be instrumental in lowering tax liabilities. Tax differentials amongst various remittance channels, for example, hold the promise of some tax reduction for the MNE, if TPM is operated judiciously.

B. *Import Duties*

Nominal import duties in LDCs are in general substantially higher than in MDCs even if one abstracts, for the latter, from the effect of EEC and EFTA schemes of integration which have significantly reduced the tariffs on trade between member countries (DeWolf, 1980). In addition, the role of import duties in LDCs differs considerable from that in MDCs.

In market-economy MDCs import duties are in essence operated as protective devices; in LDCs 'tariffs are multi-target policy instruments' (DeWolf, 1981). They are a major source of fiscal revenue, especially in the least developed countries where the lack of a sizeable industrial base does not provide other productive tax handles, such as excise duties on domestic manufactures. Tariffs are also an instrument to achieve balance-of-payments equilibrium, not only when external crises erupt and call for emergency measures, but also as a permanent feature of government policy. Tariffs are used to nurture 'infant industries', although observation shows that such protective devices tend to be maintained well beyond the initial years of new enterprises. Finally, LDCs often apply high duties to imported luxuries with a view to discouraging the consumption of such items; the use of import duties, then, serves basically distributive objectives.

Are import duty considerations likely to tempt the MNE into practising TPM in LDCs more than would be the case in MDCs? A first conclusion that emerges is that the scope for TPM appears to be limited to *ad valorem* duties. *Quantitative restrictions* do not lend themselves to TPM gambits, since they bear on quantities and normally do not affect prices of the authorized imports. Neither would underinvoicing of imports be of avail when *specific* import duties, predicated on given physical characteristics of the imports, are due; in such circumstances artificial fiddling with the intra-firm price would not affect the import duty liability for a given quantity of imports. The discussion about TPM-temptations caused by import duties, therefore, must focus on *ad valorem* import duties which raise the prices of imports to the importer (see also Itagaki, this volume).

Considering the usually much higher levels of nominal import taxes in LDCs, the conclusion readily emerges that *ad valorem* tariffs are likely to entail more temptations to practise TPM (relative to the extent of intra-firm trade) in LDCs than in MDCs. However, this prima facie inference must be qualified by several important considerations. First, the tariff-minimizing aim of TPM clashes with other conceivable motivations for TPM since successful underpricing of imports reduces the customs bill but enlarges, other factors remaining equal, the taxable profits of the importing subsidiary. The resulting decision rules for MNE have been covered in the literature (Horst, 1971), but are still too simple, in that they overlook the complex relationship between host- and home-country corporate taxation briefly sketched in the previous section. For LDCs, underinvoicing would usually result in a net tax saving for the MNE in cases where the corporate tax rate in the LDC is below that in the home country. Underinvoicing would not only score in terms of reduced customs duties, but would also result in a net saving of overall corporate tax liabilities (see also Eden, this volume).

Other trade-offs between conflicting motivations for TPM must be considered. Underinvoicing of imports by the host country subsidiary reduces the receipts that accrue to the exporting parent company. But circumstances in LDCs are often such that, due to exchange risks, the MNE wants to repatriate funds promptly from the subsidiary. If 'open' repatriation of returns is not allowed, TPM on intra-firm trade and payments flows may provide a 'covert' channel for such remittances. But this objective would call for overpricing of the LDC subsidiary's imports. (This important issue will be analyzed in section D.)

TPM is also affected by 'tariff escalation' policies, where nominal tariffs rise with the degree of domestic processing, and zero or comparatively low *ad valorem* rates apply to raw materials and intermediates. In LDCs, especially those that adopt the import-substitution strategy, these two categories of imports typically account for the bulk of import trade; consumer goods imports have generally been compressed to a minimum. In MDCs, to the contrary, nominal tariff escalation also occurs although the tariff level on final goods is usually much below that prevailing in LDCs. But final consumer goods represent a much higher percentage of total import trade than in LDCs.

In other words, not only the typical differences in import duty levels, but also the divergence between LDCs and MDCs in the composition of import trade, must be heeded when analyzing incentives for TPM. The scope of profitable underinvoicing of imports in MDCs should not be underrated. Admittedly, the comparatively low level of tariffs substantially narrows the benefits which the minimization of import duties through TPM may achieve. But the dutiable import flow to which underinvoicing could be applied is relatively much larger than in LDCs since it consists more of final goods. Besides, economic agents enjoy a greater freedom to effectuate international capital movements in MDCs than in LDCs. Hence, the desire to maximize the repatriation of profits would not flash a contrary signal and tempt the multinational into overinvoicing.

TPM-temptations can only be actually indulged in to the extent governments are unable to monitor such practices. There are few areas in which the importing country is as equipped to thwart TPM as in the customs area. Stiff penalties apply not only to smuggling but also to unacceptable declarations of values by the importer. Also, disputes with customs officials can be costly to the importer since, pending the litigation, the customs administration is entitled to withhold the release of the imported commodities.

One should add that customs regulations often impose 'posted prices'. Such price lists are intended to simplify the assessment process; they also serve as a minimum floor to the values declared by importers (IMF on taxation in sub-Saharan Africa, 1981, pp. 12-13). Such posted prices will often deviate from the prices that have actually been paid. This then is an example of artificial price tags, engineered by public authorities and not by the MNE.

C. Currency Risks

Trade deals, denominated in foreign exchange, expose economic agents to currency risks. As is the case with pure exporters or importers, MNEs are subject to 'transactions risks', when they trade with third parties in a foreign currency. Economic agents succeed in avoiding transaction risks when they convert assets in a currency which is expected to weaken, into a stronger one before devaluation actually occurs.

One time-honoured recipe to avoid exchange losses consists in accelerating prospective payments in the weak currency, and conversely, of delaying payments in strong currencies. Payment terms that were originally envisaged are thereby shortened or extended. Such 'leading' or 'lagging' can be practised amongst independent parties but operated much more readily between related units of the same MNE. Few solid data are available about the extent of leading and lagging, but there can be no doubt that the amounts of payments thus rescheduled are huge and exert an important impact on exchange markets (see Bourguinat, 1972; Holthus and Scharrer, 1973). Governments impose some restrictions on leading or lagging (see the table reproduced in Shapiro, 1982, p. 301) but they cannot push their interventions too far lest international trade becomes excessively hampered. Investigations into the financial behaviour of MNEs also document that the latter consider the recourse to leading and lagging as a major tool of exchange management (Rodriguez, 1980).

It is important to stress that TPM itself is unable to avoid exchange risks. TPM reshuffles cash balances and profits between the units of the MNE concerned but does not provide a cure for exchange risks. However, if TPM is grafted on a successful 'leading' or 'lagging' move, it amplifies the outcome as more funds in the weak currency are converted into a strong one or less units of a strong currency must be exchanged into a weak one (Plasschaert, 1979).

Three factors can be identified whereby temptations to

practise TPM are hypothesized to be stronger in LDCs than in MDCs: (1) exchange rate instability may be higher; (2) fewer facilities may be available to seek cover against exchange risks; and (3) some intra-firm payment channels may be constrained by governments so that the MNE attempts to maximize TPM with respect to payment flows which are relatively unrestricted.

First, a higher instability of exchange rates may induce MNEs to step up the flow of receipts out of a weakening currency and to strengthen this move by TPM. Second, MNEs are likely to care more for exchange risk exposure and to take advantage of the leading-and-TPM combination, when they have less opportunity to cover such risks themselves. Forward markets only encompass the currencies of MDCs, but are lacking in LDCs. Money market cover, whereby the funds needed to discharge a foreign currency debt at a later stage are borrowed immediately, is also usually inaccessible due to stringent exchange restrictions. Third, most LDCs, faced with huge import needs, suffer from chronically weak balance of payments: various restrictions on imports and on the outflow of capital are, therefore, a structural feature of LDCs. Reluctance to devalue the domestic currency also inspires governments to buttress their exchange rate by a host of specific controls on international trade and payments (Cooper, 1971).

D. Restrictions on the Remittance of Returns

In dealing with this conceivable motivation for TPM, two preliminary comments are in point. First, I purposely use the generic term 'returns' instead of 'profits', to encompass dividends, interest, and royalties and licensing fees since the MNE views these three types of return, in after-tax terms, as basically equivalent. Second, I assume that restrictions on the repatriation of returns are viewed by the parent company as a detrimental measure, so that the MNE will be tempted to circumvent that constraint by way of TPM. In actual fact, the desire by MNEs to maximize and to speed up the homeward flow of returns from LDCs is mainly predicated on fears of incurring exchange losses. The motivations which are reviewed in this paper under sections D and C, therefore, appear to be closely related.

Restrictions on remittances are comparatively rare in MDCs. Accordingly, the contrast with LDCs is rather startling. Many LDCs impose various non-tax restrictions and inflict a distinctly more severe tax treatment on remittances of returns. Some of the major non-tax limitations on repatriations of returns are worth mentioning. There may be restrictions on the payment of dividends out of profits. Thus, the Andean countries initially restricted outgoing dividends to 14 per cent of the capital registered; this limit was subsequently raised to 20 per cent. Restrictions often are more stringent as regards other non-dividend channels. Within the broader regulatory framework which governs the transfer of technology into their countries, several LDCs such as India, Brazil, the Andean Group and Mexico, subject agreements between domestic investors and foreign suppliers of technology to government supervision; the latter is empowered to bar clauses viewed as unduly restrictive and to reduce the fees paid for the use of the technology. (For a survey of government practices in Latin America, see Carlos Maria Corea, 1983.)

Tax arrangements about remittances also tend to be harsh in several LDCs. This is partly but not only a matter of rates. Appendix II shows the rates of tax which a selected number of LDCs apply to alternative channels of remittances. Several LDCs such as Colombia and Mexico apply the basic corporate tax to royalties and interests; such remittances are thereby equated with corporate profits. Bolivia metes out the same treatment to dividends. One should add that high withholding taxes on remittances in the host countries are seldom relieved by double-taxation agreements since few exist between LDCs and MDCs. Particularly noteworthy is the rule whereby intra-firm licensing fees paid by the subsidiary to its parent are not tax deductible (Andean Pact, Brazil and India). Such treatment is bound to be viewed as detrimental by the MNEs since data for the USA (Kroner, 1980) and other countries (Deutsche Bundesbank, 1982) show that royalties received by MNEs headquartered in the above-mentioned countries are overwhelmingly derived from their subsidiaries.

Other tax provisions affecting remittances should be mentioned. Often the tax on licensing fees is assessed on a gross basis and does not recognize the specific costs involved in the transfer of technology which may be rather significant (Teece, 1976). Also, payments for overhead costs made at headquarters may be disallowed (as in Mexico) or subjected to various ceilings (for practices in French-speaking Africa, see Court, 1981).

As already stressed, the treatment of remittances in MDCs is typically more lenient, both as regards the tax regime and non-tax measures (the latter, in fact, are generally absent). This more accommodative stance can be related to three MDC basic practices. First, they apply the non-discrimination rule whereby affiliates of foreign MNEs are treated in the same way as domestic firms. Second, fees for technical know-how are fully deductible for tax purposes. Finally, bilateral agreements between MDCs substantially alleviate international double taxation on remitted returns. For example, in line with the OECD model convention, they generally attribute the right to tax royalties and interests to the home country so that no withholding tax or at the most a modest one prevails.

The highly restrictive measures of many LDCs with respect to the remittance of returns can be linked to a number of arguments. One objective is to reduce the outflow of capital and improve the balance-of-payments position. Another consideration is to maximize tax revenue for the host country, since to the extent that higher withholding taxes on returns can still be credited against corporate taxes due in the home country, the more stringent treatment of remittances does not harm the MNE. It is also claimed that since royalties and interests are alternative, and allegedly frequently (ab)used channels for the remittance of profits, they should not be favoured taxwise; hence, the imposition of the basic corporate tax rate to such remittances, as in some Latin American countries.

In the early 1970s, two more subtle and related arguments were formulated which apparently inspired some of the restrictions enacted in a number of LDCs. Both are predicated on the contention that the cost of acquiring technology is unduly burdensome for the LDC. The first argument claimed that technology, once produced, displays the characteristics of a public good and should accordingly be made available at marginal cost (Robin Murray, 1981). The related argument is that the parent company should not charge royalties separately to its subsidiaries because the return on the technology deployed is already subsumed in the price of the end product, since technology often provides some degree of market power to the MNE (see Lall and Streeten, 1977).

This setting of a rather harsh treatment of various forms of remittances in LDCs, readily suggests that MNEs are likely to be tempted into TPM. But this raises the preliminary question whether and why MNEs are concerned about constraints on the remittance of returns.

Various enquiries leave no doubt that MNEs, particularly the large ones with seasoned foreign subsidiaries, attach great weight to the freedom of homeward remittances and to a modest tax burden in the host country (Robbins and Stobaugh, 1973a, p. 75). The basic reasons are straightforward. When returns are held 'captive' within the host coutry they cannot be redeployed to projects elsewhere which may fetch a higher yield. A dividend flow must be secured to remunerate the shareholders of the parent company; in a highly multinationalized firm, foreign affiliates are bound to contribute their share. And yet these rationales are not fully convincing. Actual capital-budgeting procedures within MNEs are usually not as sophisticated as the return-maximizing textbook prescriptions postulate. Besides, if one accepts the Miller-Modigliani theorem, shareholders should be indifferent as between dividends and the capital gains, nurtured by reinvested profits.

Data on the allocation of subsidiary earnings show that the reinvestment ratio is quite high; in 1981 55 per cent of earnings for US-based MNEs were reinvested (Whichard, 1982). Data for 1976 show that the reinvestment ratio was higher in Latin America than in subsidiaries located in MDCs (Brean, 1983a). Several conceivable factors may explain this rather low dividend pay-out ratio; but the point is that MNEs appear to be willing to accept a rather high ratio of earnings being ploughed back into the subsidiaries. While reinvestments in the host country do not represent the optimal allocation of profits over alternative investment projects in a world-wide perspective, they may still qualify as second-best options in the face of restrictions on the repatriation of returns.

The apparent paradox that MNEs profess to attach a high ranking to the unimpeded repatriation of returns does not seem to be related to the compelling virtues of dividend pay-outs over profit retention, but must be linked to the fact that restrictions on the remittance of returns tend to prevail in LDCs, which struggle with balance-of-payments deficits and which maintain their currency at an overvalued rate. In such circumstances, captive returns not only represent an opportunity cost but, more importantly, often involve a potential exchange loss. In other words, the remittance issue basically turns into that of exchange risks discussed in the previous section. This explanation is also suggested in the available evidence on actual TPM in LDCs. The findings of Vaitsos (1974) and Lall (1973), that parent companies were overpricing the intermediates sold to subsidiaries in Latin American countries, suggest that exchange controls and risks were the basic motivation for TPM (see also Gereffi, 1983). A similar explanation also emerges in the case of Greece, where the control of import prices through physical inspection by customs officials appears to have been integrated with exchange controls by the central bank.

If one accepts the premise that MNEs are indifferent about the channel through which returns, net of host-country tax, flow to the parent company, the additional issue arises as to which remittance vehicle is most suited to maximize the repatriation of funds in the face of restrictions on the latter. Dividends, interest, licensing fees and services charges for specific services or overhead costs at headquarters are such alternative channels. The amount and the timing of dividend payments are normally subject to a high degree of discretion by the parent company; the other returns mentioned also lend themselves to TPM, in the sense that their price tag can, in principle, be made to deviate from the arm's-length price that would prevail if the same transaction had been contracted with a non-related party.

Only solid empirical data would permit definite answers as to the extent to which TPM is practised in order to magnify the flow of returns. Unfortunately, no clear profile emerges from the meagre data that have been assembled. Data about returns flowing to US-based MNEs show that royalties and licence fees only represent a small portion, viz. 12.6 per cent in 1981, of the dividends received from developing countries.[2] Interest payments were negative, i.e. the same MNEs were net transferrers of interest. (Debts to finance companies in the Netherlands Antilles largely accounted for this surprising outcome.) Service charges and rentals for tangible property were considerably larger than royalties and licence fees and amounted to 34 per cent of dividends (Whichard, 1982, pp. 17, 19). These data, however, only have limited usefulness for our purposes; their reliability is admittedly rather weak;[3] not all royalties and interests involve intra-firm flows; and finally, they do not show to what extent these actual flows and their implicit prices contain a coefficient of TPM that is unacceptable to the host country. Another relevant consideration is that, while there are many conceivable devices to extract returns from an LDC which applies severe restrictions, the complexities involved in the 'tangled web of intra-company connections' lead MNE managements to seek ways to improve the profits performance rather than fully to exploit all opportunities which systems optimization theoretically affords (Shapiro, 1982, p. 319).

Most of the findings in the business literature, based on limited numbers of observations or on questionnaires to financial managers, relate to the channels for repatriating returns in the form of fees, interests or dividends. Obviously, the other route along which judiciously timed TPM holds the promise of enlarged return flows out of the foreign subsidiary is intra-firm trade flows, such as the sale of intermediate goods by the parent company to its foreign affiliates. Research by Vaitsos (1974), Lall (1973) and Ganiotsos (1981) suggests that this may well be the preferred route through which remittances are concealed and enlarged. This inference is a plausible one, were it only because trade flows are so much larger than those of dividends and fees. The low degree of expertise of LDCs in checking TPM adds credence to the hypothesis that, to the extent MNEs are intent upon repatriating funds out of weak-currency LDCs, the overpricing of commodities sold to the foreign subsidiary is likely to be the main channel for hidden homebound transfers when various restrictions constrain the use of more overt routes.

One final comment on the link between TPM temptations and the remittance of returns to the parent company is important. Of necessity, the MNE in designing its policies must take into account the parameters imposed by the host and home governments. To the extent such regulations cannot be circumvented without transgressing legal prescriptions and incurring a high risk of being discovered and penalized, they are bound to have some effect on the behaviour of the MNE. Thus the deferral rule and high withholding taxes on remittances are likely to reduce the rate of repatriation of returns to the parent company along official channels.[4] For example, Chudnovsky (1982) concludes that the stringent restrictions on remittances operated in a number of Latin American countries did reduce the outflow of returns. While governments tend to view this policy-induced outcome as a positive one, the question remains whether the policies and regulations adopted are optimal. Capturing more tax revenue via restrictions on remittances may have occurred at the 'cost' of lower inflow of foreign capital (see Brean, 1983a).

III. Concluding Comments

This paper has the rather limited purpose of exploring the often heard statement that problems relating to TPM by MNEs loom larger in LDCs than in MDCs, in relation to the size of intra-firm payment flows. For lack of adequate data about actual pricing patterns on internal transactions and their deviations *vis-à-vis* generally accepted norms (more particularly, the 'arm's-length' (rule), much of the analysis on transfer prices has used essentially deductive lines to assess the scope for profitable TPM.

This paper follows a similar approach, giving an overview of the structural features in LDCs and of the policies adopted in such countries. Although theoretically there exist ample opportunities for TPM, whereby the impact of adverse government measures can be avoided or minimized, MNEs do not necessarily succumb to the temptation to practise TPM since both governmental counter-moves and organizational factors act as constraints.

Generally speaking, the query addressed in this paper appears to elicit an affirmative answer. LDCs typically impose more restrictions on the MNE than is the case in MDCs. In particular, the importance of import duties and the pervasiveness of exchange controls (amongst them, the often severe restrictions on the repatriation of returns from foreign investments) which are prompted by a weak balance-of-payments position and an overvalued currency, must be singled out. LDCs generally operate fewer measures to uncover and to redress TPM since they are less well equipped for the task. Our analysis also strongly suggests that the tax variable, so prominent in the literature on TPM, ought to be downgraded, as the tax burden on corporate profits is mostly lower in LDCs than in MDCs. In a number of particular segments of tax law, however, the fiscal variable and the resulting tax differentiation between the jurisdictions involved, or between alternative ways of carrying out business operations, provides scope for judicious tax planning and TPM. As a result, we conclude that TPM is more widespread in less developed countries than in developed ones.

This paper also carries the message that in order to arrive at reliable findings, research must be willing to probe into the details of government regulations and their interrelations. Outside the field of corporate taxation, not much has been achieved in this direction. And yet, several examples in this paper show that, when extended beyond generalities, the analysis reaches nuanced conclusions. This is the case when taxes on corporate profits by the host and home countries and their interconnections are taken into account. Also, temptations to use TPM in order to circumvent restrictions on the repatriation of returns from foreign direct investment must be related to overvalued domestic currencies and the resulting exchange risks as perceived by MNEs. As regards restrictions on imports, it is important to distinguish between (pure) quantitative restrictions and 'price instruments' (such as import duties) since TPM cannot be grafted on the former. Economic circumstances and the set of regulations implemented are also bound to vary rather significantly between individual LDCs, so that generalizations must be carefully hedged.

IV. Future Research

A few suggestions are ventured as to routes that could be usefully followed in further research on transfer pricing in LDCs, even if, when data on actual prices are lacking, the analysis remains limited to a discussion of the theoretical scope for TPM. The purpose, then, would consist in relating more closely the analysis of TPM temptations to alternative policies and sets of instruments practised by LDCs. Four aspects of this broad area are briefly outlined.

First, some instruments of economic policy appear to be almost 'given', i.e. determined by structural features of LDCs. Thus, as stressed in section II.B, import duties perform an important role as generator of fiscal revenue, and endemic balance-of-payments difficulties prompt the imposition of a set of rather permanent exchange controls.

Second, these structural constraints notwithstanding, LDCs do have some 'degrees of freedom' when formulating their policies. Thus the aims, contents and implications of a strategy of import substitution, *vis-à-vis* one of export-oriented growth (as epitomized by South Korea after 1962), differ significantly. The choice amongst those broad strategies is likely to affect the theoretical scope for TPM. For example, if the export-oriented growth strategy proves successful (see Krueger, 1983), balance-of-payments pressures are likely to abate which may soften the inducement to practise TPM for purposes of avoiding exchange risks.

Third, it would also be interesting to examine the link between TPM problems and the specific policies of LDCs *vis-à-vis* the MNE. One would expect that countries with comparatively more accommodative policies towards MNEs would be less concerned about possible TPM problems. Such correlation, however, is probably a weaker one than could be expected *a priori*. LDCs which adhere to an export-oriented strategy, even if they take a more relaxed stance as regards possible TPM abuses, do not necessarily give a red carpet treatment to the foreign MNE. Thus, South Korea still restricts the entry of foreign MNEs in given sectors. The successful conquest of foreign markets by South Korea has, in fact, been engineered fundamentally by domestic manufacturers, not by the affiliates of foreign MNEs.

Finally, we conclude that much of the literature on MNEs and on TPM is not satisfactory, as it often implicitly postulates that government measures are not only legitimate (which they are since they are enacted by sovereign powers), but also conducive to an efficient allocation of resources. The connotation is often that MNEs are the villains because they not only trangress regulations of governments, but also cause economic distortions (e.g. the general tenor in Robin Murray, 1981). Admittedly, in the segmented economies of LDCs, 'market failures' are more endemic than in MDCs (see Meier, 1982). The MNE may be the origin of some of these imperfections (e.g. when their operations reduce competition within the host country). But governments often generate government (policy) failures in that they distort the optimum allocation of resources. The fixation by governments on 'posted' prices for final or intermediate goods that are traded within MNEs can be cited as an example. In given circumstances TPM 'may be market perfecting if internal prices are closer to competitive equilibrium levels' (Buckley, 1983).

Endeavours to analyze the problems in the TPM-area, not only in terms of the actual policies pursued by host countries, but also in the light of more optimal policies, are likely to entail interesting insights. Although they would still not condone unacceptable behaviour by MNEs, they would narrow the area of contention between LDCs and MNEs and redirect some energies to the overriding objective of the less developed nations, namely faster growth.

Notes

1. One should stress that these inducements are not additive, in the sense that one move, e.g. the underinvoicing of imports, does not allow the MNE to reduce the burden on all regulations listed. The last two motivations mentioned do not stem from the desire to minimize adverse repercussions from government interventions but to pursue purely business objectives.

2. Since US regulations instruct the MNE to share overhead costs with its foreign subsidiaries, the MNE is caught between two fires. A similar uncomfortable predicament occurs when, in the host country, the subsidiary is not entitled to deduct licensing fees paid to the parent company. One must add, however, that only one method of extracting returns for the use of know-how should be allowed. Thus the OECD Report on Transfer Pricing (1979) contains the sensible rule that either cost-sharing arrangements or the charging of licensing fees should apply.

3. Reporting inaccuracies in balance-of-payments statistics are now widely acknowledged; investment income figures are amongst the more opaque items, see, for example, Federal Reserve Bank of St Louis (1983).

4. The absence of a well-developed domestic capital market is another structural feature of LDCs which favours profit retention. As against this, MNEs appear eager to obtain loan financing in the host country in order to offset the exposure of their assets in the latter's currency.

Appendix I: Various Inducements for Transfer Pricing

Hypothesis: the parent company sells to the subsidiary

Motivation	Action Taken by Multinational Firm	Comments
Corporate profits tax	Underpricing	In case host country tax is lower and profits are not distributed as dividends
		Affects revenues in two countries
customs duties:		
import duties	Underpricing	Affects revenue in only
export duties	Underpricing	one country
Exchange risks:		
claim in weak currency	Overpricing plus leading	Leading or lagging
claim in strong currency	Overpricing plus lagging	allows MNE to avoid exchange risks; transfer
debt in weak currency	Overpricing plus lagging	pricing enhances the
debt in strong currency	Overpricing plus leading	benefits of leading or lagging
Repatriation of profits or capital	Overpricing	
Capitalising machinery, etc.	Overpricing	Also increases the basis of depreciation allowances and of compensation in case of expropriation
Joint ventures	Overpricing	The 'gain' from transfer pricing is, by definition, shared with the joint partner
Give support to claims for price increases by showing higher costs	Overpricing	
Avoiding anti-monopoly charges	Underpricing	
Avoiding anti-dumping charges	Overpricing	
Mollify claims for wage increases by showing lower profits	Overpricing	
Support an infant subsidiary	Underpricing	
Enlarge market share to detriment of competitors ('predatory pricing')	Underpricing	Provided lower cost is shifted into lower price to consumer

Appendix II: Rates Applying to Corporate Profits, and to Remittances of Dividends, Interests and Royalties for Selected Countries

		Germany			Canada			USA		
	CT	DI	INT.	ROY.	DI	INT.	ROY.	DI	INT.	ROY.
Latin America										
Argentina	33 *	15	11	15	18	11	18	18	11	18
Bolivia	30 *	30	30	30	30	30	30	30	30	30
Brazil	40	15	15	15	25	25	25	25	25	25
Chile	52	40	40	40	40	40	40	40	40	40
Colombia	40	20	20	40	20	20	40	20	20	40
Costa Rica	45	15	20	10	15	20	10	15	20	10
Mexico	42	21	42	42	21	42	42	21	42	42
Nicaragua	40	45	30	30	45	30	30	45	30	30
Peru	40	30	40	55	30	40	55	30	40	55
Uruguay	25	0	25	0	0	25	0	0	25	0
Asia										
India	65 *	25	75	40	25	75	40	25	75	40
Indonesia	45 *	10	10	10	20	20	20	10	10	10
South Korea	40 *	10	15	10	25	25	25	25	25	25
Pakistan	60 *	20	20	0	20	60	60	15	60	0 **
Singapore	40 *	0	10	0	0	40	40	0	40	40
Developed Countries										
Canada	49 *	15	15	15	—	—	—	15	15	15
Germany	62/44	—	—	—	15	15	10	25	0	0
United Kingdom	53 *	15	0	0	15	15	10	15	0	0
United States	53 *	15	0	0	15	15	15	—	—	—
Japan	48/60 *	10	10	10	15	15	15	10	10	10

Notes: CT = Corporate Tax.
DI = Dividends.
INT. = Interests.
ROY. = Royalties.
* = denotes existence of a double taxation agreement between the pair of countries. Germany and Japan feature split corporate rates; the first rate pertains to retained earnings, the second to distribution.
** = Singapore reduces this rate, if thereby the tax liability in the home country is not increased.
Source: Hubner (1982).

14 THE REGULATION OF TRANSFER PRICES BY DEVELOPING COUNTRIES: SECOND-BEST POLICIES?

Walter A. Chudson

I. Introduction

The regulation of transfer prices — or more broadly of the international allocation of the taxable profits ˙of multinational enterprises (MNEs) — continues to be a vexing problem for governments, economists and the MNEs themselves. It is, of course, the international or interstate dimension of the fiscal conflict between sovereign jurisdictions and global enterprises that precipitates the issue of regulation. Transfer prices — on the accounting books or so-called 'shadow' prices — adopted for managerial purposes within a multidivisional enterprise as such create no fiscal conflicts, though they continue to produce managerial headaches and conundrums.

While the basic issue of regulation is the allocation of an MNE's income among fiscal jurisdictions, the focus of regulation has been primarily on the role of transfer prices in determining this allocation. As discussed below, this approach — known as the separate entity model — has been challenged by the 'unitary theory' which, while maintaining the policy of regulation, would apportion profits without regard to specific transfer prices.

The issue of international income allocation and transfer pricing is intrinsic to the operation of all MNEs wherever they operate. Nevertheless, there is a tendency to regard it as a matter which threatens the fiscal sovereignty of developing countries more than others. For this reason the present paper examines the issue of transfer pricing mainly from the perspective of such countries.

This examination can start with the proposition that there is general agreement as to the fiscal inducements to transfer price determination, using the term fiscal in contrast to purely managerial considerations. High on the list are international tax and tariff differentials and, particularly in developing host countries, foreign exchange restrictions and other remittance controls, price controls and profit-related policies, performance requirements and the like. The record seems to support the assumption that inducements to 'manipulate' transfer pricing involving affiliates in developing countries are particularly strong because of these regulatory market imperfections, with the possible exception of international tax differentials.

No doubt the first-best solution to the problem of transfer price manipulation, however defined, would be the disappearance of the regulatory policies of host and home governments constituting such inducement. In such a Utopian world, blessed with uniform national tax regimes among other perfections, there would remain only the managerial, purely internal motivations. Invoking Utopia does not mean that a narrowing of tax differentials and a shrinkage of other market imperfections is to be excluded; some has occurred. But the extensive machinery of transfer price regulation in place testifies to the distance from Utopia that remains, as well as to an implicit official rejection of the position that deregulation is the correct second-best policy.

Before embarking on a survey of the regulatory options, account should be taken of the deregulationist approach, exemplified by Rugman (1981). The internalized transactions of the MNE are viewed as an efficient response to market imperfections arising in significant measure from government regulation. The transfer prices that overcome the costs imposed by these market imperfections make the MNE functional, thus promoting an efficient allocation of resources and production. On this view, the resulting shifting of profits must be regarded as the price of allocative efficiency in this less than most perfect of possible worlds. If some countries' tax revenues and foreign exchange receipts are eroded in the process (and others' expand), this is a matter for international consideration, leaving the optimal global allocation of production intact.

The practitioners and advocates of regulation, on the other hand, dismiss or ignore the issue of allocative efficiency, with the exception of the unitary school, discussed below. Their concern is the deprivation of tax revenue caused by the MNE's pursuit of global profit maximization and risk minimization.

In the face of many practical frustrations, governments — first in industrial countries and more recently in some developing countries — have pressed on with regulation. The outcome has been the accumulation of an armamentarium of regulatory measures (the deregulationists might call it a Procrustean bed) adopted or proposed. It is the purpose of this paper to pass these regulatory options in review.

II. Characteristics of Intra-firm Transactions

As a background for reviewing regulatory options, particularly those involving direct monitoring of prices, it is useful to survey briefly the terrain of intra-firm transactions. The statistics have been analysed, notably by Helleiner, among others (Helleiner and Lavergne, 1979; Lall, 1978b, Helleiner, 1981; Chudson, 1981). With few exceptions, the data refer understandably to the aggregate value of transactions and less so to their unit value.

The motivations and practices of corporate managers in fixing transfer prices are also documented in a body of literature based on responses to questionnaires.

A. Exports to Affiliates

The most comprehensive data on intra-firm commodity trade refer to United States MNEs in 1977 (United States, 1981a). Using a broad definition of direct foreign investment to encompass a minimum equity ownership of 10 per cent by one US person, it was found that 36 per cent of exports and 39 per cent of imports were intra-firm transactions.[1] Canada alone accounted for almost half of the MNEs' exports to industrial countries.

United States intra-firm exports to developing countries were only 4.2 per cent of total intra-firm exports, or 12 per cent of US merchandise exports. Over 60 per cent of such exports went to Latin America, mostly to Brazil, Mexico and Venezuela. In Asia four countries received the predominant share: Singapore, Hong Kong, Malaysia and the Philippines. The 'internalization ratio' (intra-firm imports or exports as a percentage of total imports or exports) in several developing countries was quite high (UN, 1983a). Brazil recorded a ratio of 50 per cent in 1972 (imports, manufacturing only) and 70 per cent (exports); in Mexico, the ratios were 58 per cent (imports) and 82 per cent (exports). The significance of these figures depends, however, on the relation of intra-firm imports and exports to domestic value-added.

The nature of the merchandise traded has a bearing on the

potential for manipulation of prices and hence of direct regulation. It is part of conventional wisdom to refer to the lack of comparable arm's-length prices for many intermediate products and to the frustration in reconstructing a market price equivalent based on costs. For finished goods destined for resale, on the other hand, deviations from conventional mark-ups can more readily indicate 'overpricing' or 'underpricing'. Also, finished goods usually bear high *ad valorem* duties, tending to restrain overpricing of imports. It is interesting, therefore, that 63 per cent of US intra-firm exports in 1977 consisted of 'merchandise for resale' without further processing. As expected, nevertheless, the ratio for developing countries is lower, about 50 per cent in the case of Latin America.

B. *Intra-firm Exports to Parent MNEs*

While declining after the petroleum nationalizations of the early 1970s, the share of intra-firm imports by US parent MNEs from affiliates in developing countries remained larger than the comparable imports from industrial countries. Nevertheless, the share of non-petroleum intra-firm imports in total US imports from the developing countries dropped from 20 per cent to 11 per cent between 1967 and 1975 (Helleiner, 1981).

Certain recent changes in the marketing of primary commodities have a bearing on transfer pricing. One is the fixing of 'notional' or 'posted' prices by host governments for certain commodities (notably bauxite) produced under conditions of international vertical integration. In other cases, a parallel independent international market price exists as a potential reference price. Also, it appears that some primary commodities exported by developing countries, whether by MNEs or domestically controlled firms, are entering the world market directly rather than through vertically integrated channels.

Manufactures have constituted an increasing share of affiliates' intra-firm exports, the major portion consisting of electrical and electronic products (UN, 1983a). This type of intermediate good gives particular trouble to authorities monitoring arm's-length prices. Yet such exports do not account for the major part of the recent expansion of manufactures exported by developing countries (Helleiner, 1981). The type of manufactures exported by developing countries that has expanded rapidly — notably textiles, clothing, footwear and other light consumers' goods — is 'less subject to management through majority-owned affiliates than is primary product trade' (Helleiner, 1981, p. 43). But a tendency for more arm's-length transactions in primary commodities has been observed (Helleiner, 1981).

In 1977 US MNE imports from their affiliates totalled $16.7 billion, of which manufactures were $3.2 billion (United States, 1981a). Since the latter were highly concentrated in a few developing countries, this suggests that the focus of any direct regulation of transfer prices of such transactions might be a few countries, a few industrial sectors and probably a limited number of commodities. The technical and administrative problems of such regulation are discussed below.[2]

C. Intangibles

Intra-firm royalties and fees, while small in relation to merchandise trade, have been growing, along with similar arm's-length transactions. Such transactions, despite being subject increasingly to substantial withholding taxes, may provide a significant alternative channel for remittances, particularly when remittance through the dividend route is blocked and transfer price remittance through commodity transactions are inhibited.

Royalties and licence fees paid to US MNEs by their foreign affiliates were estimated in 1977 at $2.2 billion. of which payments from developing countries were, surprisingly, only $155 million (United States, 1981a). Royalties and fees from these foreign affiliates comprised over 80 per cent of total US receipts from royalties and similar payments from all sources, that is including arm's-length transactions.

D. MNE's Testimony on Inducements

Assuming some form of regulation, evidence concerning the particular environmental factors that induce transfer pricing manipulation and the relative force of such inducements is of interest.

Studies of statements by managers concerning their firms' decisions on transfer prices confirm an awareness of and response to the major market imperfections — tax differentials, customs duties, exchange restrictions and the like (Arpan, 1972; Tang, 1979; Burns, 1980; Yunker, 1982). There is also evidence of the inhibiting effect of tax audits by the fiscal authorities (Greene and Duerr, 1970).

There is evidence of mixed motives as between efficiency criteria ('profit centres') and the fiscal objective of profit maximization after tax and risk minimization. For example, Tang finds that United States and Japanese multinationals tend to rank motives similarly: global profit maximization, minimization of tariff payments and motivation of profit centres. Robbins and Stobaugh (1973a) suggest that 'medium-sized' firms are more prone to centralize transfer pricing decisions than very large or small firms, but there is a question whether this evidence was controlled for degree of internalization or other industrial characteristics.

According to Brean (this volume), corporations are finding that tinkering with transfer prices is simply not worth the candle. It is not clear on what data this interesting observation is based, but three reasons are given: (1) corporate inhibitions reflecting stricter rules and administration by fiscal authorities; (2) reduction in tariff rates and international tax differentials; (3) perhaps most important, developments in intra-corporate financial manoeuvring of capital structure which allegedly offer as much if not greater prospect of minimizing a firm's global tax bill as transfer price manipulation, as well as lowering exchange risk and achieving other objectives.

These studies do not isolate inducements affecting developing countries as such. Evidence, mainly anecdotal, in this case tends to focus on non-tax factors, as indicated in the following statement by a US multinational manager:

> If I cannot get my dividends out, and my royalty rate is fixed, and I want to remit more money, then I do this by an uplift [sic] of my transfer prices on commodities (Robbins and Stobaugh, 1973a, p. 91).

Frank (1980) obtained similar responses from a sample of 90 MNEs with affiliates in developing countries. Bierstecker (1978) reports that in a small sample of Nigerian firms manipulated transfer prices did not exist and the remission of profits was not a problem. The Nigerian balance of payments was described as being at the time in a relaxed state, which could be taken as an indication of the opposite tendency of transfer pricing under less favourable circumstances.

III. Direct Regulation

The weaponry of regulation falls into two classes: (1) measures to replace directly one transfer price by another; and (2) all others, which have an indirect effect on the allocation of income. A more profound classification, perhaps, is between measures founded on the separate entity theory and those treating the MNE as a unitary entity. Other than the unitary entity model, all other regulatory measures treat the MNE as consisting of separate entities, thus focusing on intra-firm prices. Only the unitary theory conforms to the internalization-deregulationist model, in which transfer prices do not matter.

A. *Direct Replacement of an MNE's Transfer Price*

Emanating from the early concern with fiscal transfer prices affecting the allocation of taxable income among jurisdictions it has seemed reasonable, even obvious, that an appropriate price should be defined as one that would prevail if the respective national units of the international enterprise dealt with each other as if at 'arm's length'. Hence the characterization of this approach as the separate entity theory, in contrast to the integrated unitary entity whose transactions, though international, are treated as of no more concern to the fiscal authorities than those of a purely national enterprise.

Judging a transfer price by the arm's-length principle — defined as the price of a comparable transaction between unrelated parties or the equivalent thereof constructed by accounting procedures — has commended itself to advocates of regulation representing a wide range of ideology and policy. In effect, the arm's-length standard is a formula that implies that the MNE and the conditions which give rise to it do not exist, and it has been criticized accordingly (for example, Rugman, 1981; Aliber, this volume; Hennart, 1982). Here we suspend judgement on this view and confine the discussion to administrative aspects.

The arm's-length standard appears to have been enshrined in legislation first in the United States. More recently in such diverse forums as the Organization for Economic Cooperation and Development (OECD, 1979), the United Nations (UN, 1978a, 1983a) and the European Economic Commission it has been accepted as the exclusive criterion for legitimate transfer prices, as a basis both for government regulation and as a guideline for MNE managers. The principle has been extended by incorporation in numerous bilateral tax treaties.

In 1974, a United Nations advisory committee (UN, 1974a), while recommending that governments eliminate or reduce the external inducements for transfer pricing manipulation, exhorted host and home governments to enforce arm's-length pricing and formulate appropriate rules on pricing practices for tax purposes.

Nevertheless, the arm's-length standard has not been immune from vigorous criticism on both theoretical and practical grounds. The theoretical criticism emanates from the advocates of the unitary theory who themselves split into proponents of another formula for the allocation of profits, namely apportionment, and the advocates of complete deregulation ('the cure is worse than the disease'). Criticism based on practical difficulties of applying the arm's-length principle has blossomed into an extensive literature.

As a recent example, a United Nations report (UN, 1983a, pp. 100-1) cites a frequently quoted statement by the US Internal Revenue Service:

> US experience has demonstrated that even with detailed guidelines, the 'safe haven' rules and substantial disclosure requirements, an arm's-length profit margin or mark-up is still often an elusive phantom.

Nevertheless, the United Nations report proposes no alternative principle of regulation, but merely advocates moderate reinforcing action such as bilateral joint audits to augment the exchange of information provided in treaties on double taxation which already embody the arm's-length principle.

Another much-quoted report describes the enforcement experience of the US Internal Revenue Service (United States Treasury, 1973). Of almost 900 cases, reviewed under the allocation provisions of Section 482 of the Internal Revenue Code, the Service found the application of the arm's-length standard unsuitable in about 40 per cent, in any of the three sanctioned forms: uncontrolled market price, cost-plus, or resale price minus a mark-up. In these cases the government applied the 'fourth alternative', namely a negotiated settlement based on information from a variety of public and private sources, including, significantly, an element of apportionment of consolidated profits.

The theory and practice of establishing an arm's-length price for commercial technology and services have predictably given regulators greater difficulty than for merchandise trade. Comparable uncontrolled market transactions are generally lacking, almost by definition, and the reconstruction of an equivalent price by the other standard methods rarely feasible. The problem arises from the gap between the average and marginal cost of producing the service and the difficulty of allocating joint costs. This takes us into a bargaining model of welfare economics justifying an effort by the licensee and/or its government to appropriate as much of the economic rent from the supplier of technology as possible (Johnson, 1970).

Accordingly, some developing countries have fixed ceilings on intra- as well as inter-firm royalties, prohibited restrictive clauses in licences, imposed large withholding taxes on intra-firm royalties and, in several instances, disallowed intra-firm royalty payments altogether. At the same time some home governments have created the threat of double taxation by pressing resident firms to reallocate their world-wide distribution of R&D and other central office expenditures.

In 1981 a critical report on the auditing of transfer prices under the US Internal Revenue Code (Section 482) became the subject of a sharp exchange between the Comptroller General of the United States on the one side and the Department of the Treasury and the Internal Revenue Service on the other (United States, 1981b). Apart from reaffirming the need for improvement in enforcing the arm's-length standard of Section 482 (by adopting 'safe haven' ranges for prices, for example) the report is notable for officially reopening consideration of the desirability of applying the alternative of an apportionment formula (see below), reporting 'expert' opinion that the arm's-length standard is 'fundamentally flawed because it is not consistent with the economic reality of the operations of the related corporated group' (United States, 1981b, p. 50). In a sharp rejoinder, contained in the report, the Department of the Treasury rejected the formula apportionment principle on theoretical and practical grounds (see below).

The problem of inconsistent national allocations of taxable income and consequent double taxation (or possibly the opposite), has not been overlooked by governments and tax experts, irrespective of the allocation principle or definition of income of national tax systems. Apart from the inclusion of the arm's length principle in tax treaties, such treaties or informal administrative understandings may provide for 'correlative adjustment' arising from conflicting official transfer price determinations or income allocations. Shoup (1974, this volume) proposes an international 'tax court' composed of independent experts with power of binding arbitration over allocation disputes. The case for such machinery is deemed by Shoup to be particularly strong because of the disparate administrative capacity of developing countries. In Shoup's formulation the disputes to be arbitrated would be those arising only under the application of the separate entity principle, but application under the unitary principle is conceivable under certain circumstances.

It has been observed that MNEs themselves might appreciate the greater stability, particularly freedom from conflicting jurisdictions, that would ensue from an intergovernmental agreement over transfer pricing or possibly apportionment (Vernon, 1971; Bergsten, *et al.*, 1978). A supportive approach is the movement towards greater corporate financial transparency through the adoption of international standards of accounting and reporting (UN, 1983b).

Shot full of holes on theoretical and practical grounds, tattered by doubts expressed by tax authorities themselves, the arm's-length flag yet waves, if only for want of a better alternative.[3] While the unitary theory has found intellectual support and some official application notably in states *within* a federal jurisdiction, national authorities and international organizations alike adhere to the arm's-length standard despite considerable pragmatic departures, as in the US Internal Revenue Service's recourse to the 'fourth method'.

To conclude this section on a positive note, it may be asserted that a developing country bent on applying the arm's-length standard is not necessarily faced with an utterly impossible task. For one thing, the importance of intra-firm trade varies considerably from industry to industry and even within firms within a given industry (Helleiner, 1979; Mathewson and Quirin, 1979). Further, standardized intermediate goods exist in some industries to inhibit manipulation. There is also the possibility of expert arbitration advocated by Shoup (this volume).

These considerations suggest that a developing country bent on regulating transfer prices in certain industries or firms would need to take several steps. The first would be to acquire information on MNE affiliates having high internalization ratios. Secondly, these affiliates would be analyzed to determine the degree of standardization of their intra-firm merchandise transactions. Thirdly, such firms would be examined against the background of the integrated MNE as a whole and data on the global structure of the industry in question. Coupled with strengthened disclosure requirements, such procedures might tend to reverse the burden of proof of manipulation and have an inhibiting effect.

There is little doubt that the monitoring of royalties and central office expenses is more difficult than of commodity transactions in general for developing and industrial countries alike. Apart from taxing such transactions, as discussed below, regulators have tended to fall back on a 'bargaining model'. This may exert pressure to justify any price discrimination by the parent firm involving other affiliates or independent licencees (UN, 1974a; OECD, 1979). The problem may also be moderated by two practical factors. In developing countries the total value of intra-firm transactions in technology appears to be quite small compared with intra-firm merchandise transactions, although it may be high in a few particular cases. A second consideration is that royalty fees are reported by licensors to be fixed conventionally within fairly narrow limits. But the variety of non-price conditions surrounding contracts for the transfer of technology inevitably clothes this area of regulation in much uncertainty.

B. Notional Prices

The price of an intra-firm transaction has on occasion been fixed by a host country, with or without negotiation with the MNE concerned, for an extended period for the purpose of determining income subject to tax. Such so-called notional or posted prices have been fixed for primary commodities, but have been applied by some developing countries also to royalties.

Such action has been taken particularly in the absence of a comparable open market price arising from the production of an intermediate primary commodity within a vertically integrated enterprise in an industry in which this production and market structure is the general rule. In this situation host countries have been concerned not only to establish a suitable transfer price but to maximize their tax revenue by capturing a quasi-rent from the MNE. The application of the policy is facilitated by the system of tax credits employed by most industrial home countries, the result being a shift of revenue from the home to the host country.

The classic example of a posted price, though no longer relevant, is that for crude petroleum exported by MNEs from certain Arab countries. In this case the price was set by mutual agreement.

A currently functioning formula applies to bauxite exported by Jamaica and several other countries. In Jamaica, a production levy is imposed at the rate of 8.5 per cent of the price at which ingot aluminium is sold on the open market in the United States. The amount payable depends on the quantity of bauxite ore used to produce a ton of metal.

In regulating royalties a few countries, mainly in Latin America, have adopted a regime controlling prices (as well as other conditions) for arm's-length licensing contracts as well as for intra-firm royalty payments.

A somewhat comparable approach, bypassing the determination of an arm's-length price or equivalent is 'production sharing', a contractual arrangement applied thus far to several petroleum and other natural resource projects. The parties share the physical output in a predetermined way (after agreed production costs have been met) and are free to sell their share, thus eliminating the necessity of determining a transfer price for the commodity. There may be a question of pricing the inputs, but these are likely to be standardized items. Under US tax regulations a technical problem arises in that in order to qualify for a foreign tax credit, a foreign tax must be acceptable in form and substance as equivalent to the United States income tax. Accordingly, the foreign tax applied by the host country in a production-sharing agreement must be separate from royalty or similar taxes and the income subject to the host country's tax must be, in principle, comparable to a tax under United States income tax regulations, including the arm's-length standard.

IV. Indirect Measures

A. Reduction of International Tax Differentials

Minimizing its global tax liability is an obvious object of an MNE's corporate policy, and much of the literature on transfer pricing has singled out international differences in effective corporate income and withholding tax rates and the relevant *ad valorem* duties as the dominant inducement for profit-shifting (Horst, 1971, 1977; Kopits, 1976a, b; Lessard, 1979; Mathewson and Quirin, 1979).[4] Short of attaining the ideal of a common, universal income tax, a reduction in international tax differentials is generally regarded as the major object of policies designed to lessen the inducement to transfer price manipulation; or, from the deregulationist position, as a step towards market perfection.

The concern here is the relevance of international tax differentials (always taken to allow for the impact of tariffs) to profit-shifting affecting developing countries. How large and significant are tax differentials between developing (host) and industrial (home) countries, measured as effective rates? In the case of developing countries are such differentials reinforced or mitigated by other inducements, particularly restrictions on foreign exchange transfers, price controls, tariffs, and other regulatory measures and policies of host countries? Is there a systematic pattern in the tax rates of industrial home countries and developing host countries; and how does the structure of national tax systems (particularly the assertion of jurisdiction over foreign source income and deferral from tax liability accorded to unremitted profits) affect the pattern of tax differentials? In sum, what is the interest of developing countries in international tax harmonization?

A statistical analysis of tax differentials is far beyond the scope of this paper. A few comments are offered, with an awareness that such comparisons are on slippery ground.

At first glance the nominal rates of corporate income tax in the main industrial countries suggest that the comparable rates in developing countries generally could hardly be higher and might well be substantially lower. This is indicated in several studies (Kyrouz, 1975; Kopits, 1976b; Bergsten, *et al.*, 1978).[5] Data on effective rather than nominal rates are scanty and fraught with problems of comparability.

Lall (1973, p. 179) asserts that 'the cards are stacked' against developing countries because 'not only do their tax rates tend to be higher' but their duties on imported intermediates lower, thus not significantly offsetting the alleged unfavourable tax differential. There is little doubt about the duties, certainly on raw materials and semi-finished items, but Lall offers no evidence for the taxes. Plasschaert (1980, p. 179) concludes that 'various strands of analysis and elements of empirical evidence strongly suggest that profit tax considerations may be considerably less relevant than is popularly believed', noting that *within* the industrial countries, at least, tax rates (effective?) do not differ greatly. This observation is corroborated by a study of Scandinavian-based MNEs indicating that corporate tax planning has had only a limited influence on internal financial flows (Lodin, 1978/9). It has been noted above that Brean (this volume) has concluded that transfer pricing for fiscal reasons has been diminishing in favour of tax minimization measures through modifying the financial structure of MNEs, but this is attributed to easier bypassing of regulatory controls by that mechanism, not to a narrowing of tax differentials.

A recent report by the United States Senate Committee on Finance (United States, 1983) presents data for a sample of large US MNEs comparing effective tax rates on US source and foreign source income. For 1981 the companies reported effectitve rates on US source income far below nominal rates as follows (in per cent of taxable income): beverages, 28.8; chemicals, 5.0; commercial banks, 2.3; crude oil production, 3.1; electronics appliances, 29.3; food processing, 26.8; industrial and farm equipment, 24.1; metal manufacturing, 9.8; motor vehicles (an exception) 47.7; office equipment, 25.3; oil and refining, 18.6; pharmaceuticals, 35.9; tobacco, 31.3. For these industries, the foreign tax rate on foreign source income was much higher, except for tobacco, partly it seems because of the inclusion of foreign taxes not creditable under US regulations. While these data might indicate presumptive evidence of possible tax advantage on shifting profits to the United States parent firm it should be emphasized that the overwhelming portion of the foreign source income originated in industrial host countries, not in developing countries.

Even if, contrary to the general impression derived from the relatively low nominal rates in developing countries, and taking account of tax haven shelters (see below), there was some inducement for tax reasons for outward profit-shifting from developing countries, it is evident that this would be but one of several inducements operating in the same direction and not the most powerful, in general. On the other hand, the probability of shifting profits to developing countries for tax reasons seems far-fetched — except possibly to tax havens, given the strong centripetal non-tax forces at work, notably exchange restrictions.

In some cases, however, the operation of tax deferral in residence countries' tax systems might induce the reinvestment of profits in a developing country, especially in conjunction with a tax holiday — an inference which is consistent with the high proportion of US direct investment financed by reinvested earnings.

This would be an instance, rarely cited in international discussions, of an inward shifting of profits to a host developing country that might be abetted by transfer pricing. Nevertheless, developing countries have protested at the undermining of tax holidays by the unwillingness of certain industrial countries to conclude 'tax-sparing' treaties. As a final note, one may mention alleged instances of profit-shifting into developing countries to increase host-country revenue without an increase in the MNE's global tax liability due to the operation of the home country's system of tax credits.

B. *Curbing the Benefits from Tax Havens*

If it is accepted that tax differentials do not play a strong part generally in inducing profit-shifting from or to developing countries, there remains the possible escape route of tax havens. Tax avoidance through a tax haven need not necessarily involve transfer pricing, but the potential for avoiding both home and host taxes is enhanced by transfer pricing manoeuvres in a tax haven. Transfer pricing manipulation is only one aspect of the use of tax havens for tax avoidance or evasion. Even if practically uniform income tax rates in non-tax haven countries were achieved, the shunting of profits to tax havens would remain attractive.

To control tax avoidance through tax havens, including income allocations induced by transfer pricing involving a tax haven affiliate, the leading home countries have adopted regulations treating most income accruing to controlled affiliates incorporated in tax haven jurisdictions as current income (like income of a branch) and thus subject to the same tax liability in the home country as remitted funds.

This amounts, in effect, to the abolition of the privilege of deferral and can be regarded as an outgrowth of the animated debate in the United States Congress in 1962 on a proposal by the Administration and some legislators to abolish deferral entirely. If all the major home countries of MNEs did this, given their generally high tax rates, their assertion of jurisdiction over foreign source income and their granting of a credit for taxes paid abroad, this would achieve a substantial degree of international tax harmonization, in other words substantially reducing international tax differentials as an inducement for transfer pricing manipulation. It would also produce a situation of 'capital export neutrality', with the investor paying the same total tax on foreign investment as on domestic investment.

In the event, tax reform fell short of this target. Instead an amendment to the US revenue code, so-called Subpart F, was adopted in 1962 providing, with certain exceptions, that if no significant economic operations of a controlled affiliate occur within a country (presumably a tax haven) the United States will assert tax jurisdiction over the profits accruing to the affiliate even if the income is not remitted.[6]

Similar action has been taken by the Federal Republic of Germany, the United Kingdom, France, Japan, Canada, Australia, among others. Information on the effectiveness of this policy is meagre and conflicting. A recent United Nations report (UN, 1983a) calls tax havens a serious challenge to the authorities of host and home countries, citing a recent report by a consultant to the US Internal Revenue Service (Gordon, 1981) stating that '. . . taxpayers ranging from large multinational corporations to small individuals to criminals are making extensive use of tax havens' (p. 3).

Nevertheless, the report contains data suggesting a measure of caution in judging Subpart F provisions ineffective. One indication is that in 1976 manufacturing firms — the main practitioners of transfer pricing — comprised only 14 per cent of the total assets of US controlled enterprises located in tax havens, whereas non-manufacturing enterprises (offshore banking firms, 'captive' insurance companies and holding companies owning securities and real estate) held 81 per cent.[7]

Further, although the total assets of US controlled corporations in tax havens grew fivefold from 1968 to 1976, manufacturing, as indicated above, was only 14 per cent of the total in tax havens, whereas in non-tax havens it was 55 per cent; in contrast assets of non-manufacturing firms in tax havens were 81 per cent compared with 38 per cent in non-tax haven countries (Gordon, 1981). The major growth of tax haven corporations for a variety of financial reasons could be compatible with restraint on manufacturing and service corporations exercised by the 1962 legislation.

If the abolition of deferral were applied generally, not just to tax havens, it would, of course, represent a significant reduction of international tax differentials. Its importance for the manipulation of transfer prices affecting developing countries is questionable, however, if tax differentials play a minor role in this case.

C. Taxation of Intra-firm Transfer Payments (Tariffs, Royalties)

It has been frequently observed that the incentive to overinvoice an intra-firm commodity transaction to reduce taxes in a relatively high-tax jurisdiction is reduced by an increased *ad valorem* customs duty payable on the transaction. This logic can be extended to other categories of transactions which are counted as costs in the host country. If such transactions are taxed uniformly by a country with a relatively high income tax rate, the country's total revenue from the affiliate would be unaffected by shifting intra-firm transactions from one channel to another for tax reasons, say from dividends to royalties. For example, Kopits (1976a) established a significant substitution of royalty payments for dividend remittances, explained by the host countries having a higher tax rate on dividends but a lower tax rate on royalties than the US corporate income tax rate.

A number of developing countries, recognizing that intra-firm royalty payments offer an opportunity to shift profits which is difficult to detect, impose a substantial withholding tax on intra-firm royalties. A few have disallowed deduction of intra-firm royalties altogether as a business expense, treating royalty payments as profit. The economic rationale for this policy has been analysed as a proposition in welfare economics (Johnson, 1970) and development economics (Stewart, 1981).

While source country taxation of intra-firm transfer payments resists the bypassing of normal channels of income taxation, it presents certain difficulties. The most obvious is that in respect of merchandise transactions it would subordinate industrial tariff policy to taxation policy, an unlikely outcome.

Further, to treat the supply of technology as having a marginal cost of zero or nearly so, implies that the taxing (host) country has no interest in carrying any part of the burden of supporting future research and development costs of an MNE in anticipation of future benefits. Taxing or disallowing royalties as costs in effect creates a bargaining situation in which the supply function of technology to the developing country becomes indeterminate.

Another issue arises because source or 'deemed' source taxation of royalties and service income is generally not recognized by the tax authorities of the industrial countries for fear of a reduction of revenue, thus becoming a source of jurisdictional conflict and double taxation.

Most importantly, taxation of intra-firm transactions by the source country would not curb non-tax inducements for profit shifting. Since in the developing countries these inducements are generally more powerful than tax differentials or other tax motives, it is unlikely that the taxation of intra-firm transactions would effectively regulate the pricing of transactions other than royalties.

D. *Minority Interests*

As regards the monitoring and regulation of transfer pricing, certain advantages and disadvantages have been seen in joint ventures, depending on whether the perspective is that of the MNE or the host country.

It has been argued that the MNE has an incentive to extract quasi-rents from a minority partner or local shareholder by manipulating transfer prices.

On the other hand, in advocacy of joint ventures, particularly in developing countries, it has been asserted that such arrangements would inhibit manipulation by facilitating the monitoring of transfer prices by the local party, whether private or state enterprise. This judgement has been qualified by expressions of disenchantment on the ground that the local partner, not to mention the host government, probably lacks the information and technical capacity to judge the appropriateness of transfer prices. In the absence of information the matter remains moot.

E. *Apportionment*

The measures reviewed thus far assume direct or indirect regulation of transfer prices between units of an MNE considered as separate entities. Dissatisfaction with the theory of this approach and, still more, with its applicaiton in practice, particularly embodied in the arm's-length standard, has focused attention on alternatives. Short of complete deregulation, the major if not the only meaningful fiscal alternative is the apportionment of the MNE's consolidated income among its national affiliates. This requires a formula which is deemed to attribute the MNE's profits to the relevant jurisdictions and thus broadly to satisfy the test of equity.

The 'unitary entity' theory, as this approach is known, can be regarded as a corollary of the internalization theory of transfer prices as expounded, for example, by Rugman. Since it is concerned only with the consolidated profit of the MNE as an entity, the accounting profits of individual affiliates and the transfer prices that help to determine them are seen as irrelevant to the allocation of income among jurisdictions, reflecting managerial decisions that are, in principle, no different from those arising from transactions between the divisions of a purely national enterprise.

The unitary entity thus rejects the legitimacy of the separate entity theory and the arm's-length principle which is based upon it. The MNE as corporate enterprise is deemed to exist only because of its properties as an entity, the operations of whose national affiliates are organically inseparable from the integrated whole. For internalization to perform its economic function, transfer prices must respond to external transaction costs and to exogenous market imperfections such as tax differentials and exchange restrictions.

From this common footing, however, the unitary entity theory veers sharply from the benign neglect policy of internalization theorists to espouse its own form of income apportionment to solve the fiscal dilemma raised by MNEs. This is the so-called 'factor formula', which would apportion the global income of the MNE, defined by the taxing authority or authorities according to the relative size of certain variables in each jurisdiction, usually total assets, payroll and sales, computed generally as the simple average of these factors.

Apart from theoretical considerations, the factor formula has the great advantage of eliminating all the difficulties of estimating arm's-length prices or their equivalent.

On closer examination, however, serious practical pitfalls appear. To begin with, it is not always self-evident which units of a MNE should be considered interdependent, that is part of the integrated MNE, rather than purely passively linked by legal ties. This is more likely to be the case in a horizontally as distinct from a vertically integrated firm. Secondly, if one affiliate incurs losses, or very low profits, compared to the consolidated average, the losing unit would be unduly taxed. While perhaps not fatal, these difficulties would require administrative guidelines and administration for efficient execution, whether unilaterally or by international agreement. A third problem with the factor formula is that it allocates income on the assumption that the capital and labour used in the several jurisdictions are equally productive, which is not realistic. It is not appropriate to give equal weight to the factors representing capital and labour (assets and payroll) since these do not normally contribute equally to value-added (McLure, 1974). Some adjustments for these and other technical difficulties are, however, conceivable.

A difficulty with the factor formula would arise if some states remained on a separate entity basis. Profits could be shifted from a separate entity jurisdiction by manipulating transfer prices without increasing the tax liability of affiliates subject to the aportionment formula. Also, since sales are one factor entering into the formula, the allocation of income in a particular jurisdiction can be manipulated to take advantage of a tax differential, for example, by shifting the value of sales from one jurisdiction to another by manipulating transfer prices.

Varying definitions of net income in different tax jurisdictions could present a problem for the construction of an agreed figure for consolidated profits. Some advisory steps towards mitigating this particular difficulty by standardizing the accounting principles of MNEs have been taken under the aegis of the United Nations (UN, 1983a).

The factor formula can be applied by a state unilaterally or by international agreement. Obviously, unilateral application could lead to double taxation unless a correlative adjustment were made. In fairness, however, it has been pointed out that conflicts over income allocation are not eliminated by recourse to the arm's-length standard (Shoup, this volume).

Despite formal adherence exclusively to the arm's-length standard (apart from the nebulous 'fourth method'), there is some evidence in rulings of the United States Tax Court of Appeals that, when frustrated in applying the arm's-length standard, courts and tax administrators in the United States have fallen back on a rough apportionment formula as supporting evidence or, in effect, as a way of placing the burden of proof on the legitimacy of a transfer price on the taxpayer. Also, in allocating costs of research and development and other central office expenses, some rules of thumb resembling apportionment have reportedly been used.

Despite its avoidance of arm's-length estimations, its theoretical appeal and ostensible administrative simplicity, apportionment has gained only limited official support, mainly in certain states within the United States, (e.g. California), Canada and Australia. The explanation seems to be the administrative limitations stated above. Thus, while rejecting the arm's-length standard as theoretically unsound, the advocates of the unitary principle, even if some approve apportionment in principle on grounds of equity, find themselves in the same camp as the advocates of benign neglect of transfer price regulation, while aspiring to the ultimate extinction of exogenous market imperfections.

On the contrary, the United States Treasury Department in a recent statement not only does not damn the unitary principle with faint praise but attacks it on both theoretical and administrative grounds (United States, 1981b, p. 93), emphasizing several of the administrative difficulties cited above. Further, European governments, acting with the United States and other countries through the OECD, have explicitly rejected the unitary approach, citing difficulties for taxpayers and inconsistency with international tax treaties incorporating the arm's-length standard (OECD, 1979). It may be plausible to speculate that these expressions of policy reflect the attitude of a substantial segment of the business community which apparently prefers to take its chances with the uncertainties of the separate entity principle.

V. Conclusion

Given the near unanimity in identifying the inducements for fiscal transfer pricing decisions and the unlikely extinction of the underlying market imperfections that generate internalized transactions and the consequent pricing of such transactions, this paper has explored various second-best policies, focusing on developing countries.

An ambiguity is involved, since the comparison of second-best policies presupposes a single goal. In the case of transfer pricing two goals are confronted: (1) optimal efficiency in the international allocation of resources; and (2) an international allocation of the consolidated income of MNEs deemed to be equitable in a world of independent tax jurisdictions.

Widespread official consensus supports the separate entity theory of income allocation and its expression in the arm's-length standard or equivalent. Nevertheless, it has received a barrage of criticism, largely on administrative grounds but also because of its failure to confront the theoretical challenge of the unitary theory. On the other hand, the expression of the unitary theory in an apportionment formula has encountered formidable if not insuperable practical obstacles.

Despite concern over fiscal and foreign exchange erosion, few developing countries systematically regulate transfer prices or, for that matter, apply an apportionment policy. This can be attributed to administrative limitations, but some such countries appear to reject regulation for fear, rightly or wrongly, of discouraging foreign investors — a policy which could be interpreted as a crude if unselfconscious adherence to the internalization theory. In some instances, this may reflect a judgement that, given the character of the particular MNEs operating in the country and the country's liberal implementation of a policy on profit remittances, the inducement for profit shifting is not strong enough to warrant aggressive regulation. Although evidence is lacking, it is possible that a country with stringent exchange restrictions may abstain from strict regulation on the grounds that this approximates a realistic foreign exchange rate for profit remittances.

Some narrowing of international tax differentials has moderated inducements to manipulation through the operation of credits for taxes paid abroad, and more recently through the abolition of deferral privileges for 'smokestack' industries evading taxes through affiliates located in tax haven countries.

There has also been adoption in some countries of measures narrower in scope than the arm's-length standard but based on the separate entity principle, notably the taxation of specific categories of intra-firm transactions, particularly royalties.

Broadly speaking, the advocates of regulation by developing countries, both official and academic, have defined the transfer pricing problem as the inequitable loss of revenue and foreign exchange by the host country and have not addressed the issue of a trade-off between equity and efficiency.[8] On the other hand, perhaps inevitably, direct evidence of the extent of real loss of efficiency attributable to regulation is lacking — as of the extent of transfer manipulation itself, however defined, except for a few dramatic cases.

It may be good on occasion to be reminded of first principles and of how things would be in a world free of the chains of exogenous market imperfections. But to characterize the dismantling of regulation as a 'ready solution to hand' (Rugman, 1981) seems to verge on wishful thinking. The real world seems to offer an uneasy mixture of two tendencies: one, relatively inefficient regulation reinforced, perhaps, by self-regulating policies of MNEs which are inhibited by official deterrents and preoccupation with 'profit centres' and the like from fiddling with transfer prices; and two, an opposing drive towards profit maximization and risk minimization with recourse to transfer pricing and manipulation of financial structure, as argued by Brean (this volume), leading to a moderately efficient allocation of resources internationally. It seems improbable that this situation will change much in the foreseeable future.

Notes

1. Roughly corroborating data were obtained from a sample of 329 of the world's largest industrial enterprises, also for 1977, showing that one-third of all parent company exports consisted of intra-firm sales, with the shares varying from 45 per cent for the United States to 30 per cent for Western Europe and 17 per cent for Japan (UN, 1983a, based on Dunning and Pearce, 1981).

2. Mathewson and Quirin (1979), examining Canadian intra-firm trade, find that many raw materials of agricultural, forest or mineral origin are accorded duty-free or low tariff rates in Canada and hence are unusually prominent candidates for transfer price manipulation under prevailing tax differentials. On the other hand, they de-emphasize the possibility of manipulation in natural gas, metals and ores because of the 'well-directed enforcement efforts' (p. 92). The forestry industry is singled out as prone to manipulation, but the risk of manipulation is considered minimized by the fewness of companies involved. They make the point, also, that, given the offsetting nature of tariffs and taxes in the main, there is ground for apprehension if tariff reductions are negotiated while international tax differentials remain intact.

3. An attempt to establish a link between the arm's-length principle and the unitary concept underlying the apportionment formula was made by Stanley Surrey, a former Assistant Secretary of the United States Treasury. In the context of the recognition of the practical difficulty of applying the arm's-length standard, Surrey accepted with strong reserve the validity of an apportionment formula as a possibly more feasible administrative mechanism in the following terms (UN, 1978a):

> [if allocation] factors could be sought which would approximate the division of profits produced by the market place . . . these two approaches — arm's length and division of profits — become similar in theory and goal. . .

Since the basic assumption of the unitary theory is that arm's-length prices have no economic meaning or function within an internalized, multi-divisional enterprise — whether national or international — there is no basis for assuming that the two approaches have anything in common.

4. A cursory examination of textbooks on international finance, international accounting, international business and, surprisingly, several on economic development (for example, Herrick and Kindleberger, 1983; Todaro, 1981; Hagen, 1980) reveals that the issue is stated almost exclusively in terms of the incentive to shift profits, presumably out from developing countries, because of international tax differentials. Hagen, for example, merely states that 'multinational corporations . . . often regard local taxes as exorbitant, and they may have no compunction about evading them as they can' (p. 318), leaving it open whether the issue is recourse to tax havens or international tax differentials between home and host country.

5. Commenting on international tax differentials mainly from the point of view of US revenue and US 'tax neutrality' as between domestic and foreign investment income, Bergsten, *et al.* (1978, p. 1945) state the following:

> the most striking feature of the existing tax system is its complexity and, consequently, the variation of effective rates of taxation from one corporation to another and from one country to another. . . We compute a typical [foreign] tax burden of 43.8 percent for 1968. . . Because this rate is less than the 48 percent statutory rate in the United States, we conclude that American corporations might have a weak incentive to allocate taxable income to foreign rather than American affiliates. The high income and withholding taxes in Canada and most countries in Western Europe discourage allocating income to those affiliates, whereas the low rates in certain (particularly developing) countries may attract taxable income to them.

6. Under US legislation adopted in 1971 but subsequently narrowed in application, export subsidies were extended through 'export corporations' (so-called DISCs) under which a DISC was permitted not only to accumulate and invest profits from exports sales free of US income tax, but also allowed to employ transfer pricing practices in diverting profits to DISCs under rules more liberal than those applied to intra-firm transactions generally (Dworin, 1982).

7. It seems relevant to mention certain recent dramatic cases of apparent transfer price manipulation through tax havens involving non-manufacturing MNEs. One is the successful action brought by Switzerland (itself, ironically, regarded as a tax haven) against Citicorp for underpricing foreign exchange from a Swiss affiliate to an affiliate in a Caribbean tax haven. It is reported that a similar action was brought against Citicorp by Italy. Another case is the recent action by the United States against Marc Rich International, Ltd, a US subsidiary of Marc Rich & Co. AG of Switzerland, for under-reporting income arising from wholesale trade in primary commodities with its parent firm.

8. Lall (1973, p. 190) is an exception. He assumes that the investment giving rise to potential transfer pricing manipulation 'has come in for reasons of efficient resource allocation' or else that it has been attracted by uneconomic import protection. The possibility that regulation of transfer prices would itself cause inefficient allocation of resources he implicitly rejects.

15 INTERNATIONAL ARBITRATION OF TRANSFER PRICING DISPUTES UNDER INCOME TAXATION

Carl S. Shoup

I. The Proposal: Voluntary but Binding Arbitration of Transfer Pricing Disputes Involving MNEs under the Income Tax

The proposal advanced here is that there be set up a permanent board of arbitration for transfer pricing disputes involving multinational enterprises (MNEs) under income taxation. The sole assignment of the board would be to settle on a transfer price, which all parties to the dispute — typically, two countries' tax administrations, and the MNE — would be bound to use, once they had accepted the arbitration process. There would be no appeal. A dispute could be brought to the board either by the MNE (that is, by the parent company or one of its affiliates) or by any one of the tax administrations.

In a typical dispute of the kind considered here, the income taxing authorities of two countries differ on what price should be attached to a particular transfer of goods, intangibles, etc. within an MNE that operates in these countries. Commonly, income tax authorities in the country of import tend to insist on a lower transfer price than do the authorities of the exporting country. The lower the transfer price, the greater the amount of the firm's total profits that is allocated to the importing country for income tax purposes. Correspondingly, the higher that price, the larger is the profit deemed to arise within the country of export. The taxpaying MNE then finds that more than 100 per cent of its profit is allocated between the countries (for further details, see Plasschaert, 1981, especially pp. 55-6).

If income tax rates differ, the taxpayer may protest even if the two countries' taxing authorities do in fact agree on the transfer price. The taxpayer would like to see a lower transfer price accepted if the country of import levies the lower tax rate, a higher price if the low tax rate is in the country of export. The underlying cause of these transfer pricing disputes is therefore the separate accounting of MNE world-wide income required by national tax authorities.

The transfer pricing disputes would disappear if the taxing nations of the world somehow agreed to scrap the present procedure of separate accounting and used instead the allocation technique employed by the states of the United States with their income taxes. If world-wide profits of an MNE were allocated among the countries in which it operates, according to a formula, Country A, for example, would be allowed to tax that part of the MNE's world-wide profit found by applying a certain ratio to such profit, say, the average of (1) the ratio of payrolls in A to the MNE's world-wide payrolls and (2) the ratio of its sales in A to its world-wide sales. There would be no occasion for considering transfer prices.

For present purposes, however, I need not discuss the relative merits of separate accounting and allocation; it is enough to say that I see no prospect at all that the world will move to the allocation technique. Some countries might, perhaps, agree to use that technique as among themselves, but there would remain many other countries where transfer pricing problems would exist.

Similarly, if all taxing authorities in all countries would agree always to accept whatever transfer price the MNE selected, there would be no need for arbitration. But the fact is, they do not always do so, and there is no prospect that they always will. Governments do not accept for their own taxing purposes Professor Rugman's conclusion that 'transfer prices are not arbitrary numbers but are the correct internal administrative prices required to make internalization function. It is meaningless to examine transfer prices on their own . . . Instead the MNE should be allowed to use whatever transfer prices it cares to' (1981, p. 85). Accordingly, even if one accepts the argument that transfer prices as set by the MNE 'have to be respected as the prices necessary to make the MNE function efficiently' (Rugman, 1981, p. 83), the fact that the taxing countries' authorities can differ in their views on what the transfer price should be demands some kind of action to resolve disputes. The present paper neither takes issue with Professor Rugman's conclusion nor urges it; the aim here is to keep the tax mechanism moving, to prevent lengthy tie-ups, and to obviate taxation that is clearly multiple because of inconsistency in tax authorities' decisions.

The paper proceeds as follows. Section II traces the recent history of proposals for arbitration of transfer pricing disputes (or of income tax disputes generally). Sections III and IV document the need for arbitration among developed and developing countries respectively. Sections V through VIII outline the proposed arbitration procedure, and Section IX offers some conclusions.

II. Recent Discussions of Possible Arbitration

Discussion of possible arbitration for transfer pricing disputes in particular or for alleged double taxation of MNEs in general has been scanty until recently.

In 1972, a Working Party of the Organisation for Economic Co-operation and Development (OECD, 1972, p. 6) concluded that: 'There is nothing in fact to show . . . that the position of the Member States has changed since 1966 . . . and that they would now be prepared to accept that the differences or problems at which Article 25 is aimed [including transfer pricing] should, in the event of failure of the mutual agreement procedure to achieve the result, be referred to arbitration or dealt with under international law . . . . [in view of] the reluctance of the States to accept any restriction on their sovereignty in regard to this particular type of dispute.'[1] The report asserted that in fact there had been very few such disputes.

In passing, this paper (1972, p. 6, fn. 2) referred to a note, dated 1 October 1971, by the Business and Industry Advisory Committee (BIAC) set up by the OECD, which included a suggestion that arbitration be resorted to when agreement could not be reached under the mutual agreement procedure. It is of interest to observe that when this same BIAC some nine years later offered detailed comments on transfer pricing (BIAC, 1980), in the course of appraising another OECD report (OECD, 1979), it did not mention arbitration, although it had earlier outlined the advantages of arbitration 'to resolve transfer pricing controversies between national authorities' in an unpublished submission to the CFA (BIAC, 1980, p. 7).

In 1973, at the International Fiscal Association Conference, arbitration for 'permanent establishment' disputes under the income tax was suggested by the West Germany Country

Reporter, Dr A. Rädler, and by the General Reporter, Max Beat Ludwig (IFA, 1973, 78).

The next mention of transfer pricing arbitration occurred in a proposal by the Commission of the European Communities, 1976, for a Council Directive on elimination of double taxation of profits of associated enterprises. The Commission proposed setting up an arbitration commission. This proposal has not yet [as of August 1983] been adopted by the Council.

In 1981 the International Fiscal Association (IFA), at its conference in Berlin, selected, as one of the two topics for the conference, 'Mutual Agreement — Procedure and Practice'. The papers appeared in the Proceedings (*Cahiers*) for that year (IFA, 1981). One of the papers — by Francke, Lindencrona and Mattsson — proposed in some detail an arbitration commission that would handle any matter relating to international income tax disputes, not merely those arising from transfer prices. In the same year, Lindencrona and Mattsson published a greatly expanded version of that plan, entitled *Arbitration in Taxation*, with background materials, based on work that had been commissioned by the World Association of Lawyers for World Peace Through Law, and presented at the WPTL's Ninth Conference on the Law of the World in Madrid in 1979.

Finally, on 6 July 1982, the OECD's Committee on Fiscal Affairs adopted a report on 'Transfer Pricing, Corresponding Adjustments and the Mutual Agreement Procedure', aimed largely at meeting the objections to this Committee's 1979 report that had been raised by BIAC (see above). This 1982 OECD report does come to grips with the issue of arbitration, in terms of 'mandatory corresponding adjustments' (OECD, 1982, p. 2, and Part III, pp. 14-20). After a detailed discussion of the shortcomings of existing practices the CFA nevertheless concludes on p. 18 that: 'It is not in fact clear however that there is an obvious and urgent need for such an arbitration process.' Some countries had said they would find such a device 'quite unacceptable'. Yet, 'the case for an arbitration procedure has been pressed so strongly in some quarters that it seems necessary to expand the comment that the need for it has not been established', and the Committee then proceeds to such expansion, over two pages. Their main points are covered in the present paper in an analysis of arbitration as a supplement to existing procedure, to which we now turn.

III. The Need for an Arbitration Board as a Supplement to Existing Procedure in Developed Countries

Among developed countries linked by tax treaties, the need for an arbitration board may be felt more by the MNE than by either of the disputing tax administrations. In these cases, under present procedure, a taxpayer alleging double taxation because of differing transfer prices used by the different tax authorities, can request (but not compel) its domestic tax authority to consult with the authority of the other country through what is known as a 'mutual agreement procedure', if the two countries are linked by a tax treaty that allows for that procedure. The resulting consultation, if any, is simply one between the tax authorities, a consultation to which the taxpayer is not a party, though it has, in a sense, been initiated by the taxpayer. But there is no compulsion for the two sets of tax authorities to reach an agreement on the transfer price within a reasonable period, or, indeed, at all. The degree of need for binding arbitration depends, for countries linked by tax treaties, on how well the mutual agreement procedure is working. For example, if the taxpayer submits a certain figure for the particular transfer price and its domestic tax authority changes that price, for the moment the two countries differ on the transfer price. If the taxpayer then requests the mutual agreement procedure, and such procedure is started, the other country may, but does not have to, make a 'corresponding adjustment' to avoid double taxation.

It has been argued, however, that existing procedure does not need to be supplemented by arbitration. Aside from the largely spurious objection of 'loss of fiscal sovereignty', the main argument seems to be simply that the existing system is working quite well enough. The danger of double taxation in a transfer pricing dispute is said to be, in fact, small (OECD, 1982, pp. 18-20). The OECD's Committee on Fiscal Affairs believes that existing mutual agreement procedures for consultation between tax authorities, under a tax treaty, are adequate. The CFA notes, with respect to the OECD's Business and Industry Advisory Committee, that 'BIAC's practical experience of the operation of the mutual agreement procedure has been that it is normally time consuming and uncertain in its results' (OECD, 1982, p. 11). To this, the CFA replies that, while the procedure might be speeded up, uncertainty is inherent (p. 12), and concludes that 'the experience of tax authorities within the OECD at least, is that, within its limitations, the mutual agreement procedure can be a very useful instrument in resolving difficulties arising in transfer pricing cases and that, up to the present, acceptable compromises have in practice nearly always have been found. It does not appear that the experience of taxpayers has been significantly different' (p. 13).

This conclusion seems somewhat optimistic,[2] and in any event does not cover countries outside the OECD, particularly developing countries, nor does it cover countries not linked by tax treaties. We argue that a serious limitation of existing procedure is that none of the tax administrators are obligated to reach an agreement on any particular case, nor are they obliged to implement a decision, once reached. Although the competent authorities are free to ask outside advice, as from the OECD's Committee on Fiscal Affairs, they apparently have not done so (OECD, 1982, p. 11).

Also, when several disputes are settled under the mutual agreement procedure, BIAC notes that 'tax authorities tend to lump together all current cases and to negotiate a general settlement on a very rough and ready basis. Thus . . . the success of one taxpayer in his specific case may jeopardise the chances of another when States try to reach a global agreement for several open issues in a "broad-brush" approach' (BIAC, as paraphrased by CFA, in OECD, 1982, p. 12). This would not happen under arbitration; according to BIAC 'an arbitration system would obviate any danger that the merits of a taxpayer's case would be ignored and his claim abandoned by a tax authority as an expedient in order to achieve more successful results on behalf of other taxpayers' (p. 15).

Arbitration could also remedy some defects in present administrative practices within countries. For example, the tax administrator may not give the taxpayer an opportunity to present all the information that the latter believes has a bearing on the question, especially information designed to correct what the taxpayer sees as a misinterpretation or a lack of understanding on the part of the tax officials. An arbitration board would probably be more open to receipt of such information.

The arbitration board could employ impartial *ad hoc* experts to a greater degree than can the tax administrations. These experts would understand better the particular industrial or commercial environment germane to the transfer price. Their expertise would render unnecessary expensive, elaborate presentations by the taxpayer.

The board might base its decision 'less on a strict interpretation of national pricing rules and regulations than on what the arbitrator considered in the light of his (or her) experience to be a fair and equitable solution' (OECD, 1982, p. 15) (note the assumption here of a single arbitrator rather than a board).

Finally, the main advantage of arbitration for the taxpayer is that the proceedings would (1) start without undue delay, and (2) reach a decision, expeditiously. If indeed the arbitration board acted too slowly, its members could be penalized by reducing their compensation.

IV. The Special Need for an Arbitration Board in Disputes Involving Developing Countries

There is a special need for an arbitration board to settle transfer pricing disputes involving developing countries, namely to redress the balance of power between the tax authority of the developing country on the one hand, and the MNE and the developed country's tax authority on the other.

From what I saw, a decade ago, in my travels for the United Nations as Inter-Regional Adviser on Tax Reform Planning, I believe that a developing country's tax administrators often need some body to which they and the taxpayer can repair (and also, of course, the other country), if only to get all the information that the other country has on transfer price determinants. I was impressed by the disparity in technical resources for handling transfer price problems as between the developing country's tax administration and the MNE. I recall one instance that posed the following difficulty: the local authorities could do little to appraise a transfer price set by a parent of a company operating in that particular country unless the tax authorities of the home country would co-operate by sending data on prices at which the parent company sold the finished product. No such co-operation was forthcoming, the reason being the laws of confidentiality in the home country. Had there been an arbitration board available, I believe that either the information would have been forthcoming before appeal to the board or it would have been made available to the board under a more relaxed interpretation of the confidentiality laws. The mere existence of an arbitration board might well make tax administrators more willing to reach an agreement acceptable to the taxpayer. Similarly, some MNEs might be more willing to settle on terms acceptable to one or another developing country.

It is thus the feeling of helplessness of the local tax administrator as against the great power and spread of the MNE and the possibly protective attitude of the home country administrators that is one of the strongest arguments for arbitration on transfer pricing (see Brean, 1979a, pp. 35-7, 43-4). Of course both the MNE and the home country would have to volunteer to accept the board, for it to do its job, but refusal to do so might be made to look a bit embarrassing.

On the other hand, it must be admitted that in many developing countries suspicion of the expertise or even the integrity of any arbitration board, no matter how constituted, might run deep. This is why a great deal of thought would have to be lavished on the constitution of such a board, after much consultation with various developing countries' finance ministries. Some detailed proposals are offered below.

V. Some Details of Proposed Arbitration Procedure

At the risk of a summary judgement based on inadequate information, the following prescriptions are offered as to the details of an arbitration board for transfer pricing.

Only tax disputes would be considered by the board. Transfer pricing difficulties arising under anti-dumping laws, for example, would not be within the board's jurisdiction. To be sure, a board that did consider all types of disputes over transfer pricing would gain a rich experience that would carry over to the tax cases, but it seems best to start modestly. If the board proved successful in the tax field, it might later be given a broader scope of operation.

Only income tax cases would be considered, for somewhat the same reasons. Prices set by a taxpayer for customs duties reckoning, for example, or for export taxes, would not be within the board's purview (as to customs duties, see Annex B below).

The board's task would be to arrive at a transfer price, not to compute changes in tax due. That task will be difficult enough;

the board should not be diverted into interpreting the tax legislation of the several countries. Again, experience over the years might lead to the opposite conclusion, but it seems wiser to start with just one aim in view; fix the transfer price. The CFA, in contrast, considers that this limitation 'certainly in its simplest form [of arriving at an arm's-length price], would narrow down, perhaps unsatisfactorily, the area of the arbitrators' consideration' (OECD, 1982, p. 17). The CFA view seems to be shared by the Swedish group (Francke *et al.*, IFA, 1981, p. 382), whose arbitration 'court' would hear any dispute that threatened to result in taxation not in accord with a tax treaty.

Pragmatism versus principle is an issue raised by the CFA report. Should the arbitrators try merely for 'a simple compromise between the two different views expressed, or would it be more satisfactory to require them to operate by analogy with a court of law, seeking to establish which of the claims put forward was the more correct or more in accord with natural justice?' (p. 17). Surely the choice is obvious: no board would long command respect if it merely attempted to compromise. The CFA report, however, seems to waver between the two, though it does point out the effect the compromise approach would have on the ability of tax authorities to concede points to each other in preliminary negotiations.

The present proposal rests on an assumption that when a dispute occurs over a transfer price there exists a fair or appropriate price that a third party, here, an arbitration board, can ascertain, or set. The standard commonly appealed to is an 'arm's-length' price, one that would be reached if the transaction were in the open market, with buyer and seller dealing independently, 'at arm's length'.

In many cases, if not most, there will be no open-market arm's-length price that can be used as a standard for the good in question, in the market in question. In the extreme case of a market where a monopsonist (sole buyer) faces a monopolist (sole seller), the equilibrium market price is of course indeterminate. The arbitration board would be expected to do no better than to follow the procedure laid down in the United States Internal Revenue Service Regulations for Section 482 of the Internal Revenue Code. I have elsewhere analyzed these regulations (Shoup, 1975, pp. 75-82) and find that they are on the whole reasonable and, in particular, are not weighted against the interests of developing countries. To be sure, the arbitration board would be expected to develop, in time, its own set of transfer pricing principles.

Power to initiate proceedings before the arbitration board would be given to all the parties: the taxpayer, and the two or more countries concerned. Giving the taxpayer the right to initiate an arbitration procedure seems not to be a feature of the few proposals that have been made. In the Swedish plan (Francke *et al.*, IFA, 1981, p. 383) the taxpayer has only 'the right to present all the material he desires to the arbitration commission and be heard in person if he so desires'.

Which party would in fact act first would depend largely on the type of dispute. If the two countries had nearly identical tax rates, and one country notified the taxpayer that it was lowering the transfer price, and was asking the other country to make a corresponding adjustment, the taxpayer would have no reason to apply to the board if the other country agreed. If it did not, and maintained the transfer price as set by the taxpayer originally, the taxpayer would be motivated to appeal to the arbitration board. In fact, the first tax administration, upon learning that the second would not agree to a lowering of the transfer price, might itself bring the case before the board, if only to induce the second country to agree the next time.

If the two countries imposed different rates of tax, the taxpayer might want to initiate proceedings even if the second country made a corresponding downwards adjustment, if the exporting country imposed the lower rate. In this instance, if the taxpayer did not start proceedings, no one would. There is no 'double taxation', yet the taxpayer may be disadvantaged. This is the kind of case not covered by the mutual agreement procedure.

All three parties might on occasion be motivated to appeal for arbitration. One country might lower the transfer price from that set by the taxpayer, and the other, far from making a corresponding adjustment, might at the same time be raising the transfer price, both actions being detrimental to the taxpayer. Each tax administration might deem immediate appeal to the board advisable, to warn the other country from repeating its 'mistake', and the taxpayer, of course, would be inclined to act at once, since agreement between the two administrations would appear remote.

Would there be any kind of transfer price dispute that the

taxpayer would not be allowed to bring before the board? Here we may quote the OECD 1982 report: 'According to one view it would be inappropriate to allow the taxpayer the right to use the arbitration machinery as well as the domestic courts and thus perhaps have the opportunity of requiring the tax authorities to give him the benefit of whichever decision was most advantageous to him. As a practical matter, as well as to a certain extent one of equity, it could be strongly argued that before invoking an arbitration process the taxpayer should have exhausted or abandoned his domestic rights of appeal. As against this it may also be strongly argued that the taxpayer should not in any circumstances be required to give up his rights under domestic law . . .' (p. 16).

If the taxpayer first had to exhaust his rights of domestic appeal, the dispute could drag on for years, and an agreement with the other country could become correspondingly difficult. It would seem better to allow the taxpayer to appeal at once to the arbitration board, whose decision would overrule whatever the domestic courts might have said to the contrary in the interim, or might say later. This would not really be an 'abandonment of fiscal sovereignty', since no country would be forced into working with the arbitration board and, over the long run, once in, a country could probably count on as many victories as defeats.

This analysis assumes that the MNE is indeed using the same transfer price in its two income tax returns filed in the country of export and in the country of import. If it is not doing so, the case changes into one of detecting fraud, an important issue but one not covered by the present paper.

Although the 'fiscal sovereignty' issue, as noted above, is deemed important by some, the words of the Swedish group (Francke *et al.*, IFA, 1981, p. 382) reflect a more common-sense view: 'If two states have decided to conclude an agreement on the avoidance of double taxation, they have thereby agreed to refrain from the exercise of their taxing rights in certain situations. It is only logical that the states should find a solution to ensure that disputes on the contents of the agreement can be resolved in all situations.'

Membership in the arbitration process would of course be voluntary, but any country and any taxpayer wishing to use the process should have to pledge continued use of it for a certain period, say three years. Membership could then be renewed for three-year terms. Perhaps five years would be a better minimum commitment.

All members, firms or governments, would have to pledge acceptance of the board's decisions, without right of appeal.

There appears to be, however, one difficult point. In the words of the proposed EC Directive (European Communities, 1976, p. 5), the problem arises from 'the domestic legislation of certain countries, which prevents their administrations from departing from the decision of a national court or tribunal even to give effect to a decision of an international joint commission and even if to do so would be in the taxpayer's favour'. The EC proposal would solve this problem by giving the taxpayer a choice: the MNE could opt for accepting the decision of the arbitration board and give up its right of appeal to a national body, or it could opt the other way (no resort to the board, and advance acceptance of the national appeal procedure's outcome). Apparently, this option could be exercised case by case.

VI. Composition and Location of the Arbitration Board

The arbitration board would be composed of economists, accountants, lawyers and industry experts, the last perhaps being co-opted as a panel. The expertise of lawyers might seem at first not to be needed, since the only question would be, what is a suitable transfer price, not a matter of interpretation of law. But such expertise would still be needed, to weigh the evidence, to decide which of the alleged facts were indeed facts and to set up orderly procedures.

Total membership of the board would be perhaps six or seven, plus panel experts. The board would, however, be equipped with a staff, which might come to a dozen professionals.

This suggested composition of the arbitration board differs markedly from that given in certain other proposals for arbitration. A major point is, should the board include any of the tax officials engaged in the dispute? Offhand, the answer would seem to be, surely no; the very parties to the dispute should not be judging the case. There is a different view, nevertheless, in which the origins of the board itself are found in the tax administrations. Thus, both the EC and the OECD 1982 reports urge that tax officials be members.

The EC proposal is based on a widening of the present membership of the groups that consider these disputes: the tax officials themselves. Starting with 'the joint commission already provided in the OECD model convention, . . . which . . . consists only of representatives of the two national tax authorities concerned', the proposed EC Directive modifies this commission 'to enable it to make decisions which will completely remove double taxation' (p. 4), by including 'an uneven number of independent persons of standing', specifically brought in 'to avoid deadlock between the two tax authorities' (p. 6). These members would be appointed by the two tax authority groups in the commission. These independent persons could be replaced by others at any time (but presumably not during a particular case), 'since the cases submitted to the commission will have their own special features, [so that] the qualifications required of the independent persons may not always be the same' (p. 6).

Comment on this EC proposal by the OECD committee is cautious, but on the whole apparently favourable, though the committee notes that it has been argued that 'the taxpayer should be able to put the matter to a completely independent tribunal' (p. 16). This argument does not impress the OECD committee, who regard the proposed arbitration process as essentially one of arbitrating between two tax authorities, the taxpayer being only a 'third party' (p. 16).

Where should the board of arbitration be located?[3] It might be a travelling board, holding hearings and rendering decisions in one part of the world for a month or two, then in another part. Alternatively, it might start up in, say, Latin America, or South-East Asia, confining its work to cases in that area for the first year or two. Francke *et al.* (IFA, 1982, p. 338) and Lindencrona and Mattsson (1981, p. 70) recommend Stockholm, as being in a country 'which can be regarded as neutral in the political sense'.

Security of tenure for a considerable length of time might well be needed to attract qualified persons, unless, indeed, the membership of the board were to be especially constructed for each dispute, as recommended by the Swedish group (Francke *et al.*, IFA, 1982, pp. 382-3; Linderncrona and Mattsson,1981, p. 72). Under this Swedish proposal a 'permanently operating International Institute for Arbitration in Tax Disputes' would simply facilitate the appointment of an *ad hoc* commission for each dispute. Each of the two countries would appoint one member, who would agree on a third member, who would be the chairman.

This procedure would be more time-consuming than that of a permanent group of commissioners. But the Swedish proposal is more far-ranging than that of the present paper, since it would not limit arbitration to deciding what the transfer price should be, but would 'determine how the [tax] convention is to be interpreted and applied in the concrete situation which exists' (Francke *et al.*, IFA, 1982, p. 383).

VII. Legal Status and Financing of the Arbitration Board

If the arbitration board were simply an enlargement of existing conference groups of tax administrators, as suggested by the proposed EC Directive, it would be a legal unit within the governments concerned. The cost of the added members of the board would presumably be divided between the governments. So too would the additional professional, clerical and other expense incurred by this larger board. The financing problem should not be difficult.

Quite different is the case where the arbitration board is an entirely new body, composed exclusively of full-time experts chosen for long terms (accountants, economists and laywers), no tax administrators being members. Two possibilities seem open, one of them perhaps too remote to discuss seriously.

To take the latter first, some private firm or consortium engaged in rendering arbitration services to private business might set up a transfer price arbitration body, charging fees for its services. All three parties — taxpayer and the two countries — would contract to pay fees for the service over a specified period, say three years. It is not easy to see just how the charges should be computed: based on time spent, with equal one-third shares? or with shares dependent on the relative demands made by each party? Few, if any, arbitration firms might prove willing to take the start-up risks. Prhaps some seed money could be provided by a foundation or an international organization. The arbitration firm itself would have final say as to who the arbitrators would be for any particular case. So far as possible, then, the board would be insulated from pressures from one or another government or taxpayer. At the end of the three-year period, clients of the board would confer to decide whether they would renew the contract for another three years.

At the other extreme, the arbitration board might be set up, financed and staffed by some international organization. Possibilities include the United Nations[4] through its Centre on Transnational Corporations, or UNCTAD,[5] or some UN-related body such as GATT (General Agreement on Tariffs and Trade) or the International Court of Justice; joint action by regional groups, e.g. OECD and similar organizations in the developing world. Perhaps regional associations of tax administrators in various parts of the world could join to set up an arbitration board (CIAT in Latin America, the ASEAN Working Group on Tax Matters, PATA (Pacific Association of Tax Administrators)). But there appears to be no similar across-countries groups in the developed nations.

It is, however, difficult to find an international organization that commands equal trust and respect from the developing nations and the developed nations. Yet the need for an arbitration board seems greatest just where the interests of a developing country's tax administration conflict with those of a developed country or a large MNE based in a developed country.

Accordingly, what was referred to above as perhaps only a remote possibility might in fact turn out to be the most practicable procedure: the setting up of some private firm that would offer its arbitration services for a fee.

VIII. The 'Advisory Opinion (*Avis Arbitral*)'

As a step on the road towards arbitration, but without going outside the framework of the mutual agreement procedure, the OECD 1972 report proposed adoption of the 'advisory opinion (*avis arbitral*)' technique. The two states in the dispute, but not, evidently, the taxpayer, 'agree to seek the opinion of an impartial third party on a legal [*sic*] difference, while reserving their freedom of decision regarding the disposal of the matter. While the advisory opinion does not therefore have the binding force of an arbitration award, the parties to the dispute usually abide by it (cf. Suzanne Bastid, '*L'arbitrage international*, *Jurisclasseur de Droit International*, fasc. 215-8)' (OECD, 1972, p. 7).

The OECD's CFA might periodically 'draw up a list of

eminent persons from among whom the competent authorities of the two States concerned could appoint an independent person to issue an advisory opinion' (p. 7).

This might be better than nothing; it might, after some time, pave the way for the creation of a true arbitration board. For transfer pricing disputes, however, the word 'legal' in the quotation above must be replaced by 'economic' or 'business'.

A similar proposal appears at the end of the Swedish group's plan for arbitration. Admitting that some countries would find it difficult to surrender power of decision to an outside body, Francke *et al.*, (IFA, 1982, p. 383) propose that 'an Opinion Committee should be formed by the institute, consisting of persons from different countries with the best qualifications. The states could then ask these independent experts for their advisory opinion.'

IX. Conclusions

The case for arbitration of transfer pricing disputes under the income tax internationally seems uncertain, or weak, when the taxing authorities are those of developed countries, especially countries that are linked by tax treaties. Even here, however, there may be a strong undercurrent of need for arbitration that has gone unrecognized. Some further exploration seems in order.

On the other hand, many of the disputes between a developed and developing country, or a developing country and an MNE, could probably be settled much more expeditiously and more fairly if appeal to binding arbitration were possible. This statement is only a conjecture, based on some personal experience and on the logic of the situation, but its plausibility seems strong enough to warrant intensive exploration of developing countries' willingness to use arbitration. Even if the response were only lukewarm — but not widely negative — a trial run of an arbitration board for a few years might be worthwhile. If indeed no cases at all were brought before the board, or if those cases that were served only to demonstrate a real unwillingness of the parties concerned to abide by the board's decisions, we should at least have learned something that we are now not sure of. The possible reward seems great enough to warrant a modest gamble.

Annex A: International Fiscal Association Conference at Berlin, 1981: Summary of National Reporters' Views on Arbitration

The following summary of views on arbitration of international tax disputes is given in the *General Report* by Dr Karl Koch (English version, p. 125). The disputes referred to are not limited to those arising from differences over transfer pricing.

Formal Arbitration Procedure

'The National Reporters for Sweden have declared their unqualified support for a formal arbitration procedure. Further advocates of this are to be found in the Federal Republic of Germany, France, Great Britain, Greece, Portugal, Switzerland and the U.S.A. (excluding the US revenue authorities). The proposals advanced differ to some extent as to the form, set-up and composition of the arbitration authority. The National Reporters for Australia, France [*sic*] and the Netherlands support this concept, but make certain reservations. The idea is rejected by the National Reporters for Austria, Belgium, Canada, Japan and Norway. While the advocates of arbitration procedure submit detailed proposals, those who reject it do so in more general terms. Although there has long been a call for creation of arbitration procedure or an international court for tax matters, the opposition against the establishment of the required institutions is probably still too strong.' (As printed in the *Cahiers*, the National Reports of Canada, Greece, Japan, Norway, Portugal and Switzerland do not specifically address the arbitration question.)

Annex B: The GATT Procedure in Customs Valuation Disputes

For those countries adhering to the General Agreement on Tariffs and Trade (GATT), disputes over customs valuations are ultimately subject to a procedure that approaches binding arbitration but seems not quite to reach that stage. At the 1979 GATT meeting, an 'Agreement on Implementation of Article VII' of GATT was published, 26 March 1979, which specified establishment of a Committee on Customs Valuation ('Committee') and a Technical Committee on Customs Valuation ('TCCV'). It also provided for the establishment of *ad hoc*

Panels of Experts to be used at the request of any party to the dispute (but the taxpayer is apparently not considered such a party) if the matter was not referred by the Committee to the TCCV (GATT, 1979, Articles 18-20; for details on the TCCV, see Annex II, and on the *ad hoc* Panels, Annex III).

Article 20, 'Resolution of Disputes', states that if a party to the dispute 'considers itself unable to implement' the recommendations made by the Committee after the TCCV or the Panels have reported to the Committee, that party must give its reasons, and 'the Committee shall consider what further action may be appropriate', and it may 'authorize one or more parties to this Agreement to suspend the application to any other party or parties to this Agreement of such obligations under this Agreement as it determines to be appropriate in the circumstances'.

This process, evidently, is a facilitating one, not one that settles a matter for all parties concerned, with no right of appeal. I have no information on the practical working of this procedure.

In view of the special problems faced by developing countries in dealing with transfer price problems, it is of interest to note that this GATT valuation code allows developing countries a delay of five years in application of the code's provisions (GATT, 1979, Article 21, p. 21) and a further delay in acceptance of 'computed value' based on cost (pp. 3-4, 8, Article 1,2(b)(iii) and Article 6).

Annex C: The United Nations Group of Experts on Tax Treaties

In the series of reports issued by the Group of Experts on Tax Treaties between Developed and Developing Nations, set up by the United Nations, possible arbitration of transfer pricing disputes has been given little attention. The Guidelines volume, summarizing the first five reports of the Group (UN, 1974b) does not refer to arbitration at all, and the Sixth Report of the Group (UN, 1976, pp. 34-5) has only a passing reference to possible arbitration and an international tax court; neither idea evidently evoked much enthusiasm among the Group. A more sympathetic attitude was expressed towards a possible panel of 'advisory parties' (pp. 34-4).

Two recent United Nations publications on the subject

covered by the Guidelines contain no sections dealing with arbitration (UN, 1979, 1980).

Notes

I am indebted to Lorraine Eden, Charles E. McLure, Jr and Oliver Oldman for extensive comments on an earlier draft, and to the International Bureau of Fiscal Documentation for sources.

1. The mutual agreement procedure, sometimes known as the 'competent authority procedure', allows countries linked by tax treaties to consult on tax disputes. See section III below.

2. For biting comments on the insufficiency of the mutual agreement procedure, see Wolfgang Ritter, General Reporter, IFA, 1975, Vol. LXb, pp. I/67-I/68. Neither Ritter nor the Country Reporters whose papers he summarizes seem to mention arbitration as a possible alternative.

3. 'Criticism is often levelled at permanent arbitration institutions, especially in Latin American countries, because their headquarters are located in highly developed countries', leading to an arbitration 'mentality which to a certain degree and sometimes unconsciously tends to favor firms exporting capital or importing raw materials' (Cremades, 1979, p. 10).

4. As proposed by the Swedish group (Francke *et al.*, IFA, 1982, pp. 382-3). 'Putting the institute within the sphere of activity of the United Nations would eliminate the objection of the institute's being linked to a particular geographical area and to a certain political tendency. We think that the institute should be given the status of an autonmous institution under the aegis of the United Nations.'

5. United Nations Conference on Trade and Development, a permanent organization of the General Assembly, to help developing countries expand trade.

* * *

COMMENTS ON THE DIFFICULTIES IN REGULATING TRANSFER PRICES
Norman W. McGuinness

As a non-economist, a non-tax expert and a non-accountant, it was with some misgiving that I accepted the task of commenting on the papers of Chudson and Shoup. What I hope to bring to bear, however, is the many years of experience I had working in an MNE before I became an academic. In my comments I will be using some of this experience to draw attention to what I believe is an inadequate appreciation in these papers for the dilemma of the MNE itself.

Chudson and Shoup both seek equity in the way an MNE's taxes are distributed amongst the countries in which it operates.

Few would disagree with that goal. Most responsible MNEs, in my opinion, would be among the first to support it. Yet the obstacles to be overcome before equity can be attained are formidable. Chudson does an excellent job of describing the difficulties: arm's-length prices which cannot be defined; countries which refuse to exchange tax information; tax allocation arrangements which cannot be agreed to between nations. Shoup touches on additional difficulties such as developing countries having too little knowledge and insufficient bargaining power.

In such a discussion there is a tendency to assume that MNEs set their transfer prices primarily to avoid taxes. A valuable contribution of Chudson's paper is the strong suggestion that such an assumption may not be accurate. Chudson, in fact, seems to be saying that the tax allocation problem arises for many reasons other than tax differentials between countries. He questions whether it is tax differentials which cause MNEs to show low profits in developing countries. He expresses his belief that even if the tax systems of the world were in complete harmony there would still be a problem in allocating taxes equitably. Shoup, in his verbal presentation, echoed these views by stating emphatically that even in the absence of tax differentials and other imperfections there would still be major concerns with transfer prices.

Where does this leave the MNE? Are responsible MNEs to be damned for tax avoidance or worse when in fact they have been managing towards other goals? From Tang (1981) it is clear that transfer prices respond to many factors other than taxes and that some of the more important concerns to the MNE are internal ones. Must an MNE ignore these other objectives and set transfer prices with only taxes in mind?

As a simple illustration of this problem consider the MNE's normal concern with minimizing foreign exchange risk. It would be a poorly managed MNE that allowed an excessive build up of funds in a weak currency. Depending on the regulations of the country involved, manipulating transfer prices to reduce profits in the foreign market is one way for the MNE to cope with this kind of risk. But that kind of action by the MNE is exactly what is most likely to arouse the income tax authorities when in fact the real issue is not tax related. The MNE might be very willing to make payments to the government in lieu of income tax providing it is given flexibility to redeem its capital.

There are many other kinds of externalities, such as tariffs, to which transfer prices may respond and be interpreted as a form of tax evasion. Neither Chudson nor Shoup seem overly worried about such matters. Nor do they seem to be particularly interested in the significance of transfer prices to the internal management systems of the MNE. Each author acknowledges that internalization is a means of promoting efficiency, yet both show no great reluctance in having governments intervene and set the transfer prices that operate the internal system. Shoup, in having his arbitration board set transfer prices from only a tax point of view, ignores all other objectives which transfer prices must meet, and demonstrates a very narrow outlook.

The repercussions of such interventions on the operating effectiveness of an MNE are not trivial. Adjustments to transfer prices which destroy the true state of affairs can make it very difficult, for instance, to evaluate the performance of a foreign affiliate (Tang, 1981, p. 155). Keeping two sets of books, notes Tang, is an expensive remedy for this problem. Yet a theme running through this conference and an assumption that I feel underlies the views of Chudson and Shoup is that it is a relatively simple matter for MNEs to keep multiple sets of books. The transfer price set by tax authorities, therefore, need not be the transfer price used by the MNE in its internal transactions. No doubt it is easy enough to keep multiple sets of books at general levels of consolidation and reporting. But at the operating level it is, in my experience, an impossibility. Imagine the confusion inside an organization if a large number of items showed one value on invoices, another on cost tabulations for make or buy decisions and still another in profit and loss calculations. Operating effectiveness calls for consistency, accuracy and simplicity in the way transfer prices are set.

Some of the internal purposes of transfer pricing and what happens when distortions creep in are well portrayed by Barrett (1977). Using a typical but hypothetical example he describes a situation where units of an MNE in the USA, France and Ireland are all shipping identical machines to the Belgium affiliate but at considerably different prices. The situation is a potential source of serious embarrassment with customs authorities. Does the Belgium affiliate resolve the situation by purchasing from the lowest priced supplier? Not at all; it buys from Ireland whose price is the highest by far. The reason for such seemingly illogical behaviour is that the Irish plant has the benefit of a 16-year tax holiday. That, plus high start-up costs, argue in favour of the Irish plant pricing high. However, the Belgium affiliate buys from Ireland only because they are pressured to do so by the President of the European company. Meanwhile in England, the UK affiliate is dragging its feet about servicing machines that have been shipped from Spain to avoid British Price Commission regulations. The UK affiliate feels it has been inadequately compensated to perform the after-sale service work.

In this example the transfer pricing distortions have been introduced by the MNE itself. The nature of the distortions tends to confirm the worst suspicions that governments have about the evasive behaviour of MNEs. But I cite the example not for those reasons but to illustrate the chaos that 'creative' transfer prices generate for management decision making. Both the Belgium purchase and the UK after-sale service situation would have been handled routinely and autonomously by the local affiliates had the transfer prices been more normal. Instead, both situations call for careful and sustained top management attention.

If the MNE continues to set many of its transfer prices in this fashion even deeper problems arise. Can it continue to treat each affiliate as a profit centre that tries to maximize returns on a stand alone basis? One businessman commenting on the problem felt the MNE could not, when its affiliates may have very little control over their selling or transfer prices. At stake then may be a substantial reorganization and reallocation of responsibilities within the European company.

For the MNE the issues are complex and involve not just profit maximization. Very important too are relationships with country governments, and motivating affiliates to make the most of their opportunities. Two of the businessmen commentators favoured a centralized approach to setting transfer prices while the other two opted for continued decentralization. One of the proponents of decentralized authority for transfer pricing came out strongly in favour of market-based transfer prices.

There were only a few areas, in fact, where all four of these experienced businessmen commentators agreed. Such lack of unanimity testifies to the difficulty which MNEs themselves can have in setting transfer prices. Should governmnents, or boards composed mainly of lawyers and accountants, try to tamper directly with systems of such complexity, especially when they bear no on-going responsibility for operating them? Perhaps tax authorities would do better to search for methods of tax allocation which do not entail setting transfer prices.

When governments do set transfer prices, the principle of equity which guides them tends to be the arm's-length transaction price. Even though Chudson is well aware of the artificiality of the arm's-length concept both he and Shoup seem unaware that the imposition of arm's-length prices can cause serious distortions to the MNE's internal system. The basic assumption underlying the arm's-length concept is that every transaction price contains an element of profit. In normal market operations that is true. But it does not necessarily apply to the internal market since all operating units may not be profit centres. Quite a number may be sales or cost centres whose performance will be evaluated on those types of criteria. Transfer prices to and from those centres will tend to reflect the operating criteria on which they are measured.

Consider, for example, what Caves (1982, p. 15) would define as a vertically integrated manufacturing affiliate located in a developing country. Such an affiliate has not been sited in that country to capture local sales but rather to reduce production costs by gaining access to low cost labour. Product life cycle reasoning suggests that affiliates of this type tend to be established towards the mature phase of the market when the parent may be facing severe price competition in its domestic market and survival depends on reducing costs. The affiliate probably has no sales and marketing responsibilities as these activities would be conducted by the parent and its other horizontally-related affiliates.

Since it has no responsibility for revenues it becomes meaningless to evaluate that kind of affiliate on the basis of profits. Logically the affiliate is an extension of the MNE's production system and would likely transfer its output to other parts of the MNE on a cost basis. Moreover, the cost-based transfer price would be expected to be accurate and to be consistent with the way costs are measured, allocated and transferred elsewhere in the organization. The MNE will try to avoid the possible confusion that could result if the affiliate were to transfer its product to other parts of the organization on a different basis.

The government of the developing country may now regard

the transfer price that has been established as grossly unfair since it minimizes local profits. Suppose that a substantial increase in the transfer price is imposed. Throughout the rest of the MNE's organization, managers must now work with a transaction price which requires special interpretation. If the arm's-length price is taken at face value as the real cost, it will distort decisions relating to a host of factors, beginning with the perceived profitability of the domestic operations of the MNE. Pricing, advertising, make or buy considerations are but a few examples of decisions normally made by middle level managers who typically do not have sufficient information for them to allow for the profit allocations of an affiliate.

I have dealt with the foregoing examples in some detail to make the point: imposed distortions to transfer prices from any source can severely complicate internal decision making. The internal market is not necessarily a replicate of the external and cannot be treated the same way.

What then should governments, especially those of developing countries, do to levy taxes if they are to avoid regulating transfer prices? One possibility might be to change the terms of reference of the arbitration board proposed by Shoup. Instead of setting the transfer price the board could use an allocation system. The MNE would then be allowed to price to minimize total taxes but the board would allocate the total taxes raised to the countries involved in a fair way. A solution of this sort puts the problem where it properly belongs — in the international political sphere. The arbitration board would force countries to come to terms, without intervening in an excessive way into the MNE itself. The MNE would also have access to the board over issues such as double taxation.

This, of course, assumes that nations will agree to some form of arbitration board. The political problems involved are immense and this is an area to which I feel Shoup's paper could have devoted more attention. A very admirable aim of the board is to neutralize differences in bargaining power between the contending parties. But why should the stronger industrial nations give up the bargaining power they now have? What would induce them to do so? Should the developing and industrial countries be unable to agree on co-operative mechanisms such as an arbitration board, then there seems to be no alternative except direct bargaining and a variety of second-best approaches. To strengthen the hand of developing countries it may be possible for bodies such as the UN to provide them with well-informed tax experts during the bargaining process. Developing countries, whose prime attraction for foreign investment is low labour costs, may be unwise to force foreign affiliates to act like profit centres. Surely there must be taxes or fees other than an income tax which a developing country could levy and which would not require it to intervene into transfer prices.

BIBLIOGRAPHY

Abdel-Khalik, R. and Lusk, E. (1974) 'Transfer Pricing — a Synthesis', *Accounting Review* (January), 8-23

Acre, H. (1977) *The Regulation of the Financing of Foreign Investors*, BID-INTAL, Monograph Series, No. 2, Buenos Aries

Adelman, Morris A. (1972) *The World Petroleum Market*, Baltimore: Johns Hopkins

Adler, Michael (1974) 'The Cost of Capital and Valuation of a Two-Country Firm', *Journal of Finance*, 29 (1), pp. 119-32

—— (1979) 'U.S. Taxation of Multinational Corporations: A Manual of Computation Techniques and Managerial Decision Rules' in M. Salant and G. Szego (eds.), *International Finance and Trade*, Vol. II, Cambridge, Mass.: Ballinger, pp. 157-210

—— and Stevens, Guy V.G. (1974) 'The Trade Effects of Direct Investment', *Journal of Finance*, 29, 655-76

Aliber, Robert Z. (1970) 'A Theory of Direct Foreign Investment' in Charles P. Kindleberger (ed.), *The International Corporation: A Symposium*, Cambridge, Mass.: MIT Press, pp. 17-34

Anthony, Robert N. (1973) 'Accounting for the Cost of Equity', *Harvard Business Review*, 51, 8

—— (1975) *Accounting for the Cost of Interest*, Lexington, Mass.: Lexington Books

—— (1982) 'Recognizing the Cost of Interest on Equity', *Harvard Business Review*, 60, 91-6

—— N. and Dearden, John (1980) *Management Control Systems*, 4th edn, Homewood, Illinois: Irwin

Arpan, Jeffrey (1972a) 'International Intracorporate Pricing: Non-American Systems and Views', *Journal of International Business Studies* (Spring), 1-18

—— (1972b) *International Intracorporate Pricing: Non-American Views and Systems*, New York: Praeger Publishers

Arrow, Kenneth J. (1964) 'Control in Large Organizations', *Management Science*, 10, 397-408

—— (1977) 'Optimization, Decentralization and Internal Pricing in Businesss Firms' in K.J. Arrow and L. Hurwicz (eds.), *Studies in Resource Allocation Processes*, Cambridge: Cambridge University Press, pp. 134-45

—— and L. Hurwicz (1960) 'Decentralization and Computation in Resource Allocation' in R.W. Pfouts (ed.), *Essays in Economics and Econometrics*, Chapel Hill: University of North Carolina Press, pp. 34-104

Bardhan, Pranab K. (1982) 'Imports, Domestic Production, and Transnational Vertical Integration: A Theoretical Note', *Journal of Political Economy*, 90, 1020-34

Barlow, E.R. and Wender, I.T. (1955) *Foreign Investment and Taxation*, Englewood Cliffs, NJ: Prentice-Hall

Barrett, Edgar M. (1977) 'The Case of the Tangled Transfer Price', *Harvard Business Review*, *55* (May-June), 20-2, 26, 28, 32, 36, 176, 178

Batra, Raveendra N. and Hadar, Josef (1979) 'Theory of the Multinational Firm: Fixed Versus Floating Exchange Rates', *Oxford Economic Papers*, *31*, 258-69

Benke, R. and Edwards, J. (1980) *Transfer Pricing: Techniques and Uses*, New York: National Association of Accountants

Bergsten, C. Fred, Horst, Thomas and Moran, Theodore H. (1978) *American Multinationals and American Interests*, Washington, DC: The Brookings Institution

Bertrand Report (1981) *The State of Competition in the Canadian Petroleum Industry*, Director of Investigation and Research, Combines Investigation Act: Ottawa, Supply and Services

Bhagwati, Jagdish (1965) 'On the Equivalence of Tariffs and Quotas' in R.E. Baldwin (ed.), *Trade, Growth and the Balance of Payments — Essays in Honour of Gottfried Haberler*, Chicago: Rand McNally Company, pp. 53-67

—— (1968) 'More on the Equivalence of Tariffs and Quotas', *American Economic Review*, *58*, 142-6

BIAC (1980) 'Business and Industry Advisory Committee', Report by a Working Party of BIAC's Fiscal Committee, in Federation of Swedish Industries, BIAC's Response to OECD report on *Transfer Pricing and Multinational Enterprises*, and Council of Europe *Colloquy on International Tax Avoidance and Evasion*. Report, Dag Helmers, Stockholm, 8-17

Bierstecker, Thomas J. (1978) *Distortion or Development?*, Cambridge, Mass.: MIT Press

Bilsborrow, Richard E. (1977) 'The Determinants of Fixed Investment By Manufacturing Firms In a Developing Country', *International Economic Review*, *18* (3)

Bohm-Bawerk, E. von. (1891) *The Positive Theory of Capital* (trans. by W. Smart), London: Macmillan

Bond, Eric W. (1980) 'Optimal Transfer Pricing When Tax Rates Differ', *Southern Economic Journal*, *47*, 191-200

Booth, E.J.R. and Jensen, Oscar W. (1977) 'Transfer Prices in the Global Corporation under Internal and External Constraints', *The Canadian Journal of Economics*, *X*, 434-46

Bourguinat, N.H. (1972) *Maché des changes et crises des monnaies*, Paris: Calmann-Levy

Brean, Donald J. (1979a) 'Multinational Corporations, Transfer Pricing, and Tax Policy of Less Developed Countries', *Malayan Economic Review*, *24* (2), 34-45

—— (1979b) 'Taxation of Multinational Enterprise: Problems of the Host Country', unpublished PhD thesis, University of Toronto

—— (1983a) 'Taxation, Repatriation and Reinvestment by Multinational Enterprise', *Savings & Development*, *7* (2), 163-83

—— (1983b) *International Aspects of Taxation: The Canadian Perspective*, Toronto: Canadian Tax Foundation

—— (1983c) 'Host Country Taxation, Internal Finance and Reinvestment by Multinational Companies', *Savings and Development*, *III* (3)

Buckley, Peter J. (1983) 'New Theories of International Business: Some Unresolved Issues' in M. Casson (ed.), *The Growth of International Business*, London: George Allen and Unwin, pp. 34-50

—— and Casson, Mark (1976) *The Future of the Multinational Enterprise*, London: Macmillan

Burns, Jane O. (1980) 'Transfer Pricing Decisions of U.S. Multinational Corporations', *Journal of International Business Studies* (Fall), 23-39

—— and Ross (1981) 'Establishing International Transfer Pricing Standards for Tax Audits of Multinational Enterprises', *The International Journal of Accounting* (Fall)

Business International (1965) *Solving International Pricing Problems*, New York: Business International Corporation (December)

—— (1973) *Setting Intercorporate Pricing Policies*, New York: Business International Corporation

Carlson, George N. and Hufbauer, G.C. (1976) 'Tax Barriers to Technology Transfers', *Occasional Tax Paper 16*, Washington, DC: US Department of the Treasury

Carson, C.R. (1983) 'Nonresident Alien Income and Tax Witheld, 1981', *Statistics of Income Bulletin*, US Department of the Treasury Internal Revenue Service, Washington, DC: US Government Publication No. 1136, Rev. 7-83 (Summer), 35-41

Caves, Richard E. (1980) 'Investment and Location Policies of Multinational Companies', *Schweiz Z. Volkswirtsch. Statist.*, *116* (3), 321-38

—— (1982) *Multinational Enterprise and Economic Analysis*, Cambridge, UK Cambridge University Press

—— and Jones, Ronald W. (1981) *World Trade and Payments: An Introduction*, Boston, Mass.: Little, Brown and Company

Chudnovsky, D. (1982) 'Las filiales estado unidenses en el sector manufacturero de America Latina', *Comercio Exterior*, *32* (July), 748-53

Chudson, Walter A. (1981) 'Intra-firm Trade and Transfer Pricing' in R. Murray (ed.), *Multinationals Beyond the Market*, Brighton: The Harvester Press, pp. 17-30

Coase, Ronald H. (1937) 'The Nature of the Firm', *Economica*, *4* (November), 386-405

Cooper, Richard (1971) 'Currency Devaluation in Developing Countries', *Essays in International Finance*, No. 86 (June), Princeton, NJ: Princeton University

Copeland, T. and Weston, J.F. (1983) *Financial Theory and Corporate Policy*, 2nd edn, Toronto: Addison Wesley

Copithorne, Lawrence W. (1971) 'International Corporate Transfer Prices and Government Policy', *Canadian Journal of Economics*, *4* (August), 324-41

—— (1976) 'La Théorie des prix de transfert internes des grandes sociétés', *L'actualité économique*, *52*, 324-52

—— (1982) 'The Economics of the Modern Corporation', unpublished manuscript

Correa, C.M. (1983) 'Importacion de technologia en America Latina. Algunos resultados de un decenio de intervencion estatal', *Comercio Exterior*, *33* (January), 20-33

Court, J.F. (1981) 'L'imposition des entreprises étrangères et les problèmes fiscaux internationaux', *Statistiques et Etudes Financières*, (May), 58-9

Cremades, Bernardo M. (1979) 'Modernization of National Arbitration Laws in Aid of International Commercial Arbitration', *Work Paper, Madrid Conference on Law of the World*, *14* (September).

Das, Satya P. (1983) 'Multinational Enterprise under Uncertainty', *Canadian*

Journal of Economics, *XVI*, 420-8

Dasgupta, P.S. and Heal, G.M. (1979) *Economic Theory and Exhaustible Resources*, Cambridge: Cambridge University Press

—— and Stiglitz, J. (1977) 'Tariffs vs. Quotas as Revenue-raising Devices under Uncertainty', *American Economic Review*, *67*, 975-81

Dean, Joel (1951) *Managerial Economics*, Englewood Cliffs, NJ: Prentice-Hall

—— (1955) 'Decentralization and Intra-company Pricing', *Harvard Business Review*, *33* (July-August), 65-74

Deutsche Bundesbank (1982) 'Entwicklung des Patents and Lizenzverkehrs mit dem Ausland in den Jahren 1980 and 1981', *Monatsberichte* (July)

DeWolf, L. (1980) 'Determinants of the Contribution of Customs Duties to Budgetary Revenue in LDCs', *Finanzarchiv*, *III*

—— (1981) 'Customs Valuation and the Faking of Invoices', *Economica Internazionale*, *34* (February), 1-20

Diewert, Erwin (1973) 'Functional Forms for Profit and Transformation Functions', *Journal of Economic Theory*, *6*, 284-316

—— (1974) 'Applications of Duality Theory' in Intriligator, M.D. and Kendrick, D.A. (eds.), *Frontiers of Quantitative Economics*, Vol. II, Amsterdam: North Holland, pp. 106-7

—— (1982) 'Duality Approaches to Microeconomic Theory' in Arrow, K.J. and Intriligator, M.D. (eds.), *Handbook of Mathematical Economics*, Vol. II, Amsterdam: North Holland, pp. 535-99

—— (1983a) 'The Measurement of Waste Within the Production Sector of an Open Economy', *Scandanavian Journal of Economics*, *85*, 159-79

—— (1983b) 'A Dynamic Approach to the Measurement of Waste in an Open Economy', Discussion Paper 83-35 (September), Department of Economics, University of British Columbia, Vancouver, BC, Canada

—— (1984) 'The Measurement of Deadweight Loss in an Open Economy', *Economica*, *51*, 23-42

—— and Woodland, A.D. (1977) 'Frank Knight's Theorem in Linear Programming Revisited', *Econometrica*, *45*, 375-98

Dixit, Vinash and Norman, V. (1980) *Theory of International Trade*, Cambridge: Cambridge University Press

Dunning, John H. (1977) 'Trade, Location of Economic Activity and the MNE: A Search for an Eclectic Approach' in Ohlin, B., Hesselborn, P. and Wijkman, P.M. (eds.), *The International Allocation of Economic Activity*, London: Macmillan Press, 395-418

—— (1979) 'Explaining Changing Patterns of International Production: In Defence of the Eclectic Theory', *Oxford Bulletin of Economics and Statistics*, *41*, pp. 269-95

—— (1981) *International Production and the Multinational Enterprise*, London: George Allen and Unwin

—— and Pearce, R.D. (1981) *The World's Largest Enterprises*, Farnborough, Hants., Gower Press

Dworin, L. (1982) 'International Taxation' in *Handbook of International Business*. Alter, I. and Murray T. (eds.), New York: John Wiley and Sons

Eden, Lorraine (1976) 'The Importance of Transfer Pricing: A Microeconomic Theory of Multinational Behaviour under Trade Barriers', unpublished PhD dissertation, Halifax: Dalhousie University

—— (1978) 'Vertically Integrated Multinationals: A Micro-economic Analysis', *Canadian Journal of Economics*, XI, 534-46

—— (1983a) 'Transfer Pricing Policies under Tariff Barriers', *Canadian Journal of Economics*, XVI, 679-95

—— (1983b) 'The Simple Analytics of Multinational Intrafirm Trade', paper presented at the Eighth Annual Canadian Economic Theory Conference, Concordia University, Montreal, Quebec (May)

Elam, R. and Henaidy, H. (1980) 'Transfer Pricing for the Multinational Enterprise', *International Journal of Accounting* (Spring), 49-65

Errunza, Vihang and Senbet, Lemma (1981) 'The Effects of International Operations on the Market Value of the Firm: Theory and Evidence', *Journal of Finance*, 36 (2), 401-17

European Communities, Commission (1976) 'Proposal for a Council Directive on the elimination of double taxation in connection with the adjustment of profit between associated enterprises (arbitration procedure).' Submitted by the Commission to the Council. EC: Brussels, 14 (25 November): mimeograph

Federal Reserve Bank of St Louis (1983) 'International Economic Conditions', St Louis, Missouri (October)

Finnie, J. (1978) 'Transfer Pricing Practices', *Management Accounting* (December), 17-35

Fishelson, Gideon and Flatters, F. (1975) 'The (Non)equivalence of Optimal Tariffs and Quotas Under Uncertainty', *Journal of International Economics*, 5, 385-93

Fleck, Florian H. and Mahfouz, R. (1974) 'The Multinational Corporation: Tax Avoidance and Profit Manipulation via Subsidiaries and Tax Havens', *Schweiz Z. Volkswirtsch. Statist.*, 11O; (2), 145-59

Frank, Isaiah (1980) *Foreign Enterprise in Developing Countries*, Baltimore, Md: The Johns Hopkins University Press

Ganiotsos, Thomas (1981) 'The Control of Transfer Pricing in Greece: A Program Report' in Murray, R. (ed.), *Multinationals Beyond the Market: Intra-Firm Trade and the Control of Transfer Pricing*, London: John Wiley and Sons, pp. 286-303

GATT (General Agreement on Tariffs and Trade) (1979) Meeting, 12 April, Geneva. Document, dated 26 March 1979, 'Customs Valuation: Agreement on Implementation of Article VII of the General Agreement on Tariffs and Trade', mimeograph, p. 57

Gereffi, G. (1983) 'La industria farmaceutica mundial y sus efectos en America Latina', *Comercio Exterior* (October)

Goetz, Billy E. (1967) 'Transfer Prices: An Exercise in Relevancy and Goal Congruence', *The Accounting Review*, 42, 435-50

Gordon, R.A. (1981) 'Tax Havens and Their Use by United States Taxpayers — An Overview', *Report to the United States Commissioner of Internal Revenue*, Washington, DC: United States Department of the Treasury, mimeograph

Gorman, W.M. (1968) 'Measuring the Quantities of Fixed Factors' in Wolf, J.N. (ed.), *Value, Capital and Growth: Papers in Honour of Sir John Hicks*, Chicago: Aldine, pp. 141-72

Gould, J.R. (1964) 'Internal Pricing in Firms When There Are Costs of Using an Outside Market', *Journal of Business*, 37, 61-7

Green, Peter E. (1978) *Analyzing Multivariate Data*, Hinsdale, Illinois: Dryden Press

Greene, James and Duerr, Michael G. (1970) *Intercompany Transactions in the Multinational Firm: A Survey*, New York: Conference Board

Grubel, Herbert G. (1974) 'The Private and Social Rates of Return From U.S. Asset Holdings Abroad', *Journal of Political Economy*, 82 (May-June), 469-88

Hagen, Everett (1980) *The Economics of Development*, Homewood, Illinois: Richard D. Irwin, Inc.

Hanson, James S. (1975) 'Transfer Pricing in the Multinational Corporation: A Critical Appraisal', *World Development*, 3 (November/December), 857-65

Hartman, David G. (1980) 'The Effects of Taxing Foreign Investment Income', *Journal of Public Economics*, 3 (April), 213-32

—— (1981) 'Domestic Tax Policy and Foreign Investment: Some Evidence', *National Bureau of Economic Research*, Working Paper No. 784

Hawkins, P.G. and Macaluso, D. (1977) 'The Avoidance of Restrictive Monetary Policies in Host Countries by Multinational Firms', *Journal of Money, Credit and Banking*, 9 (November), 562-71

Heal, Geoffrey M. (1969) 'Planning Without Prices', *Review of Economic Studies*, 36, 347-62

—— (1971) 'Planning Prices, and Increasing Returns', *Review of Economic Studies*, 38, 281-94

Helleiner, Gerald K. (1981) 'Intra-firm Trade and the Developing Countries: An Assessment of the Data' in Murray, R. (ed.), *Multinationals Beyond the Market*, Brighton: The Harvester Press, pp. 31-57

—— and Lavergne, R. (1979) 'Intra-firm Trade and Industrial Exports to the United States', *Oxford Bulletin of Economics and Statistics*, 41 (November), 297-311

Hennart, Jean-François (1982) *A Theory of Multinational Enterprise*, Ann Arbor: University of Michigan Press

Herrick, Bruce, and Kindleberger, Charles P. (1983) *Economic Development*, 4th edn, New York: McGraw-Hill Book Company

Hirshleifer, Jack (1956) 'On the Economics of Transfer Pricing', *Journal of Business*, 29, 172-84

—— (1957) 'Economics of the Divisionalized Firm', *Journal of Business*, 30, 96-108

Holthus, M. and Scharrer, M. (1973) 'Die Rolle des Multinationalen Unternehmen im Zusammenhang mit der Deutschen Wahrungspolitik', *HWWA*, Hamburg: Institut for Wirtschaftsforschung, mimeographed

Horngren, Charles T. (1967) 'A Contribution Margin Approach to the Analysis of Capacity Utilization', *The Accounting Review*, 42, 256-64

—— (1982) *Cost Accounting: A Managerial Emphasis*, 5th edn, Englewood Cliffes, NJ: Prentice-Hall

Horst, Thomas (1971) 'Theory of the Multinational Firm: Optimal Behaviour Under Differing Tariff and Tax Rates', *Journal of Political Economy*, 79 (September/October), 1059-72

—— (1973) 'The Simple Analytics of Multinational Firm Behaviour' in Connolly, Michael B. and Swoboda, Alexander K. (eds.), *International Trade and Money*, London: George Allen and Unwin, pp. 72-84

—— (1977) 'American Taxation of Multinational Firms', *American Economic Review*, 67, 376-89

Hubner, P. (1982) 'International Corporate and Withholding Tax Rates', *Intertax*, 3, 99-100

Hufbauer, Gary and Foster, D. (1979) 'U.S. Taxation of the Undistributed Income of Controlled Foreign Corporations' in *Essays in International Taxation*, Washington, DC: United States Department of the Treasury

Hymer, Stephen H. (1976) *The International Operations of National Firms: A Study of Direct Foreign Investment*, Cambridge, Mass.: MIT Press

Imperial Oil Ltd (1982) *Second Submission to the Restrictive Trade Practices Commission on the State of Competition in the Canadian Petroleum Industry*, Imperial Oil Ltd

—— (1983) *Third Submission to the Restrictive Trade Practices Commission on the State of Competition in the Canadian Petroleum Industry*, Imperial Oil Ltd

International Fiscal Association (IFA) (1973) 'The Taxation of Enterprises with Permanent Establishments Abroad. Proceedings of the Lausanne Conference 1973: Ludwig, Max Beat. "General Report", Rädler, A. "Reporter for Germany (Federal Republic of Germany)" ', *Cahiers de Droit Fiscal International (Studies on International Fiscal Law)*, LVIIIa

—— (1975) 'Allocation of Expenses in International Arm's Length Transactions of Related Countries. Proceedings of the London Conference 1975: Ritter, Wolfgang. "General Report" ', *Cahiers de Droit Fiscal International* LXb

—— (1981) 'Mutual Agreement — Procedure and Practice. Proceedings of the Berlin Conference, 1981; Barnet, I.D. National Reporter for the United Kingdom, p. 370; Cole, Robert T., Huston, John and Weiss, Stanley, Reporters for the United States, p. 279; Francke, Jan, Lindencrona, Gustav and Mattsson, Nils, Reporters for Sweden, 'A Court of Arbitration', pp. 382-3; Koch, K. *General Report*'. Given in German, but complete versions are also in English and French. The English version is on pp. 93-129. See 'The EC Directive on Arbitration Procedure', (p. 98) and 'Formal Arbitration Procedure', p. 125.

International Monetary Fund (IMF) (1981) 'Taxation in Subsaharan Africa', Occasional Paper No. 8, Fiscal Affairs Department Washington, DC

Itagaki, Takao (1979) 'Theory of the Multinational Firm: An Analysis of Effects of Government Policies', *International Economic Review*, 20, 437-48

—— (1980) 'Vertically Integrated Multinationals', *Canadian Journal of Economics*, XIII, 176-7

—— (1981) 'The Theory of the Multinational Firm Under Exchange Rate Uncertainty', *Canadian Journal of Economics*, XIV, 267-97

—— (1982) 'Systems of Taxation of Multinational Firms Under Exchange Risk', *Southern Economic Journal*, 48, 708-23

Jenkins, Glenn P. and Wright, Brian D. (1975) 'Taxation of Income of Multinational Corporations: The Case of the United States Petroleum Industry', *The Review of Economics and Statistics*, LVII (1), 1-10

Johnson, Harry G. (1970) 'The Efficiency and Welfare Implications of the International Corporation' in Kindleberger, Charles P. (ed.), *The International Corporation*, Cambridge, Mass.: MIT Press, pp. 35-56

Karlin, S. (1959) *Mathematical Methods and Theory in Games Programming and Economics*, Vol. I, Palo Alto, Calif.: Addison-Wesley

Katrak, Homi (1977) 'Multi-National Monopolies and Commercial Policy', *Oxford Economic Papers*, 29, 283-91

—— (1980) 'Multi-National Monopolies and Monopoly Regulation', *Oxford Economic Papers*, 32, 453-66

—— (1981) 'Multi-National Firm's Exports and Host Country Commercial Policy', *The Economic Journal*, *91*, 454-65

Kemp, Murray C. and Long, Ngo Van (eds.) (1980) *Exhaustible Resources, Optimality, and Trade*, New York: North Holland

Kindleberger, Charles P. (1969) *American Business Abroad: Six Lectures on Direct Investment*, New Haven, Conn. and London: Yale University Press

Kopits, George K. (1976a) 'Intrafirm Royalties Crossing Frontiers and Transfer Pricing Behaviour', *Economic Journal*, *86* (December), 791-805

—— (1976b) 'Taxation and Multinational Firm Behaviour: A Critical Survey', *Staff Papers*, International Monetary Fund (November)

Kroner, Meryl C. (1980) 'U.S. International Transactions in Royalties and Fees 1967-78', *Survey of Current Business* (January), 29-35

Krueger, Anne O. (1983) 'The Effects of Trade Strategies on Growth', *Finance and Development* (June), 6-8

Kuhn, Harold W. and Tucker, A.W. (1951) 'Nonlinear programming' in Neyman, J. (ed.), *The Proceedings of the Second Berkeley Symposium on Mathematical Statistics and Probability*, Berkeley: University of California Press, pp. 481-92

Kyrouz, M.E. (1975) 'Foreign Tax Rates and Tax Bases', *National Tax Journal*, (March), pp. 28, 61-80

Lall, Sanjaya (1973) 'Transfer Pricing by Multinational Manufacturing Firms', *Oxford Bulletin of Economics and Statistics*, *35* (August), 173-95

—— (1978a) 'Price Competition and the International Pharmaceutical Industry', *Oxford Bulletin of Economics and Statistics*, *40* (February), 9-22

—— (1978b) 'Transnational Corporations and Manufactured Exports from Poor Countries', *Oxford Bulletin of Economics and Statistics* (August)

—— (1979) 'Transfer Prices and Developing Countries: Some Problems of Investigation', *World Development*, 7 (1), pp. 59-71

—— (1980) *The Multinational Corporation: Nine Essays*, London: Macmillan

—— and Siddharthan, N.S. (1982) 'The Monopolistic Advantages of Multi-nationals: Lessons from Foreign Investment in the U.S.', *Economic Journal*, *92*, 668-83

—— and Streeten, Paul (1977) *Foreign Investment, Transnational and Developing Countries*, London: Macmillan

Lange, O. (1937) 'On the Economic Theory of Socialism', *Review of Economic Studies*, *1 (1-2)*. Reprinted in Townsend, H. (ed.) (1971), *Price Theory*, Harmondsworth: Penguin

Lecraw, Donald J. (1981) 'The Internationalization of Firms from LDC's: Evidence from the ASEAN Region' in Kumar, K. and McLeod, M. (eds.), *Multinationals from Developing Countries*, Lexington, Mass.: D.C. Heath, Lexington Books

—— (1983) 'Performance of Transnational Corporations in Less Developed Countries', *Journal of International Business Studies*, *14*, 15-33

Lessard, Donald R. (1979) 'Transfer Prices, Taxes, and Financial Markets: Implications of International Financial Transfers Within the Multinational Corporation' in Hawkins, R.G. (ed.), *Research in International Business and Finance: The Economic Effects of Multinational Corporations*, Vol. 1, Greenwich, Conn.: JAI Press Inc.

Lindencrona, Gustaf and Mattsson, Nils (1981) *Arbitration in Taxation*, Stockholm: P.A. Norstedt & Son

Llewellen, W.G. (1969) *The Cost of Capital*, Belmont: Wadsworth

Lodin, Sven-Olof (1979) 'International Enterprises and Taxation: Some Preliminary Results of an Empirical Study Concerning International Enterprises', Nordic Council for Tax Research; reprinted in *Intertax*, No. 8

McCart, J. (1982) 'Financing U.S. Operations Through the Netherlands and the Barbados', *Canadian Tax Journal*, 30 (4), 577-87

McCulloch, Rachel (1973) 'When Are a Tariff and a Quota Equivalent?', *Canadian Journal of Economics*, 6, 503-11

McFadden, D. (1978) 'Cost, Revenue and Profit Functions', *Production Economics: A Dual Approach to Theory and Applications*', Vol. 1, Amsterdam: North Holland, pp. 3-109

McLure, Charles (1974) 'State Income Taxation of Multistate Corporations in the United States of America' in *United Nations: The Impact of Multinational Corporations on Economic Development and on International Relations*, New York: United Nations Sales No. E.74.II.A.6

Macauley, F.R. (1938) *Some Theoretical Problems Suggested by the Movement of Interest Rates, Bond Yields and Stock Prices in the United States since 1856*, New York: National Bureau of Economic Research

Malinvaud, Edmond (1967) 'Decentralized Procedures for Planning' in Malinvaud, E. and Bacharach, M.O.L. (eds.), *Activity Analysis in the Theory of Growth and Planning*, London: Macmillan, pp. 170-208

Mathewson, C. and Quirin, G.D. (1979) *Fiscal Transfer Pricing in Multinational Corporations*, Toronto: Ontario Economic Council

Mehra, Rajnish (1978) 'On the Financing and Investment Decisions of Multinational Firms in the Presence of Exchange Risk', *Journal of Financial and Quantitative Analysis*, 13 (June)

Meier, Gerald (1982) *Pricing Policy for Development Management*, Baltimore, Md: The Johns Hopkins Press, World Bank

Merville, L. and Petty, J.W. (1978) 'Transfer Pricing for the Multinational Firm', *Accounting Review* (October), 935-51

Mooney, Joseph (1982) 'A Quantitative Analysis of Market Structure and Performance in Brazil', PhD dissertation, University of Notre Dame

Murray, D. (1981) 'The Tax Sensitivity of U.S. Direct Investment in Canadian Manufacturing', *Journal of International Money and Finance*, 1 (3)

Murray, Robin (ed.) (1981) *Multinationals Beyond the Market: Intra-Firm Trade and the Control of Transfer Pricing*, New York and London: John Wiley and Sons, Brighton: Hamish Press

Mutti, John (1981) 'Tax Incentives and the Repatriation Decisions of U.S. Multinational Corporations', *National Tax Journal*, 34 (2), 241-8

Newfarmer, Richard S. and Marsh, Lawrence C. (1984) 'Industrial Structure, Market Power and Profitability in Brazil', *World Development* (forthcoming)

—— and Mueller, Willard (1975) 'Multinational Corporations in Brazil and Mexico: Structural Sources of Economic and Non-Economic Power', paper presented to the US Senate Committee on Foreign Relations, Subcommittee on Multinational Corporations, Washington, DC: US Government Printing Office

Nieckels, Lars (1976) *Transfer Pricing in Multinational Firms: A Heuristic Programming Approach and a Case Study*, Stockholm: Almqvist & Wiksell

Ohyama, M. (1972) 'Trade and Welfare in General Equilibrium', *Keio Economic*

Studies, 9, 37-73

O'Keefe, M.J. (1975) 'Management Fees and Withholding Tax', *Canadian Tax Journal*, 23, 130-7

Organization for Economic Cooperation and Development (OECD) (1972) *Additional Studies Concerning the Mutual Agreement Procedure*, Committee on Fiscal Affairs, Working Group No. 22, Report of the Working Party No. 1, Paris: OECD, mimeograph

—— (1976) *Guidelines for Multinational Enterprises*, Paris: OECD

—— (1979) *Transfer Pricing and Multinational Enterprises. A Report*, Paris: OECD

—— (1982) *Transfer Pricing, Corresponding Adjustments and the Mutual Agreement Procedure*, report adopted by the Committee on Fiscal Affairs, 6 July 1982, Paris: OECD, mimeograph

Peat, Marwick, Mitchell and Co. (1980) *The Taxation of Intercompany Transactions in Selected European Countries and the USA*, revised edn

Pelcovits, Michael D. (1976) 'Quotas versus Tariffs', *Journal of International Economics*, 6, 365-70

Penrose, Edith (1956) 'Foreign Investment and the Growth of the Firm', *Economic Journal*, 66 (June), pp. 220-35

—— (1968) *The Large International Firm in Developing Countries: The International Petroleum Industry*, London: George Allen and Unwin

Petty, J.W. and Walker E. (1972) 'Optimal Transfer Pricing for the Multinational Firm', *Financial Management* (Winter), 74-87

Plasschaert, Sylvain, R.F. (1979) *Transfer Pricing and Multinational Corporations: An Overview of Concepts, Mechanisms and Regulations*, Farnborough, Hants: Saxon House and New York: Praeger Publishers

—— (1980) 'Ways and Means to Improve European and Widen International Cooperation against Tax Evasion and Avoidance, with Particular Reference to Transfer Pricing within Multinational Enterprises', *European Taxation*, International Bureau of Fiscal Documentation

—— (1981) 'The Multiple Motivations for Transfer Pricing Modulations in Multinational Enterprises and Governmental Counter-Measures: An Attempt at Clarification', *Management International Review*, 21 (1), 49-63

Quirin, G. David (1967) *The Capital Expenditure Decision*, Homewood, Illinois: Irwin

—— and Wiginton, J.C. (1981) *Analyzing Capital Expenditures: Public and Private Perspectives*, Homewood, Illinois: Irwin

Ravenscraft, David J. (1981) 'Transfer Pricing and Profitability', manuscript (December)

—— (1982) 'Economics of Integration', manuscript (December)

Richardson, David J. (1971) 'Theoretical Considerations in the Analysis of Foreign Direct Investment', *Western Economic Journal*, 9 (March), pp. 87-98

Robbins, Sidney and Stobaugh, Robert (1973a) *Money in the Multinational Enterprise: A Study of Financial Policy*, New York: Basic Books

—— (1973b) 'The Bent Measuring Stick for Foreign Subsidiaries', *Harvard Business Review* (September-October), 80-8

Rodriguez, Rita (1980) *Foreign Exchange Management in U.S. Multinationals*, Lexington, Mass.: Lexington Books, D.C. Heath

Ronen, Joshua, and McKinney, G. (1970) 'Transfer Pricing for Divisional

Autonomy', *Journal of Accounting Research*, 8 (May), 99-112

Rugman, Alan M. (1980a) 'Internalization Theory and Corporate International Finance', *California Management Review*, 22 (2), 73-9

—— (1980b) *Multinationals in Canada: Theory, Performance and Economic Impact*, Boston, Mass.: Martinus Nijhoff

—— (1981) *Inside the Multinationals: The Economics of Internal Markets*, London: Croom Helm and New York: Columbia University Press

—— (ed.) (1982a) *New Theories of the Multinational Enterprise*, London: Croom Helm and New York: St Martin's Press

—— (1982b) Review of Lall, S., 'The Multinational Corporation', *The Economic Journal*, 92 (March), pp. 196-8

Rutenberg, David P. (1970) 'Maneuvering Liquid Assets in a Multinational Company', *Management Science* 16(10), B671-B684

Samuelson, Paul A. (1947) *Foundations of Economic Analysis*, Cambridge, Mass.: Harvard University Press

Samuelson, Larry (1982) 'The Multinational Firm with Arm's Length Transfer Price Limits', *Journal of International Economics*, 13, 365-74

Senbet, Lemma (1979) 'International Capital Market Equilibrium and Multinational Firm Financing and Investment Policies', *Journal of Financial and Quantitative Analysis* (September), 455-80

Shapiro, Alan C. (1975) 'Exchange Rate Changes, Inflation and the Value of the Multinational Corporation', *Journal of Finance*, 30 (2), pp. 485-502

—— (1978a) 'Capital Budgeting for the Multinational Corporation', *Financial Management*, 7 (1)

—— (1978b) 'Financial Structure and the Cost of Capital in the Multinational Corporation', *Journal of Financial and Quantitative Analysis*, 13 (June), pp. 211-26

—— (1982) *Multinational Financial Management*, Boston, Mass.: Allyn and Bacon Inc.

Shapiro, Daniel (1980) *Foreign and Domestic Firms in Canada: A Comparative Study of Financial Structure and Performance*, Toronto: Butterworths

Shibata, Hirofumi (1968) 'A Note on the Equivalence of Tariffs and Quotas', *American Economic Review*, 58, 137-42

Shoup, Carl S. (1974) 'Taxation of Multinational Corporations' in United Nations, Department of Economic and Social Affairs, *The Impact of Multinational Corporations on Development and on International Relations*, Technical Papers: Taxation, New York: p. 30, par. 82 ST/ESA/11. Sales No. E.74.II.A.6

—— (1975) 'Establishing Transfer Prices in Allocation of Taxable Income Among Countries' in *Tax Treaties Between Developed and Developing Countries: Report of the Group of Experts, Fifth Report*, New York: United Nations

Shulman, J.S. (1966) *Transfer Pricing in Multinational Business*, Boston, Mass.: Soldiers Field Press

—— 'Transfer Pricing in the Multinational Firm', *European Business* (January), 46-64

Singer, Stuart and Karlin, Michael (1983) 'Multinationals and New Customs Law Will Have Broad Impact on Intercompany Pricing', *Journal of Taxation* (April)

Stewart, F. (1981) 'Taxation and Technology Transfer' in Sagafinejad, Moxton and Perlmutter, Howard V. (eds.), *Controlling International Technology Transfer*, New York: Pergamon Press

Stiglitz, Joseph E. and Dasgupta, Partha (1982) 'Market Structure and Resource Depletion: A Contribution to the Theory of Intertemporal Monopolistic Competition', *Journal of Economic Theory*, *28*, 128-64

Streeten, Paul (1974) 'The Theory of Development Policy' in Dunning, John H. (ed.), *Economic Analysis and the Multinational Enterprise*, London: George Allen and Unwin

Svedberg, Peter (1979) 'Optimal Tariff Policy on Imports from Multinationals', *The Economic Record*, 64-7

Tang, Roger Y.W. (1979) *Transfer Pricing Practices in the United States and Japan*, New York: Praeger

—— (1980) 'Canadian Transfer-Pricing Practices', *CA Magazine* (March), 32-8

—— (1981) *Multinational Transfer Pricing: Canadian and British Perspectives*, Toronto: Butterworths

Teece, David J. (1976) *The Multinational and the Resource Cost of International Technology Transfer*, Cambridge, Mass.: Ballinger

Todaro, M. (1981) *Economic Development in the Third World*, New York: Longman

United Nations (UN) (1974a) *The Impact of Multinational Corporations on Development and International Relations*, New York

—— (1974b) *Guidelines for Tax Treaties between Developed and Developing Countries*, New York: Department of Economic and Social Affairs

—— (1975) *Tax Treaties between Developed and Developing Countries: Report of the Group of Experts, Fifth Report*, New York

—— (1976) *Tax Treaties between Developed and Developing Countries: Report of the Group of Experts, Sixth Report*, New York

—— (1978a) *Tax Treaties between Developed and Developing Countries: Report of the Group of Experts on its Seventh Meeting*, New York

—— (1978b) *Transnational Corporations in World Development: A Re-examination*, New York: Commission on Transnational Corporations

—— (1978c) *Dominant Positions of Market Power of Transnational Corporations: Use of the Transfer Price Mechanism*, New York: Conference on Trade and Development

—— (1979) *Manual for the Negotiation of Bilateral Tax Treaties between the Developed and Developing Countries*, New York: Department of International Economic and Social Affairs

—— (1980) *Model Tax Convention between Developed and Developing Countries*, New York

—— (1983a) *Transnational Corporations in World Development: Third Survey*, New York: Centre on Transnational Corporations

—— (1983b) 'International Standards of Accounting and Reporting', *the CTC Reporter*, New York: Centre on Transnational Corporations

United States (1973) 'Summary Study of International Cases Involving Section 482 of the Internal · Revenue Code', Washington, DC: US Treasury Department (January), mimeograph

—— (1977) 'Multinational Companies (MNCs): Tax Avoidance and/or Evasion

Schemes and Available Methods to Curb Abuse', United States Internal Revenue Service document submitted to 18th Technical Conference of the Centro Americano de Administradores Tributarios, Montevideo, Uruguay (March), mimeograph

—— (1981a) *U.S. Direct Investment Abroad, 1977*, Washington, DC: US Department of Commerce, US Government Printing Office No. 340-997-1638

—— (1981b) Report by the Comptroller General, *IRS Could Better Protect U.S. Tax Interests in Determining the Income of Multinational Corporations*, Washington DC: US General Accounting Office

—— (1983) *Taxation of Banks and Thrift Institutions*, Report by the Staff of the Joint Committee on Taxation for the Committee on Finance, United States Senate, Washington, DC: US Government Printing Office

US Senate (1974) *Government Intervention in the Market Mechanism, the Petroleum Industry*, Washington, DC: US Government Printing Office

Uzawa, H. (1958) 'The Kuhn-Tucker Theorem in Concave Programming' in Arrow, Kenneth J., Hurwicz, H. and Uzawa, H. (eds.), *Studies in Linear and Nonlinear Programming*, Stanford, Calif.: Stanford University Press, pp. 32-7

Vaitsos, Constantine (1974) *Intercountry Income Distribution and Transnational Enterprise*, Oxford: Clarendon Press

—— (1977) 'The Integration of Latin America with the Rest of the World in View of the Operations of Subsidiaries of TNCS', Institute of Development Studies, University of Sussex, England, (November), mimeograph

Varian, Hal R. (1978) *Microeconomic Analysis*, New York: W.W. Norton and Company

Verlage, H.C. (1975) *Transfer Pricing for Multinational Enterprises*, Rotterdam: Rotterdam University Press

Vernon, Raymond (1971) *Sovereignty at Bay*, New York: Basic Books

—— and Wells, Louis T., Jr (1981) *Economic Environment of International Business, Third Edition*, Englewood Cliffs, NJ: Prentice-Hall Inc.

Walras, Leon (1954) *Elements of Pure Economics* (ed./trans. by Jaffe, W.), London: George Allen and Unwin

Weiss, Leonard W. and Pascoe, George (1980) 'Adjusted Concentration Ratios in Manufacturing — 1972', manuscript

Weston, J. Fred and Brigham, E.F. (1969) *Managerial Finance*, 3rd edn, New York: Holt, Rinehart and Winston

Whichard, D. (1982) 'U.S. Direct Investment Abroad in 1981', *Survey of Current Business* (August), 11-29

Williamson, Oliver E. (1975) *Markets and Hierarchies: Analysis and Anti-Trust Implications*, New York: The Free Press

Woodland, Q.D. (1982) *International Trade and Resource Allocation*, Amsterdam: North Holland

Yadav, G.J. (1968) 'A Note on the Equivalence of Tariffs and Quotas', *Canadian Journal of Economics*, *1*, 105-10

Young, L. (1979) 'Ranking Optimal Tariffs and Quotas for a Large Country Under Uncertainty', *Journal of International Economics*, *9*, 249-64

—— (1980) 'Tariffs vs. Quotas Under Uncertainty: An Extention', *American Economic Review*, *70*, 522-7

Yunker, P. (1982) *Transfer Pricing and Performance Evaluation in Multinational Corporations: A Survey Study*, New York: Praeger

Zakour, C.P. (1981) 'The Use of Investment Incentives and Performance Requirements by Foreign Governments', Office of International Investment, US Department of Commerce (October)

NOTES ON CONTRIBUTORS

Robert Z. Aliber, University of Chicago and Williams College
Anita M. Benvignati, Bureau of Economics, Federal Trade Commission, Washington
Donald J. Brean, Institute for Policy Analysis, University of Toronto
Walter A. Chudson, School of Business, University of Connecticut (Stamford)
W. Erwin Diewert, Department of Economics, University of British Columbia
Lorraine Eden, Department of Economics, Brock University
Harry Grubert, International Economist, Office of the Secretary of the Treasury, Washington
Gerry K. Helleiner, Department of Economics, University of Toronto
Takao Itagaki, Department of Economics, Kobe Gakuin University, Japan
Donald J. Lecraw, School of Business Administration, University of Western Ontario
Norman W. McGuinness, School of Business Administration, Acadia University
Paul Natke, Department of Economics, Central Michigan University
Sylvain Plasschaert, Centre for Development Studies, University of Antwerp
G. David Quirin, Faculty of Management Studies, Universtiy of Toronto
Alan M. Rugman, Centre for International Business Studies, Dalhousie University
Larry Samuelson, Department of Economics, Pennsylvania State University
Carl S. Shoup, Professor Emeritus of Economics, Columbia University

AUTHOR INDEX

SUBJECT INDEX